THE IDEOLOGICAL FOUNDATIONS OF EARLY IRISH LAW AND THEIR RECEPTION IN ANGLO-SAXON ENGLAND, *C.* 600–*C.* 900

MEDIEVAL TEXTS AND CULTURES OF NORTHERN EUROPE

VOLUME 37

Previously published volumes in this series are listed
at the back of the book.

The Ideological Foundations of Early Irish Law and Their Reception in Anglo-Saxon England, *c.* 600–*c.* 900

KRISTEN CARELLA

BREPOLS

British Library Cataloguing in Publication Data
A catalogue record for this book is available from the British Library.

D/2024/0095/260
ISBN 978-2-503-60731-3
eISBN 978-2-503-60732-0
DOI 10.1484/M.TCNE-EB.5.134690
ISSN 1784-2859
eISSN 2294-8414

Printed in the EU on acid-free paper.

For Diggory
who was there from the beginning.
All my love, in this world and the next.

Contents

Author's Preface

This book was nearly fifteen years in the making. Before anything else, I would like to thank those individuals who made this project possible. My work on it commenced during a year-long Mellon Postdoctoral Fellowship generously granted by the Medieval Institute at the University of Notre Dame. I am particularly grateful to Thomas N. Hall and Marina Smyth whose guidance helped shape my thinking at an early stage. The Medieval Institute invited John Carey, Andrew Rabin, and Charles Wright to comment on an early draft of this volume. Their guidance and criticism during a day-long seminar was formative, to say the least. In the years that followed, Andrew Rabin heard many of my conference presentations; and the conversations that almost always followed influenced many of the ideas that I discuss herein. Several years later, I received the Morton W. Bloomfield fellowship at Harvard University, where I continued work on this project. Many thanks to Daniel Donoghue whose guidance and support were indispensable, and which continued after the fellowship ended. I am likewise in debt to Catherine McKenna for several years' access to the Fred Norris Robinson Celtic Seminar Library, which helped immensely.

Most fundamentally, I would like to thank my teachers at the University of North Carolina at Chapel Hill, where I first fell in love with Medieval Studies as an undergraduate and where I eventually finished my PhD. Special thanks to Edward Donald Kennedy, Theodore H. Leinbaugh, Craig Melchert, Richard W. Pfaff, Joseph Wittig, and, above all, to my advisor Pádraig P. Ó Néill. This volume would not have been possible without them. I am also grateful for the many scholars who have offered their advice — and their time — over the years, including (but not limited to) Dorothy Africa, László Sándor Chardonnens, Becky DiBiasio, Fr. Roger Corriveau, Bruce Gilchrist, Stephen J. Harris, Jeffrey Huntsman, Stefan Jurasinski, Kevin Kritsch, Nicole Marafioti, Joey McMullen, Britt Mize, Lisi Oliver, Dietrich Schroeer, and Kathryn Wymer. Finally, my sincere gratitude to my many students over the years at Assumption University. They, most of all, make the effort worthwhile.

All mistakes are entirely my own.

Abbreviations

Since this volume addresses several different fields of academic study, I have strived to use as few abbreviations as possible to make it more accessible. I have relied on the following abbreviations only when necessary for layout and formatting.

AM	*Audacht Morainn*
Bk	Book
cap.	*capitulum* (chapter)
CCH	*Collectio canonum Hibernensis*
CD	*Cáin Domnaig*
DxiiAS	*De duodecim abusivis saeculi*
EÍ	*Epistil Ísu*
El.	*Einleitung* (introduction)
L.	Latin
OE.	Old Engish
OIr.	Old Irish
pl.	plural
PHP	The Pseudo-historical Prologue to the *Senchas Már*
Ps.	pseudo
sing.	singular

CHAPTER 1

Introduction

First Things

Early Irish law was a deeply intellectual exercise, thoroughly grounded in thoughtful, academic exploration and esoteric knowledge of various kinds. I am convinced nonetheless, and I hope this volume will make small steps toward showing, that the goal of all this legal theorizing was eminently practical, though not always in obvious ways; that is, not always by imposing specific regulations on society proactively. Law might — indeed, must — be practical in other ways. Above all else, a functioning system of law must be sufficiently grounded in a myth (or a collection of interrelated myths) — an ideological perspective or spectrum of closely related perspectives — convincing enough that all who are a party to it are willing to ante up. All involved must believe in it to the extent that they accept the foundations of the system (at least) as axiomatic, as something integrally and transcendently real, if its day-to-day provisions are to carry sufficient weight for that legal system to operate effectually.[1]

Without question, early Irish jurists took fundamental, ideological matters head-on and often wrote about them at great length. Early Irish jurists[2] persistently raised a myriad of difficult questions for which they pursued answers at times by delving into some of the most esoteric lore available to them. Among other matters, they sought to identify the sources of law, its foundational authorities, and the relationships between different segments of society that projected legal force. They attempted to reconcile Christian and pre-Christian points of law, to systematize the proper order and method by which one should consult authorities, and to situate the place of the Irish people, historically and contemporaneously, within the broader

---

1 This point has been made commonly. Apropos to early medieval law in North-western Europe, see for example, Rabin, 'Law and Justice', pp. 85–98; Goodrich and Hachamovitch, 'Time out of Mind', pp. 159–81.

2 Most previous scholarship has assumed that Irish legal study was primarily, if not exclusively, a male endeavour. In this volume, I follow (and applaud) Boyle, *History and Salvation*, pp. 187–88, when addressing the authorship of anonymous works: 'I have deliberately avoided the use of gendered language in discussing [...] authors: the extent of female literacy and the provision of education and production of literature in female monastic communities is uncertain. In most cases, the gender of the author cannot and should not be assumed'.

scheme of Christian history. The goal of the last of these was to explain the significance of their status as converted gentiles legally and theologically within their own unique conception(s) of divine law. To be sure, Irish jurists of varying intellectual orientations (e.g., secular versus ecclesiastical lawyers, clerics with different points of view and affiliations, lay judges with different educational backgrounds, etc.; to the extent any of these various orientations were distinguishable) approached these matters from various angles and arrived at disparate conclusions. What early Irish jurists had in common was their fervent willingness to engage these questions fully, often without any explicit attempt at reconciling conflicting authorities.

This gesture is evident in the vast amount of legal literature[3] that was produced during the early period, i.e., between *c.* 600 and *c.* 900,[4] including not only the legal codes proper (written both in Latin and the vernacular) and the prologues that introduced them, but also the many tales, pseudo-histories, various religious works, and exegetical commentaries that dealt directly or indirectly with legal matters. Their energetic intellectual activity, taken collectively over these three centuries or so, resulted in a heterogeneous body of legal thought — what might aptly be described as a composite jurisprudential philosophy — that, for the purposes of this volume, I refer to as the 'ideological foundations of early Irish law', that is, the mythic groundwork, the set of axioms, upon which the pragmatic mechanisms of Irish jurisprudence depended and found bedrock. To be sure, this ideology was never unified or consistent, any more than it was the product of any aggregated, formal effort aimed at producing it. Rather, as I shall demonstrate, it was typified above all else by diversity, as one would expect of a robust and thriving system of law. The 'ideological foundations of early Irish law', emerged most of all from a tendency in Irish intellectual culture during the early Middle Ages to grapple with and attempt to explain issues of legal and theological significance dialectically and discursively; to engage with competing authorities inclusively, as opposed to rejecting some and favouring others in simplistic ways; and, what is more, to express their ideas on vellum, often in great depth and at significant length. Understood in this way, early Irish legal ideology, broadly conceived, was arguably the most important academic topic of its day, and its manifestations ripple throughout the Irish (including the Hiberno-Latin) literary corpus, sometimes in surprising ways and often in unexpected genres.[5]

---

3 Indeed, the Irish produced the largest vernacular corpus of legal materials in Western Europe during the early Middle Ages, not to mention the substantial volume of Hiberno-Latin materials, both legal and legal-theological, that were produced as well.

4 I shall discuss the reasons for these dates below.

5 Necessarily, I shall have to be selective when choosing which of these texts among the sizable corpus of Irish literature to discuss. Given the vast quantity of literary and legal

My goal in the present volume is to identify and describe these ideological foundations, at least in preliminary fashion and, secondarily, to examine how they might have been received, reimagined, and recast by Anglo-Saxon jurists. While I intend to break new ground, I hope above all else to raise some cogent questions, even as I realize that I shall not be able to answer them all. Investigating these issues will necessarily mean untangling (or rather, attempting to untangle) the Gordian knot of early Irish legal ideology or, more reasonably, a small part of it. With a few exceptions, scholarship on early Irish law since the publication of Binchy's *Corpus Iuris Hibernici*[6] (if not before) has focused, for the most part admirably, on the details of Irish law rather than on the system as a whole and the ideology that underlay it. My goal in the present volume is to attempt something different, that is, to focus on the big picture, albeit by way of and with respect for details wherever possible. So, let me rush in where scholars far more learned than me have, for the most part, declined to tread. Before going any further, however, let me begin with a concrete example that demonstrates how some of the various fields of intellectual inquiry that together constituted early Irish law might bear on important practical matters.

Notice that the case study with which I have chosen to embark treats an ecclesiastical matter of primarily theological significance, preserved exclusively in Latin texts (i.e., Columbanus's *Epistulae* regarding the paschal controversy, *c.* 600 and the decade or so thereafter). What is more, it deals with an Irish understanding (and recapitulation) of a foreign canon. While this choice will, no doubt, be surprising to many, I have chosen this point of departure with full awareness of its difficulties. While I do not mean my choice of texts to belittle or ignore the central position that early Irish vernacular law held alongside the Hiberno-Latin material, I intend this choice to affirm and emphasize my belief that we must understand Old Irish vernacular law in close conjunction with the large body of Hiberno-Latin legal and religious literature (including those texts which bear on legal matters, even if they are not explicitly legal in nature) as part and parcel of the same intellectual enterprise. In the same vein, I maintain that we cannot separate Irish theology — most of all, early Irish conceptions of divine law and Christian history — as something inherently distinct and separate from early Irish jurisprudential thought. In what follows, then, all references to 'Irish law' bear this inclusive sense. I shall address these

materials in both the vernacular and Hiberno-Latin that bear on the question(s) at hand, my goal in the present volume is only to choose those texts and passages that best exemplify the points I shall raise. I hope that others will see the theme(s) I address in other texts, and that they will both refine and correct the arguments I offer here.

6 *Corpus Iuris Hibernici.*

matters more thoroughly in what follows. For now, I shall discuss the legal sensibilities of Columbanus in the late-sixth and early-seventh centuries as a point of entry into this difficult and multifaceted discussion.[7]

Columbanus[8] and the Law for Churches *in barbaricis gentibus*

One cannot help but be struck by the overtly contentious tone with which the Irish monk and abbot Columbanus[9] (*c.* 543–615) at times

7 There are many reasons to start with Columbanus. Elva Johnston articulated some of these: 'The works of St Columbanus (+ 615) are particularly significant because they are the product of a well-attested individual who can be contextualized in a way that is virtually impossible for other Irish near-contemporaries. In addition, his career straddles the sixth and seventh centuries and while his extant writings are nearly all attributable to his time on the Continent, they also open a fascinating window into sixth-century Irish religion and learning in the monastery of Bangor. It is very likely that his impressive Latin learning was built upon native foundations. Columbanus proved not only to be a skilled writer but one who proclaimed a keen sense of his Irishness. He shows us that by the time of his intellectual formation in the second half of the sixth century there was a strong sense of Irish identity mediated by learned teachers and founded, at least partly, upon the conversion of the Irish to Christianity. It may well be that this sense of identity was enhanced, in the case of Columbanus, by the fact that he chose to pursue his religious calling outside Ireland. However, his writings help dispel various myths of Irish peculiarity. For instance, Columbanus's most distinctive divergence from accepted Christian orthodoxy was in the matter of dating Easter. His position, which he held obstinately against stiff opposition, is better described as anachronistic rather than as distinctively Irish. Certainly, many other Irishmen held firmly to the orthodox line.' Johnston, *Literacy and Identity*, p. 32.

8 Much has been written on Columbanus's life, beyond which can be catalogued here. A good starting point is Bullough, 'The Career of Columbanus', pp. 1–28.

9 The transmission history of Columbanus's letters presents certain difficulties. As Neil Wright points out in 'Columbanus's *Epistulae*', p. 30, of all the works attributed to the saint, '[...] only the authenticity of the *Epistulae* ⟨i–v⟩] [...] has never been seriously called into question'. That said, Wright continues, 'No early manuscript of *Epistulae* *i–v* now survives; modern editions rely on two comparatively late sources: first, Patrick Fleming's *editio princeps* of Columbanus's works, published in Louvain in 1667 and based [...] on a now lost Bobbio exemplar which Fleming had transcribed in 1623; and second, another transcription, made in the seventeenth century by Judoc Metzler, of a Bobbio manuscript which contained the five *epistulae* as well apparently as other material attributed to Columbanus'. Later in the same article, Wright acknowledges that 'It should not be forgotten that the *Epistulae* survive only in transcriptions made in the seventeenth century, in which anomalous forms may well have been suppressed', p. 40. That said, he argues for the authenticity of the text as it has survived, based on the observation that there is little of the '[...] kind of case-confusions, errors of accidence, and abnormal syntax which abound in the Latin of [contemporary Gallic writers]. Rather, it is grammatical correctness which is characteristic of Columbanus's *Epistulae*', p. 40. Moreover, '[...] ⟨Columbanus's⟩ taste for varied and unusual word vocabulary largely reflects techniques of amplification widely employed in late Latin texts, although a few words do seem to be indicative of the Irish milieu in which he was trained. Elaborate word-order can also be seen as an integral part

addressed the Pope in his surviving letters regarding the paschal controversy.[10] The specifics of the dispute are complex and beyond the scope of the present context to address in detail, although its general outlines are well known. For present purposes, suffice to say that the Irish *peregrini* in Gaul calculated the date of Easter differently — markedly differently — from their Continental counterparts, resulting in the awkward situation wherein one party might be celebrating Easter while the other would still be observing Lent.[11] Even more disruptively, this incongruity could render asynchronous the differently calculated ecclesiastical calendars for as long as eighteen weeks on a year-by-year basis, since a number of important feast days were determined based on the date of Easter.[12] This dispute, at least so it would appear from the surviving record, led to an emotionally infused and sometimes angry debate. To be sure, the paschal controversy was only one, albeit the most prominent and the most intractable, among several differences between the Irish Church and those of Western Christendom.[13] Here, my goal is to make a very specific point about the ideology that underlay Columbanus's challenge to the Pope concerning the proper way to calculate the date of Easter. In particular, I am concerned with his legal-theological justification for asserting Irish ecclesiastical independence in the face of Roman Apostolic authority (even if he accepted the legitimacy of that authority, albeit with

---

of the rhetorical tradition in which he worked, but there is in the *Epistulae* a degree of experimentation which can best be paralleled in certain other Insular Latin texts. Finally, Columbanus does not make as extensive a use of prose rhythm as do some continental writers', p. 58. Overall, Wright contends that the texts of Columbanus's *Epsitulae* should be taken as authentic, even in their details.

10 I do not wish to revive the opinion here that Damian Bracken described in earlier scholarship: 'Many scholars have discerned a truculence, if not arrogance, in ⟨Columbanus' s⟩ letters to the Popes', 'Authority and Duty', p. 168. In ways that extend beyond the scope of the present context to describe, Columbanus's letters are significant as much for their acceptance and sanction of Rome's and the Pope's authority as they are for any apparent challenges they pose. For a summary of early scholarship that mistakenly portrayed Columbanus as denying the Pope's authority, see Hay, 'Columbanus and Rome', pp. 315–19. For present purposes, suffice to say that, while Columbanus's views on Rome's primacy were complex, he also asserted (at times passionately) a certain degree of independence on the part of the Irish Church. See also: Bracken, 'Juniors Teaching Elders', pp. 252–73.

11 Bede, *Ecclesiastical History*, III, § 25, p. 296 (text); p. 297 (trans.), reports that this was true in Northumbria before the Synod of Whitby: 'Vnde nonnumquam contigisse fertur illis temporibus, ut bis in anno uno pascha celebraretur, et cum rex pascha dominicum solutis ieiuniis faceret, tum regina cum suis persistens adhuc in ieiunio diem palmarum celebraret' (Hence it is said that in these days it sometimes happened that Easter was celebrated twice in the same year, so that the king had finished the fast and was keeping Easter Sunday, while the queen and her people were still in Lent and observing Palm Sunday).

12 Corning, *The Celtic and Roman Traditions*, pp. 9, 13.

13 These different practices included, besides the central dispute of the date of Easter, the proper tonsure, the composition and use of penitentials, and the status of *peregrini*. See, for example, Corning, *The Celtic and Roman Traditions*, pp. 9–18.

certain exceptions). Without question, a fuller investigation of the matter I touch on here would require a significantly more thorough discussion of the topic than the current context allows.[14]

In the early days of the controversy, Columbanus wrote to successive Popes in passionate defence of Irish customs regarding how to calculate the date of Easter, therein deploying a number of arguments that relied on various kinds of authorities. In this series of letters, Columbanus demanded at first that the Pope sanction unequivocally the Irish method of calculating the date of Easter for all Christendom. Later, he backed away from this position, pleading only that the Irish be permitted to continue celebrating the holiday according to their own customs, despite its outright conflict with their Continental hosts in Gaul and most of the Western Church collectively.[15]

Between the lines of Columbanus's rhetoric, one senses a degree of desperation and, at times, what seems like frustration building to anger.[16] At one juncture in particular, it would appear that his sentiment boiled over, to the point that he seems almost to accuse the Pope of heresy, should he not change tack and back the Irish position. What is significantly more, Columbanus seems to suggest that, because of the Pope's unwillingness to support the Irish position, all the churches of the West might reject his authority and together regard him as a heretic, though it is unclear specifically what outcome he expected this putative rebuff might precipitate:

> Tua itaque consideret vigilantia, ut in fide duorum supradictorum auctorum sibi invicem contrariorum probanda, nulla sit inter te et Hieronymum in sententia promenda dissonantia, ne nobis undique sint angustiae, ut aut tibi aut illi consentiamus. Parce in hoc infirmis, ne scandalum diversitatis ostendas. Simpliciter enim ego tibi confiteor, quod **contra sancti Hieronymi auctoritatem** veniens apud occidentis ecclesias hereticus seu respuendus erit, quicumque ille fuerit; illae

14 The most recent work on the Easter debate is by Immo Warntjes. For a history of scholarship on computus generally, see his articles, including: 'Introduction: State of Research', pp. 1–42. See also, especially: Warntjes, 'Victorius vs Dionysius', pp. 33–98; Warntjes, 'Computus and Scientific Thought', pp. 285–321; Warntjes, 'The Mechanics of Lunar Calendars', pp. 273–310.

15 On this shift in Columbanus's argument from insistence that his views were universally orthodox to a plea for pluriformity, see Mackey, 'The Theology of Columbanus', pp. 235–36.

16 Though describing a different passage, Smit's observation about Columbanus's tone is apropos here and frequently throughout his letters: '⟨Columbanus⟩ attacks his opponents, but it is the despairing aggression of a cornered man'. See Smit, *Studies on the Language and Style of Columba the Younger*, p. 113.

enim per omnia indubitatam in **scripturis divinis** accomodant fidem.[17]

> (Therefore let your Vigilance take care that, in testing the faith in turn of the two above-mentioned mutually opposed authors, there be no discord between yourself and Jerome in pronouncing judgement, lest we be surrounded by difficulties on all sides, whether to agree with you or with him. Spare the weak in this, lest you reveal a stumbling block of discord. For I confess to you simply, that he who goes **against the authority of Saint Jerome** will be a heretic or a reprobate, whoever he may be, in the eyes of the churches of the West; for these ⟨place⟩ an undoubted faith in **divine scripture** in all things).[18]

Though Columbanus mitigated his tone elsewhere, his language here seems inclined toward defiance, if not outright revolt. The force of his rhetoric aside,[19] in this passage (and throughout this letter and others) Columbanus made a subtly wrought theological and legal case based on the Irish understanding of the authorities of ecclesiastical law. More precisely, he made the case that some of those authorities should be regarded as more fundamental than others, even to the extent that some of them take precedence over a papal decree; and it is to these more basic authorities that the Irish, in his view (and all Christians, for that matter), owe their obedience first and foremost. As such, Columbanus's view relied on a distinctly Irish understanding of divine law and the proper function of its agents in the world, particularly the hierarchical relationship between ecclesiastical authorities. Notice from the passage above that, for Columbanus, the writings of the Church Fathers, in this case Jerome[20] and, even more basically, *scripturae divinae* represented more fundamental authorities than Pope Gregory and the decrees of the Apostolic See generally. Should Gregory contravene these authorities, he risked falling into heresy, at least in the eyes of Columbanus. Beyond that, Columbanus argued that all the churches of the West — whose faith was grounded foundationally in *scripturae divinae* and not, we may gather by implication, the potentially

---

17 The text is from Columbanus, *Sancti Columbani Opera*, ll. 10–17 p. 8. I have followed the text in Walker except in cases where Smit suggested emendations in *Studies on the Language and Style of Columba the Younger*. Emphasis my own, in both text and translation.

18 The translation is from Stanton, 'Columbanus, Letter 1', p. 154. Compare, however, the translation in Wright, 'Columbanus's *Epistulae*', p. 66 n. 139. I have altered Stanton's translation, albeit slightly, based on Wright's rendering.

19 T. M. Charles-Edwards's observations about Columbanus's education in Latin rhetoric, style, and the scriptures are important to keep in mind in this context. See, 'The Context and Uses of Literacy', pp. 66–68.

20 On the importance of the early church fathers for Columbanus, and Jerome in particular, see especially Wright, 'Columbanus's *Epistulae*', pp. 66–75.

false, or at least less authoritative, words of the Pope — would take the same position and likewise reject the Pope as a heretic.[21] While it was likely not Columbanus's intent to threaten schism, his language would seem to entertain that peril.

Here, however, I am less interested in Columbanus's fulminating rhetoric than in the logic and nature of his reasoning. In making this argument, Columbanus appeared to regard as axiomatic — as a basic tenet of his legal and theological ideology — that some authorities were more fundamental than others, and that there existed a prescribed order for consulting these authorities when attempting to settle outstanding *quaestiones* such as this one. This order was later made explicit in the eighth-century collection of Hiberno-Latin canon law known as *Collectio canonum Hibernensis*. I shall have a great deal more to say about this collection in what follows. For now, suffice to say that, from an Irish perspective, scripture was most fundamental.[22] If, however, one could not resolve a dilemma on that basis satisfactorily, one might then proceed to look for answers in the writings of the Church Fathers. Only after these sources had been consulted exhaustively and the search had proven fruitless might one then, according to this explicit order of operations, look to the Apostolic See for an answer. Following this procedure (so it would appear), Columbanus consulted scripture first when considering this problem; and it contributed a great deal to his argument, albeit without providing him with a clear resolution. Next, he turned to patristic writings, where he found that Jerome had written conclusively on the matter, at least in Columbanus's opinion. As he explained in *Epistula II*:

> quod plus credo traditioni patriae meae iuxta doctrinam et calculum octoginta quattuor annorum et Anatolium ab Eusebio ecclesiasticae historiae auctore episcopo et sancto catalogi scriptore Hieronymo laudatam Pascha celebrare, quam iuxta Victorium [...].[23]

---

21 As bold as it may seem, this threat does not necessarily mean that Columbanus was denying the Pope's authority outright. As is clear from the context of the passage cited above and the content of his letters overall, Columbanus acknowledged the primacy of Rome. That said, he nonetheless felt that the papacy could — and indeed should — be corrected, even by junior members of the Church, when it was in error. Note that Columbanus's aggressive tone has been viewed within the context of Paul's confrontation with Peter, as reported in Galatians 2:11–12. See Bracken, 'Juniors Teaching Elders', pp. 262–67.

22 On the importance of scripture as a basic authority for Irish theologians and possible sources for this mode of inquiry, see Herren and Brown, *Christ in Celtic Christianity*, pp. 106–09. Note, however, that I disagree with the authors' claim that in early Irish (and Insular Celtic) thought, '(t)he complete law is contained within the scriptures', though I support their conclusions about the centrality of scripture in early Irish theology generally.

23 Columbanus, *Sancti Columbani Opera*, 'Epistula II', ll. 9–13 p. 18.

> (I have more confidence in the tradition of my native land in accordance with the teaching and reckoning of eighty-four years and with Anatolius, who was commended by Bishop Eusebius the author of the ecclesiastical history and by Jerome the holy writer of the catalogue, for the celebration of Easter, than to do so in accordance with Victorius [...]).[24]

In this passage, Columbanus argued that Jerome's (and Eusebius's) praise of the same method for calculating Easter adopted by the Irish provided clear testimony from a basic authority — an authority more fundamental than the Pope's — in support of his argument. For Columbanus, patristic opinion superseded the judgement of the Apostolic See; and so, for him, the matter was crystalline: There existed a more fundamental authority relevant to the topic at hand than the Pope's decree.

This understanding of the relative, hierarchical importance of the authorities of ecclesiastical law appears elsewhere in Columbanus's writings. Above all, it is clear from his letters that scripture — the Old Testament in particular, with some conditions — was a most basic authority.[25] A few citations will suffice to make the point.

> Cum Iudaeis facere Pascha non debemus. Dixit hoc olim et Victor episcopus [...] Qualis, rogo, haec tam frivola et tam impolita, nullis scilicet divinae scripturae fulta testimoniis sententia [...][26]
>
> ('We should not keep Easter with the Jews.' Bishop Victor also said this once [...] What, I ask, is this so frivolous and so unrefined judgement, supported by no testimony of divine scripture [...]?)[27]

The 'Bishop Victor' that Columbanus referred to here is Pope Victor (fl. 189?–98), who took a special interest in the Easter controversy, even to the extent that he presided over a council in Rome to adjudicate the matter.[28] More than a century later, the matter was addressed by the First Council of Nicea (325).[29] So, quite significantly, Columbanus stood vocally in opposition to both papal and conciliar judgement, arguing that the decision handed down by these authorities had no basis in *scripturae divinae*

24 Columbanus, *Sancti Columbani Opera*, 'Epistula II', ll. 10–15 p. 19.

25 On Columbanus's use of the Bible in his *Epistulae*, see especially, Wright, 'Columbanus's *Epistulae*', pp. 61–66.

26 Columbanus *Sancti Columbani Opera*, 'Epistula I', ll. 10–11 and 12–14 p. 6.

27 Columbanus, 'Columbanus, Letter 1', p. 153.

28 Pope Victor took a special interest in rooting out the Quartodeciman heresy, which held that Easter should always fall on the fourteenth *luna* (like Jewish Passover), regardless of what day of the week it fell on. See Stanton, 'Columbanus, Letter 1', pp. 162–63. For a lucid explanation of the issues surrounding this heresy and the calculation of Easter generally, see Corning, *The Celtic and Roman Traditions*, pp. 4–13.

29 See Corning, *The Celtic and Roman Traditions*, pp. 11–12.

and, in fact, had been settled by Eusebius and Jerome. For Columbanus, these were indisputably more fundamental authorities. What is more, his argument here implicitly reveals the premise that a devout Christian might legitimately abrogate both a papal decree and the decision of an ecumenical council, not only on the basis that these authorities had contradicted scripture outright but, even more sweepingly, that these authorities have no positive basis in *scripturae divinae*.

Elsewhere in Columbanus's letters, we find evidence of another procedure by which, in his view, scripture should be consulted as an authority. In particular, he constructed his arguments on the implicit notion that the weight of testimony from the scriptures was elevated when the Old and New Testaments agreed with one another. He made this point twice in *Epistula II*, addressed to an assembly of Gaulish clerics:

> quaeso vos, amantissimi patres ac fratres, et videamus qualis verior sit traditio — vestra an fratrum vestrorum in Occidente. Omnes enim ecclesiae totius Occidentis [...] non respiciunt fieri debere resurrectionem ante passionem, id est ante aequinoctium Pascha, et vigesimam lunam non excedunt, **ne sine auctoritate Veteris Testamenti sacramentum Novi Testamenti agant**.[30]
>
> > (I beseech you, my most loving fathers and brethren, and let us see which be the more true tradition — yours, or that of your brethren in the West. [...] ⟨For⟩ all the churches of the entire West do not consider that the resurrection should take place before the passion, that is Easter before the equinox, and they do not wait beyond the twentieth moon, **lest they should hold a sacrament of the New Testament without authority of the Old**).[31]

Similarly, a bit later he argued:

> Absit ergo ut ego contra vos contendam congrediendum [...] alioquin aliter inter nos potest convenire, ut aut *unusquisque in quo vocatus est in eo permaneat apud Deum* ⟨1 Corinthians 7:20⟩, si utraque bona est traditio, aut cum pace et humilitate sine ulla contentione libri legantur utrique, et **quae plus Veteri et Novo Testamento concordant, sine ullius invidia serventur**.[32]

30 Columbanus, *Sancti Columbani Opera*, 'Epistula II', ll. 10–13 and 14–17 p. 16. Emphasis my own, in both text and translation.

31 Columbanus, *Sancti Columbani Opera*, 'Epistula II', ll. 10–18 p. 17. I have used Walker's translation of Columbanus's *Epistulae*, although with caution since their accuracy has been called into question. See Esposito, 'On the New Edition', pp. 184–203 and Bieler, 'Editing Saint Columbanus', pp. 139–50.

32 Columbanus, *Sancti Columbani Opera*, 'Epistula II', ll. 17–18 and 20–24 p. 18.

> (Far be it then that I should maintain the need to quarrel with you [...] ⟨W⟩e may agree in some other way, so that either each should remain before God in the condition in which he was called, if both traditions are good, or else both books should be read over in peace and humility without any argument, and **what agrees better with the Old and New Testament should be maintained without any ill-will at any**).[33]

In these last two cases, we see a considerably more sophisticated application of the idea that holy scripture was the single most fundamental authority of ecclesiastical law. For Columbanus, the testimony of the Old and New Testaments should ideally speak with one voice and testify in accordance with one another. Moreover, it would seem from the second quotation above that, in some instances, evidence might be found in both Testaments in support of two, opposing arguments. In that case, apparently, proper procedure (in Columbanus's understanding) dictated that one should adopt the resolution that agreed better with both Testaments. I shall have more to say about this notion of concord between authorities — a basic feature of Irish legal ideology that I shall argue was pervasive — in what follows.

My point is that, by supplying authoritative justification in the manner we have seen thus far, Columbanus appealed to a series of well-established procedures in early Irish law that later were made explicit in *Collectio canonum Hibernensis* (during the first half of the eighth century). This understanding of how Christian theologians and jurists should consult authorities and how one should understand them in relation to one another was a centrally important feature of early Irish legal ideology. To be sure, this method was more intricate than simply regarding scripture as a basic authority (as is true in many Christian cultures past and present). In early Irish law, there existed a prescribed order by which one should consult authorities, starting with scripture as the most fundamental. Agreement between the Old and New Testaments (and presumably other authorities) added weight to a claim; and there were established procedures for addressing cases where equivalent authorities disagreed. I shall have more to say about the complexities of this system in what follows. For now, suffice to say that the Irish method for consulting the authorities of law was distinctive.

Returning now to Columbanus: in *The Early Mediaeval Gaelic Lawyer*, T. M. Charles-Edwards observed that:

> [...] Irish ecclesiastical lawyers worked within a tradition one of whose principal characteristics was a search for authorities, in the Bible and

33 Columbanus, *Sancti Columbani Opera*, 'Epistula II', ll. 21–29 pp. 19.

> elsewhere. They as often as not began with an existing rule or practice and then found an authority for it as *vice versa*.[34]

Here, Charles-Edwards was not describing Columbanus's reasoning, but he might just as well have been. Whether Columbanus felt that his answer was correct *a priori* is not clear (and likely not worth speculating upon). More to the point, he was able to produce evidence in the form of authoritative statements from fundamental sources that — to his mind, and from an Irish ideological perspective — made the case conclusively; more so, in any case, than his opponents had. Based on this reasoning, he believed that the Irish were right, and that the Pope needed correction. Notice, however, that his goal was ultimately practical — that is, settling the proper way of calculating the date of Easter — while his method was profoundly theoretical: for Columbanus, there existed a proper order by which one should consult authorities. Although opinions might differ, for Columbanus, the most fundamental authorities supported his argument conclusively and, moreover, those authorities corroborated one another. On this basis, he considered himself to be indisputably correct.

There is more to say on this topic. Notice how, in the passage from *Epistula I* cited above, Columbanus made a reference to the *occidentis ecclesiae*, i.e., the 'Churches of the West' (for whom he took it upon himself, in this instance, to serve as a mouthpiece) claiming that they might all collectively regard Pope Gregory as a heretic if he contradicted Jerome. With this statement, Columbanus drew an important distinction between different, post-Imperial peoples and the nature of their legal obligations to the Apostolic See. This point requires discussion. It is not immediately clear what 'churches' Columbanus had in mind beyond the Irish and perhaps the Britons (that is, the Welsh, Cornish, Cumbrian Celts, and possibly the Bretons), and possibly also the Picts.[35] Whatever *gentes* he intended to signify collectively, however, it is significant that Columbanus perceived the place of the Irish Church to possess a special status, that is, one among a group of 'Western Churches' somehow separate and distinct from the rest among those of broader Christendom, those over which the Pope, in some ill-defined, administrative/theological sense, stood at the top of the ecclesiastical hierarchy.[36] What was the special status of these 'Western Churches' for Columbanus? Generally speaking, the ecclesiastical geopolitics outside the northern and western boundaries of the old imperial West during Late Antiquity can be summed up briefly as follows:

---

34 Charles-Edwards, *The Early Mediaeval Gaelic Lawyer*, p. 2.

35 This conclusion is upheld by the distinction made by Wilfrid when attacking the Irish at Whitby, where he linked the Irish with the Picts and Britons in maintaining their obstinance. Bede, *Historia Ecclesiastica*, III, § 25, p. 300 (text); p. 301 (trans.).

36 On the significance of the 'Churches of the West', in Celtic theology, see also, Mackey, 'The Theology of Columbanus', p. 233.

> The barbarian[37] churches did not fit the pattern of the churches inside the empire, and they embodied several anomalies that required special consideration. For one thing, these churches were beyond the boundaries of the Roman empire, and therefore technically outside the formal jurisdiction of any churches within the organizational structure of the imperial church.[38]

This *status quo* put the Irish in a unique position during Late Antiquity as the only Christianized *extera gens*[39] outside the erstwhile boundaries of the Western Empire, and the only such people to have been sent a bishop by the Pope.[40] So, in his letter to Pope Gregory wherein he referred to the 'Churches of the West' (cited above), was Columbanus referring to the position of the Irish Church and its vaguely defined extra-jurisdictional status in the fifth century and thereafter — that is, its position outside the imperial jurisdiction of Rome — as a justification for defying Pope Gregory? If so, Columbanus would seem to have been making a distinction between spiritual authority, i.e., as was expressed in the scriptures, the writings of the Church Fathers, etc. (that is, the precedence of authorities discussed above), and the ecclesiastical administrative authority, i.e., the authority that the Pope (and the religious hierarchy he oversaw), inherited

---

37 I will discuss the use of the word 'barbarian' below.

38 Mathisen, 'Barbarian Bishops and the Churches "in barbaricis gentibus"', p. 668. On this point, Elva Johnston's description of Ireland as a kind of frontier zone are similarly apropos: 'Pre-Christian Ireland was, materially at least, a sub-Roman cultural zone but its encounters with *romanitas* differed from those of Roman Britain and the Continent, mainly in terms of intensity and political engagement. Ireland was both part of a Roman milieu and other than Roman. The Irish were not newcomers, but neither were they directly part of the ancient *orbis Romana*; they were neither Romans nor Germanic barbarians. Furthermore, their adaptation of Roman and Christian culture was unique, for Irish society did not have to undergo the traumatic military and political dislocations that accompanied the transformation of the Roman West and, near at hand, Britain. This is not to deny that Irish society was undergoing a process of transformation before and on the eve of Christianization. In fact, it is useful to see the island as a frontier zone, comparable to other Roman frontiers. In some respects, the role played by events on the Rhine-Danube frontier in the eventual collapse of the western Empire, have tended to overshadow the experiences of other zones such as north Africa and, indeed, Ireland. Moreover, it could be argued that changes in Irish society were influenced by the island's frontier status. These changes continued right through the missionary period and well into the sixth and early seventh centuries', Johnston, *Literacy and Identity*, p. 11.

39 Perhaps the Picts also might be considered to hold this status? In any case, the Irish Church was by far the most significant, if indeed not the only, of the western *exterae gentes*. Note that the British Church was not an *extera gens* since it was within the borders of the Empire at its inception and for some time thereafter.

40 Pope Celestine dispatched Palladius to Ireland in 431. It should be noted, however, that Palladius may have gone to Pictland during this mission as well. Note that the Britons lay inside the imperial boundaries (at least until 410), and that other converted Christian peoples on the western frontier, the Picts for instance, where converted by Irish missions.

from the secular, governmental structures of the quondam Roman Empire. As regards the latter, the so-called 'Churches of the West' might be considered to fall outside the bounds of papal administrative (as opposed to theological) authority,[41] since they never came under Roman law. This distinction, I would argue, provided a fulcrum for Columbanus's argument in the latter portion of *Epistula* III, a later missive he sent to the Pope, again addressing the paschal controversy.

In this third letter (604/607),[42] Columbanus took up a different line of argumentation than he did in his earlier letters. No longer did he assert the uncompromising position that the Irish method for calculating the date of Easter should be sanctioned for all Christendom based on the testimony of Jerome and the scriptures. This time he took a different tack, pleading only that the Irish be permitted to celebrate Easter in the way they preferred, that is, the way that had been used in Gaul and determined by their own calculus.[43] Thus, after his petition based on ecclesiastical authorities failed him, he took a different approach in this letter, seeking instead to bolster his request by citing a decree of an ecumenical council, while at the same time offering his own interpretation of it. His argument relied on the unique place that the Irish occupied within the administrative structure of the Western Church. More specifically, Columbanus invoked the special legal status of the *exterae gentes* as decreed by the First Council of Constantinople (381). One might speculate that, in this case, he sought to appeal to a kind of authority the Pope might be more inclined to recognize. In any case, Columbanus concluded his *Epistula* III with a carefully wrought, parting salvo:

> Vale, dulcissime in Christo papa, memor nostri et in sanctis orationibus iuxta sanctorum cineres et in piissimis sanctionibus iuxta Constantinopolitanae synodi centum quinquaginta auctores, **ecclesias Dei in barbaris gentibus constitutas suis vivere legibus, sicut edoctas a patribus, iudicantes.**[44]

Walker translated the passage as follows:

---

41 Save perhaps for the Britons, as former Roman provincials; but Columbanus was most immediately concerned about Irish matters.

42 As Neil Wright comments: 'The third *epistula* can be dated to 604, or perhaps to 607; it is a short missive, again concerning the paschal controversy, to one of Gregory's immediate successors as Pope (either Sabinian or Boniface III; Columbanus does not himself know the addressee)', 'Columbanus's *Epistulae*', p. 29.

43 See Dailey, 'To Choose One Easter from Three', pp. 47–64 and Warntjes, 'Victorius vs Dionysius'.

44 Columbanus, *Sancti Columbani Opera*, 'Epistula III', ll. 31–35 p. 24. Emphasis my own, in both text and translation.

> Farewell, Pope most dear in Christ, mindful of us both in your holy prayers beside the ashes of the saints, and in your most godly decisions following the hundred and fifty authorities of the Council of Constantinople, who decreed that **the churches of God planted in pagan nations should live by their own laws, as they had been instructed by their fathers.**[45]

By any measure, this is a difficult passage to translate with proper care for all its subtleties. Walker's English version requires some modifications to capture its full sense accurately. What point, specifically, did Columbanus intend to make by citing this excerpt from canon 2 of the First Council of Constantinople (i.e., the portion of the quotation in bold)? For that matter, how did he understand this canon himself?

The first point to note is that Columbanus's citation of the canon differs significantly from the accepted text which, in its widely attested form, reads as follows:

> Ecclesias autem Dei in barbaricis gentibus constitutas gubernari convenit iuxta consuetudinem, quae est patribus instituta.[46]
>
>> (But the churches of God among the barbarian peoples must be administered in accordance with the custom in force during the time of the fathers).[47]

Some explanation is necessary. As Mathisen pointed out, '[t]he phrase "institutes of the Fathers" in similar contexts often referred to (the First Council of Nicaea, AD 325) [...] and its use here perhaps was intended to create an impression that this clause, too, had received some kind of undocumented support at Nicaea'.[48] What is more, this canon sanctioned the authority of the *consuetudo*, the 'custom', *quae est patribus instituta* 'that was instituted by the fathers', i.e., not the *leges* which Columbanus referred to instead, though it is difficult to determine exactly what difference this alternative term might have held for him. No doubt, in any case, Columbanus's substitution of *lex* for *consuetudo* was loaded. What should we make of his choice of wording in this case? I shall begin by considering the canon. Although the precise meaning of this portion of canon 2 is not entirely clear, one might render its meaning somewhat more precisely (with appreciation for its broader context) as such:

> But the churches of God among **the peoples outside imperial boundaries** must be administered in accordance with the custom

45 Columbanus, *Sancti Columbani Opera*, 'Epistula III', ll. 35–40 p. 25.

46 *The Oecumenical Councils from Nicea I to Nicaea II (325–787)*, canon 2 ll. 340–43 p. 65.

47 *Decrees of the Ecumenical Councils*, canon 2 p. 32.

48 Mathisen, 'Barbarian Bishops and the Churches "in barbaricis gentibus"', p. 668 n. 24.

> **which was established** (or perhaps 'endorsed') **by the Nicene fathers during the First Council of Nicaea.**[49]

It is not clear exactly what the canonist intended to signify by *consuetudo* here, but it seems most likely that the *patres* to which it refers were the Nicene fathers, invoking (accurately or not) their sanction as a bulwark for the current provision. In effect, then, the problem that this portion of canon 2 settled was twofold: (1) The *exterae gentes* held a different jurisdictional status than those peoples inside imperial boundaries. Specifically, they did not fall under the jurisdiction of bishops of another diocese within those imperial boundaries. Therefore, the internal affairs of the *exterae gentes* should be determined internally, presumably by provincial synods or — if any such authority existed[50] — by the bishop of their own *gens*. (2) The *exterae gentes* were to be governed by the 'custom' established — or, more likely, 'endorsed' — by the authority of the First Council of Nicaea. Most reasonably, thus, the primary intent of this canon was to protect the *exterae gentes* (particularly those outside the boundaries of the Eastern Empire, which were more numerous, and where the question had an immediate context) from extra-jurisdictional authority exerted by Roman bishops outside their dioceses. This canon underscored the notion that provincial matters, even among the *exterae gentes*, should be decided internally by provincial synods, not imposed by any authority from without.[51]

Note, however, how much more expansively Columbanus seems to have interpreted this provision:

> **From canon 2 of the First Council of Constantinople (381)**
> Ecclesias autem Dei in barbaricis gentibus constitutas gubernari convenit iuxta consuetudinem, quae est patribus instituta.
>
> **From Columbanus, *Epistula* III**
> Vale, dulcissime in Christo papa, memor nostri et in sanctis orationibus iuxta sanctorum cineres et in piissimis sanctionibus iuxta Constantinopolitanae synodi centum quinquaginta auctores, **ecclesias**

49 The translation, with emphasis, is my own.

50 The situation was quite complex, as Mathisen summarized it: 'The barbarian churches did not fit the pattern of churches inside the empire, and they embodied several anomalies that required special consideration. For one thing, these churches were beyond the boundaries of the Roman Empire, and therefore technically outside the formal jurisdiction of any churches within the organizational structure of the imperial church. Secondly, the bishops of these barbarians were bishops, not of cities, but of *gentes*. Furthermore, some Roman bishops for some time had been exercising a most uncanonical authority over some of these barbarian churches, which were not only not in their provinces but not even in their dioceses', 'Barbarian Bishops and the Churches "in barbaricis gentibus"', p. 668.

51 Mathisen, 'Barbarian Bishops and the Churches "in barbaricis gentibus"', p. 668.

> **Dei in barbaris gentibus constitutas suis vivere legibus, sicut edoctas a patribus,** iudicantes.

First of all, notice how the phrase *ecclesias [...] Dei in barbaricis gentibus constitutas* ***gubernari [...] iuxta consuetudinem*** (the churches [...] of God among the peoples outside imperial boundaries **must be administered [...] according to custom**) as it is stated in canon 2, is transformed in Columbanus's paraphrase. For Columbanus, the *exterae gentes* (in this case, the Irish) have sanction *suis vivere legibus,* that is, 'to live according to their own laws'. While the precise meaning (and the implications) of Columbanus's recasting of this phrase is difficult to determine, his use of the possessive *suis* (here in the ablative agreeing with *legibus* and referring back to the subject accusative *ecclesias Dei*) would appear to suggest that he understood this passage to signify Irish legal practices — probably ecclesiastical but, conceivably, Irish law generally[52] — not the jurisprudential custom of the Church (as sanctioned in the original canon). Whatever his intent (and whatever the precise meanings of the technical terms involved), it is certainly a very different matter for a church 'to be administered' (*gubernari*) 'according to custom' (*iuxta consuetudinem*), than 'to live according to its own laws' (*suis vivere legibus*). At the very least, Columbanus's paraphrase appears to assert that native law (ecclesiastical, at least, and perhaps secular, too) was not only something to which the Irish church had a right (in the face of external authorities, even that of the Apostolic See), but potentially also that it constituted a legitimate legal system that, in some cases, might be regarded as distinct and independent from the law of the Church as a whole. I shall have more to say about this point in what follows.

Other questions, more tangential to the point at hand, but no less important, arise. More difficult to know is what Columbanus meant by the phrase *sicut edoctas a patribus.* Walker renders it 'as they had been instructed by their fathers', taking the sense of the reflexive possessive *suis* from the previous clause to carry over semantically and modify *patribus.* Thus, he adds a further possessive 'their' modifying *patres* in his translation, giving the sense (which I alter here somewhat for emphasis) that the Irish should live by **their own** laws as instructed by [**their own**] *patres.* This translation would seem to suggest that the *patres* Columbanus indicated were Irish 'fathers'. If this rendering is correct, then the question immediately arises: who were these Irish *patres*? Did Columbanus mean clerical teachers within the Irish Church? More radically, did he intend to signify his Irish predecessors generally, in the sense of 'ancestors', such

52 As I shall argue in what follows, early Irish jurists sometimes viewed native law, both ecclesiastical and secular, as part of an overall Christian tradition. It is not inconceivable, therefore, that Columbanus might have intended to signify all Irish law collectively.

as the *Féni*[53] (or, perhaps even pre-Christian ancestors) who passed down the Irish laws? If so, then in what sense does his claim favour the primacy of native Irish law (ecclesiastical? Secular? Left intentionally vague?) in relation to external — in this case papal — prerogative? This question is informed, if not resolved, by other curious references Columbanus made to 'ancient' Irish scholars, most notably in his *Epistula 1*. Addressing the Pope, he claimed:

> Scias, namque **nostris magistris** et **Hibernicis antiquis philosophis** et sapientissimis componedi calculi **computariis** Victorium non fuisse recpetum, sed magis risu vel venia dignum auctoritate.[54]
>
> > (For you should know that Victorius has not been accepted by **our teachers** nor by the **ancient Irish savants**, nor by those **computists** most skilled in the reckoning of chronology, but is more worthy of laughter or indulgence than authority).[55]

It is not clear at all what Columbanus meant by *nostri magistri* (our teachers, i.e., presumably given the next phrase, 'our ⟨ancient, native Irish⟩ teachers'), *Hibernici antiqui philosophi* (⟨our⟩ ancient Irish savants, scholars, or philosophers?), and *computarii* (⟨our ancient, native Irish⟩ computists). What class of learned individuals in Irish society might have been appropriately described by an early seventh-century cleric as '**ancient** Irish savants', whose opinions, moreover, could be invoked legitimately as evidence before the Pope in a dispute over ecclesiastical matters? At the very least, Columbanus had confidence in his Christian education, even though he received it at the edge of the known world, as Elva Johnston has noticed:

> Columbanus, easily the most famous Irishman on the Continent of his generation, made this point forcefully. For him, Irish learning was equal with, if not in fact superior to, the best that could be found on the Continent. His admittedly somewhat murky role in the Three Chapters controversy showed that he saw himself as someone capable of making informed judgements on matters of Christian doctrine. He might have come from the ends of the earth but he evidently thought that Christianity put him on a par with his most illustrious contemporaries and enabled him to claim the Christian heritage just as

53 F. Kelly, *A Guide to Early Irish Law*, p. 311, defines *Féni* as follows: 'freemen of full legal capacity; *la Féniu*, among the Irish, according to Irish law; *bélrae* (later *bérla*) *Féne* the language of the *Féni*, legal language'. Moreover, he defines *fénechas* as 'the law of the *Féni*, customary or traditional law; native law (as opposed to Canon law, or later, English common law)', p. 311.

54 Columbanus, *Sancti Columbani Opera*, 'Epistula 1', ll. 2–5 p. 6. Emphasis my own, in both text and translation.

55 Columbanus, 'Columbanus, Letter 1', p. 153.

> much as those who came from the cities and lands that surrounded the central sea.[56]

And yet, there would appear to be more going on in the passage above than merely an expression of Columbanus's intellectual confidence. Regarding Columbanus's statement above, Esposito queried:

> Who were these 'ancient Irish philosophers and most wise calculators', and what exactly did Columbanus, writing to Pope Gregory about 595–600, mean by 'ancient'? Further, in his second letter[57] written in 603 or 604, he refers — quite wrongly — to Victorius [189?–198] as 'nuper dubie scribens' ⟨writing recently and in a doubtful manner⟩,[58] and obviously the *ancient* Irish philosophers and chronologists could not have treated with derision a *recent* writer.[59]

Thus, Esposito concludes, I think too hastily, that '⟨t⟩his passage may be regarded as a mere piece of rhetoric'.[60] Though unclear to a modern audience, I do not believe Columbanus's statement here can be dismissed so lightly. More likely, I would argue, Columbanus had some class of Irish intellectuals in mind who could indeed be described as more ancient than the second-century Pope Victorius, and who — in his understanding of Christian history — might nonetheless speak with some authority on Christian matters. More needs to be discussed, however, before I can address this topic fully. For now, suffice to say that Columbanus apparently believed in an ancient class of Irish intellectuals who were Christian in some sense (but perhaps with some secular, traditional role as well?) who passed down some body of knowledge relevant to Christian matters and whose testimony was pertinent to resolving technical *quaestiones* within the Church, and which might legitimately (from his perspective) be offered as evidence to the Pope as a point of argument on the Easter controversy.

To return to the question of Columbanus's paraphrase of canon 2: reading the text of *Epistula III* closely (in the context of his other letters) and considering the evidence adduced so far, I am inclined to believe in this case that with the term *patres* Columbanus meant to signify clerical teachers within the Irish church. Some evidence is found for this interpretation in two places immediately preceding the citation in question. First, Columbanus asked the Pope:

---

56 Johnston, *Literacy and Identity*, p. 3.
57 Columbanus, *Sancti Columbani Opera*, 'Epistula I', ll. 13 p. 18.
58 Columbanus, *Sancti Columbani Opera*, 'Epistula II', l. 15 p. 19.
59 Esposito, 'On the New Edition Edition', p. 185.
60 Esposito, 'On the New Edition Edition', p. 185.

> [...] ut nobis peregrinis laborantibus tuae pium sententiae solatium praestes, quo si non contra fidem est **nostrorum traditionem** robores **seniorum**, quo ritum Paschae sicut accepimus a **maioribus** observare per tuum possimus iudicium in nostra peregrinatione.[61]
>
> > ([...] that you would grant to us pilgrims in our travail the godly consolation of your judgement, thus confirming, if it is not contrary to the faith, **the tradition of our predecessors**, so that by your approval we may in our pilgrimage maintain the rite of Easter as we have received it from **generations gone before** ⟨or perhaps, '**from our ancestors**'⟩).[62]

Immediately thereafter, he continues:

> Constat enim nos in nostra esse patria, dum nullas istorum suscipimus regulas Gallorum, sed in desertis sedentes, nulli molesti, cum **nostrorum regulis manemus seniorum** [...].[63]
>
> > (For it is admitted that we are in our native land,[64] while we accept no rules of your Frankish friends, but dwelling in seclusion, harming no one, **we abide by the rules of our predecessors** [...]).[65]

Like the passage wherein he cited the First Council of Constantinople, here too, Columbanus referred to native Irish authorities, twice using the designation *seniores*, and once *maiores* to identify them. As they are used in the passages cited here, all of these terms would seem to signify clerical authorities. If we assume, then, that Columbanus intended these terms in the same (or similar) sense as *patres* in his paraphrase of canon 2 (i.e., in the citation from canon 2 under discussion) — and, admittedly, that is an assumption — then some light may be shed. In Hiberno-Latin, *senior* and *maior* had a wide sematic range that included both ecclesiastical

61 Columbanus, *Sancti Columbani Opera*, 'Epistula III', ll. 16–19 p. 24. Emphasis my own, in both text and translation.

62 Columbanus, *Sancti Columbani Opera*, 'Epistula III', ll. 17–21 p. 25.

63 Columbanus, *Sancti Columbani Opera*, 'Epistula III', ll. 19–22 p. 24. Emphasis my own, in both text and translation.

64 Columbanus, *Sancti Columbani Opera*, p. 25 n. 3, suggests that this phrase means, 'i.e., that we are outwith the jurisdiction of the French hierarchy'. Smit suggests: '[...] ⟨Columbanus⟩ gives a remarkable reason for his obstinate clinging to his own customs: *Constat enim nos in nostra esse patria, dum nullae istorum suscipimus regulas Gallorum* [...] as long as the Irish in Gaul did not adopt any of the Gallic customs, they remained outside the jurisdiction of the Gallican episcopate, they remained *Irish* [italics Smit's]', *Studies on the Language and Style of Columba the Younger*, p. 90. He further suggests, 'Homesickness may have been a factor here' (!), p. 90 n. 3. To the best of my knowledge, no-one has examined his reference to the First Council of Constantinople, p. 381.

65 Columbanus, *Sancti Columbani Opera*, 'Epistula III', ll. 21–24 p. 25.

and secular authorities.[66] Context, I would argue, favours the former interpretation, however: here, it seems most likely that, in his paraphrase of canon 2 of the First Council of Constantinople, Columbanus intended to signify his ecclesiastical predecessors with the word *patres*, i.e., those Irish clerics who celebrated Easter before him, according to their own method of calculating the date. Thus, I propose the following translation of Columbanus's paraphrase (loosely rendered to capture the implicit sense of his words):

> Vale, dulcissime in Christo papa, memor nostri et in sanctis orationibus iuxta sanctorum cineres et in piissimis sanctionibus iuxta Constantinopolitanae synodi centum quinquaginta auctores, **ecclesias Dei in barbaris gentibus constitutas suis vivere legibus, sicut edoctas a patribus,** iudicantes.
>
>> (Farewell, Pope most dear in Christ, mindful of us both in your holy prayers beside the ashes of the saints, and in your most godly decisions following the hundred and fifty authorities of the Council of Constantinople, who decreed that **the churches of God planted in pagan nations should live by their own laws, as they had been instructed by ⟨their own⟩ clerical elders** ⟨or perhaps, '**and decided in their own provincial synods**'⟩).

This is how I am inclined to read the passage but, to be sure, I am a bit uneasy about it. Without question, these words are loaded: perhaps Columbanus intended to leave the matter somewhat vague,[67] or perhaps to veil some kind of tacit threat? On the other hand, perhaps he was thinking about the Irish people and Irish law and their place within Christian history in some particular way that, to a modern audience is (and indeed, perhaps also to a contemporary audience was) not immediately clear.[68] At the very least, the evidence discussed so far would suggest that

---

66 See, for example, *The Dictionary of Medieval Latin from British Sources*, s.v. *maior*, 5d '[...] (pl.) ancestors, forebears', 7 (as sb. m. pl.) predecessors, elder in time, higher in authority, but also 8f '(eccl., also sg.)'; s.v. *senior*, 6d '(of cleric)' and 6e (of teacher), but also 5 'elder, ancestor, forefather, predecessor'.

67 On other occasions, Columbanus recast the wording of his sources significantly. See, for example, Wright, 'Columbanus's *Epistulae*', p. 79.

68 To be sure, one point seems clear: Columbanus was likely appealing to the Pope with respect to the notion that the conversion of the Irish — the *exterae gens* at the end of the world (known at that time) — was, in the words of Damian Bracken, '[...] the point at which Rome realized its claim to universal responsibility for all churches [...] and became the *universalis ecclesia*', 'Juniors Teaching Elders', p. 255. And yet, there was a view expressed from the Apostolic See emphasizing the insignificance of the Irish as but *mentagrae orbis terrarum* (pimples on the face of the earth), Cummian, *'De controversia paschali' and the 'De ratione conputandi'*, p. 72 (text); p. 75 (trans.). See also: O'Reilly, 'Islands and Idols at the End of the Earth', pp. 119–45.

a clerical elder (*senior, maior, philosophus, magister*, etc.) as Columbanus understood the role, would have signified something different than it did to Pope Gregory. For Columbanus, it appears there was an Irish tradition of Christian learning that might be described as 'ancient'; more so, as we have seen, than Victorius toward the end of the second century (and so well before the historical fifth-century conversion of the Irish). For him, this tradition was 'Christian', if not straightforwardly in a historically literal sense, then in some other way, sufficiently canonical and theologically sound that it could be invoked as evidence in the paschal controversy roughly four centuries later.

This debate raises important questions. For now, however, let me set them aside. A full treatment of them must await matters I discuss below. For present purposes, suffice to say that, however one takes Columbanus's statement in his passage from *Epistula III* recasting the decision made at Constantinople in 381 — conservatively (as I have), as a claim for native Irish ecclesiastical privilege over papal authority in some cases or, more radically, as an endorsement of native Irish law in some broader sense — it seems that Columbanus attempted to accomplish two things in *Epistula III*. First, he sought to assert the independence of the Irish Church in the face of Roman authority and, second, to sanction the jurisdiction of Irish ecclesiastical law where it pertained to internal affairs (as adjudicated, presumably, in Irish provincial synods) above decrees from without, even those issued by the Apostolic See. By any measure, Columbanus's claim was bold, and the skill with which he made his argument and the technical knowledge upon which he relied is impressive. That said, questions arise. Foremost among them: was his rendering of the decision at Constantinople simply a misunderstanding, or was it an intentional equivocation of the provision? While it is impossible to know for certain, I am inclined toward the latter conclusion. In the canon proper, the churches outside the former Empire must *gubernari* [...] *iuxta consuetudinem* (be administered [...] in accordance with custom), where *gubernari* is in the passive and refers to no explicitly stated agent. So, for anyone reading the canonical statute, the question might arise: who or what governing body was to administer law according to custom? This potential lack of clarity, I would argue, provided a convenient opening for Columbanus to interpret the phrase opportunistically. In his paraphrase, he recast the provision so that the agent was clear: the churches *in barbaris gentibus* — i.e., the Irish, in this case — were not 'to be administered' (*gubernari*), passively, 'according to custom', but rather should live (*vivere*) — actively — 'according to their own laws'. Cast in this syntax, Columbanus's version of the canon supported the idea that the Irish church was its own master, and — at least where internal matters were concerned — should determine its own legal fate; in this case, when calculating the date of Easter. The implications of his argument, however, were significantly more far-reaching.

Many more questions arise about Columbanus's paraphrase of the canon. For example: What, for Columbanus, was the distinction between *consuetudo* (in the canon) and *lex* (as it was rendered in Columbanus's paraphrase)? Does the verb *edocere,* which Columbanus used in the phrase *sicut edoctas a patribus,* signify something intentionally distinct — perhaps something different about the way he understood Irish law (Christian or secular) to have been transmitted — than the verb *instituere* from the canon, in the parallel phrase *est patribus instituta*? Might, for example, Columbanus have conceived of law as something that was taught (*edocere*) as opposed to what was 'established' (or 'decreed', or 'endorsed' = *instituere*)? These are important questions, albeit ones which I shall not be able to address here.

Enough for now. Let me wrap up this portion of the discussion. For my present purposes, I am most interested in the way Columbanus presented his argument. In the citations from his *Epistulae* I have discussed so far, he deployed two different arguments based on two distinct types of legal ideology. First, as we have seen, he relied on the notion — made explicit in later Hiberno-Latin canon law — that there existed a prescribed order of precedence by which one should consult authorities. And so, Columbanus pointed to fundamental authorities supporting his case and, what is more, that they agreed with one another. When this tactic fell on deaf ears, he shifted his tactics and subsequently built his case on different grounds. Namely, he argued that the technicalities of the Western Church's administrative structure — and what he believed to be the special place of the Irish within that structure based on his interpretation of the decree of an ecumenical council — endowed the Irish with a certain degree of independence from papal authority. Although Columbanus's arguments were highly theoretical in nature, his goal was eminently pragmatic. The date upon which one celebrated Easter represented a basic expression of the Christian faith. For Columbanus, proper conduct of the rituals associated with it might well affect the status of his immortal soul, not to mention those for whom he served as pastor. His method, thus — though heavily technical — bore directly on matters that, from his theological perspective, carried real-world (and perhaps real-afterworld) implications. In what follows, I shall explore this relationship more thoroughly as I seek to identify and define the ideological foundations of early Irish law.

Part One

Early Irish Law

CHAPTER 2

Background

Early Irish Law

Nowhere in the early medieval West did the relationship between ecclesiastical and pre-Christian, native law receive more attention than in Ireland. There, debate over how to harmonize these radically diverse bodies of jurisprudence provoked repeated consideration and re-consideration. The surviving evidence points to continuous, ongoing discussion about how to resolve this multi-layered, legal-theological dilemma, which might aptly be described as a protracted collision of ideologies fomenting an ongoing discourse that lasted for several centuries, at least. Over the course of the early Middle Ages, various provisional frameworks designed to address this problem emerged, none of which ever became predominant. Irish *literati*[1] of different intellectual orientations and with varying agendas proposed diverse solutions, while redactors of the same text would appear to have disagreed on major points of doctrine. All evidence suggests that explanations of the relationship between ecclesiastical and pre-Christian, native law were very much in flux throughout the early Middle Ages and beyond, rendering it impossible to identify a single model intended to explain the complex interrelations between these legal ideologies that one could designate as unequivocally 'Irish'.

From the outset, it is necessary to define some of the terms I use to describe early Irish law and those who practised it, some of which I use differently than other scholars and some of which I have coined. First, by 'pre-Christian, native law' I intend to signify the unwritten, customary law rooted in the legal system that predated the introduction of Christianity to Ireland. This body of law did not disappear entirely after conversion, despite being encompassed within an overall Christian legal framework that influenced it on nearly every level. Thus, in what follows, by 'pre-Christian, native law' I mean to signify both the customary law that existed in Ireland prior to the advent of Christianity and the legal system based on it that continued to develop post-conversion. Of course, we only have direct textual evidence of the latter. Very soon after the introduction of Christianity, the new faith began to influence pre-Christian,

1 I intend the term *literati* to be a neutral term designating all members of the Irish intellectual elite, whether primarily secular or ecclesiastical in their orientation and affiliation.

native law; and by the time the first texts emerged, the two systems had already blended to a significant degree. Since all written records post-date the introduction of the new faith, this distinction is, to some extent, a hypothetical reconstruction. That said, the surviving texts indicate that such a distinction existed in the minds of the early Irish *literati*, even if what I refer to here as 'pre-Christian, native law' had become significantly Christianized by the time the first written texts emerged.

Second, I use the term 'native' as opposed to 'secular' because, for reasons I shall discuss at length below, the simple opposition 'secular versus ecclesiastical' is insufficient to describe early Irish law, at least given the way these terms are understood in modern scholarship. To equate pre-Christian, native Irish law with secular law unaccompanied by a flurry of explanatory statements would be misleading. First and most importantly, I do not intend to signify 'pagan' with any of these terms. What I refer to as 'pre-Christian, native law' had become deeply Christianized by the historical period. Second, pre-Christian law — while, by definition, not 'Christian' — might nonetheless be perceived in retrospect as being situated within a Christian ideological framework. For example, pre-Christian, native law might be construed as 'natural law' and, as such, oriented toward an overtly Christian *telos*. For accuracy, therefore, I distinguish between (what was originally foreign) ecclesiastical law and pre-Christian, native law, since in the surviving record, both systems of jurisprudence (to the extent they were separate at all) contain, to a greater or lesser extent, features that might, in modern scholarly terms, be designated 'secular' or 'ecclesiastical'. This, in any case, is what I mean by 'pre-Christian, native' law and 'secular' law. More broadly, by describing the different and sometimes distinct bodies of law that existed in early medieval Ireland with these terms, I seek to be more precise than other commonly used categorizations, such as those T. M. Charles Edwards enumerated as '[the] three characteristic oppositions — Latin versus Irish, ecclesiastical versus secular, and international versus native [...]' that 'generally coincided' in early medieval Ireland.[2]

Third, I use the hyphenated term 'legal-theological' as a technical designation here and throughout to signify a concept more specific than what any alternative designation I could devise, such as 'legal and theological', 'juridical theology', or 'law informed by theology' (or vice versa), might signify. By 'legal-theological', I intend to emphasize the connection, even the unity, between these modes of thought in the mind of early Irish intellectuals. Part and parcel of my thesis in the present volume is that ideologically (if not always pragmatically) speaking, for the medieval Irish *literati*, law and Christian theology were not merely aspects of the same

2 Charles-Edwards, *The Early Mediaeval Gaelic Lawyer*, p. 5.

effort in a joint endeavour. Rather, in the early medieval Irish worldview, these fields (separate in the modern mind, but not in early medieval Ireland) were practically indistinguishable. So, what we think of now as the separate fields of law and theology were conceived of as one intellectual category in early medieval Ireland operating together, not conjointly but identically, in a single, unified gesture with the same goal(s).

I will clarify my use of these terms as they bear on certain arguments I make below. For now, let me return to my main argument. While common themes can be identified, Irish views about the relationship between ecclesiastical and pre-Christian, native law evolved over time with entirely new solutions (or at least re-formulations, partial or complete) surfacing periodically. From the outset, it is important to accept that contradictions, real and apparent, will characterize evidence derived from the primary texts. Regarding this point, Claire Stancliffe's observation about a related genre seems apropos here as well: '[...] while the Irish loved categorizing their material at a superficial level, beneath this they were often happy to live with two or more variants, even when these seem contradictory'.[3] While, in this instance, Stancliffe was describing a feature of early Irish homiletic literature, her remarks apply equally to the legal materials. Generally speaking, therefore, we should not expect to unearth a single, unified resolution to this multifaceted dilemma upon which the Irish *literati* ever settled. As is often true in debates of central importance to a culture's perception of its own identity within the context of a broader ideological framework — especially when elements are introduced from foreign sources (as was Christianity in this case) — anxiety inevitably arises about any number of critical issues. As a result, heterogeneous, even antithetical responses periodically emerged, submerged, and later re-emerged without any single one ever achieving permanent buoyancy, at least not during the early period. So, questions about the relationship between ecclesiastical and pre-Christian, native law in early medieval Ireland failed to achieve

3 Stancliffe, 'Red, White and Blue Martyrdom', pp. 21–46. In this context, Josef Falaky Nagy's points in *Conversing with the Angels* should be kept in mind. Even though his points were intended to address belletristic literature primarily (rather than law proper), his insights about the ideological heterogeneity that typifies medieval Irish literature nonetheless resonate in the present context: 'It may seem quixotic to seek ideological consistencies in a literature that is the product of such seemingly disparate strands and layers of literary tradition. The cultivation of heterogeneity can be a legitimizing tactic, however, and signs that seem unrelated or even conflicting can often add up to a continuum, not chaos, in this literature', p. 15 and 'The profound thematic consistencies, as well as inconsistencies, among texts from many different sources ⟨in Irish literature⟩ [...] constitute evidence, therefore, not only for extensive literary borrowing but also for a productive ideological substructure to medieval Irish literature and to the culture that in producing this literature reproduced itself', p. 22.

unequivocal resolution, despite the often-confident rhetoric that typically contextualized essentially provisional answers.

What is more, certain legal-theological questions bearing on (and sometimes derivative of) this underlying ideological dilemma likewise eluded straightforward, widely accepted, or consistent answers. Such questions raised implicitly by the early Irish *literati* and apparent in early Irish legal literature included, for example: (1) What was the place of the Irish within Christian history[4] prior to and after conversion? From whom (within the timeline of Christian history, as they understood it) were the Irish descended, and what implications might such a lineage entail in biblical law? Did Christian law, given the Irish understanding of their place in Christian history, supplant pre-Christian, native law and, more broadly, native juridical traditions generally; and, if not entirely, then to what extent? Was there room in the Christian understanding of history within which the Irish might situate the narrative of their own ethnogenesis that did not abjure crucial ideological pillars of their own self-perceived, pre-Christian history, and that might even provide a context for it? (2) What was the legal-theological status of the Irish as converted gentiles within the Christian faith and its concomitant implications in biblical law? Were the Irish subject to the Law of Nature, the Law of Noah, the Law of Moses, the Law of the Prophets, or the Law of Christ, and — if any (or all) of these — then in what sense specifically? How did these 'Laws' relate to one another in a practical sense that the Irish could apply pragmatically to lawgiving? What about their ancestors, whose condition in the afterlife, from the perspectives of these new converts, hung in the balance? And, perhaps most vitally, (3) what was the role of the Church in Irish secular jurisprudence and vice versa? How should these interconnected bodies of law relate to one another and coexist, if both were to continue in this newly Christianized environment? Elizabeth Boyle addresses many of these questions in her recent volume *History and Salvation in Medieval Ireland*. While her volume stands out as a fundamental starting point for considering these questions, my approach differs in minor, but significant ways. For example, while Boyle emphasizes (but does not limit herself to)

---

4 In the context of this volume, by 'sacred history' I intend to signify the Christian understanding of universal history, beginning with the creation as expressed in Genesis and continuing, in this worldview, through the events described in the Bible to the present day and ultimately to the Apocalypse, as expressed in the biblical book of Revelation. I shall provide a fuller explanation of patristic and Irish understandings of this worldview in what follows. As related in the Bible — and particularly in the Old Testament — the account of sacred history largely focused on the Israelites. In the New Testament, and particularly in the Pauline Epistles, questions surrounding the place of gentiles in this broader narrative was considered at length, but still left many questions unanswered from an Irish perspective. For the Irish, pseudo-historical accounts filled the gap. I shall have a great deal to say about these stories in what follows. See also, Boyle, *History and Salvation*, pp. 16–19 and 188.

literary sources, I focus on (but do not limit myself to) legal materials. Most of all, I am sceptical of the claims — made by Boyle and others[5] — that the Irish envisioned themselves, literally, as 'God's Chosen People', and that early Irish jurists saw themselves as Old Testament Levites, as I shall discuss at length below. That said, the similarities between our conclusions far outweigh their differences; and I believe my arguments here, with only a few exceptions, amplify hers.

Although primarily theoretical in nature, these matters were nonetheless pressing since they bore directly on day-to-day, practical jurisprudence. If, for example, Irish society embraced the New Testament idea of forgiveness (in whatever sense) as a practical replacement for the Old Testament (and similar, pre-Christian, native) notions of retribution, however theologically sound the rationale underlying any such justification might be, the impact of this putative decision on the legal culture of Irish society would likely be devastating (as the author of the Pseudo-historical Prologue to the *Senchas Már* realized, and which I shall discuss at great length below). More broadly, how would the proper relationships between individuals and institutions within society be regulated? As in any culture, chaos would ensue if fundamental societal interrelations were not clearly defined and controlled. Indeed, the late seventh-century Irish legal text *Córus Bésgnai* begins by expressing this very concern:

> § **1.** *Córus Bésgnai co háragar? I coraib bél, ar is bailedach in bith mani astaitis cuir bél?*[6]
>
> (§ **1.** The arrangement of discipline, how is it secured? By contracts, for it would indeed be a chaotic world if contracts were not held fast).[7]

Simply put, without enforced laws governing relationships between individuals and institutions, society would fail; but what would it mean to enforce the law in this new, Christianized world, especially in matters where it bore on practices and social interactions unique to Irish culture and which might come into conflict with Christian doctrine?

A multiplicity of solutions emerged to define the relationship between pre-Christian, native and ecclesiastical law, none of which ever resolved into a single, predominant, or officially sanctioned position. Throughout the early Middle Ages, Irish legal-theological ideology was as rife with thoughtful questions as it was lacking in generally accepted resolutions. To be sure, given the highly decentralized, local nature of both the Church

5 For references to recent scholarship on this point, see, for example, Brady, *The Origin Legends of Early Medieval Britain and Ireland*, p. 67 and n. 15.

6 The text is from *Córus Bésgnai*, p. 26.

7 The translation from *Córus Bésgnai*, p. 27.

and lay authority in early Irish culture and their intellectual sphere of influence abroad, perhaps such unanimity of thought would not have been conceivable.

Despite these complications and the disagreements they precipitated — in fact, because of them — Ireland provides fertile ground to begin investigating the early medieval reception and adaptation of late-antique, Christian ideas (patristic and otherwise) by the non- or only thinly Romanized cultures of Northwestern Europe. As the first literate culture in the West among those converted peoples outside the immediate geographical hegemony of either the former Empire or the Church — that is, those cultures described by Roman Christians as *gentes barbaricae* (or collectively as *barbaricum*)[8] — Ireland provides a rare glimpse into the transitional, newly-Christianized ideology of the cultures in Northwestern Europe soon after conversion.[9] Ireland stands out as a unique example of how those peoples outside erstwhile imperial boundaries, and hence outside the formal ecclesiastical administrative structures that endured teeteringly for a time after Rome's secular government disintegrated, understood their place within Christendom (a geographical identity that was essentially one and the same with the Roman Empire, at least in the West, until Ireland's inclusion) and, perhaps more importantly, how they understood their role in their broader narrative of Christian history.

In the chapters that follow, I shall examine how the Irish received the legal-theological heritage of late antique Christendom and transformed it into something uniquely their own, particularly in light of residual pre-Christian, native ideologies. I shall also consider, albeit in limited fashion, how the Irish exported their legal-theological ideologies abroad. Since the Irish were among the first of the northwestern European peoples to convert, and since they played an active role in early efforts to missionize Britain and the Continent, it stands to reason that their treatment of

8 For use of these terms, see, for example, Mathisen, 'Barbarian Bishops and the Churches', pp. 665 and 669. I here use the term 'barbarian' in the same sense as Mathiesen: 'It should [...] be noted that the word "barbarian" will be used here as a convenient, nonpejorative term to refer to all the non-Latin- and non-Greek-speaking *exterae gentes* who dwelt around, or eventually settled within the Roman Empire during late antiquity', p. 665. See also, Mathiesen, *Roman Aristocrats in Barbarian Gaul*', pp. 1–6 and 39–49, and Ladner, 'On Roman Attitudes toward Barbarians', pp. 1–25.

9 In fact, as Ralph W. Mathisen points out in 'Barbarian Bishops and the Churches', p. 667 and n. 19, the Irish were the only people in Western Europe to whom the Church made direct overtures in the early period: 'In the West [...] the situation was somewhat different. In only one instance is a bishop, or a cleric of any kind, known to have been dispatched to western barbarians beyond the frontier. According to the chronicle of Prosper, in 431 Palladius was sent as *primus episcopus*: "Ad Scottos in Christum credentes ordinatus a papa Celestino Palladius primus episcopus mittitur" ("Palladius, appointed as ⟨their⟩ first bishop, was sent by Pope Celestine to the Irish believing in Christ")', Prosper Tiro, 'Epitoma chronicon', p. 473.

late-antique Christianity in the centuries immediately following the slow dissolution of the Roman Empire would provide a bridge to understanding later medieval Christian thought, not only in Ireland itself, but also in the wider world with which they maintained close contacts. Much work remains to be done in this fruitful area of research and, no doubt, much awaits discovery. Given the extensive contacts between the early Irish *literati* and the broader European world, opportunities for comparative study abound. Unfortunately, I shall be able to accomplish little more than to scratch the surface here. In this study, I shall restrict myself to exploring how certain legal-theological ideas developed in early medieval Ireland (and in Irish foundations on the Continent) were exported to Anglo-Saxon England and played a role in shaping legal thought there.

At present, our understanding of this period during which the *gentes barbaricae* situated beyond the northern boundaries of the old Roman Empire received and adapted Christian ideologies — arguably the most adumbral period in both Irish and, more broadly European, history after the Iron Age — remains severely limited by a number of factors. By 'this period', I mean those centuries between roughly 600, when the first written texts of Irish origin emerged (whether in Old Irish or Hiberno-Latin) and 900, by which time most of the basic legal material[10] (here again, regardless of language) had been set to vellum.[11] Moreover, by 900, the influence of the Irish missions throughout Western Christendom had mostly, albeit incompletely, been subsumed by intellectual offshoots of the Carolingian *Renovatio* which, by 900, had already taken over, with increasing momentum, the leading role as the principal voice of European Christian thought, legal and otherwise. At the same time, these approximate dates demarcate the first of the three chronological periods into which Irish vernacular literature has conventionally been divided (i.e., 'Old Irish', to *c.* 900, as opposed to the later divisions 'Middle Irish', *c.* 900–*c.* 1200, and 'Early Modern Irish', *c.* 1200–*c.* 1650). Across the Irish Sea in Anglo-Saxon England, which I shall discuss later in this volume, these dates mark roughly that period from the introduction of Christianity and the advent of the first written texts (including the Laws of Æðelberht, king of Kent, d. 616) to the end of King Alfred's reign (871–899), under whom Anglo-Saxon England was first united under a single ruler. So, these dates — fuzzy and imprecise as they are — will provide the rough *termini* within which I shall delimit the present study. That said, the implications

10 By 'basic legal material', I mean what scholars have referred to as the 'base text' of the laws, as opposed to glosses and commentary. These latter two categories — the value of which for the history of Irish law should not be underestimated — remained a robust feature of Irish jurisprudence throughout the Middle Ages and well into the early modern period.

11 Most of the basic legal material was likely produced in a single century, between *c.* 650 and *c.* 750.

as well as the main objects of my arguments will quickly breach these boundaries, both early and late. My intent in proposing them is merely to set an approximate temporal focus for the study that follows, lest it span beyond what can be addressed reasonably in a single, initial study of this fascinating, problematic, and intellectually forbidding period in Irish and European history.

Argument and Method

Many fundamental questions pertaining to the reception and transformation of Christian thought in early medieval Ireland (pertinent not just to legal matters) remain unresolved in modern scholarship and require fuller investigation including, above all, questions concerning the Irish export of their ideas abroad. While acknowledging that a fuller understanding of these issues would likely affect or at least nuance the conclusions I shall draw in the present volume, I nonetheless propose here to break new ground by examining a very specific set of questions. In particular, my purpose is to identify the ideological foundations of early Irish law, first by investigating the Irish reception of the Christian ideological framework(s) transmitted to them via the scriptures, the Church Fathers, and other, mostly late-antique legal (and quasi-legal)[12] documents that fundamentally affected Irish legal thought as it had existed from well before the emergence of the first written texts in Old Irish or Hiberno-Latin. Second, I shall explore how the Irish transformed these ideologies, particularly as they sought to formulate and define the relationship between pre-Christian, native law and this (mostly Roman and, often more immediately Romano-British)[13] Christian inheritance. Thus, I shall focus on the various ideological frameworks developed in medieval Ireland (and in religious foundations of Irish origin in Britain and on the Continent) constructed expressly to harmonize ecclesiastical and pre-Christian, native

12 By 'quasi-legal', I intend to signify documents that are regulatory in nature, but which are not traditionally considered to be 'law' in contemporary scholarship, such as penitentials, prologues to law codes, monastic rules, and other such texts that explicitly (or implicitly) prescribe, prohibit, limit, sanction, or define certain behaviours.

13 The impact of the British Church on early Irish legal thought, although poorly understood, was significant. On this topic, Charles-Edwards, *The Early Mediaeval Gaelic Lawyer*, p. 4, commented: 'The Irish Church needed its own law. Because Roman law had lost its authority in Britain, the missionaries had not introduced Roman law; and yet they did not accept that Irish law should, quite simply, be their law. In Western Christendom, therefore, the Irish Church was apparently the first to develop what one could call a full canon law, a developed legal system with a wide jurisdiction [...] ⟨T⟩his ecclesiastical law was also of interest to those who had brought Christianity to the Irish, the Britons. Indeed, the beginnings of the tradition may go back to fifth-century Britain'. See also pp. 1–2.

law.[14] To a lesser extent, I shall examine the rhetorical strategies that legalists employed when addressing these issues and the disputes that arose surrounding them. Finally, I shall examine some specific aspects of this legal ideology that were transmitted to Anglo-Saxon England during the early Middle Ages. Unfortunately, it lies beyond the scope of this present volume to examine the influence of ideologies which the Irish exported further afield.

Let me emphasize that my intent here is to explore the foundational ideologies that underlay the relationship between ecclesiastical and pre-Christian, native law, not to (re)define or to work out the multifaceted and complex associations between particular statutes, institutions, or learned professions within early medieval Irish society, which would require a much larger and significantly more complicated project, to say the least. Nor is it my goal to (re)examine the technical features of Irish law, to catalogue every similarity or point of contact between different systems of jurisprudence (pre-Christian native, ecclesiastical, etc.), nor to survey the many legal-theological and other intellectual issues that informed early Irish legal thought beyond those which bear directly on my topic. Many a worthy article and several volumes have been written on these matters, and there remains yet an enormous amount of work to be done. In the present volume, I intend not to make a great leap forward, but only to take a small step. While certain peripheral details will at times enter into the discussion by way of example or to provide evidence for my broader claims, I set out only to describe the ideology or, more precisely, the competing ideologies, that both provided a framework for and guided Irish lawgiving in all its various manifestations during the early Middle Ages, particularly as it bears on how the Irish *literati* reconciled the relationship between pre-Christian, native and ecclesiastical law. Above all, I want to emphasize that it is not my main purpose to describe Irish law as it was practised.[15] For the most part, I am less concerned here with what actually happened in early medieval Irish courts or other real-world, legal milieux,

---

14 While my focus will be on explicit treatment of the relationship between ecclesiastical and pre-Christian, native law, I shall at times selectively include discussion of texts which treat this problem implicitly.

15 In this sense, my methods and goals differ from other recent approaches, such as Stacey, *Dark Speech*. See especially pp. 7–14, where Stacey explains her methodology, arguing that texts like the Old Irish vernacular codes, which she aptly describes as 'written, stylized, and largely descriptive in nature', p. 7, can productively be mined for information about how law was performed in early medieval Ireland. Like Stacey, I too acknowledge the important connections between legal and non-legal literature in early Ireland, both vernacular and in Latin. For example, she points out that: '⟨L⟩aw tracts of all traditions and regions [...] ⟨drew⟩ on characters from the literary realm like Finn, Cú Chulainn, or Conchobar's jurist Sencha on the one hand, or characters from the Bible like Lucifer, Adam, or Cain and Abel on the other', p. 10.

than with how Irish jurists of all ranks and affiliations described — and, presumably, prescribed — how law should function as an ideal; how it was imagined and, most of all, on what bases it was imbued with authority. Certainly, these prescriptive ideologies affected the day-to-day practice of law in a plethora of ways; and while I am interested in such phenomena secondarily (and shall at times discuss them), they are not the primary object of this study.

Necessarily, this task will lead me to consider pertinent theological issues, albeit selectively. Law and Christian theology, while tightly connected throughout the Middle Ages and often thereafter, were especially close — indeed, virtually indistinguishable — in early medieval Ireland. Certainly, one cannot understand Irish law without a thorough knowledge of the theology that underlay it and played an integral role in constructing it. That said, much remains yet to be unearthed in the closely related field of early Irish theology as well, particularly in the fifth and sixth centuries, the poorly understood intellectual developments of which laid the groundwork for the period of intense legal activity in the centuries that followed.[16] As briefly as possible, I shall discuss the relevant issues as they arise but, regrettably, it lies beyond the scope of this study to address them fully. Throughout, my purpose shall be to maintain focus as strictly as possible on the specific question of how Irish jurists explained the relationship between the law that existed in Ireland prior to conversion and continued residually to some extent afterward, and the Christian legal system, introduced later, that increasingly circumscribed it.

To this end, I shall discuss a wide variety of textual witnesses that bear on the question at hand. Among these witnesses, two legal texts will be especially important: one written in Latin, the other in vernacular Irish. These include, first, the early collection of canon law known as *Collectio canonum Hibernensis* compiled under Irish auspices during the first half of the eighth century. The second, the so-called Pseudo-historical Prologue to the *Senchas Már* (hereafter, the Pseudo-historical Prologue), is an eighth-century composition adapted from earlier material to provide a pseudo-historical context for the collection of Old Irish vernacular legal tracts known and the *Senchas Már* (The Great Tradition).[17] Part One will culminate with a close study of the Pseudo-historical Prologue. Of course, a great number of texts from a variety of literary and utilitarian genres will enter the discussion, including but not limited to those with legal, historical, belletristic, pseudo-historical, and religious orientations; these two documents, however, will hold a place of special importance throughout. Unfortunately, in a study as wide-ranging as this one, I cannot

16 See, for example, Herren and Brown, *Christ in Celtic Christianity*, pp. 1–19.

17 See especially: 'An Edition of the Pseudo-historical Prologue', p. 10. See also: Charles-Edwards, 'Early Irish Law', pp. 342–43, and F. Kelly, *A Guide to Early Irish Law*, p. 245.

claim that my survey is exhaustive. The evidence I shall adduce in what follows is merely that which I have discovered to best make the case.

From the outset, I must address an idea now widely accepted in contemporary scholarship on early Irish law that needs revision. In what follows, I shall encourage thoughtful reconsideration of a claim made most prominently by Donnchadh Ó Corráin, Liam Breatnach, and Aidan Breen in a seminal article entitled 'Laws of the Irish'.[18] Here, the authors make the arresting claim that early Irish jurists consciously identified themselves with the Israelite lawyers of the Old Testament and considered Mosaic Law not only to be alive and well, but — for all intents and purposes — to be one and the same with Irish law. In the quotation that follows, the authors specifically address early Irish views concerning the Pauline conceptualization of Law of Nature; but their implicit claims — which are startling and which they do not fully explicate — are significantly more expansive when fully considered:

> [...] in the second half of the seventh century, if not before, there existed in Ireland an extremely influential school of exegetes and canon lawyers who regarded the Mosaic law as living law, based many of their own detailed prescriptions directly upon it, and consciously identified the clerics, men of learning and their dependents with the priests and levites of the Old Testament. For persons of such attitudes, Paul's arguments cut both ways and explicit use of them was best avoided, particularly (and this may well have been the case) if there were contrary opinions about the place of Old Testament law in the life of the Christian.[19]

This claim is at least as shocking as it is far-reaching, even though it has generally not been received as such. Here, the authors posit that early Irish jurists envisioned themselves almost, if not actually, in literal terms as Old Testament priests who consciously modelled their juridical institutions on those of ancient Israel. I say 'almost, if not actually' because the authors are not entirely clear, in this article or elsewhere, about the degree of truth-value they believe this identification held for the Irish jurists to whom they attribute this worldview.[20] Whether literal, metaphorical, or otherwise, such an ideologically momentous position would necessarily have had profound ramifications for Irish law and theology, not to mention nearly every field of academic interest to the early medieval Irish Christian

18 Ó Corráin, Breatnach, and Breen, 'The Laws of the Irish', pp. 382–438.

19 Ó Corráin, Breatnach, and Breen, 'The Laws of the Irish', p. 394.

20 'Truth-value', that is, in a multi-valued system of logic where more than two possibilities, true and false, exist. For the medieval Irish *literati*, the truth-value of this proposition would have been informed by a number of coexisting ideologies including, for example, pre-Christian, native ideas and Christian doctrine.

literati. The authors go even farther, however, as is clear in the quotation above. They claim, stunningly, that these jurists were in some sense more comfortable with the Law of Moses than with later Christian law to the extent that, in the view of the authors, these jurists deliberately ignored New Testament doctrines (specifically the Pauline doctrine of natural law) that might undermine their putative, self-perceived, levitical identity, preferring instead, so the authors argue, to apply Old Testament paradigms to contemporary legal issues.

These are extraordinary claims, to say the least; claims which, though frequently repeated, have not been properly regarded as such nor sufficiently evaluated and challenged. The question must be raised: could early Irish jurists have willfully abjured New Testament doctrine in this manner, even if only on certain occasions, or as an acceptable theological peccadillo? Given the profound importance of scripture in early Irish learning and both the care and meticulousness with which Irish scholars engaged with it, I am deeply sceptical about this claim. I suspect that the authors of the abovementioned article anticipated such a response, too, since they append parenthetically the curious hedge, 'and this may well have been the case', to their theory about Irish jurists' conscious willingness to avoid Pauline doctrine. More likely, it was not the case; at least not exactly. Indeed, how could such have been the case in a thoroughly intellectualized and literate Christian culture like early medieval Ireland, where the implications of such a blatantly unorthodox doctrine would immediately come under scrutiny by religious scholars of all professions?

Let us succinctly consider the implications of these authors' view. Above all, how could a thoroughly Christianized judiciary, working in a Latin ecclesiastical milieu — indeed, a judiciary best conceptualized as an arm of the Irish church establishment — fixate on the Old Testament to the virtual exclusion of the New? What ideological standpoint, informed by mainstream Christian theology to any extent, could accommodate it? Any such claim relies on a presumption of ignorance or, what is more, willing, agenda-driven self-deception on the part of the early Irish *literati*. After all, even if the jurists responsible for setting Irish vernacular law to vellum were not one and the same individuals who composed the Hiberno-Latin biblical commentaries, certainly they rubbed shoulders with them on a regular basis in the *scriptoria*.[21] Given the close contact — or, what is more likely, the identity — between jurists of secular and ecclesiastical orientations, it is by any analysis unimaginable that the early Irish *literati*,

21 Consider, for example, Liam Breatnach's conclusion about eighth-century Munster in 'Canon Law and Secular Law in Early Ireland', p. 459: '[…] we can hardly speak of law schools uninfluenced by Christianity. Rather, the evidence […] provides firm support for the integration of the churches into Irish society as a whole, the involvement of churchmen in the law, and their close family connections with the secular learned orders […]'.

jurists or otherwise, would have intentionally and consciously overlooked or disregarded the teachings of the New Testament, or that they could have done so without significant objection that would have left some detectable mark in the written record. The fact is, no such mark is detectable.

Rather, all the available evidence attests that Irish exegetes engaged — not merely preserved and transmitted, but engaged — sincerely and meticulously with the writings of the Church Fathers, including not only major authors such as Augustine, Hilary, Jerome, Ambrose, Cassiodorus, Gregory, Isidore, etc., but also minor but nonetheless significant authors such as Eucharius, and even formally heretical ones like Origen and Pelagius.[22] Lamentably, and by any measure inaccurately, the work of these Irish exegetes has often been dismissed unfairly as merely compilatory, that is, as little more than the rote marshalling of authoritative quotations addressing a given theological problem, without thoughtful consideration for the implications of their content, nor their relationship to one another. Such ungenerous and uninquisitive assessments have been rightly called into question, though perhaps not often enough.[23] Given their intimate and extensive knowledge of patristic doctrine, as is well-attested in the corpus of Hiberno-Latin exegesis and elsewhere in Irish literature, it is by any measure inconceivable that a thoroughly literate monastic culture like that in early medieval Ireland — a culture that engaged robustly with patristic literature both major and minor — could admit, without significant controversy at the very least, such a doctrinally aberrant and unorthodox notion as Ó Corráin, Breatnach, and Breen propose. Without question, re-evaluation is necessary.

Given these objections — and they are significant — let me hasten to emphasize that Ó Corráin, Breatnach, and Breen produced a great deal of evidence supporting their thesis; evidence which cannot be ignored or dismissed. In a series of articles, Ó Corráin argued that the Pentateuch provided a fundamental model for early Irish jurists.[24] These claims have been summarized by Pádraig P. Ó Néill:

> The biblical title of 'levite' and its attendant privileges seem to have been extended in Gaelic society to all members of the learned classes, secular as well as religious. The biblical notions of the levitical city with

22 The Irish interest in Pelagius's writings and the doctrines attributed to him, which I shall discuss at length below, should not be surprising merely because he was anathematized. Early Christian writers such as Origen were also anathematized, but nonetheless played a formative role in Christian and Catholic religious thought in early medieval Ireland.

23 See for example, O'Loughlin, 'Tradition and Exegesis in the Eighth Century', and B. Carella, 'Divine Law'.

24 Such claims can be found frequently throughout the writings of the authors mentioned so far in this context. However, see especially: Ó Corráin, 'Irish Law and Canon Law', pp. 157–66 and Ó Corráin, 'Irish Vernacular Law and the Old Testament', pp. 284–307.

> its carefully measured environs and the city of refuge where asylum was given to those who had committed involuntary manslaughter (Numbers 35:1–15) were applied to major Irish church-sites such as Armagh and Kildare. Offerings made to the Church could not be rescinded, in accordance with Leviticus 27:28. A problem of prohibited degrees of consanguinity in marriage was solved by reference to a story in Numbers. When Salphaad died without male issue, his five daughters begged Moses for 'a possession among their father's kindred' (Numbers 27:6). Moses judged that women could inherit their father's property but only if they married within their tribe; at the same time the ban on marriage within the prohibited degrees was circumvented by having them marry 'sons of their paternal uncle' (Numbers 36:11). For Irish jurists this story provided a legal precedent to justify the Gaelic practice of parallel cousin marriage and with the same end in view — to avoid alienation of family property.[25]

Without question, the Old Testament provided a fundamental model for early Irish law.[26] A fuller context for this gesture is required, however, if we are to understand accurately the significance of Mosaic Law in early Irish jurisprudential ideology. From the outset, it is important to note that, to the majority of the early Irish *literati*, any such application of Old Testament law to Christian society over and above the New Testament (i.e., as Ó Corráin, Breatnach, and Breen suggest) would, at best, have seemed a dangerous challenge to orthodoxy and, at worst, heretical. This is a matter of high doctrinal significance that simply could not have been swept under the rug.

In fact, there is considerable evidence that early Irish intellectuals understood the orthodox position regarding the relationship between Old Testament and New Testament Law, and that they contemplated it in detail. This does not mean that they refrained from using the Mosaic Law as a model for their own laws; but it does mean that their reliance on the Old Testament was more nuanced than previously understood. One example will suffice to make the point. Consider, for example, the commentary on Galatians from the eighth-century, Hiberno-Latin *Reference Bible*. The portion covering Galatians includes only two verses, 2:14 and 4:25. I shall focus on the first of these, Galatians 2:14, since it is a scriptural *locus classicus* for the Pauline rejection of Judaizing (as it is referred to in scholarship and sometimes in the primary sources),[27] that is, Paul's rejection of the

25 Ó Néill, *Biblical Study and Mediaeval Gaelic History*, pp. 25–26.

26 This is true of Irish literature, as well. See most recently Boyle, *History and Salvation*.

27 I concur with Boyle, *History and Salvation*, p. 22, that 'the term (and indeed the concept of) "Judaizing" [is] a potentially unhelpful one, not least because it inevitably carries with it resonances of the abhorrent antisemitism that has been directed at Jewish people over many centuries'. Here, I use the term cautiously and strictly in its technical and historical senses,

idea that Old Testament law should apply fully to newly converted gentile Christians. For obvious reasons, this discussion bears directly on the topic at hand.

Here is the short commentary on the verse in the *Reference Bible*:

> **Ad Galatas** · I · DIXI PETRO CORAM OMNIBUS · SI TU CUM IUDAEUS SIS GENTILITER *ET* NON IUDAICE UIUIS QUOMODO COGIS GENTES IUDAIZARE quod est hoc id est quasi dixisset si tu non tenis quod natus es quomodo illos facis tenere quod nati non sunt rationem reddit non iniuriam facit·
>
> (**To the Galatians** I. 'I said to Peter before them all: If you, being a Jew, live after the manner of the Gentiles, and not as the Jews do, how do you compel the Gentiles to live as do the Jews' ⟨Galatians 2:14⟩ What is this? It is as if he had said: 'If you do not keep what you are born into, how do you compel those to keep what they were not born into?' He provides a reason that does not cause offense).[28]

First, notice that the *Reference Bible* commentator does not attempt to challenge Paul's anti-Judaizing position. On the contrary, their commentary appears to emphasize it. What is more, their choice to include it as one of only two verses from Galatians for comment suggests that they took it to be especially important.

Significantly, this comment did not originate in the *Reference Bible*, but was adapted in slightly truncated form from the early fifth-century, Pelagian commentary *Expositiones* XIII *Espistvlarvm Pauli*, where the issue of Judaizing and the relationship between the Old and New dispensations is a primary topic.[29] Later, in the mid-ninth century, Sedulius Scottus commented on this passage also, borrowing from Pelagian writings even more heavily than the *Reference Bible* commentator did. For example, on the portion of Galatians 2:14 reading *et non Iudaice*, Sedulius included the Pelagian comment 'non ex operibus legis sed sola fide, sicut et gentes uitam in Christo inuenisse te nosti' (you know that you found life in Christ not by works of the law, but by faith alone, just as the Gentiles too).[30] Clearly, Sedulius Scottus interprets the verse as a condemnation of Judaizing, while emphasizing that Christians are saved by their faith alone, not by adherence to the Old Law.

---

particularly as it describes Pauline doctrine in biblical law, and especially as it pertains to (accusations of it) in Pelagian doctrine and, more broadly, in the teachings of Ascetic Movement.

28 The *Reference Bible* remains mostly unedited. The text comes from my own transcription of the primary witnesses, i.e., Munich, Bayerische SB, MS Clm 14277 and BnF, MS lat. 11561 both *in situ* and using electronic reproductions. The translation is my own.

29 Pelagius, *Expositions*, p. 315.

30 The text and translation are from Sedulius Scottus, *The Harmonious Organ*, p. 160.

This matter is not quite so straightforward as it might appear at first, however. Some veins of early Irish theology apparently did not accept straightforwardly the orthodox position that salvation was achievable *sola fide* nor that works were irrelevant. For example, Sedulius Scottus, again borrowing from Pelagius verbatim for his comment on Ephesians 5:5, appears to counter the notion that one can be saved by faith alone:

> ⟨Ephesians⟩ 5:5 HOC ENIM SCITOTE ⟨INTELLIGENTES QUOD OMNIS FORNICATOR AUT INMUNDUS AUT AVARUS QUOD EST IDOLORUM SERVITUS NON HABET HERIDITATEM IN REGNO CHRISTI ET DEI⟩.[31] Hoc contra illos agit, qui solam fidem posse sufficere dicunt.[32]
>
> (⟨Ephesians⟩ 5:5 FOR YOU SHOULD KNOW THIS ⟨AND UNDERSTAND THAT, NO FORNICATOR, OR UNCLEAN, OR COVETOUS PERSON (WHICH IS A SERVING OF IDOLS) HAS INHERITANCE IN THE KINGDOM OF HEAVEN⟩.[33] He writes this against those who say that faith alone can suffice).[34]

In his *Expositiones*, the text continues, explaining:

> [...] qui[a] huius modi actus non [ex] deo, sed daemoni[o] exhibentur: hereditas autem regni caelorum dei filiis, non diaboli praeparatur.[35]
>
> ([...] because acts of this kind are not from God, but rather are offered to the Devil; for the inheritance of the kingdom of heaven is prepared for the children of God, not of the Devil).[36]

Admittedly, this is just one example (albeit one of many) that express strong anti-Judaizing sentiments, not only in the *Reference Bible* and Sedulius Scottus's commentary, but commonly throughout early Irish biblical exegesis. There is a great deal that remains to be understood about medieval Irish Christian belief regarding the role of grace versus good works as a means to attain salvation, the relationship between the Law of Moses and the Law of Christ, not to mention their reception of Pelagian doctrines. A thorough examination of this topic, however, would

---

31 I have provided the rest of the verse from the *Biblia Sacra Iuxta Vulgatam Versionem*. All quotations of the Vulgate, unless otherwise stated, are from this edition.

32 The text is from Sedulius Scottus, *The Harmonious Organ*, p. 218. Compare: Pelagius, *Expositions*, p. 315.

33 All English translations of the Bible are from the Douai-Rheims version unless otherwise specified. I have updated obvious archaisms, albeit sparingly.

34 The translation is from Sedulius Scottus, *The Harmonius Organ*, p. 219.

35 The text is from Pelagius, *Expositions*, p. 374.

36 The translation is my own.

extend well beyond the scope of the current volume. What is clear by any measure, however — as this example of three Insular Celtic exegetes writing during a period of more than four centuries indicates — is that Irish theologians fully understood orthodox notions of the relationship between the Law of Moses and the Law of Christ, that they thought about this question deeply, and that they grappled with it actively until at least the middle of the ninth century. Simply put, they understood what was at stake and would not likely have admitted the view that the Old Testament was straightforwardly living law, at least not in the manner that Ó Corráin, Breatnach, and Breen postulate. Medieval Irish Christians engaged with and understood relevant theological opinions on the relationship between Old and New Testament Law, and therefore would have been fully aware of the theological consequences of abjuring the latter in Christian society. This fact is unavoidable and remains unexplained; and so, a measured reassessment of Ó Corráin, Breatnach, and Breen's claims is now imperative.

Let me emphasize, however, that such reassessment need not, and in my view does not, undermine the substantial body of evidence that Ó Corráin, Breatnach, and Breen adduced in support of their thesis that the Old Testament served as a fundamental source of inspiration for early Irish jurists and that, at times, they used it a model for Irish lawgiving. Rather, I set out here to explain how this apparent, anti-orthodox treatment of the Law of Moses as living law — as many contemporary Irish Christians, steeped in Pauline doctrine on the matter, no doubt would have regarded it — was explained by Irish jurists. That is, I seek to explain how a thoroughly Christianized, intellectual elite fully immersed in orthodox teachings (which they understood, even if they did not always follow to the letter) justified their heavy reliance on the Old Testament as a model for their own Christian lawgiving. As I shall demonstrate, the key to understanding early Irish views on the continued significance of Old Testament law in Christian society lies in their distinctive view of sacred history and their own place within it. In what follows, I shall propose a revised interpretation of the evidence gathered by Ó Corráin, Breatnach, and Breen, particularly the evidence in support of their claims about the centrality of the Old Testament to the *de facto* exclusion of the New in early Irish law.

More specifically, I shall examine their claims as they are informed by contemporaneous Irish theology which, I shall argue, was deeply infused with Pelagian doctrines (both those directly attributable to Pelagius and those which reflect similar ideas), including, above all, those teachings that defined the relationship between Old and New Testament law. Pelagian thought featured prominently in early Irish genres ranging from biblical exegesis to early pseudo-historical accounts of their ethnic origins and played a formative role in early Irish theology generally. In light of this evidence, I shall argue that the apparent centrality of Old Testament law for early Irish jurisprudence was not, despite appearances, out of sync with other, essentially orthodox views concerning the relationship between the Old and New Testaments. On the contrary, far from ignoring the New Testament or avoiding its precepts where they contradicted Old Testament law, early Irish jurists embraced their role as converted gentiles who were, in their own understanding, subject to the Law of Christ. What is more, these jurists were at pains to situate the origin of their traditional, pre-Christian legal system within the broader context of Christian history (as they conceived of it), in such a way that their role as a Christianized gentile people did not in any way contradict what they understood to be direct Mosaic influences on their native legal system prior to Ireland's conversion. In early Irish pseudo-historical literature, we find an elaborately wrought myth of the Irish ethnogenesis in which the Law of Moses was taught in pre-Christian Ireland without the Irish ever entering into the Mosaic Covenant, since doing so would have rendered them subject to the Law of Moses in the same sense as Jews. In essence, early Irish jurists constructed a narrative of their ethno-religious past with which they could both point to formative Mosaic influences on their pre-Christian legal system while simultaneously maintaining their theological place within sacred history as converted gentiles. I shall discuss these matters in what follows.

In summary, these will be my goals: first, in Part One, I shall examine (1) the Irish reception of Christian ideological frameworks as expressed first and foremost in the scriptures, but also selectively in the Church Fathers and other legal and quasi-legal documents from Late Antiquity, and (2) how the Irish transformed these ideologies with respect to native concerns. Then, in Part Two, I shall consider how some of these Irish ideas about law, particularly about the relationship between ecclesiastical and pre-Christian native law, developed in early medieval Ireland, were transmitted to Anglo-Saxon England.

Primary Documents

I shall not undertake here to provide a full account of the history of medieval Irish law or the scholarship which has unearthed it and continues to unearth it. Such a thorough recounting of the field would extend well beyond the scope of the present work and has been expertly narrated elsewhere.

I shall begin with the vernacular codes. As is the case with most Indo-European cultures, the metrical-mnemonic character of the earliest written evidence suggests that the earliest law in Ireland was oral-poetic. Similarities with what little is known about Continental Celtic law (virtually all culled from the writings of classical ethnographers) would seem to indicate that the more conservative aspects of Irish jurisprudence have analogues dating back well into prehistory.[37] Legal activity is reported by the first Christian missionaries to the Island, beginning with St. Patrick's report of dealings with individuals who rendered judgements about unspecified matters.[38] With the advent of Christianity came literacy; and by at least the mid-seventh century (and possibly earlier) Irish jurists began to record legal materials in writing, with most of the primary documents set to vellum in the seventh and eighth centuries.[39] While the majority of the law codes can be dated on linguistic and historical grounds to this early period,[40] the manuscripts in which they survive invariably date from no earlier than the twelfth century,[41] with most dating from the fourteenth to the sixteenth centuries.[42] In the manuscripts, the laws themselves are commonly, though inconsistently, written in large letters with surrounding commentary and interlinear/marginal glosses, accumulated over the course of the texts' transmission, in smaller script.[43] Finally, most of the laws that survive are grouped in codes that address a particular legal topic or, less frequently, are ascribed to a famous legendary or ecclesiastical personage. Virtually none are associated with kings or other real-world, historically attested secular figures. Some scholars have taken this apparent lacuna in the extant record as evidence that royal codes never existed, which is explained in their view by the relative weakness of the institution of kingship in early Irish society. On the other hand, more recent opinion holds that Irish kings participated actively in the legislative process.[44]

By far the largest collection of vernacular Irish law is the *Senchas Már*. Until recently, this extensive and diverse collection of law tracts was thought to have been the work of compilers bringing together originally separate tracts from a variety of sources. In his 2010 E. C. Quiggin Memorial Lecture,[45] however, Liam Breatnach argued convincingly that

---

37 See Binchy, 'Distraint in Irish Law', p. 27 and F. Kelly, *A Guide to Early Irish Law*, pp. 231–32.

38 '[...] illis qui iudicabant [...]' ([...] those who judged [...]), § 53 of St Patrick's *Confessio*. See: *Libri Epistolarum Sancti Patricii Episcopi*, pp. 86–87.

39 See Charles-Edwards, 'Early Irish Law', p. 331, and F. Kelly, *A Guide to Early Irish Law*, p. 225.

40 See Breatnach, *A Companion to the Corpus Iuris Hibernici*, pp. 354–55.

41 As Fergus Kelly pointed out, 'There are two law-texts [...] in the early twelfth-century manuscript Rawlinson B 502 in the Bodleian Library, Oxford [...] The earliest surviving manuscript which contains mainly legal material is H 2. 15A in Trinity College Dublin, dating probably form the early 14th century', *A Guide to Early Irish Law*, p. 225 n. 1.

42 F. Kelly, *A Guide to Early Irish Law*, p. 225, and n. 1. See also Charles-Edwards, 'Early Irish Law', pp. 331–32 and n. 4.

43 F. Kelly, *A Guide to Early Irish Law*, p. 226. Glosses and commentary range from the ninth to the sixteenth centuries. See also: Charles-Edwards, 'Early Irish Law', pp. 331–32.

44 Wadden, 'The Pseudo-Historical Origins of the *Senchas Már*', pp. 141–58. See also: Charles-Edwards, 'Early Irish Law', pp. 332–33; Charles-Edwards, 'Celtic Kings: "Priestly Vegetables?"', pp. 65–80; MacCana, 'The Three Languages and the Three Laws', pp. 77–78.

45 See Breatnach, *The Early Irish Law Text Senchas Már*.

the *Senchas Már* was a product of a unified effort by ecclesiasts working in the north of Ireland. As summarized by Patrick Wadden:

> Breatnach offered a completely revised interpretation of the origins of the most important collection of early Irish law tracts, the *Senchas Már*. Since Rudolf Thurneysen first proposed (in 1926) that it was produced at much the same time as the *Collectio canonum Hibernensis*, that is in the early eighth century, the *Senchas Már* has been perceived as a compilation of tracts of different dates, written in one or more locations in the northern half of Ireland, compiled as a single lawbook in the early eighth century. Breatnach's alternative view, the seeds of which are apparent in some of his earlier publications, sees the *Senchas Már* as a unitary whole, 'an integrated coherent text, rather than a loose assemblage of individual tracts or groups of tracts', written, in its entirety, between 660 and 680 at Armagh. Breatnach's study adds further weight to the growing body of evidence that the Church played a central role in the production of the oldest written texts of Irish vernacular law, and while it is probably necessary to distinguish between the separate processes of composition and writing, it seems increasingly likely that in Ireland, as in much of western Europe, the Church took a leading role in writing and preserving *lex scripta*, and may, in fact, have provided the ideological motivation for doing so.[46]

Despite his claim that the text was set to vellum by clerics working in Armagh, Breatnach is quick to point out that, although the text has an ecclesiastical origin, it should not be regarded straightforwardly as church law:

> [...] *Senchas Már* cannot be described as a canon law text. That its main concern is with secular law will be immediately obvious from the titles of [its] component tracts [...] At the same time, however [...] the influence of Christianity is tangible throughout the text, and the interests of an established church are well represented.[47]

Later, he continues, expanding on this point:

> The tracts we have looked at [in the *Senchas Már*] are not to be seen as an afterthought, as adding a Christian veneer to a text that was originally different in nature, as the themes in them permeate the text as a whole, although not in quite such an obvious fashion.[48]

Thus, in Breatnach's view, the *Senchas Már* is a collection of Irish law and legal traditions brought together and set to vellum as a unified work with

---

46 Wadden, 'The Pseudo-Historical Origins of the *Senchas Már*', pp. 141–42.
47 Breatnach, *The Early Irish Law Text Senchas Már*, p. 13.
48 Breatnach, *The Early Irish Law Text Senchas Már*, p. 14.

unified themes (many of them Christian) by churchmen working in an ecclesiastical setting, specifically at Armagh in the late seventh century. Moreover, although Breatnach does not explicitly say so, it is likely that the genesis of other vernacular Irish legal tracts (i.e., those not considered part of the *Senchas Már*) emerged in similar fashion, that is, that they were first set to vellum by clerical jurists working with and adapting customary Irish traditions in an ecclesiastical milieu. Their end products, therefore, cannot be described as somehow 'purely' native Irish law to which later Christian interpolations were added. Rather, what is sometimes referred to as 'secular' Irish law emerged in its first written form within an ecclesiastical context.

The nearly complete corpus of medieval Irish vernacular law, including accompanying glosses and commentary, has been edited in D. A. Binchy's diplomatic, six-volume *Corpus Iuris Hibernici*. While this work stands out as an unparallelled milestone for the study of early Irish law, it is not without problems. As one recent commentator described it:

> Binchy's Corpus is without translations. Its sparse table of contents merely lists the manuscripts transcribed (without description) [...]. What lay between the covers of CIH was indeed a desert, a bewildering wilderness, without signposts or recognizable landmarks (though it was rumoured that its hidden hills were full of gold).[49]

In all cases, Liam Breatnach's *A Companion to the Corpus Iuris Hibernici*[50] is an indispensable tool when working with the *Corpus Iuris Hibernici*. Critical editions and translations of individual law tracts, where they exist, can be found published in journals or separate volumes, though many are now out-of-date.[51] The only thoroughgoing attempt to translate a large portion of the surviving material is the nineteenth-century *Ancient Laws of Ireland*, which set out to translate the *Senchas Már* in its entirety.[52] Though without question a respectable achievement for its era, *Ancient Laws of Ireland* was flawed from the beginning and by now is hopelessly inaccurate

49 McLeod, 'A True Companion to the *Corpus Iuris Hibernici*', p. 136.

50 Breatnach, *A Companion to the Corpus Iuris Hibernici*.

51 See the 'Concordance of Published Tracts' in Binchy, *Corpus Iuris Hibernici*, I, pp. xxiii–xxv; F. Kelly, *A Guide to Early Irish Law*, pp. 264–83, 'Appendix 1: List of Law-Texts'; and the catalogue of documents (as extensive as it is indispensable) in chapter 5, 'Old Irish Texts', in Breatnach, *A Companion to the Corpus Iuris Hibernici*, pp. 160–337. Since Breatnach's *Companion*, several other editions and translations have been published, including, for example, *Córus Bésgnai*, *Cáin Lánamna*, *A Raven's Battle-Cry*, *Lost and Found in Early Irish Law Aidbred*, *Marriage Disputes*, and *Bretha Comaithcheso*.

52 *Ancient Laws of Ireland*.

and out-of-date.[53] Although recently reprinted,[54] modern scholars must be leery not only of the badly outmoded introductions to the primary texts, but also of the transcriptions and especially the translations that accompany them.

The situation is a little better with the Hiberno-Latin documents, though the corpus of this material, too, is not without significant problems. *Collectio canonum Hibernensis*, the largest single compilation of early Irish ecclesiastical law[55] (and the first collection of its kind in early medieval Western Europe),[56] was assembled sometime between the years 669 and 748,[57] though its contents are considerably older. The collection seems to have been the collaborative effort of two monastic legalists, one named Ruben who is associated with the monastery in Dairinis (in County Waterford) and another named Cú Chuimne who dwelt at Iona (in the Inner Hebrides, off the western coast of Scotland).[58] Despite its Insular origins, it has survived exclusively in manuscripts of continental production, albeit widely dispersed (Brittany, France, Germany, Austria, Switzerland, and Italy),[59] a fact which attests to its high level of importance, not only for Ireland itself but also for Irish missions to Europe. Significantly, its contents are organized by topic, under which the opinions and judgements of various authorities — including the scriptures, patristic authors, papal decrees, and the decisions of both ecumenical and provincial councils — are listed often without discussion and typically without any attempt to reconcile apparent contradictions.[60] The text survives in two, or possibly

53 For an assessment of the problems with the *Ancient Laws of Ireland* see Binchy, 'The Linguistic and Historical Value', pp. 197–98.

54 *Ancient Laws of Ireland* was reprinted in 2000 by William S. Hein & Co.

55 Although, *Collectio canonum Hibernensis* is often considered to be ecclesiastical law, see *The Hibernensis*, Bk I, p. 48*, where Flechner points out that, in some respects, *Collectio canonum Hibernensis* 'appears close to vernacular secular law and can often be seen to seek compromises between ecclesiastical ideals and customary law, some of which, perhaps goes back to a pre-Christian legal culture'. From its ostensible beginnings, thus, a central concern of early Irish jurisprudence was reconciling these disparate bodies of law.

56 Charles-Edwards, *The Early Medieval Gaelic Lawyer*, p. 4 notes: 'In Western Christendom [...] the Irish Church was apparently the first to develop what one could call a full canon law, a developed legal system with a wide jurisdiction'.

57 *The Hibernensis*, Bk I, p. 61. See also: Charles-Edwards, *The Early Medieval Gaelic Lawyer*, p. 5 and Hughes, *The Church in Early Irish Society*, p. 123 and p. 133 n. 3.

58 *The Hibernensis*, Bk I, p. 56*.

59 L. M. Davies, 'The Biblical Text of the Collectio Canonum Hibernensis', pp. 17–41. For a catalogue of most of the surviving manuscripts, etc., see Kéry, *A Bibliographical Guide to the Manuscripts*, pp. 73–80.

60 I shall have more to say about this topic below. I do not mean to suggest that the authors/compilers of the text were in any way sloppy, or that they lacked thoroughness or a consistent plan. Quite the contrary, their methods for marshalling authoritative testimony from a variety of sources adhered closely to a well-developed process witnessed elsewhere in Irish texts, particularly in Hiberno-Latin biblical exegesis.

three recensions, designated A, B, and C. Of these, C (if indeed it represents a separate recension at all) is an apparent work in progress attested in only one manuscript, probably emanating from Brittany.[61] Until recently, only the A-text had been edited,[62] and that in a late nineteenth-century edition now generally considered out-of-date. A new critical edition and translation by Roy Flechner is now available, based on both the A and B recensions.[63] I shall have a great deal more to say about *Collectio canonum Hibernensis* below.

In addition to *Collectio canonum Hibernensis*, a sizeable quantity of other Hiberno-Latin legal and quasi-legal material has survived; and although no single compendium of these documents yet exists, many individual texts have been edited in journals or separate volumes. Unfortunately, much remains unedited. Scholars not familiar with the field should be aware that, in this context, 'legal material' is defined somewhat more broadly and inclusively than in other disciplines. On this point, Robin Chapman Stacey's observation about the vernacular legal materials applies to the Latin texts as well:

> The tracts of which the ⟨early Irish⟩ lawbooks are composed are not the records of legislation, but rather extended discussions of the structures and practices prominent in Irish society of the period: clientship. Fosterage, social status, regulations concerning animal behavior, dues owed to and by the church [...].[64]

Here, 'law' is taken to include classes of documents not always considered legal in other areas of study, such as penitentials, wisdom texts, certain kinds of commentaries, etc., in addition to primarily statutory material.[65] Even *Collectio canonum Hibernensis* might be best described as an assemblage of authoritative quotations on selected legal *quaestiones*.[66] What is more, there exists at present no complete, up-to-date catalogue of Hiberno-Latin legal texts.[67] Michael Lapidge and Richard Sharpe's

---

61 For recent discussion, see Dumville, *A Palaeographer's Review*, II, pp. 219–20. See also: Stokes, 'Old Breton Glosses', pp. 326, 328, and 342–45; d'Arbois de Jubainville, 'Le manuscrit cottonien Otho E.xiii', pp. 238–40.

62 Wasserschleben, *Die Irische Kanonensammlung*.

63 See *The Hibernensis*, Bk I, p. 51*. See also the highly critical review by Russell, '*The Hibernensis. Book 1*'.

64 Stacey, *Dark Speech*, p. 7.

65 For a thorough description of the Irish law books and their see, Qiu, 'Law, Law Books, and Tradition'.

66 Perhaps nowhere else is T. M. Charles-Edwards's observation about Irish law generally more apropos: 'Irish ecclesiastical lawyers worked within a tradition one of whose principal characteristics was a search for authorities, in the Bible and elsewhere', *The Early Medieval Gaelic Lawyer*, p. 2.

67 F. Kelly, *A Guide to Early Irish Law*, pp. 282–83, for example, 'Appendix 1: List of Law-Texts', contains only seven texts under the headings 'Ecclesiastical Legislation' and 'Canon Law'. Of

Bibliography of Celtic-Latin Literature, 400–1200 remains an indispensable tool,[68] as is Richard Sharpe's *A Handlist of the Latin Writers of Great Britain and Ireland before 1540*.[69] Likewise, an important collection of legal and quasi-legal documents, focusing on penitentials but including early synodal materials, etc., has been edited and translated with an introduction by Ludwig Bieler in *The Irish Penitentials*. In addition to these important volumes, there is a handful of other important collections that contain Hiberno-Latin law and related materials.[70] Above all, the digitized *Archive of Celtic-Latin Literature*, an ongoing project of the Royal Irish Academy begun as part of the *Dictionary of Medieval Latin from Celtic Sources*, published by Brepols and now linked via the *Cross-Database Searchtool* to the *Library of Latin Texts*, also published by Brepols (and other databases such as the *Digital Monumenta Germaniae Historica*), provides an unparallelled collection of electronically searchable primary documents, though it is unfortunately of limited use to a scholar who does not come to it knowing what he, she, or they are seeking *a priori*.

Modern Scholarship

It would be gross understatement to claim that our contemporary understanding of early Irish law and its mechanisms has evolved steadily over the course of the past one-hundred years. During the first half of the twentieth century and beyond, scholarly interest in the Irish law codes centred above all on their relative antiquity, and especially their comparative value as witnesses to Indo-European language and culture. To be sure, research of this kind continues today. However, investigation of these matters did little to promote deeper knowledge of the law codes themselves, or — just as lamentably — their synchronic function within medieval Irish society. Even where interest extended to such matters, early scholarship was hindered by several beliefs about the surviving corpus of Irish law

these, only two are written in Latin, both listed under 'Canon Law', (1) *Canones Hibernensis*, I–IV, Bieler, *The Irish Penitentials*, pp. 160–75 and (2) *Collectio canonum Hibernensis*, ed. Wasserschleben, *Die Irische Kanonensammlung*. A new edition and translation is now available. See: *The Hibernensis*. See also the highly critical review by Russell, '*The Hibernensis. Book 1*', pp. 116–27.

68 Lapidge and Sharpe, *Bibliography of Celtic-Latin Literature*.

69 Sharpe, *A Handlist of the Latin Writers of Great Britain and Ireland*.

70 Besides those already mentioned, a partial list of the most important collections includes the following works (of course, some of these works supersede others): *Concilia, Decreta, Leges, Constitutiones*, ed. by Spelman; *Concilia Magna Britanniae et Hiberniae*, ed. by Wilkins; *Councils and Ecclesiastical Documents relating to Great Britain and Ireland*, ed. by Haddan and others; *Councils and Synods with Other Documents relating to the English Church*, ed. by Whitelock; *Cáin Adomnáin and the Canones Adomnani*, ed. and trans. by Ó Néill and Dumville.

which have since been called into question, and which are now sometimes referred to (derogatorily) as 'nativist'. These include: (1) the notion that early Irish vernacular law was primarily the product of professional lay jurists,[71] (2) the notion that these professional jurists were members of a secular class in Irish society distinct from clerical jurists, and (3) the related notion that the vernacular law codes, originally — if not in the form that they have come down to us — emanated from independent, secular law schools separate from the institutions of the Church, and in particular from monasteries. While some scholars have inferred the existence of such schools, all concrete evidence connects such centres of legal activity with monastic foundations. This point is often apparent even in the writings of scholars who believe that secular law schools flourished in early medieval Ireland. Fergus Kelly, for example, states:

> It is reasonable to assume that there were a number of centres of legal knowledge at which such instruction [in Irish vernacular law] could be obtained, but there is no firm evidence of their location at the period of the composition of the law-texts (7th–8th centuries). In the 9th century *Triads of Ireland*, however, there are references to the monasteries of Cloyne, Cork, and Slane as legal centres.[72]

Elsewhere, Kelly points out: 'The annals provide no information about lawyers or law-schools during the main period of the compilation of the law-texts (7th–8th centuries)'.[73] So, if a class of secular, lay jurists existed before circa 900 (a claim about which I remain sceptical), then they almost certainly received their education within a monastic sphere of influence, both physically and culturally.[74]

Anti-nativists reacted against nativist premises, arguing that no positive evidence indicates the existence of a class lay jurists working in secular law schools, at least not during the early period. Instead, they argued that the vernacular law codes, just like Latin collections of canon law such as *Collectio canonum Hibernensis*, owed their existence to a 'mandarin class'

---

71 For a reconsideration of this position see: Charles-Edwards, 'Celtic Kings: "Priestly Vegetables"?', pp. 65–80.

72 F. Kelly, *A Guide to Early Irish Law*, p. 242.

73 F. Kelly, *A Guide to Early Irish Law*, p. 248.

74 This debate has been ably summarized by Stacey, *Dark Speech*, pp. 58–59. Prominent voices in the debate, in addition those already mentioned, include (but are not limited to) Ó Corráin, Breatnach, and Breen, 'The Laws of the Irish'; Breatnach, 'Canon Law and Secular Law in Early Ireland'; Breatnach, 'The Ecclesiastical Element in the Old Irish Legal Tract *Cáin Fhuithurbe*'; Charles-Edwards, 'The Context and Uses of Literacy'; Ó Corráin, 'Nationality and Kingship in Pre-Norman Ireland'; Ó Corráin, 'Irish Law and Canon Law'; Ó Corráin, 'Irish Vernacular Law and the Old Testament'; Ó Corráin, 'Early Irish Churches: Some Aspects of Organisation'; McCone, 'Dubthach maccu Lugair and a Matter of Life and Death'; McCone, *Pagan Past and Christian Present in Early Irish Literature*, pp. 84–106 and Gerriets, 'Theft, Penitentials and the Compilation of the Early Irish Laws'.

of poets and jurists drawn from the clergy, working not in secular law schools but in monastic *scriptoria*.[75] More recently, this notion of a unified Christian learned caste 'whose members sang from the hymn sheet always and everywhere'[76] has come under fire by Elva Johnston, who points out that

> ⟨d⟩espite its implausibility, this model has received widespread acceptance and has mostly replaced older, even more flawed notions that emphasized the importance of so-called pagan oral traditions at the expense of written texts. While it does rightly stress the importance of Christian literacy, this scheme has a number of drawbacks. Most damagingly, it ignores or underplays the variety of person and product that distinguishes the Irish communities of learning; it misses out on the way that this variety fostered creative links between the literate and non-literate in elite environments.[77]

Most agree, in any case, that Latin Christian learning centred in monasteries was the apogee of literacy in early medieval Ireland, even if it existed (albeit in the same, Christianized milieux) alongside other kinds of literacy, including oral and vernacular literacy.

Ultimately, scholars of the anti-nativist movement collectively demonstrated that Latin Christian sources and themes underlay many of the vernacular legal tracts, even those passages which, in many cases, previous scholars had identified as the unadulterated patrimony of Ireland's Celtic and Indo-European heritage. Eventually, however, the anti-nativist reaction intensified and broadened to the extent that some came to believe, at the most extreme, that virtually all early Irish law, secular or ecclesiastical — indeed, all Irish literature and learning generally — was produced solely in monastic *scriptoria*, composed by the abovementioned mandarin class of clerics with a predominantly, if not exclusively, ecclesiastical orientation. As evidence for their claims, anti-nativists pointed out biblical, patristic, and other Christian sources for legal, literary, and other texts formerly thought to be predominantly secular in origin. The movement, still well-represented today, has succeeded in demonstrating that the influence of the Church was profound to say the least, shaping all aspects of learning in early medieval Ireland. As a result of such research, few today adhere to a purely nativist position.

---

75 In 'The Laws of the Irish', Ó Corráin, Breatnach, and Breen suggest that: 'One can, perhaps, go further and suggest that a large party in the Irish church in the seventh and eighth centuries consciously conceived of the mandarin caste of churchmen, scholars, jurists, canon lawyers, historians and poets, to which they belonged, as priests and levites in the strict Old Testament sense of these terms', p. 394.

76 Johnston, *Literacy and Identity in Early Medieval Ireland*, p. 23.

77 Johnston, *Literacy and Identity in Early medieval Ireland*, p. 23.

With respect for their accomplishments, however, the anti-nativist reaction, like many scholarly movements, at times went to extremes, 'identifying' Christian sources and allusions behind virtually every line of medieval Irish text, at times thinly justified by only the vaguest similarities or the dimmest parallels with the Bible or other Latin ecclesiastical material. Elva Johnston provided a measured assessment of the nativist/anti-nativist debate:

> As it happens the two approaches share similarities. The opposing theories presuppose a set of simple binary oppositions composed of pagan/Christian, oral/written and secular/ecclesiastical, although these are interpreted differently in each model. Nonetheless, both employ the idea of a single literate caste, created through triumphant assimilation, in order to account for vernacular narrative literature. Nativists collapse druid, *fili* and cleric into a pagan-dominated learned class which is greatly indebted to oral culture and secular concerns. On the other hand, anti-nativists draw all categories together into a Christian ecclesiastical elite which, in its turn, remakes Irish culture in its own image. The situation was far less clear-cut than either of the pair will allow. Fortunately, in practice, the actual complexity of the situation has informed a good deal of the writing on both sides of the debate. Naturally, when studying medieval written sources emanating from monasteries, it is important not to minimise the role of literate churchmen in their organisation and diffusion. At the same time, it may be asked whether such a role was exclusive or whether these literate churchmen, in any sense, formed a single dominant and cohesive caste.[78]

Later she adds:

> The disagreement between nativist and anti-nativist positions has the potential to lead scholars into an intellectual cul-de-sac. It asks questions about origins which, given the state of our knowledge, are either unanswerable or only circumstantially answerable. The speculation can be fascinating but does not directly allow for an in-depth examination of the operation of literacy as a whole within Irish society and the huge implications of that literacy for Irish expressions of self-identity.[79]

Johnston's criticisms of both sides of the debate are well taken. While anti-nativists have made a strong case for the pervasive influence of Christian learning on medieval Irish law, that does not mean it lacked influence from residual pre-Christian, native traditions as well, nor that other forms of

---

78 Johnston, *Literacy and Identity in Early Medieval Ireland*, p. 18.
79 Johnston, *Literacy and Identity in Early Medieval Ireland*, p. 23.

literacy, including vernacular literacy and oral learning, were nonexistent or unimportant. At the very least, it seems reasonable to posit that the literate Irish elite were not necessarily part of a single, homogenous, 'mandarin' caste without significant internal variation.

The implications of Johnston's arguments go farther, however. Whatever distinction there was, if any, between specialists in vernacular law versus those who produced the Latin materials is a complicated question. Johnston points to the existence of

> [...] solid evidence for ecclesiastical participation in the practice of law. Bishops were involved in secular cases alongside *brithemain* and could be expert in native and Church law. It is arguable, on the other hand, that the *scriba* should be differentiated from bishop and *brithem*. Significantly, the chronicles discriminate between those clerics expert in vernacular law, who could be called a *iudex* or *brithem*, and those who are named as *scribae*. This makes sense if the latter were distinguished by their authority in cases under canon law jurisdiction [...]. At one point it even states explicitly that the king should call upon the scribe to declare a legal judgement [...]. In Irish terms this neatly pairs with its native law sibling, where judgement is expounded by the *brithem* but promulgated by the king or in his presence. The *scriba*'s role is analogous to that of the *brithem*.[80]

Quite likely, there was significant overlap between both parties.

On the other hand, the question of whether the laws were produced in secular schools or monastic *scriptoria* seems more settled. Until concrete evidence for the existence of secular schools is forthcoming, we must assume that the earliest Irish laws were written in the only centres of literacy known to have existed — and, for that matter, the only institutions known to possess both the technology and the wealth necessary to produce vellum in significant quantities — that is, in Christian monastic foundations. No question, Latin Christian learning stands out as the dominate influence, even though other kinds of learning — including vernacular literacy and oral learning — may have existed alongside of it. For the purposes of the present volume, I shall refer to secular and ecclesiastical 'interests', 'orientations', and 'milieux', fully aware that, in the real workaday world of early medieval Ireland, any such distinction between these concerns would not likely have been easily delineated, to the extent that they were distinguishable at all.[81] Furthermore, I wish to emphasize that by secular 'interests' (etc.), I do not intend to suggest that these existed

80 Johnston, *Literacy and Identity in Early Medieval Ireland*, pp. 123–24.

81 This is not to suggest that certain points of law were not regarded as 'secular' or 'ecclesiastical' in nature, nor that there were not distinctions between 'secular' and 'ecclesiastical' mechanisms of justice. On the contrary, the evidence suggests otherwise.

outside of an overarching Christian framework. No evidence suggests that a pagan intellectual elite survived conversion to any manifest extent. That said, elements of pre-Christian knowledge could persist, including certain legal ideas, where they did not contradict or threaten Christian doctrine. Indeed, that is a major theme of the Pseudo-historical Prologue to the *Senchas Már*, as I shall discuss at length below. Presumably, however, such knowledge was preserved by Irish Christian *literati* working in *scriptoria*. Thus, by 'pre-Christian' and 'secular', I do not mean 'pagan'; and by 'interests' (etc.), I do not intend to suggest that these existed independently of an ecclesiastical structure.

With the complexities of this issue fully in mind, it is apparent that there was ongoing debate between secular and ecclesiastical interests regarding, for example, the proper role, if any, of pre-Christian, native law under the New Dispensation. Whether this debate should be characterized as mere theorizing or whether it bore substantively on real-world judicial practice remains uncertain. What seems clear is that the issue was debated primarily within the Church between separate parties in a thoroughly Christianized milieu. Unsurprisingly, whenever relicts of pre-Christian, native legal practice came under scrutiny, the concerns of the Church dominated in virtually every instance. That said, the evidence suggests that native, secular interests had bearing on the discussion as well.[82] To be sure, we should not imagine that differences between adherents of these two orientations invariably led to conflict. On the contrary, it seems there was a marked attempt within the Church to accommodate certain pre-Christian, native legal practices. Although it is difficult to assess the extent of such influences, it would seem that the time-honoured knowledge of the native learned classes, exemplified by (1) the traditional body of customary, oral-poetic legal lore known as *fénechas* (or *bélrae Féni*, 'the language of the Féni', i.e., customary or native law)[83] and (2) *filidecht*,[84] the traditional body of knowledge of the *filid* (sing. *fili*)[85] continued to affect Irish jurisprudence well into the Christian period. Indeed, there is

That said, the intellectual community that gave rise to early medieval Irish law were situated in monastic *scriptoria* where the laws were set to vellum.

82 See, for example, *The Hibernensis*, Bk 1, pp. 47*–48*.

83 Per p. 25 n. 53 above: Fergus Kelly defines *Féni* as follows: 'freemen of full legal capacity; *la Féniu*, among the Irish, according to Irish law; *bélrae* (later *bérla*) *Féne*, the language of the *Féni*, legal language'. Moreover, he defines *fénechas* as 'the law of the *Féni*, customary of traditional law; native law (as opposed to Canon law, or later, English common law)': *A Guide to Early Irish Law*, p. 311.

84 See *eDIL*, s.v. *filidecht*, 'the art, office, or practice of the *fili*; poetry; also, divination; a poetic composition; charm'.

85 Etymologically, *fili* meant a 'seer, or diviner', but came to signify a learned individual with a wide variety of intellectual skills. *eDIL*, s.v. *fili*, also includes the following definitions: '⟨p⟩oet (historian, panegyrist, satirist, man of learning [...] a learned man, one skilled in literary composition in Irish [...]'.)

evidence that *filidecht* could be, at least under certain circumstances, part of a cleric's body of knowledge. For example, Elva Johnston points out that '*Fili* and cleric shared a learned tradition: the legal tract *Míadshlechta* stipulated that the third highest-ranking ecclesiastical scholar should be competent in *coimgne, filidecht* and *léigend*'.[86] Thus, to some now largely unknowable extent, elements of pre-Christian, native Irish learning and beliefs survived Christianization, influencing the new order, if only as a muted substratum.

That said, it is important to acknowledge from the outset that this substratum, where observable, manifests itself only via written texts produced in a Christian milieu. Anti-nativists correctly point out that literacy arrived in Ireland with the Church and remained exclusively within the purview of clerics throughout the early Middle Ages. To be sure, other kinds of non-literate, oral knowledge persisted throughout the period, and these interests interacted with those of the *literati*:

> [E]arly Irish literacy functioned within a secondary-oral environment, an environment in which the oral and written were in continual interaction. At one end was the monastic *literatus* whose writings were part of the intellectual world of Christianity and who relied on a whole infrastructure of literacy based on ecclesiastical institutions, books and pedagogy. At the other were more transient contributors to this culture, individuals such as the *baird* and the lower ranked among *filid*. These, despite their limited literate skills, still partook of the accepted social realities articulated by the literate elite.[87]

The expression of knowledge in writing, however, remained a predominantly monastic endeavour. Knowledge of letters aside, the complicated and expensive processes involved in the manufacture of vellum and the production of manuscripts could only have been conducted at wealthy monastic foundations. There is no evidence, in any case, that such technology existed elsewhere in early Irish society. These facts notwithstanding, it appears that in the early years following conversion, at least during the late fifth century and in the centuries thereafter, native learning and Christian ideologies began to accommodate one another, blend, and adapt so that eventually they became virtually indistinguishable. One would do best, in my view, to envision this process as the absorption of pre-Christian, native Irish institutions by the Church, not as a union of equal parties. Yet, it seems likely, though ultimately speculative, that during the very first years after the advent of Christianity, many of the Irish *literati* with native skills began to populate Irish monasteries; and those elements of their traditional skill set that did not contradict Christian doctrine, even if

86 Johnston, *Literacy and Identity in Early Medieval Ireland*, p. 142.
87 Johnston, *Literacy and Identity in Early Medieval Ireland*, p. 157.

not actively practised, nonetheless shaped their thinking and, presumably, that of their students. The existence of a class of jurists known as *brithem téora mbreth*, 'a judge of three judgements', that is, of *fénechas*, *filidecht*, and scripture would seem to indicate this kind of fusion.

Possibly the best way to understand the more than two-and-a-half centuries between the coming of Christianity with the arrival of Palladius and, soon after, Patricius, and the flurry of legal activity that occurred *c.* 650 to *c.* 750 and thereafter, is as an extended process in which the learned classes, both native intellectuals and Christian clerics, adapted to one another, became ever more commensal and, at least in some cases, merged. Earlier scholarship supported this view. As Robin Chapman Stacey put it, '[...] ⟨t⟩here can be little doubt that what ⟨early Irish law⟩ remains to us today is the product of the joining of two great legal traditions, native and Christian, each with its own mythology, specialists, and sense of the past'.[88] Similarly, Kathleen Hughes, writing in the mid-twentieth century claimed:

> It looks to me as if, for the first 250 years of its life in Ireland, Christianity made steady inroads. By 700 the position had stabilised. It is clear that by this time Ireland was nominally Christian; there were scores of monasteries which must have been serving a considerable part of the country, providing baptism and Christian burial. But it is also clear that by about 700 the church had adjusted itself to secular law. When the canons of the first synod of Patrick, Auxilius, and Iserninus were drawn up (I think towards the mid sixth century), Christians were being encouraged to keep clear of the secular courts. By the time the 'Collectio Canonum Hibernensis' was published in the early eighth century, the situation had changed. These canons provide rulings on the law of evidence, on surety, on inheritance. They reflect the principles of secular law, and show how the church, which had been a Roman institution, has now been brought into line with native legal practices.[89]

Hughes' now dated statement mut be weighed against the more recent scepticism of Colmán Etchingham, who — describing Irish society as a whole (not just legal matters) — posits that:

> [...] the point at which Christianity first arrived and the determining factors, time-scale, and extent of conversion over the course of the fifth century and the comparably obscure sixth are largely the subjects of no more than reasonable inference and conjecture. Much ink has been spilt on the initial process of conversion, much of it to little profit.[90]

88 Stacey, *Dark Speech*, p. 7.
89 Hughes, *The Church in Early Irish Society*, pp. 315–16.
90 Etchingham 'Conversion in Ireland', p. 181.

The matter remains unresolved, though not unaddressed. Currently, there are two different schools of thought about how deeply Christianity penetrated early Irish society, including matters regarding law. Elizabeth Boyle ably summarizes the debate as follows:

> Put simply, two broad schools of interpretation exist for the role of the Church in early Irish society: one, which we might term the 'minimalist' school, advocated most notably in recent years by Colmán Etchingham, suggests that the depth of Christianisation in Ireland was minimal and superficial, that pastoral care was administered only to a para-monastic ecclesiastical élite and that the majority of the population was left mired in its own sinfulness without the possibility of salvation [...].[91] By contrast, the 'maximalist' school, whose leading advocates included the late Richard Sharpe, see the Church in Ireland as providing pastoral care to the entire population who, whatever the vagaries of individual belief and morality, would have regarded themselves as Christian, with as good a chance as any of gaining entry to heaven. This would seem to be supported by the archaeological evidence, which suggests a radical social transformation in fifth- and sixth-century Ireland coinciding with the conversion era [...].[92]

These different views aside, what can be said with confidence is that by the year 700, a large portion of the Irish elite was Christianized. To some unknown extent, however, pre-Christian learned classes were, to a certain degree, absorbed into the Church; and in this environment, native learning endured, particularly in Irish monastic foundations — which, by that time, had in many cases become wealthy and powerful centres of intellectual activity — including the study and production of law. Pre-Christian ideologies still mattered, and were to a certain extent preserved, albeit reinterpreted and circumscribed by Christian doctrine, at least where they did not contradict canonical teachings prominently.

Early on, this merger of secular and ecclesiastical interests — especially given the resilience of certain native legal practices troublesome to the Church — fomented an ever-more pressing need for reconciliation between the two legal systems, at the very least between their most blatant points of contradiction. As a result, debate concerning how to explain the relationship between pre-Christian, native, and ecclesiastical law consumed a great deal of creative energy among early Irish jurists, if the number of extant texts addressing the topic is any indicator. As one might imagine, a working resolution to this issue was crucial to achieve, so that Irish jurists might claim an unshakeable ideological foundation for their laws. On the most basic level, establishing a theoretical groundwork

91 Etchingham, 'Bishops, Church and People'.

92 Boyle, *History and Salvation*, pp. 154–55.

was critical for society to function; and Irish jurists of all backgrounds realized how much was at stake. We might speculate that, in the earliest years post-conversion, Christianity posed a challenge, if not an outright threat, to the continuity of early Irish traditions, especially the native legal system. To contemporaries, particularly the pagan elite, the success of the Christian missions in Ireland must have seemed like the end of an age, the roots of which reached deep into the imagined age of their mythical origins.

Unlike other Celtic lands, late antique and early medieval Ireland had been a relatively stable society, free from external conquest, persistent foreign invasion, and other kinds of upheaval that typically precipitate fundamental changes to basic cultural institutions.[93] The advent of Christianity in the fifth century and its steady rise to prominence soon thereafter, however, was an exception. While not an invasion *per se*, the heralds of Christ introduced challenges that were in many ways akin to foreign occupation. To all parties, Christian and pagan alike, the future must have seemed unclear and profoundly threatening, not just to certain abstract and theoretical questions of faith, but to such concrete and utilitarian matters as the practical application of law.

What did this ideological *coup d'état* mean for the native Irish legal system? In whatever form law existed in pre-Christian Ireland, its processes were categorically essential for society. Arguably, nothing is more crucial for a civilization than an effectively functioning system of justice. Customary systems of jurisprudence, not just in early medieval Europe but around the globe, tend to evolve over time so that they become an elemental part of the fabric of a culture. Thus entrenched, wholesale replacement by a foreign legal system or wide-scale purgation of all provisions not obviously compatible with the new order are typically disastrous and, for contemporaries, literally inconceivable. Generally speaking, rapid change leads to catastrophe, at least in the short term. In medieval Ireland, thus — as anywhere else — rapidly overturning the established legal system would almost certainly have led to a prolonged period of chaos. Besides the civil disorder that necessarily would have ensued, change of this magnitude would have dispossessed native legalists on the one hand, while on the other leaving complete responsibility for the conduct and execution of justice to the fledgling Irish Church. Neither outcome, presumably, was desirable to anyone. Both parties, therefore, had something to gain by compromise; and it seems that ecclesiastical interests, though dominant, nonetheless accommodated secular concerns, at least to an extent. Here, Roy Flechner's observation about the secular elements in *Collectio canonum Hibernenesis* is apropos:

---

93 This is true until the advent of the viking raids, which began in 795 and became more frequent in the early 820s and thereafter.

> When viewed against the backdrop of such 'typical' canon-law collection, ⟨*Collectio canonum Hibernensis*⟩ stands out as a glaring exception for its preoccupation with ostensibly secular matters such as kinship, theft, inheritance, treason, and even fair wages for workmen. In dealing with these matters, ⟨*Collectio canonum Hibernensis*⟩ appears close to secular vernacular law and can often be seen to seek compromises between ecclesiastical ideals and customary law, some of which, perhaps, goes back to pre-Christian legal culture.[94]

In this effort, Hermann Moisl has seen the Church as driven primarily by utilitarian — as opposed to sentimental or preservationist — concerns:

> Irish law dealt with quite a variety of subjects, many of them basic to the functioning of early Irish society. It stands to reason that a Church which was an integral part of the Irish social system would have to articulate its interests within the legal framework which defined that system, and all the indications are that it did.[95]

The fundamental importance of a functioning system of law, solidly grounded on an ideology that was generally accepted by society at large, meant that some kind of accommodation was necessary. Any such compromise would inevitably involve tackling the delicate task of reconciling obvious contradictions between two very different legal doctrines. As Proinsias MacCana expressed it:

> [...] the position in sixth-century Ireland was that there were two laws, on the one hand native, secular law, on the other the law of the Church. These two codes were distinct, if not indeed antithetical, in point of origin, form, and ultimate aim, but the public to whom they applied was by and large the same. This in itself is not an unfamiliar situation, but the problems to which it gives rise must have presented themselves especially clearly and bluntly in this particular setting. The Irish legal system was stubborn and conservative, its position in Irish society solidly buttressed by time-old usage; whereas the law of the Church, for all its power and vigour, was still an innovation, its roots in Irish social custom as yet shallow and delicate. Even if the clerics were to display the utmost toleration and goodwill towards the native system, which would in any case have seemed part of the natural order to most of them, they must have realized very early on that it was going to be extremely difficult to establish a satisfactory *rapprochement* with a 'code' which consisted merely of memorized tradition, and in which the 'letter of the law' had no meaning.[96]

---

94 *The Hibernensis*, Bk I, pp. 47*–48*.

95 Moisl, 'The Church and the Native Tradition of Learning', p. 262.

96 MacCana, 'Three Languages and the Three Laws', p. 70.

Conflicts between individual statutes and differences over matters such as the nature and severity of prescribed punishments might simply be glossed over, at least in most cases, without ostensible reconciliation; the underlying ideology, however, demanded unequivocal resolution. Not surprisingly, therefore, we see in early Irish legal literature a number of attempts to establish and define such a resolution. These attempts will be the object of study in the chapters that follow. First, however, some background is necessary.

CHAPTER 3

Biblical Law

The Scriptures

As early Irish jurists no doubt realized, this situation in which ecclesiastical law came into potential conflict with pre-Christian law had precedent. For those Jews who converted and who were the first Christians, the transformation from Judaism to Christianity involved, among other changes, a shift from a geographically circumscribed, mostly ethnic religion to an expansionist and proselytizing faith aimed (eventually) at widespread conversion. As a result, the missionary activities of the Church from its very inception sparked dilemmas about whether or not non-Jews who converted to Christianity should be subject to the full injunction of the Law of Moses. Resolving the problem, however, required working out a host of thorny legal-theological issues which became some of the main themes of the Pauline Epistles. Questions that arose included: what is the status of gentiles and their pre-existing law in the new Christian religion? Are gentiles subject to Law of Moses? Does the Law of Moses still apply under the New Dispensation, and if so, what was its relationship to the Law of Christ? Such problems, and others that necessarily emerged when early Christian communities began to consider the implications of these matters in fine detail, penetrated straight to the heart of biblical law. Before examining how early Irish jurists addressed these questions, however, I shall begin with a brief discussion of how they were treated in scripture since, as few would disagree, the Bible provided the foundation for many later developments in Irish law.[1] Since my purpose is to lay the groundwork for a discussion of Irish legal thought, however, I shall focus on matters that are relevant to that later tradition. I do not intend what follows, therefore, as a substitute for a more thoroughgoing, objective survey of biblical law with the rigour of modern theological scholarship. Rather, I intend this brief discussion merely as a bare-bones introduction to the

1 The central role of the Bible and biblical study for Irish learning in all fields can hardly be overstated. This point is amply demonstrated throughout Boyle, *History and Salvation*. See also: Ó Néill, *Biblical Study*, p. 1, who put it thus: 'In the early mediaeval Gaelic Churches the study of the Bible was preëminent. That preëminence reflects the strongly monastic character of Gaelic ecclesiastical learning and, more importantly, the central role accorded to biblical studies. All branches of learning in the monastic curriculum were subservient to it [...]'.

relevant legal-theological issues in the Bible as they pertained specifically to Ireland in the early Middle Ages.

Questions about the appropriate application of biblical law to various newly converted communities, including the legal procedure by which such matters should be adjudicated, emerged early in the Christian mission. Most notably, Acts 15 recounts the decision of the so-called 'Synod of Jerusalem', which addressed the controversy concerning whether newly converted gentiles should be required to undergo circumcision as required by the Law of Moses. The importance of this episode for Christian jurisprudence cannot be overstated. Major points of doctrine were at stake, with implications extending far beyond the issue at hand. Above all, the settlement reached in this assembly defined the legal requirements of Jews and gentiles under the New Dispensation, specifically whether the Law of Moses as a whole, that is, not just as regards circumcision, applied fully to non-Jewish converts. Just as important, the process employed to adjudicate this dispute became a *primum exemplum* for synodal procedure in the Church generally, by which disputes involving matters not treated in scripture could be decided. On both points, the Synod of Jerusalem became a leading case. I shall consider both matters, that is, the role of the Law of Moses in Christian society and the establishment of synodal procedure, since both became important legal issues for the medieval Irish Church.

How was the dispute in Acts 15 resolved? First, as the text explains, the appropriate authorities gathered in a council to consider the matter at hand, specifically the *apostoli* and *seniores* (Acts 15:6), in the presence of the local Christian community. One party, represented by Pharisees who were apparently intent on pressing this issue as a test case, insisted not merely that new converts be circumcised, but also that the Law of Moses be applied strictly for all Christians, both Jews and gentiles alike. Simply put, they maintained that the scriptures required literal adherence to the Law of Moses to obtain salvation (Acts 15:5). In the debate that followed, Peter, invoking his special status as God's designated evangelist to the gentiles (Acts 15:7), offered the first recorded opinion:

> et qui novit corda Deus testimonium perhibuit dans illis Spiritum Sanctum sicut et nobis et nihil discrevit inter nos et illos fide purificans corda eorum (Acts 15:8–9).
>
> > (And God, who knows hearts, gave testimony, giving unto them ⟨i.e., the gentiles⟩ Holy Ghost, as well as to us; and he put no difference between us and them, purifying their hearts by faith).

Peter went on to urge a more lenient approach, wherein Mosaic precepts would be applied only in a limited manner to gentiles. He argued that for Christians, whether Jews or gentiles, salvation is achieved through grace, not through strict compliance with the Law of Moses (Acts 15:10–11).

Next, after hearing testimonial evidence from the missionaries Barnabas and Paul, James offers his opinion. He, too, argued that leniency was best, citing the prophet Amos 9:11–12 as confirmation that God held gentiles in favour (Acts 15:16–18); and so, like Peter, he also recommended a milder injunction. In James's view, newly converted gentiles should be forbidden three things only, that is, from eating sacrifices offered to idols, from eating animals that have been strangled and from blood, and from fornication (Acts 15:19–20). Procedurally, the debate was resolved when all members of the synod, the *apostoli* and *seniores* along with Church as a whole, decided by consensus that the advice of Peter and James should be adopted (Acts 15:22).

Acts 15 is a *locus classicus* in the scriptures for the proper conduct of synodal procedure, and it would appear to have influenced early Irish legal ideology on a number of levels. Importantly, the Synod of Jerusalem is the first instance outside of the gospels where the Christian community adjudicated a basic dispute in biblical law, in this case: what is the relationship between the Old Law of Moses and the New Law of Christ? Jesus himself addressed the matter on a number of occasions in the gospels, most notably in Matthew 5:17 where he stated: 'nolite putare quoniam veni solvere legem aut prophetas non veni solvere sed adimplere' (do not think that I have come to destroy the law or the prophets. I have not come to destroy, but to fulfill). Although clear enough in the context he uttered it, from a legal perspective Christ's statement is somewhat ambiguous, leaving significant room for questions about important practical matters of law (for example, whether gentiles must be circumcised). The decision of the Synod of Jerusalem, therefore, provided a clarification of Christ's position in Matthew 5:17, implicitly acknowledging, therefore, that scripture might at times require clarification. Furthermore, it established a procedure for resolving similar disputes within Christian communities that would inevitably arise in the future as the Church grew, i.e., the ecclesiastical synod. Note, too, that this episode also established a procedure for presenting evidence, namely, one in which the parties involved sought guidance from authorities within the broader Christian tradition (e.g., Peter's appeal to the idea of grace and James's citation of the prophet Amos), both from the New Testament and, very significantly, from the Old Testament as well.

Taken together, Acts 15 and Matthew 5:17 express the basic scriptural doctrine concerning the relationship between the Old Law of Moses and the New Law of Christ. These two laws, however, were not the only levels of biblical law to warrant consideration. Alongside the Law of Moses and the Law of Christ there exists in scripture the idea of the 'Law of Nature', a complex notion including those legal precepts accepted and promulgated by non-Christians prior to their conversion. The fundamental basis for the Law of Nature rests on the idea that humankind's innate reason has the potential to lead them to righteous jurisprudence. The idea finds its most basic scriptural expression in Romans 2:14–15,[2] where Paul described it as follows:

> (14) cum enim gentes quae legem non habent naturaliter quae legis sunt faciunt eiusmodi legem non habentes ipsi sibi sunt lex (15) qui ostendunt opus legis scriptum in cordibus suis testimonium reddente illis conscientia ipsorum et inter se invicem cogitationum accusantium aut etiam defendentium.
>
> > ((14) For when the gentiles, who do not have the law, do by nature those things that are of the law; these having not the law are a law to themselves (15) Who show the work of the law written in their hearts, their conscience bearing witness to them, and their thoughts between themselves accusing, or also defending one another).

Early on, this statement led to the important notion of the *naturale bonum*, discussed in patristic writings and widely expressed by theologians of the Ascetic Movement,[3] which posited that pre-conversion gentiles and their laws have the capacity for natural, innate righteousness even though they are ignorant of the Law of Moses and faith in Christ. Ali Bonner for example points out that in his *Epistula ad Demetriadem*, Pelagius expressed the notion that

> [...] man's nature was innately good [...] 'There is, I say, a kind of natural sanctity (as I would put it) in our souls'. ⟨*Est enim, inquam, in anmis nostris naturalis quaedam, ut ita dixerim, sanctitas*⟩. He referred

---

2 For an Irish use of this scriptural passage, see especially: Ó Corráin, Breatnach, and Breen, 'The Laws of the Irish', pp. 390–94 and Scowcroft, '*Recht Fáide* and Its Gloss', pp. 147–48.

3 This idea was especially important to the so-called 'Ascetic Movement', of which Pelagius was an exponent. I shall have a great deal to say about this topic below. For example, Ambrosiaster (a fourth-century exegete of the Ascetic Movement) 'asserted that there was a "natural law" (*lex naturalis*) that guided man to correct belief. He characterised belief as something to which individuals came through their own choice. This natural law played a part in coming to salvation. It taught men not to do to others what they did not want to suffer themselves. Ambrosiaster discussed at length how there were men before Moses: "Who had not sinned in the likeness of Adam", and he cited Abraham as one such who was "guided by nature". This was the same argument that Pelagius later expounded about the natural goodness of some Old Testament figures. Ambrosiaster [...] referred to "nature" and the "natural law" (*natura, lex naturalis*), where Pelagius later referred to "the good of nature" (*bonum naturae*), but the argument that there had been "righteous men" (*iusti*) before Moses and before Christ's advent was the same in both authors', Bonner, *The Myth of Pelagianism*, pp. 190–92. Likewise, Apponius, another adherent to the Ascetic Movement, '[...] suggested that human initiative played a part in coming to belief. God gave man's nature, made in the image and likeness of God, a rational sense: Through which he may know to seek good and to reject evil', Bonner, *The Myth of Pelagianism*, pp. 192–93.

> to 'the good of nature' ⟨*naturae bonum*⟩, 'the riches of nature' ⟨*naturae diuitiae*⟩, and 'that treasure-store of the soul ⟨*ille thesaurus animae*⟩'.[4]

So, according to Pauline doctrine, the laws of the gentiles — under certain conditions and where they did not contravene anything in scripture — might continue to hold value in Christian society,[5] especially where they addressed matters not explicitly covered elsewhere in Christian law. This notion held a place of great importance in Irish theology and law,[6] as it did elsewhere in the medieval West generally and beyond.

Exegesis on biblical law has a long and complicated history, spanning the period from ancient rabbinical teachings which influenced early Christian exegetes to modern theological scholarship.[7] At every stage, biblical law was systematized differently and often with labyrinthine complexity. On the most basic level, medieval Christians recognized three divisions: the Law of Nature, the Law of Moses and the Law of Christ. This tripartite conceptualization of divine law parallelled the received understanding of the successive stages of Christian history as reflected in the patristic formula that described

> [...] the division of sacred history in to three periods, *ante legem, sub lege, et sub gratia*, i.e., the period before the Mosaic Law, the period under the Law, and the period of grace inaugurated by Christ. This formula apparently originated with Augustine. It appears in his discussion of biblical number symbolism in *De doctrina Christiana*, as well as in his letters, often in his exegetical works and in one of his sermons [...] The formula is also found several times in the works of Quodvultdeus, and in Cassiodorus' *Commentary on the Psalms*. It was further spread through Gregory the Great's *Homilies on the Gospels*, and its inclusion in Isidore's *Etymologies* and his *De ecclesiasticis officiis*. The formula became part of the Insular homiletic tradition, occurring in Bede's *Homilies on the Gospels*, in Hiberno-Latin homilies, and several

---

4 Bonner, *The Myth of Pelagianism*, p. 37. The portions in angle brackets are from p. 37 n. 17.

5 See, for example, Donahue, 'Beowulf, Ireland, and the Natural Good', pp. 267–71 and Scowcroft, '*Recht Fáide*', p. 147.

6 I shall have more to say more about natural law below. For a few examples of its understanding in Irish thought, see Herren and Brown, *Christ in Celtic Christianity*, pp. 95–96.

7 I intend these very general statements (both here and those that follow) only as a basic overview of biblical law and sacred history from the perspective of a medieval Irish Christian. I do not intend them to substitute for a complete interpretation of the scriptures informed by modern theological scholarship.

> times in the homilies of Ælfric, who retained the Latin formula from his English homiliaries.[8]

Views of the relationship between these laws were intricately complicated and variously conceived by exegetes and theologians throughout the Middle Ages and beyond. Certainly, more and finer distinctions could, and were in fact often made. These three divisions, however, described as 'Laws', reflect the most basic understanding of the historical development of biblical law as a series of covenants between God and mankind over the span of sacred history, beginning with prelapsarian humanity who, in the beginning, lived without written law (that is, according to the Law of Nature), then under the written law of the Old Testament (that is, according to the Law of Moses), until the coming of Jesus and the New Dispensation (that is, according to the Law of Christ). In the most common medieval view (though, again, there were variations), each successive law was understood to supersede its predecessor, though no law was never considered to have been rescinded.[9] Rather, each law was thought to prefigure its successor just as it fulfilled what came before.[10] As such, divine law was viewed both historically and theologically: divine law evolved according to the Christian view of history, through a series of stages, each fulfilling the latter, from Creation until Doom.[11]

According to this religious view, each successive period in sacred history inaugurated a new covenant between God and mankind, in which God revealed more of his divine plan, making certain promises in return for obedience to his dictates. The ultimate source for this understanding of history, that is, as a series of divine dispensations in God's evolving relationship with humanity, was the Bible:

> [...] the basic bipartite division of sacred history between the 'old law' (i.e., the law of Moses) and the 'new law' of the Gospel is proclaimed in the Prologue of John's Gospel: 'For the Law was given through Moses, grace and truth have come through Jesus Christ' (John 1:17; cf. John 13:34). The phrase 'new law' does not occur here, of course, and in

8 Martin and Hall, 'The Enumeration of Laws Motif', pp. 53–55. I am extremely grateful to Thomas N. Hall for drawing my attention to this material. Martin and Hall provide extensive references to occurrences of this formula in the works of these patristic authorities.

9 How the succession of Laws was understood in various cultures and, for that matter, different patristic writers, is a matter of great complexity. For one view of how the progress of divine history was understood in early medieval Ireland, see Herren and Brown, *Christ in Celtic Christianity*, p. 114. Note, however, that I am sceptical of some of their conclusions, as I shall discuss below.

10 The implications of this doctrine provoked a great deal of controversy. For a brief discussion, see Herren and Brown, *Christ in Celtic Christianity*, pp. 106–09.

11 See also, Boyle, *History and Salvation*, pp. 16–19. Note that Boyle uses the designation 'salvation history' to signify what I call 'sacred history'. These are equivalent terms.

> fact it does not occur anywhere in the New Testament, but in using the expression 'the pure law of liberty', the author of the Epistle of James can be regarded as referring to the Gospel as a new law (James 1:25) [...].[12]

With the Mosaic Covenant, God was understood to have given the Decalogue to the Jews, who then became his Chosen People and were led to the Promised Land in return for their compliance with his law. Historically, therefore, only the Jews ever fell under the Law of Moses; during the same period, gentiles (according to this understanding) remained subject to the Law of Nature, which may or may not have been formally codified within any given culture. Subsequently, with the advent of Christ, God was believed to have made a new covenant with mankind (understood as the fulfillment of the prior Mosaic Covenant), wherein all humanity — not just Jews but gentiles as well — received divine grace and remission of their sins in return for their faith in Christ and their acceptance of his new law of forgiveness (that is, the Law of Christ). This succession of stages in Christian history represents the most basic Christian conceptualization of God's unfolding relationship with mankind: each consecutive stage in the historical progression toward final judgement and salvation was thought to herald a new covenant, a reconstituted relationship between God and humankind, and — most importantly for the present study — a new, fuller, and more sophisticated understanding of divine law.

To this basic view of sacred history, some exegetes added the Noahide (or Noachide, or Noachic) Covenant, a concept I shall mention here since it will be important for my later discussion of Irish law. The Noahide Covenant refers to the promise God made to Noah on Mount Ararat after the great flood, as described in chapter nine of the book of Genesis. In the most basic formulation, God established his covenant with Noah, promising that he would not destroy the world again by means of a flood (Gen 9:9–17). In return, he laid down the following injunctions for Noah and his offspring: (1) that they should increase and multiply (Gen. 9:1,7), (2) that they should not eat flesh with blood (Gen. 9:4), and (3) that they should require capital punishment for murderers: 'quicumque effuderit humanum sanguinem fundetur sanguis illius ad imaginem quippe Dei factus est homo' (Whosoever shall shed man's blood, his blood shall be shed: for man was made in the image of God) (Gen. 9:6). These basic statutes, sometimes thought to include other requirements of divine law that appear in the book of Genesis, constitute what some exegetes have referred to as the 'Noahide Law'.

For several reasons, this stage in the Christian understanding of sacred history is important for the present discussion. First, since the Noahide

12 Martin and Hall, 'Enumeration of Laws Motif', p. 51.

Covenant preceded the Mosaic Covenant — that is, since it preceded the time when the Jews were believed to have become God's Chosen People — the Law of Noah, within a Christian view of sacred history, likewise preceded the biblical distinction between Jews and gentiles. Thus, the Law of Noah was sometimes understood by early Christian legal scholars and exegetes as the divine law of all righteous gentiles. As such, it was sometimes, though not always, considered to be one and the same with the Law of Nature. Secondly, many have noticed that the Noahide injunctions bear strong resemblance to the decision of the Synod of Jerusalem, where it was decided that newly converted gentiles would not be subject to the full sanction of the Law of Moses. The only substantive differences were that (1) Noahide law included no explicit prohibition of idolatry, and (2) the Synod of Jerusalem did not require capital punishment for murderers. Based on its overall similarities with the decision in Acts 15, the Synod of Jerusalem could be taken not as a reduced version of the Law of Moses, but rather as a requirement that gentiles obey the Law of Noah to which they would have been most appropriately subject anyway, given the common understanding of their place in sacred history as descendants of Noah, but not of Moses and the other Israelites. I shall have more to say on this point as it pertains to Irish law below.

Biblical Law in Early Ireland

How was biblical law understood in early medieval Ireland? The answer to this question is quite involved but reveals much about how Irish jurists confronted the problem of reconciling ecclesiastical and pre-Christian, native law. Here, we should not expect to find a monolithic tradition. Rather, the evidence suggests that the divisions of biblical law recognized in the Irish tradition and the relationship between them were variously conceived at different times and in different contexts.[13] In the vernacular, there were a variety of terms referring to successive stages of sacred history and biblical law, for example *recht aicnid* (the Law of Nature), *recht litre* (the Law of the Letter, or written law, usually signifying the Law of Moses, but sometimes Christian law generally, including the Law of Christ).[14] In certain contexts *recht* by itself signified the Law of Moses (compare the use of L. *lex*, e.g., in *Collectio canonum Hibernensis* to signify the Law of

13 My references to 'the Irish' and 'the Irish tradition' should be understood in this light. I do not intend to suggest that early Irish Christianity was without variation and internal controversy. My claims, therefore, should be taken only as my interpretations of doctrine as represented in particular texts which, in all cases, were part of a larger, more diverse intellectual milieu.

14 On the possible meanings of *recht litre*, see McCone, *Pagan Past and Christian Present*, p. 95.

Moses, where the phrase *in utraque lege* signifies the Laws of both the Old and New Testaments, i.e., the Law of Moses and the Law of Christ). Other terms commonly used include: *recht bérlai báin* (literally, the Law of the 'White Language', i.e., the Law of Scripture),[15] *recht fetarlaice* (the Law of the Old Testament), *recht fáide* (the Law of Prophecy, sometimes distinguished from *recht litre* when the latter was used to signify its specialized meaning as the Law of Moses, sometimes not), *recht nuafiadnaise* (the Law of the New Testament), and *recht in spiruta nóim* (literally, the Law of the Holy Spirit, usually signifying the Law of Christ, but occasionally the Law of Nature or Law of the Prophets). This short catalogue is by no means a comprehensive list.

In the most idealized formulations, early Irish jurists conceived of biblical law as somewhat more finely divided than the more common threefold system described above. As Kim McCone,[16] Lawrence T. Martin and Thomas N. Hall,[17] and, more recently, R. Mark Scowcroft[18] have discussed, in addition to the Law of Nature, the Law of Moses, and the Law of Christ, the most completely formulated Irish understanding of biblical law consisted of a quadripartite division including the so-called 'Law of Prophecy' or the 'Law of the Prophets' (L. *lex prophetiae*, OIr. *recht fáide*), understood to follow the Law of Moses and precede the Law of Christ in the scheme of Christian history. Presumably, this additional, fourth Law emerged from the preeminent place the scriptures held in Irish theology. The admonitions of the Old Testament prophets, while most often derivative of levitical precepts, nonetheless exhibited a somewhat different character, especially as they looked forward and anticipated the coming of the messiah. Thus, given their legal or at least sometimes legalistic nature, the nomothetical aspects of the prophetic books of the Old Testament apparently warranted separate consideration in the minds of Irish jurists, apart from the Law of Moses. Indeed, their choice to categorize the 'Law of the Prophets' as a distinct period in sacred history would seem to suggest that they understood the legal and theological ideologies expressed in these books to represent a significant expansion upon the Law of Moses.

Occasionally, Irish jurists seem to have regarded their own pre-conversion, native judges and wise men as equivalent to the Old Testament prophets, and the 'prophecies' they uttered to carry the same force of

---

15 See especially Ó Néill, *Biblical Study*, p. 26: '⟨The Pseudo-historical Prologue to the *Senchas Már*⟩ relates that after the arrival of Christianity the authority and language of the native learned classes became subject to those who possessed *bérlae bán*, literally "the white (or clear) language". Elsewhere this odd phrase is more precisely defined as "the white/clear language of the *Beati*" (Psalm 118)'.

16 McCone, *Pagan Past and Christian Present*, pp. 92–94.

17 Martin and Hall, 'Enumeration of Laws Motif', pp. 57–65.

18 Scowcroft, '*Recht Fáide*', pp. 148–50.

law as those in scripture. Consider, for example, this passage from the late seventh-century vernacular tract *Córus Bésgnai*:

> § 35. Ro ráidi Dubthach maccu Lugair in fili bretha fer nÉrenn a recht aicnid ⁊ a recht ḟáide. Ar ro follnastar fáidsine i recht aicnid i mbrithemnas inse hÉrenn ⁊ inna filedaib, toch-airrchechnatar fáidi leo do-n-icfad bérlae mbán .i. recht litre.[19]
>
> (Dubthach maccu Lugair the learned poet stated the judgements of the men of Ireland ⟨delivered⟩ out of the law of nature and the law of the prophets. For prophecy in accordance with the law of nature had ruled in the judgement of the island of Ireland and her learned poets, and prophets among them had foretold that the pure language of the *Beati* would come, that is the law of the letter).[20]

Here, we are told that Dubthach maccu Lugair, a native Irish jurist infused with natural goodness (about whom I shall have a great deal to say below), recited laws and judgements in accordance with divine law, specifically the Law of Nature and the Law of the Prophets. This is a startling claim. A Middle Irish gloss in one manuscript goes even farther, naming two other mythical Irish figures who also uttered such prophecies, including Morann, to whom *Audacht Morainn* (*The Testament of Moran*),[21] is attributed and Fíthal, to whom *Senbríathra Fíthail* (*The Ancient Sayings of Fíthal*) (associated with Aldfrith of Northumbria) is attributed.[22] By situating early Irish wisdom literature within the framework of sacred history in this way, they imbued it with the force of biblical law, an equivalence that significantly increased the body of native learning that Irish jurists could regard as 'divine law'. Moreover, although speculative, it is tempting to wonder if Columbanus's reference to 'Hibernicis antiquis philosophis' (ancient Irish savants), in his *Epistula 1*, might in some way refer to pre-Christian figures like Dubthach, Moran, and Fíthal who, despite being pagan, nonetheless issued judgements based on the Law of Nature and the Law of the Prophets and foresaw the coming of the Law of Christ.

Whatever the status of their native prophets, Irish jurists and theologians appear to have preferred this fourfold division of divine law that included the Law of the Prophets. McCone, Martin and Hall, and Scowcroft all cite a series of early Irish commentaries upholding this fourfold division. The most thorough catalogue of both Latin and vernacular examples, however, is found in Martin and Hall.[23] Given the importance of this

19 The text is from Breatnach, *Córus Bésgnai*, p. 34.

20 The translation is from Breatnach, *Córus Bésgnai*, p. 35.

21 *Audacht Morainn*.

22 *Old Irish Wisdom*.

23 Martin and Hall, 'Enumeration of Laws Motif', pp. 57–65.

idea for the present discussion, I shall reproduce a portion of the most important evidence these scholars have assembled.

The first example is from the still (mostly) unedited, eighth-century, Hiberno-Latin biblical commentary known as the *Reference Bible*:[24]

> Quot sunt leges principales et unde incipit et finit unaquaque de eis? Leges quattuor sunt principales: **lex naturae** et **lex littere, lex prophetiae**, et **lex euangelii**. Incipit lex nature ab Adam usque Moysen; lex littere a Moysen usque ad Samuhel; lex prophetiae a Samuel usque ad Iohannem Babtistam; lex euangelii ab Iohanne usque ad finem mundi.[25]
>
>> (How many are the principle laws and when does each begin and end? There are four principle laws, the **Law of Nature** and the **Law of the Letter** [= the Law of Moses], the **Law of Prophecy** and the **Law of the Gospel**. The Law of Nature extends [*lit.* begins] from Adam to Moses. The Law of the Letter from Moses to Samuel, the Law of Prophecy from Samuel to John the Baptist, and the Law of the Gospel from John until the end of the world).[26]

Next, as both Martin and Hall and Scowcroft point out, a similar division occurs in the Old Irish *Litany of Jesus*:

> Ateoch frit huile thuicsenchu **rechta aicnid**, im Aibel, im Sheth, im Heli, im Enoc, im Nói, im Abraham, im Isaác, im Iacob; Ateoch frit huili thuicsenchu **rechta litre**, im Moysi, im Iesu, im Chalep, im Aron, im Elizar, im Ionass; Ateoch frit huli thuicsinchu **rechta fatha**, im Eliam, im Elisium, im Dauid, ⁊ im Sholmáin; Ateoch frit huile thuicsenchu **rechta nua-fiadnaise** im do noeb-abstalu uadessin, ⁊ im na huile noebu, co deired in domuin.[27]

---

24 The so-called 'Reference Bible' (known also by its German appellation 'das Bibelwerk') is a series of excerpts from the Bible with interspersed commentary. On this important text, see especially: Bischoff, 'Wendepunkte in der Geschichte der Lateinischen Exegese', pp. 189–279 (repr. Bischoff, *Mittelalterliche Studien*, I, pp. 206–73; translated by Colm O'Grady, 'Turning-points in the History of Latin Exegesis', pp. 74–160). See also: J. Kelly, 'Das Bibelwerk: *Organization and Quellenanalyse*', pp. 113–23; McNamara, 'Plan and Source Analysis of *Das Bibelwerk*', pp. 84–111; and B. Carella, 'Divine Law'. The only portion so far edited, covering Genesis through Leviticus, is found in *Pauca problesmata de enigmatibus ex tomis canonicis*. The two complete manuscript witnesses are BnF, MS lat. 11561, and Munich; Bayerische SB, MSS Clm. 14276 and 14277, and there are several fragments. See also: Martin and Hall, 'Enumeration of Laws Motif', p. 60. I have added the bold.

25 *Pauca problesmata de enigmatibus ex tomis canonicis*, ll. 10–15 p. 25. Emphasis my own, in both text and translation.

26 The translation I have included here is Scowcroft's, '*Recht Fáide*', p. 148 n. 18.

27 The text is from *Irish Litanies*, p. 32. I have added the emphasis. See also: Ó Corráin, 'Irish Vernacular Law and the Old Testament', p. 292.

> (I beseech Thee, by those wise in the **Natural Law**, such as Abel, Seth, Elijah, Enoch, Noah, Abraham, Isaac and Jacob; I beseech Thee, by those wise in the **Law of the Letter**, such as Moses, Joshua, Caleb, Aaron, Eleazar and Jonah; I beseech Thee, by those wise in the **Prophetic Law**, such as Elijah, Elisha, David and Solomon; I beseech Thee, by those wise in the **Law of the New Testament**, such as Thy own holy apostles and all the saints, to the end of the world).[28]

Similarly, McCone points to a mention of the Law of Prophecy distinguished from the other biblical laws in a Middle Irish pseudo-historical prosimetric narrative from the Yellow Book of Lecan known as *Do Suidigud Tellaich Temra* (The Settling of the Manor of Tara),[29] attributed to the legendary figure Fintan mac Bóchra. Presumably, the fourfold division in this *c.* tenth- to *c.* twelfth-century text reflects earlier tradition. In this poem, Moses is said to have made *bretha lánmaithi litre* (perfect judgements of the letter), David *bretha fíra fáitsine* (true judgements of prophecy), before the coming of Christ, who made judgements *tria núfíadnaise nóemgloin* (through his holy, pure New Dispensation).[30] As another example, McCone points out that both Muirchú and Tírechán in their respective, late seventh-century lives of St Patrick portray the great saint and lawgiver typologically, likening him to Moses, Elijah, and Christ, thus representing the Law of Moses, the Law of Prophecy, and the Law of Christ respectively. A clear example of this pattern is found in Tírechán's *vita*, where we are told that '[...] perrexit Patricius ad montem Egli, ut ieiunaret in illo quadraginta noctibus, Moysaicam tenens disciplinam et Heliacam et Christianam' ([...] Patrick proceeded to *Mons Aigli*, intending to fast there for forty days and forty nights, following the example of Moses, Elijah, and Christ).[31]

Next, Martin and Hall point to the fourfold division of divine law in the ninth-century Stowe Missal:

> Acanar dind off*riund* for*sen* it*er* i*n*troit ⁊ orthana ⁊ tormach corrigi liacht nap*stal* ⁊ Ψalm ṅdig*r*ad isfigor **recto aicnith** i*n*sin inroaithnuiged cr*ist* tria huili baullo ⁊ gnímo · Liacht ap*stal* im*murgu* ⁊ salm dig*r*ad ⁊ hoṡuidiu codinochtad is foraithmet · **rechta litre** i*n*rofiug*ra*d cr*ist* acht nadfess cadacht cidrofiug*r*ad and ·

28 The translation is Scowcroft's, '*Recht Fáide*', p. 149 n. 19.

29 The text is edited in 'The Settling of the Manor of Tara'. See also: Ó Corráin, 'Irish Vernacular Law and the Old Testament', p. 293.

30 McCone, *Pagan Past and Christian Present*, p. 93.

31 McCone, *Pagan Past and Christian Present*, p. 89. The text and translation are from *The Patrician Texts in the Book of Armagh*, p. 152 (text); p. 153 (translation).

Indinochtad corrici leth i*nn*a oblæ ⁊ *in*cailich ⁊ acanar occo it*ir* sos*cél* ⁊ aillóir corrici oblata isfora*ithm*et **rechta fáthe** hitarchet cr*ist* cofoll*us* acht nath naiccess coregénir:~

Tocbál *in*cailich iarnalándiurug q*uando* canit*ur* oblata is for*aithm*et gene cr*ist* *in*sin ⁊ áin*d*ocbale tre airde ⁊ firto ·[32]

> (What is chanted of the Mass thereafter, both introit and prayers and addition, as far as the Lesson of the Apostles (the Epistle) and the Gradual, *that* is the figure of **the law of Nature**, wherein Christ has been renewed, through all His members and deeds.
>
> The Epistle, however, and the Gradual, and from this to the uncovering (of the chalice), it is a commemoration of **the law of the Letter** wherein Christ has been figured, only that what has been figured therein was not yet known.
>
> The uncovering so far as half, of the Host and the Chalice, and what is chanted thereat, both Gospel and Alleluia as far as *oblata*, it is a commemoration of **the law of the Prophets** wherein Christ was manifestly foretold, save that it was not seen until He was born).[33]

The authors continue:

> The elevation of the chalice is interpreted as 'a commemoration of Christ's birth', which is not here referred to as a 'law', but nevertheless the passage as a whole is obviously an application of the four laws variety of the enumeration of laws motif [...].[34]

Finally, turning to legal materials proper, apparently heretofore unnoticed in this context is mention of four laws in *Collectio canonum Hibernensis*, Liber II, *De prespitero uel sacerdote* (Concerning the presbyter and *sacerdos*), cap. 10 *De diuerso sacrificio per IIII, leges* (Concerning the varied offerings in the four laws):[35]

> Melchisedech uinum et panem obtulit, Iob holocaustomata, Aaron agnos et uitulos columbasque et turtures, Christus corpus et sanguinem obtulit.[36]

32 The text is from *Thesaurus Palaeohibernicus*, II, pp. 252–53.

33 The translation is from *Thesaurus Palaeohibernicus*, II, pp. 252–53.

34 Martin and Hall, 'Enumeration of Laws Motif', p. 63.

35 See also: Ó Corráin, 'Irish Vernacular Law and the Old Testament', p. 293. Ó Corráin's interpretation of this passage differs significantly from my own.

36 *The Hibernensis*, Bk I, p. 23.

> (Melchisedech offered wine and bread, Job holocausts, Aaron lambs and calves and doves and turtledoves, Christ offered his body and blood).[37]

In this passage, Melchisedech represents the mode of sacrifice practised according to the Law of Nature, a conclusion upheld in an earlier chapter of the same book (Liber II, cap. 5), entitled *De causis, quibus immolabant sacerdotes legis naturae, quorum primus Melchisedech* (Concerning the reasons why the *sacerdotes* of the law of nature, the first of whom was Melchisedech, were offering).[38] Christ, obviously enough, represents the practice according to the Law of Christ. The references to Job and Aaron, however, are less straightforward. Aaron's sacrifice certainly represents proper sacrificial practice according to the Law of Moses, though one would expect him to follow immediately after Melchisedech on historical grounds. What does Job represent? Based on the process of elimination, Job would seem to represent the Law of Prophecy. Why Job, however, who is not usually regarded as a prophet? As it turns out, Job's treatment as a prophet is well-precedented in medieval exegetical literature. Gregory the Great's well-known *Moralia on Iob*, for example, discussed Job in this capacity, specifically '⟨i⟩n light of Job 19:25–27[39] [...] ⟨and on this account⟩ is typical of medieval commentators in regarding Job as a prophet of the general resurrection of the dead'.[40] Understood in this light, therefore, Job would seem to represent the Law of Prophecy in this context.

Confusingly, however, a passage from Gregory is cited in an earlier chapter of the same book of *Collectio canonum Hibernensis* (Liber II, cap. 5) that seems to regard Job not as a prophet but rather as a representative of the Law of Nature. In this chapter, Job is held up as one of two examples of sacrifices made according to the Law of Nature. His inclusion here would seem to indicate that Gregory, at least in this context, did not regard Job as prophet. Despite this apparent incongruity, only four individuals are listed in the former citation (Melchisedech, Job, Aaron, and Christ) as representatives of the four biblical laws, one each, presumably, to represent the Four Laws specified in the chapter's title. The process of elimination leaves only Job to represent the Law of Prophecy; and yet, just a few

---

37 *The Hibernensis*, Bk II, p. 494.

38 *The Hibernensis*, Bk I, p. 21 (text); Bk II, p. 493 (trans.).

39 Job 19:25–27: (25) scio enim quod redemptor meus vivat et in novissimo de terra surrecturus sim (26) et rursum circumdabor pelle mea et in carne mea videbo Deum (27) quem visurus sum ego ipse et oculi mei conspecturi sunt et non alius reposita est haec spes mea in sinu meo ((25) For I know that my Redeemer lives, and in the last day I shall rise out of the earth. (26) And I shall be clothed again with my skin, and in my flesh I will see my God. (27) Whom I myself shall see, and my eyes shall behold, and not another: this, my hope, is laid up in my bosom).

40 Boadt, *The Book of Job*, p. 30. For an alternative interpretation of Job's role in this passage see Ó Corráin, 'Irish Vernacular Law and the Old Testament', p. 292.

chapters earlier he was unambiguously held up as a representative of the Law of Nature in a citation from the same authority. What are we to make of this apparent contradiction? Perhaps the problem can be resolved if we understand that symbolically, the figure of Job was polysemic. As a gentile of the Old Testament, Job's pious sacrifice (Job 1:5) might be read as innately righteous behaviour according to the Law of Nature. On the other hand, his apparent prognostic abilities, foretelling the raising of the dead on Judgement Day (Job 19:25–27), for example, may have suggested to an Irish audience that, depending on context, he might be regarded as a prophet as well. It would seem, then, that the compilers of *Collectio canonum Hibernensis,* like Gregory himself, understood Job in both capacities. For an Irish audience fully aware of their inherent status as gentiles, Job (himself a gentile) may have seemed a particularly fitting choice to represent the Law of Prophecy, since his prognostic abilities might be taken as evidence that the Holy Spirit could — and did — speak through the mouths of pious non-Jews, at least on occasion, prior to the advent of Christianity.[41]

Based on these passages, an idealized, if by no means monolithic, Irish conceptualization of the divisions in biblical law can be summarized as follows:

1 The Law of Nature (L. *lex naturae,* OIr. *recht aicnid*), signifying unwritten law prior to Moses emanating from the innate goodness of human reason. It is historically biblical (i.e., applying to Jews during the period from Abel to Moses, though see '1a' below), but can also describe pre-Christian gentile law, covering the periods from Abel up to the point of a given gentile people's conversion to Christianity.
2 The Law of the Letter (L. *lex litterae,* OIr. *recht litre,* etc.), signifying the written Law of Moses as expressed in the Pentateuch. In a Christian view of sacred history, this Law applied in unmediated fashion only to Jews prior to the advent of Christ.
3 The Law of the Prophecy (L. *lex prophetiae,* OIr. *recht fáide*), a somewhat less well-defined notion, perhaps ultimately derivative of the common biblical pairing of *lex et prophetae,* signifying the 'law' expressed in the prophetic books of the Old Testament. Historically (like the Law of Moses), this Law applied only to Jews.
4 The Law of the New Testament (L. *lex euangelii,* OIr. *recht nuafiadnaise,* etc.), signifying the Law of Christ as expressed both in the Gospels and in the remainder of the New Testament. Historically, this Law applied to both Jews and gentiles alike from the point of their conversion.

41 As, in fact, is asserted in the Pseudo-historical Prologue to the *Senchas Már,* as I shall discuss below.

To this list, as item (1a), we might add the Law of Noah, signifying the injunctions God set down for Noah and his offspring on Mount Ararat after the flood. Historically, the Law of Noah applied to both Jews and Gentiles alike, from the point of God's Covenant with Noah on Mount Ararat to Moses' reception of the Decalogue. Although Noahide Law seems to have been important for early medieval Irish legal thought as part of the Law of Nature (as I shall discuss below), it is not to the best of my knowledge included in any formal catalogue of the biblical laws in early medieval Ireland. Rather, Noahide Law seems typically to have been regarded as one and the same with, or at least subsumed within the Law of Nature.

It is important to emphasize that this fourfold model was by no means the only one to which medieval Irish exegetes subscribed. Clearly, there was a great deal of variation in the early Irish conceptualization of biblical law and Christian history. The fourfold system I have described here constitutes only one of several versions found in early Irish texts. Other formulations existed which we need not see as necessarily contradicting one another, but rather as adaptations for a particular purpose within a specialized theological or legal context. Sometimes variations can be found even within a single text, a phenomenon common in Irish literature, as we have seen. Often, for example, the Law of Nature and the Law of Prophecy were left unmentioned; and where the latter was included, its practical application (other than to provide supplemental confirmation for a decision made in accordance with one of the other Laws) — if it had any such function at all — seems at best only vaguely conceived.[42] Despite this high degree of variation, the fourfold division seems to represent the Irish understanding of biblical law and sacred history in its most idealized, fully-conceived, and widespread form.

This model of biblical law, as McCone and Scowcroft rightly point out,[43] though originating with Jerome, likely found its way to Ireland via Isidore's divisions of the Old Testament in his *Etymologiae* VI.i.3, directly or indirectly:

> Hebraei autem Vetus Testamentum, Esdra auctore, iuxta numerum litterarum suarum in viginti duos libros accipiunt, dividentes eos in tres ordines: Legis scilicet, Prophetarum, et Hagiographorum.[44]

---

42 Pelagius, a fifth-century British or Irish heretic, whose views may or may not represent those of his native land, recognized the Law of Nature, the Law of Moses, and the Law of Christ, though his views on them — particularly the significance he attributed to the Law of Nature — may be idiosyncratic. I shall have more to say about this matter below. For recent discussion, see in particular: Herren and Brown, *Christ in Celtic Christianity*, p. 70.

43 McCone, *Pagan Past and Christian Present*, p. 93; Scowcroft, '*Recht Fáide*', p. 146–47.

44 The text is from Isidore of Seville, *Etymologiarum*, I, V.i.3–4.

> (The Hebrews take the Old Testament, with Ezra as its redactor, as consisting of twenty-two books, corresponding to the number of letters in their alphabet. They divide the book into three classes: Law, Prophets, and Sacred Writings).[45]

In Ireland, the addition of a fourth law — the Law of Prophecy — seems to have been an innovation, presumably based on the organization of the Old Testament according to Isidore, and perhaps also the common biblical phrase *lex et prophetae* to signify Old Testament Law.[46] According to the Irish understanding of biblical history, these divisions within the Old Testament marked not merely separate sections of the Bible, but successive dispensations within sacred history, in which God made a covenant with humankind wherein he revealed more of his divine plan (= Law) in return for certain promises from mankind to obey his precepts. As such, these 'dipensations', 'covenants', or 'Laws' had real-world legal implications.

Such implications are apparent from a close reading of Acts 15. Let me now return to it. It is possible, I would argue, that Irish jurists derived this notion of four laws, at least in part, from a close reading of this biblical episode. Although it is not explicitly mentioned in the primary sources (for reasons I shall explore below) it is revealing to examine the procedures of this first, paradigmatic synod from the perspective of an early Irish jurist. At the Synod of Jerusalem, the legal question at hand centred on whether or not newly converted gentiles should be circumcised, and — more broadly, for this was the real question — whether or not they should be held subject to the full sanction of the Mosaic Law (Acts 15:1). Apparently, this debate fomented a dispute of some magnitude within the early Church; and, as a result, two representatives, Paul and Barnabas, were designated to go to Jerusalem to raise the matter for adjudication at a gathering of *apostoli* and *seniores* (Acts 15:2). The debate began when some of the Pharisees argued that converted gentiles must be circumcised, and — distilling the underlying principle of the question under consideration — that they should be ordered to keep the Law of Moses in full (Acts 15:5). So, the point of law to be decided was whether or not the Law of Moses applied to gentiles in the same way and to the same extent that it applied to Jews. The first to speak was Peter who argued against enforcing the Mosaic Law in its fullness, reasoning as follows (Acts 15:7–11):

> (7) cum autem magna conquisitio fieret surgens Petrus dixit ad eos viri fratres vos scitis quoniam ab antiquis diebus in nobis elegit Deus per

45 The translation is from Isidore of Seville, *The Etymologies*, p. 135.

46 There may be influence of Pelagian doctrine here as well. Herren and Brown note, for instance, that 'Pelagian texts refer to four sources of the divine law: the law (Pentateuch), the prophets, the gospels and the apostles', *Christ in Celtic Christianity*, p. 106. See also in the same volume, p. 72 and n. 19.

os meum audire gentes verbum evangelii et credere (8) et qui novit corda Deus testimonium perhibuit dans illis Spiritum Sanctum sicut et nobis (9) et nihil discrevit inter nos et illos fide purificans corda eorum (10) nunc ergo quid temptatis Deum inponere iugum super cervicem discipulorum quod neque patres nostri neque nos portare potuimus (11) sed per gratiam Domini Iesu credimus salvari quemadmodum et illi.

((7) And when there had been much disputing, Peter, rising up, said to them: men, brothers, you know that in former days God made choice among us, that by my mouth the Gentiles should hear the word of the Gospel, and believe. (8) And God, who knows hearts, gave testimony, giving unto them the Holy Spirit, as well as to us, (9) and put no difference between us and them, purifying their hearts by Faith. (10) Now therefore, why do you tempt God to put a yoke upon the necks of the disciples, which neither our fathers nor we have been able to bear? (11) But by the grace of the Lord Jesus Christ, we believe to be saved, in like manner as they also).

Peter's reasoning is complicated. To an Irish audience it may have appeared that he was making an argument, at least in part, based on the Law of Nature. His claim in Acts 15:8 that 'qui novit corda Deus testimonium perhibuit dans illis Spiritum Sanctum sicut et nobis' (And God, who knows the hearts, gave testimony, giving unto them the Holy Spirit, as well as to us), would seem to suggest that the Holy Spirit was present among virtuous gentiles before their hearts were purified by the faith (Acts 15:9). This argument reflected a basic tenet of the Christian concept of the Law of Nature, that is, that the Holy Spirit often manifested its will to righteous non-Christians prior to their conversion. This doctrine is expressed explicitly elsewhere in Irish literature.[47] As recipients of the gift of the Holy Spirit (under the Law of Nature), Peter continued, gentiles are the same as Jews

47 For example, the author of the Pseudo-historical Prologue the *Senchas Már* explains: 'Ar in Spirut Naem ro labrastar ⁊ doaircechain tria ginu na fer fíréon ceta-rabatar i n.-inis Érenn [...]' (For the Holy Spirit spoke and prophesied though the mouths of the righteous men who were first in the island of Ireland [...]). The text and translation are from Carey, 'An Edition of the Pseudo-historical Prologue', p. 12 (text); p. 18 (trans.). This notion parallels the idea expressed in Matthew 18:20 'ubi enim sunt duo vel tres congregati in nomine meo ibi sum in medio eorum' (For where there are two or three gathered together in my name, there am I in the midst of them) and is cited *Collectio canonum Hibernensis*, Liber XIX, *De ordine inquisitionis causarum* (Concerning the order of invoking authoritative sources) where instructions are given on the proper method for consulting the sources of religious authority when adjudicating disputes of Christian doctrine. Herren and Brown list more examples in *Christ and Celtic Christianity*, pp. 95–96.

(Acts 15:8). Peter concluded, probably referring to Matthew 23:1–4,[48] that the *iugum* (yoke) of the Law of Moses was overbearing and unnecessary because both Jews and gentiles have been saved by the grace of Christ (Acts 15:11).

Peter's argument, surely not lost on an Irish audience, implicitly acknowledged that the Law of Nature and the Law of Christ applied to converted gentiles; and, moreover, it expressly made the case that the Law of Moses, which applied historically to Jews alone, should not be expanded retroactively and imposed upon gentiles who converted to Christianity. He began by outlining the relationship between Jews and gentiles within sacred history, arguing that, in the first instance, there was no difference between them under the Law of Nature: both received the gift of the Holy Spirit from God, who knew (and presumably judged worthy) all human hearts (Acts 15:8–9). Jews, on the other hand — unlike gentiles — had been subject to the Law of Moses from the time of Moses' epiphany on Sinai until the advent of Christ, and so their legal status within Christian history differed during that period. However, this difference between them had passed since, under the New Dispensation — *per gratiam Domini Iesu* (by the grace of the Lord Jesus) — the yoke of the Mosaic law had been lifted, and all Christians — Jews and gentiles alike — were, in his view, now subject to the Law of Christ.

James offered the next opinion, acknowledging Peter's statement and arguing that it agreed with the prophets (Acts 15: 15-18), citing Amos 9:11-12. Acts 15:15: 'et huic concordant verba prophetarum sicut scriptum est' (And with this agree the words of the prophets, as it is written):

Acts 15:15–18 (16) *post haec revertar et aedificabo tabernaculum David quod decidit et diruta eius reaedificabo et erigam illud* (17) *ut requirant ceteri hominum Dominum et omnes gentes super quas invocatum est nomen meum dicit Dominus faciens haec* (18) *notum a saeculo est Domino opus suum* (16) After these things I will return, and will

COMPARE: Amos 9:11–12 (11) *in die illo suscitabo tabernaculum David quod cecidit et reaedificabo aperturas murorum eius et ea quae corruerant instaurabo et reaedificabo eum sicut diebus antiquis* (12) *ut possideant reliquias Idumeae et omnes nationes eo quod invocatum sit nomen meum super eos dicit Dominus faciens haec* (11) In

48 Matthew 23:1–4: '(1) tunc Iesus locutus est ad turbas et discipulos suos (2) dicens super cathedram Mosi sederunt scribae et Pharisaei (3) omnia ergo quaecumque dixerint vobis servate et facite secundum opera vero eorum nolite facere dicunt enim et non faciunt (4) alligant autem onera gravia et inportabilia et inponunt in umeros hominum digito autem suo nolunt ea movere' ((1) then Jesus spoke to the multitudes and to his disciples, (2) saying: the scribes and the Pharisees have sat on the chair of Moses. (3) All things therefore whatsoever they will say to you, observe and do: but do not behave according to their works; for they say, and do not. (4) For they bind heavy and insupportable burdens and lay them on men's shoulders; but with a finger of their own they will not move them).

rebuild the tabernacle of David, which is fallen down; and the ruins thereof I will rebuild, and I will set it up: (17) That the residue of men may seek after the Lord, and all nations upon whom my name is invoked, says the Lord, who does these things. (18) To the Lord was his own work known from the beginning of the world.

that day I will raise up the tabernacle of David, which is fallen: and I will close up the breaches of the walls thereof, and repair what was fallen: and I will rebuild it as in the days of old. (12) That they may possess the remnant of Edom, and all nations, because my name is invoked upon them: says the Lord who does these things.

Here, James invoked the authority of the prophet Amos as testimony in support of Peter's argument. To an Irish audience, thus, James's statement would have seemed implicitly to acknowledge the Law of Prophecy, whose practical value in a legal procedure was that it could be cited as evidence to show agreement and corroboration (or, if such had been the case presumably, disagreement) with the Law of Nature, the Law of Moses, or the Law of Christ (as this example from Acts 15 suggests). James' opinion, based on Peter's testimony and his own interpretation of the prophets, was that gentiles should only be held accountable to a reduced set of Mosaic injunctions. In particular, they must refrain from eating offerings made to idols, from fornication, from things strangled, and from blood (Acts 15:19–20), requirements that bear a strong resemblance to the basic features of Noahide Law.[49] Finally, as a procedural matter, the resolution of the debate was decided upon and formally enacted only after it was accepted by the unanimous consent of the 'apostoli, seniores, and omni ecclesia' (apostles, elders, and the entire church) (Acts 15:22).

James' reflex to consult the prophets for legal precedent after the Law of Moses and the Law of Christ had already been invoked may have been inspired by scripture itself. As I mentioned above, the words *lex* and *prophetae*, commonly paired in both the Old and New Testaments, was used as a formula to express the idea that to be in accordance with both 'the law and the prophets' was tantamount to being in accordance with all applicable Old Testament law. Significantly in a similar legal context, Christ himself invokes *lex* and *prophetae* in Matthew 5:17, 7:12 and 22:37–40. It seems reasonable, thus, to speculate that the Irish doctrine of the Law of Prophecy might have been derived from the biblical text itself.

An Irish jurist familiar with biblical exegesis might well have deduced the four laws from this text, if indeed they were not already predisposed

---

49 As has often been noticed, the provisions considered binding on gentiles that were decided at the Synod of Jerusalem bear close resemblance to the Noahide injunctions. Whether or not the imposition of Noahide law on Christians of gentile (as opposed to Jewish) origin was the intent of the synod is a matter of theological debate.

to see it in this way as a result of the influence of patristic doctrine. Perhaps even more importantly, the Synod of Jerusalem provided a model of ecclesiastical legal procedure: it established a pattern for how a synod should be conducted in both practical and ideological terms. Practically, consensus seems to have been important: not just the ecclesiastical elite, but the entire Church as well, should agree about any given verdict. Furthermore, ideologically, decisions should accord with divine law on all of its successive dispensations, so that each agrees with and corroborates the others, as upheld by evidence, above all else, from cited scripture. In this way, the Synod of Jerusalem exemplified how biblical law should be applied to resolving legal-theological disputes. Notice that this desire for agreement between scripture *loci* representing the various 'Laws' in sacred history was reflected in Columbanus's reasoning as well, as I discussed in the introduction to this volume.

Moreover, this procedure upheld synods, perhaps even provincial synods, as the foremost legitimate mechanism in ecclesiastical law for adjudicating *quaestiones* whose resolution could not be deduced from scripture.[50] It tacitly acknowledged, therefore, that scripture alone was not in and of itself sufficient to settle every problem that might arise within the Christian community, and established a mechanism for deciding points of contention that eluded resolution based solely on the biblical text. From an Irish perspective, the reasoning implicit to Acts 15 acknowledged four laws: the Law of Nature, the Law of Prophecy, the Law of Moses, and the Law of Christ. Moreover, it provided a template for how these should be applied in an actual legal setting, i.e., one should look for testimony in scripture — in the Law, the Prophets, and the New Testament — that pointed to the same conclusion; and that conclusion should then be accepted and endorsed by the whole church in consensus.[51]

The question must be addressed, however, as to why the Synod of Jerusalem is never explicitly held up in Irish literature as a source or example of the four laws, given that it is such an obvious choice.[52] One possibility is that the idea of the four laws was considered so fundamental

50 Note that this reasoning may have informed Columbanus's argument (described in the introduction) that the Irish should be permitted to celebrate Easter according to their own calculation of the date as decided and adjudicated by them.

51 One will notice how similar reasoning appears throughout Columbanus's arguments to successive popes about the proper way to calculate the date of Easter. In the example I discussed in the introduction to this volume, for instance, he (1) sought corroboration between authorities, first in scripture and then elsewhere, and (2) asserted the authority of the provincial synod.

52 To be sure, Acts 15 is cited, albeit not to express the relationship between Laws in Christian history. For example, Acts 15:29 is invoked twice in *Collectio canonum Hibernensis*, Liber LIII, *De carnibus edendis* (Concerning eating meats), once in cap. 14 and once in cap. 16, both in regards to dietary restrictions. See *The Hibernensis*, Bk I, p. 422 ll. 8–9 and p. 423 ll. 9–10.

that it hardly required explanation. Another possibility is that the Synod of Jerusalem had the potential to seem a dangerous abjuration of the Law of Moses to Irish clerics who were deeply invested in Mosaic statutes as living law. This possibility, as mentioned above, was first suggested by Ó Corráin, Breatnach, and Breen as an explanation for why Romans 2:14 was never cited in Irish documents as a biblical justification for the Law of Nature. Instead, as these authors have pointed out, Irish jurists looked to the Old Testament for an explanation of the Law of Nature. Specifically, they chose the example of Jethro, Moses' father-in-law, whose advice Moses sought out and enacted, despite the fact that he was a foreigner and a pagan priest:[53]

> Ubi sunt in lege praecepta quae Deus non praecipit? Iethro socer Moysi elegere .lxx. principes qui iudicarent populum cum Moysi, et hoc iudicium est, quia si inuenerimus iudicia gentium bona, que natura bona illis docet, et Deo non displicet, seruabimus.[54]
>
> > (Where are there precepts in the ⟨Mosaic⟩ law which God did not command? Jethro, the father-in-law of Moses, told Moses to choose seventy *principes* who should judge the people with Moses, and this is a judgement ⟨i.e., a precedent for the view⟩ that if we find the law of the nations good, which their good nature teaches them, and if it is not displeasing to God, we shall keep it).[55]

The importance of the Law of Moses in early Irish jurisprudence, as Ó Corráin, Breatnach, and Breen among others, point out, can hardly be over-stated.[56] That said, the reception of the Law of Nature and the Law of Moses in early Irish jurisprudential thought (particularly as regards its relationship with the Law of Christ) has not been fully understood, including in the aforementioned, seminal article by Ó Corráin, Breatnach, and Breen. A thorough re-examination of this topic will provide a main theme of what follows. For my present purpose, however, suffice to say that for early Irish jurists who perceived themselves to be in some sense analogous to the Christian spiritual recipients of the law promulgated

53 Ó Corráin, Breatnach, and Breen, 'The Laws of the Irish', p. 392.

54 This passage is from: *Synodus Sapientium*. The text is from Bieler, *The Irish Penitentials*, p. 168.

55 Translation is by Ó Corráin, Breatnach, and Breen 'The Laws of the Irish', p. 392.

56 A classic study is Kottje, *Studien zum Einfluss des Alten Testamentes*. Textual evidence for the importance of the Old Testament for medieval Irish jurisprudence can be found in the use of the so-called *Liber ex lege Moysi*, a Hiberno-Latin collection of excerpts from the Pentateuch, as an apparent preface to several witnesses of the A-text of *Collectio canonum Hibernensis*. On the *Liber ex lege Moysi*, see Bradshaw, *The Early Collection of Canons Known as the Hibernensis*, p. 25 (an excellent, relatively untapped study which should not be discounted on account of its age); Fournier, '*Liber ex lege Moysi*', pp. 230–31; Kottje, 'Der *Liber ex lege Moysis*'; and B. Carella, 'The Source for the Prologue to the Laws of Alfred'. The text has been edited by Meeder, 'The *Liber ex lege Moysi*: Notes and Text'.

by the jurists of the Old Testament (a reception which, in early Irish thought, was more complicated than previously realized), any potential abjuration of the Law of Moses was a potential threat to their fundamental conceptualization of lawgiving. For such individuals, Acts 15 might well have seemed a serious challenge to — if not outright retraction of — the Law of Moses under the New Dispensation; and their idea of law relied heavily on Old Testament precepts. As such, these matters would best be left uncited and reserved, instead, for fuller discussion in a more apropos scriptural context. To understand how early Irish jurists perceived the Law of Moses to be living law while simultaneously regarding themselves as converted gentile Christians subject to the Law of Christ, however, requires a subtle understanding of Pelagianism and the broader theology of the Ascetic Movement which, I posit, suffused Irish legal-theological ideologies.

Pelagius and Early Ireland

Another, closely related possibility is that this decision to release gentiles from the strict requirements of the Law of Moses (i.e., to release them from precepts laid out in scripture) on the authority of what is essentially a conciliar decree, was deeply troubling to Irish clerics influenced the theology of the fourth- and fifth-century Ascetic Movement, often (but perhaps ahistorically, as Ali Bonner has argued) referred to as 'Pelagianism'.[57] Irish clerics of this persuasion might also have found problems with the other implications of the Synod of Jerusalem, above all any possible misunderstanding of Peter's claim that all Christians are saved by grace, without any obligation to obey God's commandments as expressed in the Law of Moses (Acts 15:10–11). Of course, jurists with these sensibilities would not have argued that Peter was wrong; just that his statement might easily be taken, in their view incorrectly, to undermine the authority of Old Testament Law. More context would be needed to explain how, in the Ascetic Movement's understanding of Christian history, both the Old Law and the New Law provided a path to salvation. It will be necessary to examine this point in more detail since the role of the Ascetic Movement's theology in early Irish legal thought is central to my argument.

Some background on the Ascetic Movement will be necessary before proceeding, since recent scholarship has called into question our understanding of what is typically referred to as 'Pelagianism'. In her book *The Myth of Pelagianism*, Ali Bonner argued that Pelagianism as a formal heresy never existed, because (1) Pelagius actually taught very few of

57 Bonner, *The Myth of Pelagianism*.

the doctrines ascribed to him by his opponents; (2) Pelagius's teachings had already been expressed by others in the so-called Ascetic Movement, such as Athanasius, Evagrius, Ambrosiaster, Apponius, and even Jerome; and (3) there was no organized Pelagian movement of theologians who shared a common set of ideas.[58] While Bonner's arguments raise important questions, some critics have pointed out flaws in her method, and ultimately her conclusions. Most problematic is Bonner's narrow definition of the Pelagian corpus of writings to just a handful of texts she considers representative of Pelagius fully, without corruption or later interpolation. For example, she excludes from this corpus all of the *Expositiones XIII epistularum Pauli* (of which at least the commentary on Romans is typically considered authentically Pelagian).[59] These criticisms aside, Bonner's overall argument warrants careful consideration. At the very least, her contention that Pelagius was an exponent of a broader theological movement (which she calls the Ascetic Movement) likely describes the widespread occurrence of what have been called 'Pelagian ideas' without attribution in some early medieval British and Irish texts (though he is often cited by name as well). In what follows, I shall refer to the Ascetic Movement as equivalent to what has traditionally been called Pelagianism, though I shall not alter references in cited scholarship. Also, when discussing works attributed to Pelagius (other than the handful considered to be authentic,[60] which is itself a matter of widespread disagreement), I shall refer to them as 'Pelagian writings', since they largely reflect views of the theological tradition he was associated with, even if he did not write them himself, or if they have become corrupted over the course of their transmission.

Although the weight of scholarly opinion has tended to minimize Pelagius's legacy in Ireland (and, concomitantly, that of the Ascetic Movement),[61] recent scholarship has shown that doctrines associated with

58 Bonner, *The Myth of Pelagianism*, p. xiii.

59 Bonner's argument has received a great deal of criticism. See, for example, Daniel Watson's extensive review of her book *The Myth of Pelagianism*. I shall not add my voice to this debate here, except to say that I find plausible Bonner's argument that Pelagius was not the only purveyor of ideas now typically considered 'Pelagian', but rather that he was an exponent of a larger theological tradition. I have for the most part adopted her use of the term 'Ascetic Movement' here, though be aware that I still use 'Pelagianism' as well, for example, when I refer specifically to writings attributed to him. For the purposes of this volume, I am less interested in what Pelagius himself thought or said than I am in the theological ideas associated with him and the Ascetic Movement collectively.

60 I generally follow Bonner here, accepting that the canon of Pelagius's authentic work include: his *Epistula ad Demetriadem, Epistula ad Celantiam, De virginitate, De diuina lege*, possibly *Epistula ad quondam Matronam*, and his *Libellus fidei*. Bonner, *The Myth of Pelagianism*, p. xvii. I follow most other scholars, however, in that I consider the commentary on Romans in his *Expositiones XIII epistularum Pauli* to be a genuine work of Pelagius.

61 The nature and extent of the Pelagian legacy in Ireland has been a matter of some controversy. For recent discussion, see: Herren and Brown, *Christ in Celtic Christianity*,

Pelagius and the Ascetic Movement played a greater role in shaping early Irish (and also early Welsh and Northumbrian) religious thought than has been previously acknowledged, detectable well into the ninth century.[62] While there was never an organized group of avowed, dogmatic Pelagians to endorse his teachings outright,[63] Pelagius's own writings and those of theologians in the Ascetic Movement nevertheless seem to have circulated widely (both pseudonymously and otherwise) adding, at the very least, a distinctly Pelagian flavor to early Irish theological doctrine.

The opinions of those scholars persuaded by the argument that Pelagianism (as separate from the Ascetic Movement) significantly affected early Irish theology vary widely on how thoroughgoing they believe his influence was. Generally, those scholars who have considered the matter agree that the influence of Pelagian thought — at its height in Late Antiquity and during the early Middle Ages — laid the groundwork for later intellectual developments in the Irish Church, so that subsequent Irish clerics who perhaps knew nothing of Pelagius and the theology of the Ascetic Movement firsthand were influenced by these teachings. As evidence, Michael Herren and Shirley Ann Brown have shown that texts expressing distinctly Pelagian ideas appear consistently in Ireland from the fifth through the ninth century:[64]

> [...] ⟨T⟩he influence of Pelagianism in the British Isles throughout the period ⟨from the fifth to the tenth centuries⟩ was substantial — indeed, 'defining' [...] We know too little about Church affairs in

---

pp. 9–13 and 69–103. For various other opinions, see: Zimmer, *Pelagius in Irland* (translated by Meyer, *The Celtic Church in Britain and Ireland*); Pelagius, *Expositions*, p. 1; Gougaud, *Christianity in the Celtic Lands*, pp. 22–26 and 292–93; Kenney, *Sources for the Early History of Ireland*, pp. 661–63; Nerney, 'A Study of St. Patrick's Sources: II'; Nerney, 'A Study of St. Patrick's Sources: IV'; Donahue, 'Beowulf, Ireland, and the Natural Good'; Donahue, 'Beowulf and Christian Tradition'; Hughes, *The Church in Early Irish Society*; Hardinge, *The Celtic Church in Britain*, p. 2; J. Kelly, 'Augustine in Hiberno-Latin Literature'; J. Kelly, 'Pelagius, Pelagianism, and Early Christian Ireland'; Ó Néill, '*Romani* Influences on Seventh-Century Hiberno-Latin Literature'; Dumville, 'Late Seventh- or Eighth-Century Evidence for British Transmission of Pelagius'; Ó Cróinín, 'New Heresy for Old'; Markus, 'Pelagianism: Britain and the Continent'; O'Loughlin, *Celtic Theology*; Charles-Edwards, *Early Christian Ireland*, pp. 185 and 202–05.

62 Herren and Brown, *Christ in Celtic Christianity*, pp. 80–103.

63 See Kelly, 'Pelagius', p. 115: 'Available evidence links the Irish somehow to every known use of Pelagius by name in the early Middle Ages and to considerable anonymous use as well. There are a number of ways to explain this phenomenon. One way, however, not to explain it is as a formal Pelagian party or movement in the Irish Church. Most of the Irish use of Pelagius was selective and for explication of certain passages. Nowhere was Pelagius used to the exclusion of orthodox Fathers, especially not to his adversaries Augustine and Jerome. His use simply does not reflect "Pelagian" attitudes'.

64 For a list of specific texts containing Pelagian ideas, see Herren and Brown, *Christ in Celtic Christianity*, 'Additional Texts', pp. 101–03.

> fifth-century Britain to argue that Pelagians were numerically in the majority or exercised control over the whole region — we may simply have a case of the 'tail wagging the dog' [...] We know that important Pelagian texts were copied and circulated throughout ⟨Britain and Ireland⟩, sometimes pseudonymously, sometimes not, into the ninth century. But most significantly, throughout our entire period we find numerous citations from writers on both islands that either support or attack the chief tenets pf Pelagianism. Pelagius continued to be a 'talking point among the faithful'! It is fair to say that Pelagian thought influenced — and disturbed — the Churches of the British Isles for more than four centuries [...] An understanding of British, Irish and even Northumbrian Christology requires the acceptance of this basic fact.[65]

Herren and Brown's claim that Pelagian theology exerted a heavy influence on early Irish thought is not new. To assess it as 'defining', however, marks a significant break from past scholarship, where most scholars — even among those who acknowledge that Pelagius had some measurable impact — considered his influence to be relatively minor. Yet, in an appendix to *Christ in Celtic Christianity,* the authors provide a list of Pelagian-influenced texts from early medieval Ireland that makes a strong case for his pervasive influence. Thus, although the weight of scholarly opinion historically has tended to minimize his legacy in Ireland, recent scholarship has shown that Pelagius's doctrines, along with those expressed by the Ascetic Movement more generally, played a greater role in shaping early Irish religious thought than has been previously acknowledged, extending at least into the ninth century.

Let us look at one example that demonstrates the prevalence of Pelagian thought in early Irish theology. In the passage that follows, James F. Kenney discusses the sources for the Würzburg glosses on the Pauline Epistles, specifically those in Latin (as opposed to Old Irish). He states:

> [...] The great source of this Irish commentary was Pelagius, and consequently it has become, (in turn), a most valuable source for the reconstruction of Pelagius's exposition of the Epistles of St Paul. Pelagius is quoted 957 times (in ten of which the attribution is erroneous). Moreover, 16 extracts attributed to other authorities were really derived from Pelagius, as well as 348 anonymous quotations. Thus, there are in all 1311 glosses of Pelagian origin.[66]

The Pelagian influence on the Würzburg glossator was substantial; and this is merely one example of what Herren and Brown convincingly

65 Herren and Brown, *Christ in Celtic Christiantiy*, pp. 100–01.

66 Kenney, *The Sources for the Early History of Ireland*, p. 636.

demonstrate to be the extensive and defining influence of Pelagianism and the theology of the Ascetic Movement on early Irish Christian intellectual culture.

What explains this widespread influence of the Ascetic Movement in early Ireland and, for that matter, throughout the geographical and cultural areas that fell within the purview of what Herren and Brown refer to as the 'Celtic Church'? One major problem with their claim is that no Irish manuscript witnesses survive that include any primary Pelagian writings in full (though short citations are attested). Given the sheer volume of references to his writings, not to mention the many indirect expressions of his ideas in works of Irish cultural origin, one would expect to find a significant number of primary-text witness; but none have been identified. Of course, it is possible that these manuscripts were destroyed later by pious Christians who wished to snuff out an old heresy. If so, they bore no such animus toward works by authors who cite Pelagius, even when he is invoked by name. References to Pelagius, Origen, and other heretics occur often enough in other works, and remain untouched. So, how can we explain the sheer volume of both Pelagius and Pelagianism in early Irish literature?

On this matter, Ali Bonner's thesis that Pelagius taught doctrines widely attested by others in the fourth- and fifth-century Ascetic Movement may shed light on this question. Perhaps Pelagius was not the main source of what has been called 'Pelagianism' in Ireland? Instead of being the font of his theology, perhaps he was merely a vocal exponent of it; a prominent voice that went to Rome and preached ideas typical of the Ascetic Movement (as Bonner argues) and therefore also typical of fifth-century Irish (and likely also British) theology that was influenced by it? Certainly, we know little enough about Irish religious thought in the latter half of the fifth century, just after conversion began, to say with any confidence what the fundamental tenets of its beliefs were. This theory would explain why Pelagius was cited by name relatively infrequently while other heretics suffered no such exclusion. Likewise, it may explain why what has been called Pelagianism was so widespread in early Irish literature of all kinds. It would be astonishing indeed if one man, or one idea, had such an extensive influence across all genres of Irish literature that persisted for centuries. To Irish exegetes working in the poorly attested decades and centuries after Pelagius's death, ideas that we think of as distinctly 'Pelagian' may not have seemed so to them. Rather, these so-called 'Pelagian ideas' might well have been ideas held widely by Irish (and perhaps Insular) theologians steeped in the theology of the Ascetic Movement and expressed by any number of adherents, of whom Pelagius is among the more well-known. While ultimately speculative, I would argue that this theory best explains the apparent pervasiveness of 'Pelagian' thought in all aspects of Irish Christian culture. In any case, to whatever extent Pelagian theology and the theology of the Ascetic Movement influenced early Irish religious doctrine — and it was significant, by any measure — it had, as Herren and Brown claim, a defining impact on Irish intellectual thought.

Before going any farther, it will first be necessary to discuss some of the ideas that constituted Pelagian and Ascetic Movement dogma, since they are not well known and often misconstrued. Although a full treatment of the topic lies beyond the purview of this chapter (and, indeed, this volume), a brief discussion relevant to the present argument will lay some necessary groundwork for what follows. For my present purpose, I shall focus on those works attributed to Pelagius, whether they are genuine or not, since my goal is not to elucidate what Pelagius actually believed himself, but rather more generally what doctrines came to be associated with his theology. The basic tenets of this dogma include (among other beliefs),

> [...] the assertion of the natural goodness of human nature, the possibility of a sinless life, the denial of transmitted original sin, categorical denial of predestination, a marked tendency to discount the miraculous [...] the reliance on the scriptures as the sole source of religious authority [...] ⟨and the idea that s⟩alvation could be achieved by all through strict obedience to God's law as revealed by the scriptures [...].[67]

as opposed to grace alone. These doctrines might have been difficult for Irish jurists to reconcile with certain ideas expressed in Acts 15, at least without a great deal of laborious and inconvenient explanation. How, for example, would a cleric influenced by such doctrines have explained Peter's argument in Acts 15:7–11 (cited above) favouring a reduced injunction of the Mosaic Law on the grounds that neither Jews nor gentiles could bear its yoke (Acts 15:10) and which explicitly linked salvation to grace (Acts 15:11), when Irish law relied on a sophisticated understanding of the continued relevance and application of Mosaic Law under the New Dispensation? For an Irish jurist influenced by the doctrines of Pelagius and the Ascetic Movement, these statements might raise questions better left unasked, since a full understanding of the topic would necessarily entail providing substantial context: for example, Peter might be (mis)understood to have argued that scripture (at least the Old Testament) was flawed since, in his view, mankind is unable to live according to it and, for that reason, could only be saved by grace. All these ideas run counter to Ascetic Movement theology, which taught (1) that all the scriptures were perfect and applied without exception, (2) that mankind had not only the innate potential but also the responsibility to uphold divine law as expressed in *all*

67 Herren and Brown, *Christ in Celtic Christianity*, p. 5.

the scriptures (which, according to Pelagian and Ascetic Movement belief, was possible with proper instruction, albeit with extreme difficulty), and (3) that by doing so one could save themself though the merit of their good works apart from grace, at least theoretically, if not in actual practice. The last point is very subtle, but especially important. For Pelagians, all God's laws and covenants are complete and perfect, and so it follows that all of them have the potential to lead to salvation. That said, Pelagius acknowledged that living perfectly according to the Mosaic Law was all but impossible, so that salvation by grace was the only practically achievable path. As such, his main point had more to do with affirming the perfection of all scripture and the completeness of each divine covenant in Christian history than it was about asserting the Mosaic Law as a path to salvation.

Ascetic Movement doctrine on the relationship between the Law of Moses and the Law of Christ was intricately complex and will require more explanation.[68] While neither he nor his followers ever denied that the Law of Christ fulfilled the Law of Moses (Matthew 5:17 was often quoted in this context), nor that Christians were released from the 'yoke' of the Mosaic Law (as Peter asserts in Acts 15:10, and which becomes a main them of the Pauline Epistles),[69] they vigorously resisted any suggestion that the duty of a Christian to obey the scriptures in their entirety was thereby reduced or in any way lightened. Throughout the corpus of extant writings associated with Pelagius, there is emphasis on the idea that a Christian bears a greater load under the Law of Christ than under the Law of Moses because he or she is liable, now, to an increased injunction. A few citations will suffice to make the point:

68 For a more thorough and detailed discussion of this important question, see especially: Herren and Brown, *Christ in Celtic Christianity*, pp. 106–15.

69 Despite commonly held notions to the contrary, Pelagius apparently believed that the Law of Christ did in fact remove the 'yoke' or burden of the Old Law. This position is clearly stated and widespread throughout his writings. See, in particular, the three references to Acts 15:10 in Pelagius, *Expositions*, p. 312: '[...] absoluti sumus[, hoc est,] a iugo legis' ([...] we are released, this is, from the yoke of the law); and p. 322: 'Si in lege spem ponitis et iustifcari posse uos creditis, infirmam Christi gratiam iudicatis, et quod iam gratis consecuti estis, tamquam non habentes propriis uultis laborabis adipisci' (If you put your hope in the Law of Moses and you believe that you can be justified, you adjudge the Grace of Christ to be feeble; and what you have already achieved by Grace, just as those who have it not, you wish to acquire by your own works). But, note the interesting qualification at the end of the following citation, p. 529: 'Coinquinati et infideles sunt qui non credunt iugum legis a colle credentium dominum abstulisse; id est, omnia quae temporaliter fuerant instituta' (They are defiled and unbelievers who do not believe that the Lord removed the yoke of the Law of Moses from the neck of believers; that is, everything which has been established *temporally*(?) *temporarily*(?)).

> [...] nescio, quomodo Christus Dominus non uenit soluere legem, sed adinplere, si per eius credulitatem disciplina non aucta est, sed minuta.[70]
>
> > ([...] I cannot understand how the Lord Christ can be said to have come not to destroy the law but to fulfill it, if this means that through belief in him discipline has not been increased but diminished).[71]

Similarly, elsewhere:

> [...] intentius peruidendum est, utrumne post Christi aduentum solis inpiis futurae beatitudinis spes abnuatur, quando etiam illis, qui uniuersa legis iussa conpleuerint, nisi etiam addita gratiae mandata seruauerint, denegetur. In hoc enim discipulorum Christi plus quam scribarum et Pharisaeorum poterit eminere iustitia, si non ea tantum, quae per Moysen et prophetas scribis Pharisaeisque praecepta sunt, uerum etiam, quae per Christum sunt mandata, subpleuerint.[72]
>
> > ([...] We can see that we have to give more careful consideration to the question whether, after Christ's coming, the hope of future blessedness is denied to the ungodly only, when it is refused even to those who have fulfilled all the commandments of the law, unless they have also kept the additional commandments of grace. For the righteousness of Christ's disciples will be able to stand out above the scribes and the Pharisees, as long as they have fulfilled not only the precepts given to the scribes and Pharisees by Moses and the prophets but also the commandments given by Christ).[73]

Compare also a statement, claimed to have appeared in a book by Coelestius (Pelagius' outspoken student), which Pelagius was called upon to recant in the Synod of Diospolis (415): '[...] lex sic mittat ad regnum quemadmodum euangelium' ([...] thus the Law of Moses may send one to the kingdom of heaven just as the Gospel).[74]

And yet, Ascetic Movement doctrine did not advocate adherence to the Law of Moses without understanding it within the context of the Law of Christ:

> Adinplet enim legem, cum eam ueram ostendit. Ueram enim ostendit, quando per se cessare facit, quae illa cessatura praedixerat. Et

---

70 The text is from: Pelagius, *Epistola de malis doctoribus et operibus fidei et de iudicio futuro*, IV.1. It is edited in *Briefe, Abhandlungen und Predigten*, p. 71.

71 The translation is from: Pelagius, *Life and Letters*, p. 217.

72 From: *Briefe, Abhandlungen und Predigten*, X.1, p. 82.

73 Translation is from Pelagius, *Life and Letters*, p. 227.

74 Augustine of Hippo, *De perfectione iustitiae hominis*, XI.23, p. 76.

> de antiqua lege legem produxit nouam, et nouum testamentum promulgauit ex uetere, ut magis ac magis legis et prophetarum praedicta subpleret [...] In quibus omnibus aduertendum est, nos iam non antiquorum imitatores oportere esse, sed Christi, nec tam ueteris testamenti praecepta seruare debere, quam noui.[75]
>
> > ([...] ⟨F⟩or ⟨Christ⟩ fulfils the law by revealing it to be true, and he reveals it to be true by making to cease what the law had foretold would cease. And out of the old law he brought forth the new, and out of the old covenant he promulgated the new, so that he might make good the prophecies of the law and the prophets [...]. In all these matters we must now observe that we are not to imitate the men of old but Christ and that we are to keep not the commandments of the old covenant but the new).[76]

Likewise, clarifying his position:

> Quid ergo proderit mihi eius rei obseruatio, per quam iam caelestis regni possessor esse non possum? Ob hoc tantum nunc nobis uetus legendum est testamentum, ut Dei in eo facta miremur, omnipotentiam operum, mysteriorum rationem, signa uirtutum, et ut Christum nouissimis temporibus promissum, eodem testamento adnuntiante, noscamus. Caeterum ad uitae conuersationem noui praecipue testamenti doctrina spectanda est [...]. Si uetus semper celebrandum erat, cur successit nouum? Aut si succedere debuit, quomodo celebrandum est uetus? Quamquam et in nouo uetus celebretur, dum, quod uetus fore adnuntiauit, celebratur.[77]
>
> > (What will it profit me to observe a rite which can no longer enable me to possess the heavenly kingdom? The sole reason for our reading the Old Testament now is in order to marvel at the acts which God did in it, at the omnipotence of his works, at his mysterious plan, at wonders and signs, and to know the Christ promised in the last days and announced in the same Testament. But for the conduct of our lives we must pay special attention to the New Testament [...]. If the Old was always to be observed, why did the New supersede it? Or if it had to be superseded, why is the Old to be observed now? Nevertheless, it is true that the Old is observed in the New, since what the Old announced is still observed).[78]

---

75 From: *Briefe, Abhandlungen und Predigten*, '*Tractatus de diuitiis*', x.5, p. 39–40.

76 Translation is from Pelagius, *Life and Letters*, p. 187.

77 Caspari, *Briefe, Abhandlungen und Predigten*, '*Epistola de castitate*', xii.4, p. 151.

78 Translation is from Pelagius, *Life and Letters*, p. 284.

Although this doctrine was formulated somewhat variously, the underlying principle seems to have been that, for a Christian, the burden of biblical law is heavier than before the advent of the Christ, since the New Law in no way releases one from prior obligations. Yes, Christ removed the 'yoke' of the Law of Moses, but he did not repeal or replace it; rather, he fulfilled it. Thus, according to the Ascetic Movement's understanding, the Law of Christ superseded the Law of Moses only in the sense that it provided a new context for it, i.e., the 'Old is observed in the New'. For those like Pelagius, therefore, a Christian remained bound by the obligations of the Law of Moses in addition to the requirements of the Law of Christ. They believed, thus, that Christians carried a greater burden than Jews before the coming of Christ; and because of this more onerous responsibility, Christians were even more liable to fall into transgression.

So, for early Irish jurists with these theological views, the apparent rejection of the Mosaic Law in Acts 15 — while not an abnegation of Ascetic Movement doctrine when fully understood — would, from their perspective, require a great deal of explanation to avoid the very kind of misunderstanding they were expressly at pains to prevent, that is, the mistaken idea that Christians were under a lesser injunction than Jews. Moreover, the apparent rejection of the Law of Moses in Acts 15 would have troubled Irish jurists for whom the Law of Moses, as understood by adherents to Ascetic Movement doctrine, remained in force. Equally problematic would have been the idea that the decisions of a synod or council could override scripture,[79] if the Synod of Jerusalem were seen to reduce or remove certain requirements of the Law of Moses. No question, the fifteenth chapter of Acts was itself biblical and therefore not denied by those in the Ascetic Movement. As Herren and Brown point out:

> ⟨For Pelagians, t⟩he whole of God's law is promulgated in the scriptures. It consists of the 'law' (pentateuch), the prophets and the gospels; one text, *On Bad Teachers*, adds the apostles. Despite the greater textual emphasis given the first three parts, there can be no question that 'the Apostles' was given equal status by Pelagius as part of the divine law. This is shown by the particularly heavy weight accorded the authority of the Pauline epistles.[80]

For those with such sensibilities, Acts 15 may well have seemed a topic most conveniently left undiscussed, lest it lead to the misapprehension that Christians might evade their responsibility to fulfill scriptural law in its entirety, and find salvation through grace alone without recourse to their own personal accountability.

---

79 Pelagians denied the right of the ecumenical councils to legislate anything that might conflict with scripture. See Herren and Brown, *Christ in Celtic Christianity*, p. 8.

80 Herren and Brown, *Christ in Celtic Christianity*, p. 72.

Regardless of whether the Four Laws ultimately derive at first remove from a close reading of Acts 15 (as I speculated above, and which Herren and Brown may be suggesting in the passage just quoted), it is apparent that early Irish legal ideology was closely derivative of legal thought and procedure as represented in scripture, and particularly in Acts 15. Thus, whatever the primary doctrinal orientation of those Irish jurists who formulated models to explain the relationship between ecclesiastical and pre-Christian, native law, they possessed a thorough knowledge of the Bible and of scriptural exegesis, including Pelagian exegesis.

Before moving on, it is important to emphasize one last point. For early Irish jurists of all orientations, the Law of Nature provided a convenient justification for the continued application of pre-Christian, native law, albeit with some alterations. Irish jurists with various agendas seized upon the framework of the Four Laws, and the Law of Nature in particular. Before I discuss this highly important concept in early Irish law, however, I shall first have a bit more to say about synodal procedure and its practical application in Irish law.

Collectio canonum Hibernensis

Since Acts 15 provided a basic, scriptural model for the proper conduct of ecclesiastical synods, it may be instructive to compare it to what is known about the conduct of early Irish conciliar practice. *Collectio canonum Hibernensis* provides some insight into the methods used by Irish judges to investigate doctrinal disputes within the Church. Here, for the first time in canon law, a set of guidelines prescribing the order jurists should follow when consulting legal authorities was defined. In the sole chapter of Liber XIX, *De ordine inquisitionis causarum* (Concerning the order of invoking authoritative sources),[81] the following order or precedence is established, spuriously attributed to Pope Innocent I:

> Innocentius dicit de causis in quibus soluendi ligandique auctoritas est: XXII librorum ueteris testamenti, IIII quoque euangeliorum cum totis apostolorum scriptis. Si non appareat, ad diuina recurrito scripta, que grece agiographa dicuntur. Si nec inuenies in illis, ad catholicę æclesiae historias catholicas doctoribus catholicis scriptas manum mitte. Si nec in his, canones apostolicæ sedis intuere. Si nec in istis, sanctorum exempla perspicaciter explorata inspice. Quod si his omnibus inspectis huius questionis qualitas non lucide inuestigatur, seniores prouinciae congrega et eos interroga. Facilius namque inuenitur, quod a plurimis

81 For discussion, see: *The Hibernensis*, Bk II, pp. 847–88 nn. 150–53. See also Brasington, '*Congrega seniores provinciae*', pp. 1–4. This chapter is later cited by Gratian.

in unum sentientibus queritur. Verus enim repromissor Dominus ait: Si duo ex uobis conueniant super terram in nomine meo de omni re quamcumque petierint fiet illis.[82]

> (Innocent says concerning sources in which there is authority to loose and bind: The twenty-two books of the Old Testament, and the four gospels together with all the writings of the apostles. Should an answer not present itself, turn to the divine texts that are called *hagiographa* in Greek.[83] If you do not find the answer in them, reach for the catholic histories of the catholic church written by catholic doctors ⟨*ecclesiae historias catholicasque a doctoribus catholicis*⟩. If they do not have it, examine the canons of the apostolic see. If they do not have it, consult examples of saints ⟨*sanctorum exempla*⟩, which have been acutely examined. But if, after consulting all of these, the essence of the matter is not clearly revealed, convene the elders of the province ⟨*seniors provinciae*⟩ and ask them. For that which is sought by many giving an opinion on one issue is more easily found. For the true surety, the Lord, said: Should two of you come together upon the earth in my name, concerning any thing whatsoever they shall ask, it shall be done for them [Matthew 18:20–19]).[84]

The first set of authorities — all biblical — would seem to derive from Jerome-Isidore's division of books of the Bible. It is noteworthy that the scriptures come first as the fundamental legal authority and primary source for both legal knowledge and precedent. Next, comes 'ecclesiae historias catholicasque a doctoribus catholicis', by which the canonist likely intended to signify certain patristic writings on the history of the Church, including the historical works by authors such as Tertullian, Cyprian, Eusebius, Sulpicius Severus (whose *Chronicorum* was known at Iona),[85] Orosius, etc.,[86] and possibly biblical exegesis.[87] Only after these authorities were thoroughly examined does the canonist instruct judges to consult

---

82 This is the complete text of *Collectio canonum Hibernensis*, Liber XIX. See: *The Hibernensis*, Bk I, p. 111.

83 Not 'hagiography' in the modern sense, but rather 'sacred writings'. These are defined by Isidore of Seville in the *Etymologiae* VI.i.7 as containing nine books, including Job, the Psalms, Proverbs, Ecclesiastes, Song of Songs, Daniel, Paralipomenon, Ezra, and Esther. See also *The Hibernensis*, Bk II, p. 848 n. 151.

84 *The Hibernensis*, Bk II, p. 556.

85 O'Loughlin, 'The Library of Iona', p. 41.

86 Cummian's *Epistola ad Segienum Hiensem abbatem de controversia paschali*, which follows this order of authorities, includes as *historiae* witnesses such as '[...] decrees of Church councils, scriptural exegesis, and general dogmatic commentary such as Cyprian's *De unitate ecclesiae*'. Cummian, *De controversia paschali*, p. 16.

87 *The Hibernensis*, Bk II, p. 848 n. 152 argues that *historiae* may signify, among other things, biblical exegesis in this context.

the 'canones apostolicae sedis'.[88] 'Sanctorum exempla' come next, by which saints' lives were likely indicated, including not only their *vitae* proper, but also their actions and deeds as known from other sources not strictly hagiographic.[89]

Most striking, however, is the final authority in the list, namely a gathering of 'seniores provinciae'. The idea, supported by a citation of Matthew 18:20–19, appears to stipulate that, in cases where all other authorities fail to resolve a dispute, a synod should be convened to decide the matter wherein Christ, speaking though his ministers on earth via the Holy Spirit, will make the true and proper judgement apparent to all, as he did, for example, in the Synod of Jerusalem. A number of questions immediately arise. Who were the 'seniores provinciae'? What did this phrase signify in an Irish cultural context? Did it include only ecclesiasts, or could secular authorities participate as well? The answers to these questions have the potential to reveal much about who in early Irish society was considered qualified to adjudicate points of law. As Bruce Brasington points out, the word *senior* has a wide range of meaning, not only in early medieval Latin generally but specifically in early Hiberno-Latin. His suggestion that the phrase 'seniores provinciae' in this passage unambiguously indicates secular *filid*, however, seems unlikely.[90] Who, then, were these '*seniores*'?

From the outset, it is important to acknowledge that the legal process described above seems intended to guide synodal procedure adjudicating disputes arising specifically within the Church. As stated in the text, this particular method applies in '[...] causis in quibus soluendi ligandique auctoritas est [...]' (sources in which there is authority to loose and bind), echoing the language of Matthew 18:18:[91] 'Amen dico vobis quaecumque alligaveritis super terram erunt ligata et in caelo et quaecumque solveritis super terram erunt soluta et in caelo' (Amen I say to you, whatsoever you shall bind upon earth, shall be bound also in heaven; and whatsoever you

---

88 In Cummian's letter, *De controversia paschali*, the phrase 'canones apostolicae sedis' signifies decrees, letters, and various statutory materials not only issued from Rome but '[...] quaternae sedis apostolicae, Romanae, uidelicet Ierosolimitanae, Antiochenae, Alexandrinae [...]' ([...] of the fourfold Apostolic See, namely that of Rome, Jerusalem, Antioch and Alexandria [...]). The text and translation are from Cummian, *De controversia paschali*, p. 70 (trans. p. 71), ll. 90–93. In the notes to line 179 (p. 81), however, the editors point out that in letters by Columbanus and Ps-Columbanus, Rome alone is signified with this phrase.

89 For example, Cummian's famous letter on the Easter controversy, which follows this order of precedence for consulting religious authorities, invokes the computus used by St Patrick as evidence within the category of *sanctorum exempla*. Cummian, *De controversia paschali*, p. 84 (text); p. 85 (trans.), ll. 208–09.

90 See: Brasington, '*Congrega seniores provinciae*', p. 3 n. 9.

91 Compare Matthew 16:19, where Christ describes this authority when speaking to Peter alone, with Matthew 18:18, where Christ gives the authority to all the apostles. Also compare John 20:23.

shall loose upon earth, shall be loosed also in heaven). This stipulation appears to indicate, therefore, that the procedure here described applied expressly to ecclesiastical gatherings. There is further evidence for this conclusion. In the Synod of Jerusalem, the prototypical church council, the term *seniores* is used four times to describe certain members of the gathering, always paired with *apostoli* (Acts 15:4, 6, 22, and 23); and in at least two of these verses (Acts 15:6, 22) the individuals so designated appear to participate in the decision making. As noted in the introduction, Hiberno-Latin *senior* can signify both ecclesiastical and secular elders. Given this context, however, *senior* most likely signified a ranking member of the clerical community. Cummian, for example, uses the term *senior* in his letter *De controversia paschali* where he decries those who hold out for the Irish system of dating:

> **Seniores** uero nostri, quos in ⟨ue⟩lamine ⟨repulsionis habetis, quod optimum in diebus suis esse nouerunt simpli⟩citer et fi⟨deli⟩ter sine ⟨culpa⟩ contradictionis ullius ⟨et animositatis obs⟩eruauerunt [...].[92]
>
> (Our elders ⟨ = ***seniores***⟩, however, whom you hold as a cloak for your rejection, kept simply and faithfully, without blame of any contradiction or animosity, that which they knew to be best in their day).[93]

Here, the context unambiguously suggests that the term *seniores* should be taken to signify 'ecclesiastical forbears'. Likewise, in early medieval Ireland, a mid-sixth-century synod improperly excommunicating Columba (as described by Adomnán, his hagiographer)[94] consisted of a group (presumably of clerics) described as *seniores*. Similarly, David Dumville has pointed to the use of a vernacular parallel, *senudh sruith*[95] (synod of seniors) to describe an ecclesiastical gathering, the Synod of Inis Aingen (899), in the *Chronicum Scotorum*.[96] Also, in the Irish penitentials, the word 'senior' bears a technical meaning, invariably designating senior members of a monastic community.[97] While these examples show that there is some variation of usage, they would all seem to indicate a typical ecclesiastical

92 The text is from Cummian, *De controversia paschali*, p. 74, ll. 114–17.

93 The translation is from Cummian, *De controversia paschali*, p. 75.

94 Adomnán, *Life of St Columba*, III.3, pp. 184–85.

95 Though the semantic range of Old Irish *sruith* appears to be as broad as Latin *senior*, encompassing both secular and ecclesiastical senses, it seems never to designate a *fili*. See: *eDIL*, s.v. *sruith*.

96 *Chronicum Scotorum*; Evans, *The Present and the Past*; McCarthy, 'The Chronology of the Irish Annals'; Grabowski and Dumville, *Chronicles and Annals of Medieval Ireland and Wales*; and Mac Niocaill, *The Medieval Irish Annals*.

97 See the list of references in Bieler, *The Irish Penitentials*, p. 332 (index rerum uerborum locutionum).

signification of *senior* in early Hiberno-Latin, at least when the term is used within an ecclesiastical context.

Admittedly, the sources I have examined so far are all ecclesiastical in orientation, so perhaps it should be no surprise that they point to a clerical identity. Is there evidence that *senior* could also indicate a secular elder? Elsewhere, even in some ecclesiastical sources, there is evidence to suggest it could. For example, *Collectio canonum Hibernensis*, Liber XXI, *De iudicio* (Concerning judgement), cap. 1, *De personis dignis ad judicandum* (Concerning the ones worthy of judging), distinguishes between ecclesiastical and secular cases,[98] prescribes who should participate in each gathering, and specifies what responsibilities their roles should entail. Very significantly, individuals described as *seniores* appear in both lists. Specifically, this chapter lays out the following instructions:

> Gregorius Nazanzenus ait: In omnibus causis æcclesiasticis III persone eligende sunt ad iudicandum: episcopus, scriba, contemtibilis omnis negotis secularibus. Episcopus conuocet **seniores** et scribam. Scriba interroget scripturam. Inde ait Faustinus: Scrutatus sum et interrogaui et constitui iudicium. Contemtibilis conuocet omnes peritos, maxime conscientiam suam.
>
> Gregorius Nazanzenus: In negotis secularibus rex et senex et iuris peritus iudicent. Rex conuocet scribam et scriba statuat iudicium coram rege. Senex conuocet omnes hos et statuat. Iuris peritus conuocet **seniores** et conprouinciales, ne temere iudicauerint.[99]
>
> > (Gregorius Nazianzen said: In all ecclesiastical cases three people must be chosen as judges: a bishop, a *scriba*, and a man who is contemptuous of all secular transactions. Let the bishop summon the elders ⟨ = ***seniores***⟩, and the *scriba*. Let the *scriba* consult scripture. Hence Faustinus said: I have examined and questioned and reached a verdict. Let the one *contemptibilis* summon all the legal experts, especially his own conscience.

98 Some gatherings included both ecclesiastical and secular magnates, such as those promulgating the ecclesiastical *cánacha* (sing. *cáin*) or *leges* (sing. *lex*). See Charles-Edwards, 'Early Irish Law', pp. 334–37. However, *Collectio canonum Hibernensis* proscribes judgements by laymen in these gatherings. Liber XXI, cap. 28, for example, states: '[…] Si æpiscopus uel scriba presentes sint, statuant iuditium; quia inlicitum est laicis disputare presentibus æpiscopis, aut scribis, aut sanctis' (If a bishop or a *scriba* should be present, let them pass judgement; because it is not proper for laymen to dispute in the presence of bishops or *scribae* or holy men), *The Hibernensis*, Bk I, p. 137 (text); Bk II, p. 575 (trans.). Likewise, Liber XXI, cap. 28 specified that laymen are never to judge clerics, though clerics can judge laymen, *The Hibernensis*, Bk I, p. 137 (text); Bk II, p. 575 (trans.).

99 *The Hibernensis*, Bk I, p. 116. Emphasis is mine.

> Gregorius Nazianzenus: In secular legal disputes let a king and an elder and a legal expert sit in judgement. Let the king summon the *scriba*, and the *scriba* pronounce judgement in the king's presence. Let the elder assemble all those and pronounce judgement. Let the legal expert summon the elders ⟨ = ***seniores***⟩, and fellow-provincials ⟨ = ***conprovinciales***⟩, lest he should judge rashly).[100]

So, in both ecclesiastical and secular proceedings, individuals described as *seniores* did in fact participate. However, it seems that in neither gathering were *seniores* assigned the role of judge. Though it is not made exactly clear in the text, it appears that their role (in secular cases at least, and presumably also in ecclesiastical ones), was to ensure fairness. Whether or not they provided any positive counsel to those sitting in judgement, I would speculate that their presence was intended to lend an overall sense of gravity to the event, lest those making the decisions *temere iudicaverint* (judge rashly). In any case, the pairing of *seniores* and *conprovinciales* in this citation, closely echoing the phrase *seniores provinciae* in the passage from *Collectio canonum Hibernensis*, Liber XIX (cited above) may support the claim that these gatherings typically included both clerics and lay people.

Whatever the precise status of individuals signified by the phrase *seniores provinciae*, they seem to have been considered essential participants in both the ecclesiastical and secular legal procedures of a province,[101] at least by the canonists who compiled *Collectio canonum Hibernensis*. Apparently, their role was not active in the sense that they did not legislate or make decisions *per se*; rather, I suspect their purpose was to provide counsel, lend support, and bring the overall weight of their collective opinion to bear on the proceedings. I do not mean to suggest, however, that their role was entirely passive. General consensus — preferably unanimous consent in support of the judgements handed down — seems to have been the desired outcome of these legal procedures, as it was at the Synod of Jerusalem (Acts 15:22). There is no positive indication, however, that such decisions were made on the basis of a vote, majority or otherwise, as in a modern jury; consensus, rather (real or perceived), seems to have been the guiding principle for arriving at a verdict. Thus, similarly, when picking a person worthy to serve as judge, one of the three qualities listed in *Collectio canonum Hibernensis*, Liber XXI, *De iudicio* (Concerning judgement), cap. 5, *De III, quibus indiget iudex* (Concerning the Three Things that a Judge Needs) is *consensu plurimorum* (the consensus of the majority).[102] From this evidence we might infer that the role of the *seniores* in all

100 *The Hibernensis*, Bk II, p. 560.

101 Here, Brasington is probably correct that *provincia* is equivalent to Old Irish *túath*, '*Congrega Seniores*', p. 3 and n. 10. It is defined in ecclesiastical terms in *The Hibernensis*, Liber XX, *De provincia, The Hibernensis*, Bk I, pp. 112–15 (text); Bk II, pp. 557–59 (trans.).

102 *The Hibernensis*, Bk I, p. 119 (text); Bk II, p. 562 (trans.).

these proceedings was similar: they could affix their collective imprimatur, tacitly or otherwise, on those procedures they felt were sufficiently fair and proper; and — presumably — when a judgement was generally considered unfair, they could utilize the weight of public opinion (and perhaps other kinds of influence) to exert pressure for justice (or the outcome they desired).[103]

As described in *Collectio canonum Hibernensis*, such gatherings, whether or not they were convened to adjudicate ecclesiastical or secular cases, functioned according to an ecclesiastical model analogous to the procedure described in Acts 15.[104] Comparison of the two reveals how influential the model of the Synod of Jerusalem was for Irish conciliar practice: first, the appropriate magnates were gathered, with the actual constituency of the assembly depending on the nature of the case (whether ecclesiastical, secular, or possibly both). Like the procedure described in the Synod of Jerusalem, these included not only individuals specifically assigned active roles in the procedure, e.g., *scriba*, *peritus*, etc., but also *seniores*, i.e., the various ecclesiastical and possibly secular magnates of the province, as well. Next, the matter was investigated according to the authorities prescribed in Liber XIX of the *Hibernensis* until a satisfactory answer was found. In Liber XXI, *De iudicio* (Concerning judgement), cap. 1, *De personis dignis ad judicandum* (Concerning persons worthy to judge) (cited above), primary responsibility for the investigation of these authorities seems to have been delegated to a *scriba*.[105]

103 There is evidence that public opinion was a factor in secular law as well. Consider, for example, the public ritual of fasting against a legal opponent as a means to sue for justice. On this practice, see F. Kelly, *A Guide to Early Irish Law*, pp. 182–83.

104 Importantly, it must be mentioned that an order of operations analogous to that expressed in Liber XIX of *Collectio canonum Hibernensis* appears in vernacular law as well, for the purposes of application to secular cases. Charles-Edwards, *The Early Mediaeval Gaelic Lawyer*, p. 23, summarizes and translates the text as follows: 'On what is the judicial role founded in Irish law? Not difficult: on justice and entitlement and nature. Justice is established on the basis of *roscada* and *fásaige* and truthful texts. Entitlement is based on verbal contracts and acknowledgement. Nature is based on remission and communal order. Justice and entitlement are both founded on the holy. Any judgement not based one of these has no force at all. Any judgement of the Church is based on justice and entitlement and Scripture. A judgement by a poet, however, rests on *roscada*. A judgement by a ruler, on the other hand, is based on them all: on *roscada*, on *fásaige*, and on truthful texts ⟨ = *Corpus Iuris Hibernici*, 2256.13–2257.11 and 2261.18–36⟩'. It seems likely, in any case, that this provision for ascertaining the proper authorities of law derives ultimately from earlier principles of ecclesiastical law.

105 In Hiberno-Latin, *scriba* had a complex range of meaning that extended beyond merely 'scribe'. See: Johnston, *Literacy and Identity*, pp. 120–28, especially, pp. 123–24. In the penitentials, the word (according to Bieler) is equivalent to OIr. *fer légind*, literally 'a man of learning', with the technical meaning 'the director of studies in a monastic school' (Bieler, *The Irish Penitentials*, p. 251), or 'professor of sacred scripture and theology in a monastic school, often a bishop, abbot […]' (*eDIL*, s.v. *léginn*). Elsewhere, *scriba* glosses Old Irish *suí*,

An important feature of the decision in Acts 15 was that it harmonized with biblical law on all levels as demonstrated by specific references to the scriptures. Similarly, according to *Collectio canonum Hibernensis*, a proper judgement must be in accordance at least with the Law of Nature, scripture, and the sensibilities of the wise. This requirement is made explicit in *Collectio canonum Hibernensis*. For example, in Liber XXI, *De iudicio*, cap. 6, *De tribus modis, quibus debent judices judicare* (Concerning the three methods by which judges ought to judge) the following requirement is set out:

> Augustinus: Tribus modis iudicibus iudicandum: Natura, hoc est indagatione rerum, {et similitudine rerum} et similitudine precedentium, et ex verbis scripture.
>
> Item: III modis agnoscitur omne uerum, cum non ueniat contra naturam, et verbis scripturæ conueniat, et animis prudentium non desistet.[106]
>
>> (Augustine: Judges must judge in three ways: According to nature, namely by investigating facts and by corroborating facts, and by the correspondence with precedents, and according to the words of scripture.
>>
>> Likewise: Every truth is recognized in three ways: When it does not contravene nature, and when it is consistent with words of scripture, and when it does not depart from the words of the wise).[107]

Here, as in the Synod of Jerusalem, accordance with law on multiple levels constituted evidence of truth. Thus, in this canon, not only must a judgement accord with biblical law, it must also be announced publicly, in front of *seniores* and *conprovinciales*, whose consent and support, as in Acts 15, validated the decision.[108]

Of course, *Collectio canonum Hibernensis* presents an idealized description of judicial procedures in which ecclesiastical interests predominated. There is evidence that in the period soon after the conversion of Ireland

---

'man of learning, scholar, wise man, sage' (*eDIL*, s.v. *suí*). Apparently, the term indicated a clerical scholar of some sort, though what particular kind of clerical scholar it signified in a legal context is uncertain. See also, *The Hibernensis*, Bk II, p. 851 n. 172.

106 *The Hibernensis*, Bk I., p. 120. Note that he second part of this dictum is repeated almost verbatim in Liber XXII, cap. 4, *De III-bus modis quibus agnoscitur ueritas* (Concerning the three ways of identifying truth), *The Hibernensis*, Bk I, p. 142 (text); Bk II, p. 579 (trans.).

107 *The Hibernensis*, Bk II, p. 562.

108 It will be obvious to the reader how this method informed much of Columbanus's argument to successive popes that the Irish should have the right to celebrate Easter on the date of their own calculations (as described in the introduction to this volume).

and for a considerable time thereafter, both ecclesiastical and secular courts (in whatever form they existed) heard cases and administered justice separately. The existence of secular courts can be inferred, for example, from an often-cited provision in the so-called First Synod of Patrick, where penance is required of all Christians who make oaths at such secular proceedings, presumably in some pagan ritual:

> Christianus qui occiderit aut fornicationem fecerit aut more gentilium ad aruspicem iurauerit, per singula cremina annum penitentiae agat [...].[109]
>
> > (A Christian who has committed murder, or committed adultery, or sworn before an *aruspex*[110] according to the custom of the Gentiles ⟨i.e., pagans⟩, shall do a year's penance for each of these crimes [...]).[111]

Further evidence for the continuing existence of secular courts can be found in the eighth-century vernacular law tract *Uraicecht Becc* (the Small Primer), which draws a distinction between the kinds of evidence used in the decisions made by different authorities, including secular as well as ecclesiastical judges:

> NACH BREAT ECALSA DOCHUISIN [...] IS FOR FIR ⁊ DLIGED SCREPTRA CONSUITER [...] BRETH FILED IM̄ FO ROSCADAIB CONSUITER [...] BREATH FLATHA IM̄ CONSUITER FORAIB UILI FOR ROSCADAIB [...] ET FASAIGIB [...] ET TEISTEMNAIB.[112]
>
> > (Whatever judgement of the Church there is, it is based on *fír* ⟨probably 'truth;' but possibly 'justice, oath, proof'. Less likely in this context 'ordeal'⟩[113] and the law of scripture [...]. The judgement of a *fili*, however, is based on legal verse [...]. The judgement of a secular ruler, however, is based on all: legal verse,

109 The text is from Bieler, *The Irish Penitentials*, p. 56. Note that my translation departs somewhat from Bieler's.

110 Bieler translated *aruspex* as 'druid'. The reservations expressed by Faris concerning this identification in *The Bishop's Synod*, pp. 44–45, which were later echoed by Charles-Edwards in 'Early Irish Law', p. 350 n. 91, are well taken. Whatever profession this term signifies, however, it would appear to designate a non-Christian individual.

111 The translation is based on Bieler, *The Irish Penitentials*, p. 57. Note, however, that my translation departs somewhat from Bieler's.

112 *Corpus Iuris Hibernici*, 1592.8–20. Compare 635.24–636.1.

113 These are the definitions posited by F. Kelly, *A Guide to Early Irish Law*, p. 312. *eDIL* generally agrees with Kelly's definition, but includes 'compurgation', which seems unlikely in this context.

> ancient legal maxims, and *teistimin* ⟨probably 'written text' or 'scriptural quotation'⟩).[114]

This passage would seem to distinguish between ecclesiastical, secular, and royal courts; or — if not courts in some physical manifestation — then at least different mechanisms of jurisprudence under the predominant sway of these (separate or to some degree overlapping) authorities, whatever these distinctions might have meant in actual practice.

Yet, despite this apparent assertion of separation between secular and ecclesiastical interests, significant overlap between them was not only possible but apparently common. Later in the same text, for example, there is reference to a *brithem téora mbreth* (a judge of three judgements) who was apparently qualified to make decisions based on all three kinds of evidence:[115]

> [...] BREITEM TEORA MBRET [...] .I. BRET FENI [...] ⁊ BRETH FILED [...] BREATH BERLA BAIN BIAS [...][116]
>
> (A judge of three judgements [...] i.e., judgement of the *Féni* ⟨i.e., traditional lore⟩ [...] and judgement of a *fili*, ⟨and⟩ judgement of the White Language of the Beati ⟨i.e., the scriptures⟩).[117]

In fact, there is a great deal more evidence for this kind of intersection between secular and ecclesiastical jurisprudence. Kim McCone, for example, points to the Middle Irish story of Cenn Fáeled (which, he argues, originates in an earlier period), who received an injury in the Battle of Mag Raith (637) famously destroying the part of his brain that allowed him to forget.[118] After his injury, Cenn Fáeled was taken to the monastic foundation of Túaim Drecain,[119] where he studied and memorized learning from three schools: [...] *scol leigind ⁊ scol feinechais ⁊ scol filed* [...] ([...] a school of written ⟨Latin Christian⟩ learning, and a school of traditional learning, and the school of the poets [...]).[120] Here too, we have evidence for ecclesiastical and secular learning at the same location, in this case a

114 The translation is my own. F. Kelly, *A Guide to Early Irish Law*, p. 322, posits that *teistimin* should be translated 'testimony, written text', while *eDIL*, s.v. *teistimin*, defines it as '(a) testimony, written evidence [...] (b) text, scriptural quotation, passage'. Given the broader context, I would suggest 'scriptural quotation', is the best translation.

115 Compare the reference in *Bretha Nemed Toísech* to a 'brithem téora mbreth', *Corpus Iuris Hibernici*, 2221.29. Elsewhere in *Uraicecht Becc*, there is reference to a *BREITHEAM TRI MBERLA* (a judge of three language, ora judge of three laws), *Corpus Iuris Hibernici*, 1614.31, 2331.15, 2279.12.

116 *Corpus Iuris Hibernici*, 1612.23–26.

117 On *bias*, *eDIL*, s.v. *biait* (b). The translation is my own.

118 McCone, *Pagan Past and Christian Present*, p. 23. See also the discussion in MacCana, 'Three Languages and the Three Laws', pp. 61–66.

119 See Gwynn and Hadcock, *Medieval Religious Houses, Ireland*, p. 407, s.v. 'Tomregan'.

120 *Corpus Iuris Hibernici*, 250.42. The translation is my own.

religious house, undertaken by a formerly royal personage who, in this context, is not readily classifiable as either cleric or laymen. As McCone explains:

> Whatever the proportion of fact and fiction in this narrative, it was clearly intended as the charter for a literate monastic legal tradition applied to society as a whole and believed to combine poetic teaching and practice with ecclesiastical doctrine and techniques [...]. The story about Cenn Fáeled is thus likely to involve the projection of relevant contemporary conditions into the more distant past for authoritative justification, and this suggests that alongside the central *scol léigind* schools of law and *filedacht* or *senchus* ⟨ancient tradition⟩ were a common enough feature in pre-Norman Irish monasteries.[121]

McCone, thus, sees the monasteries as centres of gravity attracting and, over the course of the Middle Ages, eventually absorbing the various bodies of Irish learning, secular/traditional as well as ecclesiastical.

While this idealized picture of cooperation might mark a later stage of development in the relations between secular and ecclesiastical legal interests, judicial affairs were likely not always so equitably congenial. According to *Collectio canonum Hibernensis*, it would seem that the Church — while perhaps to some extent recognizing the legitimacy of secular jurisprudence outside its immediate purview — nonetheless sought to protect its pride of place as the superior and final authority. Consider, for instance, the provision in Liber xxi, *De iudicio*, cap. 3, *De incerto iudicio a minoribus iudicibus a maioribus querendo* (Concerning lesser judges seeking advice from senior judges on an uncertain judgement), which asserted the final authority of ecclesiastical courts:

> Deuteronomium[122] Cum perspexeris ambiguum iudicium et uerba iudicum uideris uariari, surge et uade et ascende ad locum, quem elegerit Dominus Deus tuus, et ad iudicem, qui in illo tempore fuerit, et iudicabit tibi ueritatem.[123]

---

121 McCone, *Pagan Past and Christian Present*, pp. 23–24.

122 Compare Deuteronomy 17:8–9: '(8) si difficile et ambiguum apud te iudicium esse perspexeris inter sanguinem et sanguinem causam et causam lepram et non lepram et iudicum intra portas tuas videris verba variari surge et ascende ad locum quem elegerit Dominus Deus tuus (9) veniesque ad sacerdotes levitici generis et ad iudicem qui fuerit illo tempore quaeresque ab eis qui indicabunt tibi iudicii veritatem' ((8) If you perceive that there be among you a hard and doubtful matter in judgement between blood and blood, cause and cause, leprosy and leprosy: and you see that the words of the judges within your gates do vary: arise, and go up to the place, which the Lord thy God shall choose. (9) And you shall come to the priests of the Levitical race, and to the judge, who shall be at that time: and you shalt ask of them, and they shall show you the truth of the judgement).

123 *The Hibernensis*, Bk I, p. 118.

(Deuteronomy: When you perceive an ambiguous judgement, and you see that the words of the judges vary, arise, and go and go up to the place, which the Lord your God has chosen, and you shall come to the judge who shall be at that time, and he shall judge truthfully for you).[124]

In this reduced citation from scripture, reference to the Levites is removed; but — that said — the identification of the place where court was to be held as *locum quem elegerit Dominus Deus tuus* suggests that the procedure described was primarily ecclesiastical. With this canon, the Church seems to have been intent on establishing its courts as the final authority and on asserting its right to overrule the decisions of other legal proceedings that it had not officially sanctioned.[125]

To what extent do these prescriptions reflect the reality of Irish jurisprudence in the early Middle Ages? On the one hand, it seems clear that there was some distinction between separate bodies of law, based on the kinds of individuals to whom it applied, who promulgated it and under what authority, and how it was administered. Thus, in the predominantly secular category, there was (1) the Law of the *Féni* (or *fénechas*) which constituted the oldest stratum of customary law based on ancient poetic lore and maxims. Next, there was (2) the Law of the *filid*, whose judgements were usually delivered in *roscada*, or legal verse, cast (at least on occasion) as interpretations of the Law of the *Féni*. In addition to these bodies of law, there is evidence of (3) royal law (*bretha flatha*), promulgated on the authority of kings and based on a variety of different kinds of evidence. Alongside, and eventually overshadowing all of these was ecclesiastical law, the statutes of which were drafted by clerics. The last of these rested on the authority of scripture and other religious authorities cited above, and explained in *Collectio canonum Hibernensis*, Liber XIX, *De ordine inquisitionis causarum* (Concerning the order of invoking authoritative sources). On the most basic level, ecclesiastical law applied to clerics and addressed matters of religious doctrine. More broadly, it appears that the Church increasingly sought to expand its jurisdiction to matters otherwise dealt with in predominantly secular proceedings, either on their own prerogative

124 *The Hibernensis*, Bk II, p. 561.

125 A similar notion is expressed in the Pseudo-historical Prologue to the *Senchas Már*: 'Co tánic Pátraic trá, ní tabairthe erlabra acht do t[h]riur: fer comcni cumnech fri aisnéis ⁊ scélugud, fer cerda fri molad ⁊ aír, brithem fri brithemnas a roscadaib ⁊ fásaigib. Ó thánic Pátraic immurgu, is fo mámmus atá cach erlabra donaib í-seo do ḟíur in bérlai báin .i. inna canóine' (Until Patrick came, ⟨authority in⟩ speaking was only granted to three men: the historian with a good memory for explanation and narration; the man of art for praise and satire; the judge for giving judgements with *roscada* and maxims. After Patrick's coming, however, all these ⟨kinds of authoritative⟩ speech are subject to the possessor of the white language, i.e., of the scriptures). Carey, 'An Edition of the Pseudo-historical Prologue', p. 12 (text); p. 19 (trans.).

or in co-operation with secular authorities. This process was accelerated in situations where the Church was the more powerful institution and thereby most capable of enforcing law and order.

The citations from legal documents in the discussion immediately above — and many more could be called to witness — present a picture in which the various practitioners of jurisprudence, regardless of their predominant orientations, existed alongside one another in an overall ecclesiastical milieu. This intersection is evidenced, for example, by the existence of a class of judges known as a *brithem téora mbreth* (judge of three judgements) and the statement in *Uraicecht Becc* that secular rulers based their judgements on all the various sources of law, both traditional and religious (both cited above). I suspect, however, that such finely measured distinctions should be understood as idealizing attempts to systematize a complex and fluid reality rather than as accurate, normative depictions of real-world legal practice. Different centres of power held sway in medieval Irish society at different times and in different locales, each with its own respective mechanisms to enforce justice: these included kings, traditional figures like *filid* and *brithemon*, as well as clerics of varying degrees. More than likely, the jurisprudential authority of each waxed and waned with the strength of their overall position in society. No doubt also, since governance in medieval Ireland was highly decentralized, the relative power of these authorities varied from time to time, and from locality to locality, i.e., from *provincia* to *provincia* and from *túath* to *túath*. As T. M. Charles-Edwards described it:

> [...] whatever their background, the authors of the ⟨Old Irish vernacular⟩ tracts claimed an authority to instruct by virtue of their expertise in law which they rightly perceived as native and secular, even though it could and did borrow from a different law. This ecclesiastical law, in its turn, had no doubt that it should be contrasted with secular law, and its learned men with secular men. It drew its authorities from the Church at large, not just from Irish synods and Irish exegetes. [...]. For some centuries in the central middle ages it was the law of the new Gaeldom north of Forth and Clyde [...].[126]

As this assessment suggests, multiple authorities wrote, copied, and preserved law in early medieval Ireland. It was a time and place where law, both as a matter of practical application and of intellectual theorizing was in perpetual flux. Of course, the ultimate victor in this saga was the Church. That said, a careful assessment of the written record suggests that lawgiving during this period was typified above all else by a dynamic

---

126 Charles-Edwards, *The Early Mediaeval Gaelic Lawyer*, pp. 42–43.

hybridity, its constituent elements waxing and waning both geographically and temporally.

This point necessitates an important observation that will inform some of the basic claims I shall make in this volume: Given the nature of the evidence, no individual voice can testify authoritatively, nor should be regarded confidently as a trustworthy, unbiased witness to the overall picture. As modern scholars, we have only fragments representing a tiny portion of the record, all of which represent and are contextualized by culturally situated points of view, the significance of which we can never fully discern. Understood as such, then, early Irish law might be seen as a diverse collection of increasingly interdependent legal ideologies revolving around a common centre of gravity — at times co-operating with one another, at others vying against each other — but progressively evolving into a multifaceted, heterogeneous legal system ultimately based on a loosely amalgamated bedrock of culturally ingrained, tacitly accepted axioms. Like all axioms, they were taken for granted as true *a priori*, though in actuality they congealed over time as a multiplex admixture consisting of both pre-Christian, native ideas and foreign influences introduced via Christianity. These axioms are the ideological foundations of early Irish law.

To be sure, this aggregation was a protracted process which ultimately never came to an end, in the sense that no single body of law, unified under and executed by a central authority, ever emerged in early medieval Ireland. So, during the early period and perhaps for a considerable time thereafter, I imagine that individuals within society petitioned whatever legal authorities seemed most willing — and, above all, most capable — of resolving their legal problems effectively. Further speculation is unwarranted; for those documents that survive preserve virtually no concrete evidence concerning how disputes were resolved in practice.

CHAPTER 4

The Law of Nature

The Law of Nature in Early Medieval Ireland

It would be difficult to overstate the importance of the Law of Nature (L. *lex naturae*, OIr. *recht aicnid*) for early Irish jurisprudence. The basic concept, which has analogues in many cultures around the globe, centres on the notion that there exists within the cosmos a fundamental set of innate precepts enshrined by a higher power, divine or otherwise, that applies to all peoples everywhere in common, and which are derivable by observation without explicit religious instruction. In Western Europe, various expressions of this idea can be traced back to Aristotle, with numerous subsequent iterations in Roman, and later Christian, legal, patristic, and philosophical circles. Likely, its entry into Irish thought as a named concept depended on Isidore,[1] perhaps in conjunction with a close reading of the scriptures. From whatever source Irish Christian jurists first encountered the concept of *lex naturae* (and the closely related idea of the *naturale bonum*),[2] they frequently and inventively adapted it to local circumstances to explain and resolve various ideological dilemmas in their native legal system. Indeed, with the possible exception of pseudo-history, nothing else seems to have engaged the imaginative energy of early Irish jurists so completely.

For the present study, an investigation of the early Irish understanding of *lex naturae* has the potential to reveal much about early Irish legal thought, since it represents a point of relatively unproblematic agreement between secular and ecclesiastical perspectives. For predominantly secular jurisprudence, the concept of natural law (albeit with some adaptations) provided a ready explanation for the continuing validity of age-old, customary legal practices within a Christian milieu. For clerical jurists, it had the advantage of casting native Irish law as the first stage in a teleologically conceived evolution of sacred history through a series of dispensations that culminated with the Law of Christ and looked toward Judgement

1 See Isidore of Seville, *Etymologiarum*, I, v.iv. For a translation, see Isidore of Seville, *The Etymologies*, p. 117.

2 'Natural good', that is the idea that innate goodness that can be present in individuals before their conversion to Christianity.

Day.[3] As such, it circumscribed pre-Christian, native jurisprudence within a thoroughly Christianized view of history defined in purely ecclesiastical terms. The idea allowed secular interests to retain some aspects of the native legal system in exchange for their acceptance of an overall Christian ideological framework. To be sure, this compromise was never so openly stated nor so cynically conceptualized by Irish jurists of any orientation, who no doubt regarded their beliefs about law and theology as revealed truth, not as some imperfect-but-functional compromise worked out to appease various interests within Irish society. Nonetheless, this understanding describes the end state after an extended period of contact between secular and ecclesiastical jurisprudential interests in early medieval Ireland: Residual secular ideas and practices were accommodated to a significant extent, but only within a thoroughly Christian legal framework.

That said, ideas and influences could, and occasionally did, travel both ways; and the early Irish understanding of *lex naturae* provides a prime example of how native legal ideas could be accommodated within a Christian framework. As we have already seen, judgements according to the Law of Nature were sometimes ascribed to certain mythical, pre-Christian wisemen, including Dubthach, Morann, and Fíthal. Collections of their wise sayings, moreover, were regarded as prophecy of a kind analogous to the prophets of the Old Testament, that is, as native expressions of the Law of Prophecy and, more fundamentally, as expressions of the Law of Nature. What is more, ideas ascribed to them, and hence to Ireland's pre-Christian past, were echoed in later Christian legal texts, sometimes nearly verbatim. For this reason, it will be necessary to explore the relationship between Irish wisdom literature and ecclesiastical jurisprudence in this chapter.

One area of early Irish law influenced by pre-Christian thought in this manner, and expressed in wisdom literature such as *Audacht Morainn*, concerns native Irish belief in the connection between human behaviour and the natural order, specifically the complex set of ideas upholding that the cosmos maintained a fragile balance immediately dependent on the equitable conduct of, and harmonious interrelations between its inhabitants. Neil McLeod has described this belief in detail.[4] According to this view of the universe, the regular, properly ordered operations of the natural world (including calm weather, freedom from disease, the fertility of land and animals, etc.), of which human society was considered an integral part, simultaneously reflected and affected this balance. When humans, particularly the ruler, behaved properly and equitably, peace and prosperity ensued, not just among humans, but in all aspects of the nature and society. On the other hand, when humans acted improperly or unjustly — that is, unnaturally — their behaviour had immediate repercussions

3 See also Boyle, *History and Salvation*, p. 184.
4 McLeod, 'The Concept of Law', pp. 356–67.

that resonated throughout the physical world, setting it out of balance and leading directly to multifarious natural catastrophes, both large and small. Disasters of this sort were not attributed to divine vengeance or any other consciously motivated, moral reckoning; and, strictly speaking, they were not seen as punishment. Rather, they were understood as the necessary, cause-and-effect outcome of human disruption of the cosmic equilibrium. To act unjustly was to act, in the most literal sense, unnaturally (or inordinately, in the etymological sense); and chaos would inevitably ensue. There are many episodes reflecting this belief in Irish literature, too numerous to catalogue here. Examples with bearing on legal practice include the notion that blemishes would rise on the face of a judge or king who pronounced an unjust decision and the belief that satire (a practice regulated by law) — provided it was truthful and warranted — could inflict actual, physical harm on the object of derision, including disfigurement and even death.[5] Irish literature, including the law codes, is replete with such episodes:

> It would appear the [Irish] jurists acknowledged a natural order and acknowledged further that man-made rules could depart, in error, from its parameters — with disastrous consequences not only to the promulgator but to the physical environment. There was an intrinsic connection between the regulation of the physical and spiritual world and the regulation of human society. The law was an element of true order. Its breach could be readily identified by the resultant supernatural evils.[6]

On this point, early Irish belief was not unique. As has often been discussed, versions of this perceived relationship between human conduct and the retributive power of nature can be traced to Indo-European prehistory, and similar reflexes have been identified in many cultures around the world.[7] What distinguishes the Irish version of this idea is how it remained a living, productive, legal concept well into the Christian era, even among ecclesiastical jurists who — rather than rejecting the idea as a relic of paganism — embraced it whole-heartedly instead, and adapted it for their own purposes within the Christian ideological framework of *lex naturae*.

On this point also, the Irish were not unique. Analogues of this idea were absorbed by Christianity in many European cultures, especially in the early Middle Ages. That said, the enthusiasm which it inspired among Irish clerical jurists, and the extent to which they applied it at an early

---

5 See Breatnach, 'Satire, Praise and the Early Irish Poet' and Meroney, 'Studies in Early Irish Satire I–II' and his follow-on article, 'Studies in Early Irish Satire III'.

6 McLeod, 'The Concept of Law', p. 360.

7 For a discussion of this phenomenon with special attention to the Irish evidence, see Hartmann, 'Was Ist "Wahrheit"?'.

stage, however, stands out. In Ireland, as Neil McLeod asserts, this juridical understanding of the natural order

> [...] was the pre-Christian view of law. Breaches against the inherent truth comprised in the natural order could only bring disorder. Therefore, Truth could be revealed in a tradition of rulings which had proved to preserve harmony. To this Christianity added the element of the divine author: while natural law was essential to the scheme of things, its origin was to be found on a higher, external plain — it was not only natural, it was deliberate. This theory opened the door to a further way of uncovering compatible formulations: divine revelation. With the acceptance of Christ as the Divine Planner, they were to be found in the testaments of the apostles and in such specific divine formulations as the Decalogue.[8]

These ideas were heavily developed by the Church at a very early stage in medieval Ireland. After the conversion, ecclesiastical absorption and accommodation of native legal ideology went on in earnest; perhaps nowhere more markedly than where this notion is concerned. Synthesizing this concept with the Latin Christian idea of the *lex naturae*, both secular and ecclesiastical jurists (where, in fact, they can be distinguished) accepted this view of the cosmic order earnestly and developed it productively as a living mechanism of law.

What textual evidence is there for mutual accommodation between jurists of secular and ecclesiastical orientations regarding the legal implications of this belief? To address this question, it will be necessary to examine an array of texts from different genres. Focusing on legal and quasi-legal material (without attempting to be exhaustive), I shall begin by discussing three texts that exemplify this idea. These texts all contain a complex series of (often nearly verbatim) parallels pointing to some connection between them that is not only ideological, but textual as well. Significant for my purpose here, the similarities between them suggest that there was close contact, even identity, between scholars of different skills and orientations in early Irish society that composed these various kinds of treatises, despite any differences in their overall ideological perspectives.[9]

The three texts I shall consider first include: (1) *Collectio canonum Hibernensis*, Liber XXIV, *De regno* (Concerning kingship), cap. 4, *De eo quod bonorum regum opera ædificentur* (That the deeds of a good king are efficacious)[10] which dates from the first part of the eighth century, (2) the

---

8 McLeod, 'The Concept of Law', p. 362. See also: Meens, 'Politics, Mirrors of Princes and the Bible', pp. 350–52.

9 See Meens, 'Politics, Mirrors of Princes and the Bible', p. 352.

10 *The Hibernensis*, Bk I, p. 148 (text); Bk II, pp. 583–84 (trans.). Cap. 3 of the same book in *Collectio canonum Hibernensis*, 'De eo quod malorum regum opera distruant' (That the deeds

Hiberno-Latin *De duodecim abusivis saeculi*,[11] (On the Twelve Abuses of the World)[12] attributed to Ps.-Cyprian, dating from the middle third of the seventh century, cap. 9, *Rex Iniquus* (An Unjust King), and (3) the Old Irish wisdom tract *Audacht Morainn* (the *Testament of Morann*),[13] dating from *c.* 700, 'though much of the text must have had a previous oral or possibly manuscript existence'.[14] All three tracts deal intimately with the concept of the 'king's truth' (OIr. *fír flaith*, L. *iustitia regis*), that is, the notion that the conduct of the king, as the preeminent representative of human society, directly influenced all aspects of the order and balance of his realm: if a ruler lied, judged inequitably, or behaved in any manner unjustly, the kingdom itself — both human society and the natural world — would consequently descend into chaos and disaster. Conversely, if the king was truthful, judged justly, and conducted himself righteously, he would preside over a prosperous and fertile realm, free from disease, natural catastrophes, and attacks from foreign invaders.[15]

All three texts date from roughly the same period and all deal with essentially the same topic. Although the similarities between them have been noted elsewhere, it is important to emphasize just how much they have in common with one another, despite some notable scepticism about whether these points of contact resulted from direct borrowing.[16] For example, addressing the points of comparison between the tradition represented in both *Collectio canonum Hibernensis* and *De duodecim abusivis saeculi* on the one side, and *Audacht Morainn* on the other, Fergus Kelly asserts that, although '[...] the two traditions have much in common [...] there is nothing that would imply influence in either direction'.[17] I am dubious of this assertion, though it is beyond the scope of the present

of bad kings are destructive) covers similar territory, albeit expressed in the negative. Both chapters are worthy of close consideration, but given my present purpose, I have focused on cap. 4 in order to avoid repetitiveness.

11 Hereafter, *DxiiAS*; on Hiberno-Latin, see Breen, 'Pseudo-Cyprian *De duodecim abusivis saeculi* and the Bible', p. 231.

12 Ps.-Cyprian, *De xii abusivis saeculi*.

13 Edited and translated in *Audacht Morainn*.

14 *Audacht Morainn*, p. xxix.

15 The similarities between these texts have often been noted, but to my knowledge never explored in detail. Neil McLeod noticed these correspondences in 'Concept of Law', p. 360 n. 14. See, however, the somewhat fuller, though still rather brief, discussion in *Audacht Morainn*, pp. xv–xvi.

16 See, for example: *Audacht Morainn*, p. xv.

17 *Audacht Morainn*, p. xv. See also, Meens, 'Politics, Mirrors of Princes and the Bible', p. 352: 'Though the correlation between Ps.-Cyprian and Audacht Morainn does not imply a direct dependence of one text on the other, the resemblances are striking: the encompassing ideal of justice, the connection with cosmological consequences, and the character of those consequences. These similarities show that the two texts stem from an identical cultural background'.

context to examine this matter in depth. For my present argument, it will suffice to show that these texts express a common ideology, regardless of the reason for their affinity or any textual connections between them. In what follows, I shall point out the similarities between these three texts in order to show how closely they represent the notion that a king's behaviour bore a direct relationship to the cosmic order.

I shall begin by providing the complete text and a translation of *Collectio canonum Hibernensis*, Liber XXIV, *De regno*, cap. 4, *De eo quod bonorum regum opera ædificentur* alongside those portions of cap. 9 of *De duodecim abusviis saeculi*, where the close, almost verbatim relationship between them is apparent. After that, I shall catalogue the close similarities between this portion of *Collectio canonum Hibernensis* and specific provisions in *Audacht Morainn*. Laid out in this manner, the close relationships between the texts will be apparent and will make the case that early Irish intellectuals of various orientations who produced these texts shared a common ideology, at least as far as this idea is concerned.[18]

Comparison of *Collectio canonum Hibernensis* Liber XXIV, *De regno*, cap. 4, *De eo quod bonorum regum opera aedificent* and *De duodecim abusivis saeculi*, cap. 9, *Rex Iniquus*

In the table that follows, I provide the complete text of Liber XXIV, cap. 4 of *Collectio canonum Hibernensis* in the first column, alongside close parallels in cap. IX of *De duodecim abusivis saeculi*, in column 2.

Collectio canonum Hibernensis*, Liber XXIV, *De regno*, cap. 4, *De eo quod bonorum regum opera ædificentur[19] Patricius: Iusticia uero regis iusti hæc est: neminem iniuste iudicare, aduenis et uiduis et pupillis defensore esse, furta cohibere, adulteria punire, inpudicos et istriones non nutrire, iniquos non exaltare, impios de terra perdere, parricidas et periurantes	**from *De Duodecim Abusivis Saeculi*, cap. 9 *Rex Iniquus***[22] [...] Iustitia vero regis est neminem iniuste per potentiam opprimere, sine acceptione personarum inter virum et proximum suum iudicare, advenis et pupillis et viduis defensorem esse, furta cohibere, adulteria punire, iniquos non exaltare, impudicos et striones non nutrire, impios de terra perdere, parricidas et

18 Note that another parallel, which I do not include here, is the Hiberno-Latin *Collectanea* of Pseudo-Bede. Also, the previous chapter in *Collectio canonum Hibernensis*, Liber XXIV, cap. 3, *De eo quod malorum regum opera distruant* (That the deeds of bad kings are destructive), *The Hibernensis*, Bk I, p. 147 (text); Bk II, p. 583 (trans.), expresses many of the same images, albeit expressed in the negative. Also, a close comparison of these witnesses with *Audacht Morainn* would admit a few more parallels than those I catalogue below but would add little to my present argument.

uiuere non sinere, æcclesias defendere, pauperes elimosinis alere, iustos super regni negotia constituere, senes et sapientes et subrios consiliarios habere, magorum et phithonistarum et augoriarum superstitionibus non intendere, patriam fortiter et iuste contra aduersarios defendere, per omnia in Deo confidere, de prosperitate animum non eleuare, cuncta aduersa patienter ferre, fidem catholicam in Deo habere, filios suos impie agere non sinere, certis horis orationibus insistere, ante horas congruas non sumere cibum. (Salamon: Ve tibi ciuitas, cuius rex iuuenis est).[20] Iustitia regis pax populorum est, tutamen patrie, immunitas plebis, munimentum gentis, cura languorum, gaudium hominum, temperies aeris, serenitas maris, terre fecunditas, solatium pauperum, hereditas filiorum, spes future beatitudinis, segetum habundantia, arborum fecunditas. Alibi legitur: Prosperitas est regni regis in misericordia et exaltatio nominis eius in largitate, longitudo dierum eius in uero iudicio est. Salomon: Misericordia et ueritas custodiunt regem, et roboratur clementia tronus eius **_Collectio canonum Hibernensis_, Liber XXIV, cap. 4, _That the deeds of a good king are efficacious_**[21] Patrick: This is, therefore, the justice of a just king: he does not judge anyone unjustly, he is a defender of strangers and widows and orphans, he prevents thefts, punishes adultery, he does not sustain the unchaste and the buffoons; he does not exalt the iniquitous, he casts out the impious from the land, he does not allow killers and perjurers to live, he defends churches, he feeds the poor with alms, he appoints the just over the affairs of the kingdom, he has elders and wise men and sober men as counselors, he does not heed the

periurantes vivere non sinere, ecclesias defendere, pauperes elemosynis alere, iustos super regni negotia constituere, senes et sapientes et sobrios consiliarios habere, magorum et hariolorum et pythonissarum superstitionibus non intendere, iracundiam differre, patriam fortiter et iuste contra adversarios defendere, per omnia in Deo confidere, prosperitatibus animum non elevare, cuncta adversaria patienter ferre, fidem catholicam in Deum habere, filios suos non sinere impie agere, certis horis orationibus insistere, ante horas congruas non gustare cibum. (Vae enim terrae, cuius rex est puer [...])[23] [...] Pax populorum est tutamen patriae, munitas plebis, munimentum gentis, cura languorum, gaudium hominum, temperies aeris, serenitas maris, terrae fecunditas, solacium pauperum, hereditas filiorum et sibimet ipsi spes futurae beatitudinis [...] **from _On the Twelve Abuses of the World_, cap. 9, _An Unjust King_**[24] [...] Truly, the justice of the king is this: he oppresses no-one unjustly by means of power; he judges between a man and his neighbor impartially; he defends strangers, the destitute, and orphans; he represses thievery; he punishes adultery; he does not exalt evil men; he does not sustain the shameless or buffoons; he drives impious men from the land; he does not allow murderers or perjurers to live; he defends the Church; he supports the poor with alms; he places the needs of just men before the business of the kingdom; he keeps wise and sober counselors; he pays no attention to the superstitions of magicians, soothsayers, or snake-handlers; he withholds his wrath; he strengthens the land, and justly defends it against enemies; he trusts in God for all things; he does not superstitions of magicians, oracles and augurs, he bravely and justly defends the homeland against its enemies, he has faith in God through all things, he does not puff up his mind out of prosperity, he bears all hardship with patience, he has catholic faith in God; he does not allow his sons to behave impiously, he persists in prayer at fixed times, he does not eat before the designated hour. [Solomon: Woe to you, O city, whose king is a child]. The king's justice is the people's peace, the fatherland's protection, the commoner's freedom, the nation's defence, the welfare of the weak, the joy of men, the temperance of weather, the serenity of the sea, the fertility of the land, the consolation of the poor, the sons' inheritance, hope of future blessing, abundance of crops, the fecundity of trees. Elsewhere one reads: The kingdom's prosperity is in the king's mercy, the exaltation of his name in his generosity, and his longevity in his truthful judgement. Soloman: Mercy and truth preserve the king, and his throne is strengthened by clemency.

disparage the good fortune of the soul; he remains patient in all adversity; he maintains the catholic faith in God; he does not permit his sons to act impiously; he keeps the hours of prayer; he does not consume food before the proper hours ([...] For woe is the land, whose king is a child [...]) [...] The peace of the people is the defence of the land, the relief of workers, the protection of tribes, the care of the sick, the joy of men, the tranquility of the weather, the serenity of the sea, the fertility of the land, the consolation of the poor, the inheritance of sons, and, for he himself, the hope of future beatitude [...]

---

19 The text is from *The Hibernensis*, Bk I, pp. 148–49.

20 I have inserted this short excerpt from the immediately following chapter, Liber XXIV, cap. 5, *De eo quod non oportet iuuenum regnare* (That it is not proper for a young man to reign), *The Hibernensis*, Bk I, p. 149 (text); Bk II, p. 584 (trans.), to highlight the parallelism between these two texts.

21 The translation is from *The Hibernensis*, Bk II, pp. 583–84.

22 The text is from Ps.-Cyprian, *De xii abusivis saeculi*, pp. 51–53.

23 This partial citation of Ecclesiastes 10:16, 'Vae enim terrae cuius rex est puer [...]' (For woe to the land whose king is a child [...]), while not included in *Collectio canonum Hibernensis*, Liber XXIV, cap., 4, is one of two citations in cap. 5, immediately following: *De eo quod non oportet iuuenum regnare* (That it is not proper for a young man to reign). *De duodecim abusivis saeculi* cites the entire verse: 'Vae enim terrae, cuius rex est puer et cuius principes mane comedunt' (Woe to thee, O land, when thy king is a child, and when the princes eat in the morning), while *Collectio canonum Hibernensis* cites only the fragment.

24 The translation is my own.

Comparison of *Collectio canonum Hibernensis*, Liber XXIV, cap. 4 and *Audacht Morainn*

The close textual relationship between *Collectio canonum Hibernensis* and *De duodecim abusivis saeculi* is readily apparent. Their connection with *Audacht Morainn*, however, is less well understood. On this point, one must acknowledge that *Audacht Morainn* is generically a very different kind of text. While the two Latin witnesses emerge from related intellectual milieux (*Collectio canonum Hibernensis* is considered legal, and *De duodecim abusivis saeculi* can be considered philosophical), *Audacht Morainn* represents an Irish reflex of the gnomic, sapiential literature known elsewhere as *speculum principi* (a genre possibly of Irish origin),[25] where the qualities of a good king are espoused (and, likewise, sometimes the qualities of a bad king are decried). Despite their generic differences, however, the similarities in their content and ideology are clear. In the comparison below, I have catalogued the closest verbal parallels between the above-mentioned chapter of *Collectio canonum Hibernensis* and *Audacht Morainn*. To avoid repetitiveness, I have not included *De duodecim abusivis saeculi* in this comparison since, with the exception of any specific message of the fruitfulness of trees, it matches *Collectio canonum Hibernensis* in every point.

Comparison of Collectio canonum Hibernensis *and* Audacht Morainn

(1) CCH: ⟨Iusticia uero regis iusti hæc est⟩ patriam fortiter et iuste contra aduersarios defendere [...] tutamen patrie [...] munimentum gentis.[26]
(⟨This is, therefore, the justice of a just king⟩: he bravely and justly defends the homeland against enemies [...] the fatherland's protection [...] the nation's defence).[27]

25 See *Audacht Morainn*, p. xv. See also: F. Kelly, *A Guide to Early Irish Law*, pp. 235–36. In the latter, Kelly points out that *Audacht Morainn* has close relationships with legal texts other than those mentioned here, albeit on different grounds than I discuss in the present argument: '[...] there is good evidence that *Bretha Nemed Toíseach* and *Bretha Nemed Déidenach* [...] draw from the same learned tradition as the 7th century wisdom-text *Audacht Morainn* [...]'. Kelly, however, finds it unlikely that *Audacht Morainn* was composed by a cleric.

26 The text is from *The Hibernensis*, Bk I, pp. 148–49.

27 The translation is from *The Hibernensis*, Bk II, pp. 583–84.

AM § 15: Is tre ḟ⟨ir ⟩fl⟨athemon⟩ ath- ⟨mór⟩cathu fri crícha comnámat -cuirethar.[28]
(It is through the justice of the ruler that that he dispatches ⟨great⟩ battalions to the borders of hostile neighbours).[29]

(2) CCH: ⟨Iustitia regis est [...]⟩ hereditas filiorum.[30]
(⟨The king's justice is [...]⟩: the sons' inheritance).[31]

AM § 16: Is tre ḟ⟨ir⟩ fl⟩athemon⟩ cech comarbe con a chlí ina chainorbu clanda.[32]
(It is through the justice of the ruler that that every heir plants his house post in his fair inheritance).[33]

(3) CCH: ⟨Iustitia regis est...⟩ segetum habundantia.[34]
(⟨The king's justice is [...]⟩: abundance of crops).[35]

AM § 19: Is tre ḟ⟨ir⟩ fl[athemon⟩ ro-bbí(?) cech etho ardósil imbeth.[36]
(It is through the justice of the ruler that there is (?) abundance of every high, tall corn).[37]

(4) CCH: ⟨Iustitia regis est [...]⟩ arborum fecunditas.[38]
(⟨The king's justice is [...]⟩: fecundity of trees).[39]

AM § 17: Is tre ḟ⟨ir⟩ fl⟨athemon⟩ ad- manna mármeso márḟedo -mlasetar.[40]
(It is through the justice of the ruler that abundances of great tree-fruit and great wood are tasted).[41]

It is not my purpose here to argue that there was direct borrowing between any of these witnesses. That said, the similarities between them point to a close, albeit complex relationship that remains to be worked out. At the very least, however, the evidence indicates a connection between the Latin witnesses on the one hand and *Audacht Morainn* on the other that is more

28 The text is from *Audacht Morainn*, p. 6.
29 The translation is from *Audacht Morainn*, p. 7.
30 The text is from *The Hibernensis*, Bk I, pp. 148–49.
31 The translation is from *The Hibernensis*, Bk II, pp. 583–84.
32 The text is from *Audacht Morainn*, p. 6.
33 The translation is from *Audacht Morainn*, p. 7.
34 The text is from *The Hibernensis*, Bk I, pp. 148–49.
35 The translation is from *The Hibernensis*, Bk II, pp. 583–84.
36 The text is from *Audacht Morainn*, p. 6.
37 The translation is from *Audacht Morainn*, p. 7.
38 The text is from *The Hibernensis*, Bk I, pp. 148–49.
39 The translation is from *The Hibernensis*, Bk II, pp. 583–84.
40 The text is from *Audacht Morainn*, p. 6.
41 The translation is from *Audacht Morainn*, p. 7.

substantial than can be explained by vague ideological analogy or their unrelated, simultaneous emergence from a common literary or intellectual tradition. At this point, however, little can be said about the relationship between them with certainty, beyond the obvious fact that they express a similar view of kingship and its connection with the prosperity of the realm. Thus, while their ideological affinity is clear, any textual relationship between them remains putative.

The close affinity between these texts becomes even more complex when one looks more broadly for analogues in the early Irish legal tradition. Similar lists of reverberating natural disasters, in this instance recounting harm to the natural world resulting from violations of the so-called 'Law of Sunday' (as opposed to unjust leadership in the texts discussed previously), are found in the closely related vernacular legal tracts *Cáin Domnaig* (The Law of Sunday) and the *Epistil Ísu* (The Epistle of Jesus). Here too, verbal parallels are apparent. In both cases, these parallels correspond closely to the highly rhetorical final section of the passages excerpted from *Collectio canonum Hibernensis* and *De duodecim abusivis saeculi* cited above, organized around the repeated phrase *justitia regis pax populorum est* [...] (the justice of the king is the peace of the people [...]), in the case of *Collectio canonum Hibernensis*, or *Pax populorum est* [...] (the peace of the people is [...]), in the case of *De duodecim abusivis saeculi*, the former echoing the repeated Old Irish phrase in *Audacht Morainn*: *is tre fír flathemon* [...] (it is through the justice (or 'truth') of the king [...]). A comparison of the relevant portions shows how close the similarities are:

Comparison of *CCH*, *DxiiAS*, *Cáin Domnaig*, and *Epistil Ísu*

CCH[42]	*DxiiAS*[43]	*Cáin Domnaig*[44]	*Epistil Ísu*[45]
Iustitia regis pax populorum est, tutamen patriae, immunitas plebis, munimentum gentis, cura languorum, gaudium hominum, temperies aëris, serenitas maris, terrae fecunditas,	Pax populorum est, tutamen patriae, munitas plebis, munimentum gentis, cura languorum, gaudium hominum, temperies aeris, serenitas maris, terrae fecunditas,	Ar is ar tairmthecht Domnuig do-beir Día plága forsna gurta. Is ed beres for cúlu cech torath do-cuirethar muir ⁊ tír eter ith ⁊ mblicht ⁊ mes. ⁊ is ed di-gní íascratha ambriti. Is ed do-beir nauna ⁊ gortai ⁊ sína sóeba for tótha cloéna. Is ed do-beir cenéla echtranna co claidbib díglae dia	'Mani forcmaid in domnach', ol Fíadu, 'ina críchaib córaib, dobicfat anbthine móra ⁊ lochait immdai tenntide ⁊ torann ⁊ srobtene dóidfes na clanna ⁊ na cenéla ⁊ casra troma ailchide ⁊ nathraig lúamnig

CCH[42]	*DxiiAS*[43]	*Cáin Domnaig*[44]	*Epistil Ísu*[45]
solatium pauperum, hereditas filiorum, spes future beatitudinis, segetum habundantia, arborum fecunditas.	solacium pauperum, hereditas filiorum et sibimet ipsi spes futurae beatitudinis.	mbrith hi fognam i tíre geinte. Is ed dobeir catha ⁊ choicthiu et*er* na cenéla cona bí síd na subæ na cairde i cech dú. Is ed immefolgni ír ⁊ ingar ⁊ debaith i cach tegdais co llína brón ⁊ dubæ ⁊ doichell cride cech duini.	⁊ dobicfat gennti úam-si', ol Día fessin, '.i. cenél na pagán nobbérat i mbrataib as bar tírib ⁊ atobopérat dia n-deeb fesne'.
The king's justice is the people's peace, the fatherland's protection, the commoner's freedom, the nation's defence, the welfare of the weak, the joy of men, the temperance of weather, the serenity of the sea, the fertility of the land, the consolation of the poor, the sons' inheritance, hope of future blessing, abundance of crops, fecundity of trees.	The peace of the people is the defence of the land, the relief of the workers, the protection of tribes, the care of the sick, the joy of men, the tranquility of the weather, the serenity of the sea, the fertility of the land, the consolation of the poor, the inheritance of sons, and, for he himself, the hope of future beatitude.	For on account of the transgression of Sunday God brings pestilences on the fields. This it is that sets back every produce that the sea and earth bring forth, including corn, milk, and mast. This it is that makes fisheries barren. This it is that brings famines, hungers, and unseasonable weathers on perverse peoples. This it is that brings foreign races with avenging swords to bear them in bondage into pagan lands. This it is that brings battles and wars among peoples so that nowhere is there either peace or happiness or friendship. This it is that causes anger, impiety (?) and discord in every dwelling so that sorrow, gloom, and ill-will fill the heart of everyone.	'Unless you observe Sunday', says the Lord, 'within its proper boundaries, there shall come great tempests, and many fiery lightenings, and thunder, and sulphurous fire, which shall burn peoples and nations, and heavy stony hailstorms, and flying serpents, and heathens shall come to you from Me', says God Himself; 'that is, even a race of Pagans, who will carry you into bondage from your own lands, and will offer you up to their own gods'.

It is important to point out that, just as *Collectio canonum Hibernensis* and *De duodecim abusivis saeculi* likely have a direct textual relationship to one another (at least in the particular section which is the focus of this comparison), so do *Cáin Domnaig* and *Epistil Ísu*.[46] So, with this table, I am really comparing two sets of related texts, that is, *Collectio canonum Hibernensis* and *De duodecim abusivis saeculi* with *Cáin Domnaig* and *Epistil Ísu*.

As above with *Collectio canonum Hibernensis*, it is enlightening to compare *Cáin Domnaig* and *Epistil Ísu* with *Audacht Morainn*. Here again, the verbal parallels are apparent:

Comparison of *Cáin Domnaig*, *Epistil Ísu*, and *Audacht Morainn*

(1) CD: [...] is ar tairmthecht Domnuig do-beir Día plága forsna gurta.[47]
([...] it is on account of the transgression of Sunday God brings pestilences on the fields).[48]

Here, the opposite idea, stated about a good ruler:
AM § 19: Is tre ḟ⟨ir⟩ fl⟨athemon⟩ ro-bbí(?) cech etho ardósil imbeth.[49]
(It is through the justice of the ruler that there is (?) abundance of every high, tall corn).[50]

(2) CD: is ed di-gní íascratha ambriti.[51]
(This it is that makes fisheries barren).[52]

42 The text is from *The Hibernensis*, Bk I, pp. 148–49.
43 The translation is from *The Hibernensis*, Bk II, pp. 583–84.
44 The text and translation are from 'Cáin Domnaig', ed. and trans. by Hull. I have made a few minor changes to the translation.
45 The text and translation are from 'Cáin Domnaig', ed. and trans. by O'Keefe, though I have made a few minor changes to the translation.
46 On the borrowing by *Epistil Ísu* from *Cáin Domnaig*, see: Hull, 'Cáin Domnaig', pp. 152–53.
47 The text is from *Cáin Domnaig*, ed. and trans. by Hull, p. 170.
48 The translation is from *Cáin Domnaig*, ed. and trans. by Hull, p. 171.
49 The text is from *Audacht Morainn*, p. 6.
50 The translation is from *Audacht Morainn*, p. 7.
51 The text is from *Cáin Domnaig*, ed. and trans. by Hull, p. 170.
52 The translation is from *Cáin Domnaig*, ed. and trans. by Hull, p. 171.

Here, the opposite idea, stated about a good ruler:
AM § 20: Is tre ḟ⟨ir⟩ fl⟨athemon⟩ to- aidbe ⟨uisce⟩ éisc i sruthaib -snáither.[53]
(It is through the justice of the ruler that abundance of fish swim in streams).[54]

(3) CD: Is ed do-beir [...] sína sóeba.[55]
(This it is that brings [...] unseasonable weathers).[56]

EÍ: [...] dobicfat anbthine móra ⁊ lochait immdai tenntide ⁊ torann [...] ⁊ casra troma ailchide [...].[57]
([...] there shall come great tempests, and many fiery lightning, and thunder...and heavy stony hail-storms [...]).[58]

Here, the opposite idea, stated about a good ruler:
AM § 12: [...] is tre ḟír flathemon [...] márlóchet di doínib dingbatar.[59]
(It is through the justice of the ruler that [...] great lightnings are kept from the people).[60]

On this point, compare also *Collectio canonum Hibernensis*, Liber xxiv, cap. 3, *De eo quod maliorum regum opera distruant* (That the deeds of bad kings are destructive),

CCH: Iniquitas iniqui regis [...] potestates aereis suscitat [...] fulmina succendit.[61]
(The iniquity of the iniquitous king [...] stirs up storms [...] sets lightening on fire).[62]

(4) CD: Is ed do-beir cenéla echtranna co claidbib díglae dia mbrith hi fognam i tíre geinte.[63]
(This it is that brings foreign races with avenging swords to bear them in bondage into pagan lands).[64]

---

53 The text is from *Audacht Morainn*, p. 6.
54 The translation is from *Audacht Morainn*, p. 7.
55 The text is from *Cáin Domnaig*, ed. and trans. by Hull, p. 170.
56 The translation is from *Cáin Domnaig*, ed. and trans. by Hull, p. 171.
57 The text (of *Epistil Ísu*) is from *Cáin Domnaig*, ed. and trans. by O'Keefe, p. 196.
58 The translation (of *Epistil Ísu*) is from *Cáin Domnaig*, ed. and trans. by O'Keefe, p. 197.
59 The text is from *Audacht Morainn*, p. 6.
60 The translation is from *Audacht Morainn*, p. 7.
61 *The Hibernensis*, Bk i, pp. 147–48. Note that I did not include *Collectio canonum Hibernensis*, Liber xxiv, cap. 3 in my initial comparison, since it largely states the contents of cap. 4 in the negative. This image of lightning storms is not included in cap. 4, however.
62 *The Hibernensis*, Bk ii, p. 583.
63 The text is from *Cáin Domnaig*, ed. and trans. by Hull, p. 170.
64 The translation is from *Cáin Domnaig*, ed. and trans. by Hull, p. 171.

EÍ: [...] cenél na pagán [...] bérat i m-brataib as bar tírib ⁊ atobopérat dia n-deeb fesne.[65]
([...] a race of Pagans [...] will carry you into bondage from your own lands, and will offer you up to their own gods).[66]

Here, the opposite idea, stated about a good ruler:
AM § 15: Is tre ḟ⟨ir⟩ fl⟨athemon⟩ ath-⟨mór⟩cathu fri crícha comnámat -cuirethar.[67]
(It is through the justice of the ruler that that he dispatches (great) battalions to the borders of hostile neighbours).[68]

The similarities between these two groups of texts suggests a close ideological relationship and a complex, possibly direct textual relationship as well.

With the evidence considered thus far (and without breaching the question of direct textual influence), it is possible to draw some conclusions about the relationship between these documents. All of these texts — the selections from *Collectio canonum Hibernensis, De duodecim abusivis saeculi, Audacht Morainn, Cáin Domnaig,* and *Epistil Ísu* — warrant comparison on the grounds that they posit a direct, causal link between various earthly calamities that might befall a kingdom or a people when their king (or, potentially, others of rank within the community) abrogates certain, abstractly conceived injunctions of natural law, envisioned variously as violations of *iustitia, pax, fír,* or — more concretely when expressed in unambiguously Christian terms — the sanctity of the sabbath. Conversely, these texts attribute the prosperity of land and people to the righteous conduct of their leader(s). The idea is that the normal, balanced processes of the cosmos both depend upon and reflect the proper, lawful conduct of all its inhabitants and that, under certain conditions, it can be disrupted by unnatural (here equated with 'unjust' or 'improper') human behaviour. Violation of the natural order was thought to be the immediate cause of such catastrophes as are enumerated in these texts.

All these documents reflect early Irish belief in the causal connection between human (in)justice and (im)balance with the physical universe. As such, the common set of ideas found in these texts — ideas that go beyond mere generalities, to include a similar and at times almost formulaic list of specific effects (positive or negative) on grain, fish, weather (especially lightning), and foreign invasion possibly, though not certainly, originated in early pre-Christian, native Irish wisdom literature. The five texts dis-

65 The text (of *Epistil Ísu*) is from *Cáin Domnaig*, ed. and trans. by O'Keefe, p. 196.
66 The translation (of *Epistil Ísu*) is from *Cáin Domnaig*, ed. and trans. by O'Keefe, p. 197.
67 The text is from *Audacht Morainn*, p. 6.
68 The translation is from *Audacht Morainn*, p. 7.

cussed here, I would argue, are ultimately derivatives of that tradition.[69] Of relevance to the present discussion, however, is where and how these ideas have survived. In terms of genre, the two Latin texts would appear to be the most pragmatic: *Collectio canonum Hibernensis* is canon law, presumably intended for practical application, while *De duodecim abusivis saeculi* belongs to a broadly defined class of early Irish philosophical-wisdom tracts, in this instance with a clear religious orientation. *Cáin Domnaig* and the *Epistil Ísu*, on the other hand, both written in the vernacular, are usually considered legal texts, though this generic classification (and their actual purpose) has been questioned. As Vernam Hull noted in his edition of *Cáin Domnaig*:

> Strictly speaking, ⟨*Cáin Domnaig*⟩ is not a law tract. It does not form part of the *Senchas Már*, nor was it apparently ever enforced. Its author also remains unknown. Presumably he was not a brehon. Rather he would seem to have been a member of a monastic establishment which he perhaps served in the capacity of a legal adviser. How versed he actually was in Irish ecclesiastical law is, however, a matter for conjecture. Thus, for example, assuming that the received text of ⟨*Cáin Domnaig*⟩ has been correctly transmitted, it is, nevertheless, impossible to form a clear picture of the actual procedure that takes place on the basis of the account in § 3 ⟨which attributes practical legal penalties and procedures to *Cáin Domnaig*⟩.[70]

Despite J. G. O'Keefe's questionable description of *Cáin Domnaig* as 'a highly technical law tract',[71] a sentiment later echoed by Robert McNally,[72] Hull's reservations concerning the practical legal value of the text warrant consideration. For similar reasons, one might also question the pragmatic legal status of the *Epistil Ísu*, which comes across more as a work of imaginative fiction than practical jurisprudence.

Caution is warranted, however. Questions about their practical legal value notwithstanding, a large excerpt from the *Epistil Ísu* (in Latin)[73]

---

69 This same relationship between just and proper human behaviour and the cosmic order is also found in a tenth-century text *Immacallam in dá Thuarad* (The Colloquy of the Two Sages). Many of the same disastrous effects representing disorder in nature (i.e., disasters related to corn, fish, weather, and foreign invasion) are found in this text as well. The text, currently available only in Whitley Stokes's early twentieth-century edition, *The Colloquy of the Two Sages*, needs a new edition.

70 '*Cáin Domnaig*', ed. and trans. by Hull, p. 152.

71 '*Cáin Domnaig*', ed. and trans. by O'Keefe, p. 189.

72 McNally, 'Dies Dominica', p. 357.

73 Robert McNally asserts that: 'The *Cáin Domnaig*, though itself composed in Old Irish, undoubtedly rests upon a Latin tradition, at least as far as the *Epistil Ísu* is concerned', but offers no evidence in support of this claim, 'Dies Dominica', p. 357. Without textual evidence, it is impossible to determine in which language the original document was composed.

is found in two related Hiberno-Latin legal collectanea (both of Breton provenance):[74] BnF, MS lat. 3182 and Orléans, Médiathèque, 221. Both of these collections contain Hiberno-Latin and Breton-Latin texts whose status as practical law has not been questioned: including, for example, *Collectio canonum Hibernensis, Excerpta de libris Romanorum et Francorum* (formerly known as *Canones Wallici*),[75] and *Canones Adamnani.*[76] Their inclusion in this manuscript context among other ostensibly pragmatic documents (in what, by all appearances, seem to be unadorned, utilitarian codices), raises the possibility that these texts may in fact have been regarded as practical, living law despite the objections just raised.

Of the five texts discussed so far, all of them except *Audacht Morainn*, whether written in Latin or the vernacular and despite other differences, contain clear Christian references and would seem, therefore, to have taken shape within a Christian milieu. Why does *Audacht Morainn* lack overt Christian references? How does it relate to the other documents in this group? Despite its obvious similarities to the other Christian texts apparent in the comparisons above, there is very little to suggest that the author of *Audacht Morainn* was a cleric, or that the text was intended for use in a Christian setting. On this point, Fergus Kelly (following Daniel A. Binchy) explains that, in the oldest recension of *Audacht Morainn*, just as in the oldest law codes,

> [...] there is a noticeable lack of specifically Christian sentiments and very few Latin loan-words. Though one cannot rule out the possibility of outside influence in a text that must have taken roughly its present form over 200 years after the arrival of Christianity, it has yet to be shown that any of the ideas which it expresses are of Christian provenance.[77]

To be sure, it is possible to overstate the case. Later in the same volume, for example, Kelly notes that, '⟨a⟩s *A⟨udacht⟩ M⟨orainn⟩* seems untouched by Christian influences (apart from a few Latin loans [...]), it is interesting to find the word *dúilem* ("creator") which is otherwise attested only in Christian contexts'.[78] Also, though the Latin loanwords are few, all of them are ecclesiastical in nature.[79] Thus, however thin it may be, a stratum of Christian influence can be detected. Nonetheless, *Audacht Morainn* stands

74 The Latin text is edited in McNally, 'Dies Dominica', pp. 355–61.

75 Edited in Bieler, *The Irish Penitentials*, pp. 136–49 and pp. 150–59.

76 A Latin version of part of the *Epistil Ísu* is also found in MS Vatican Reg. lat. 49, the so-called *Catechesis Celtica*, a collection of religious, not legal materials (although some of the surrounding texts are concerned with divine justice). See McNamara, 'Sources and Affiliations', p. 235 (#55).

77 *Audacht Morainn*, pp. xiv–xv. See also: F. Kelly, *A Guide to Early Irish Law*, pp. 235–36.

78 *Audacht Morainn*, p. 43, note on § 32 '*dúilemon*'.

79 *Audacht Morainn*, pp. xxxix–xl.

out as notably distinct from the other texts in that its outlook does not appear to be primarily ecclesiastical in orientation, a fact which raises questions about the ideological tradition that ultimately gave rise to this group of related texts.

What explains the relative lack of Christian orientation in *Audacht Morainn*? Granted, of the five texts discussed in this section, *Audacht Morainn* is the most generically distinct: the others might be classified loosely as legal-philosophical tracts with overt ecclesiastical agenda, while *Audacht Morainn*, on the other hand, is a *speculum principi* text more broadly associated with Old Irish wisdom literature.[80] Though vernacular Irish sapiential texts at times discuss matters of ecclesiastical interest,[81] and though one might find analogues in biblical wisdom literature possibly underlying individual proverbs, generally speaking, Irish reflexes of this genre tend to reflect secular interests.[82] One might point out that, since the intended audience of a *speculum principi* text are individuals with a stake in secular authority (a king in the case of *Audacht Morainn*), one might expect the themes expressed within it to be somewhat less clerically centred. And yet, generic expectations, to the extent these can be confidently defined in the early Irish tradition, do not suffice to explain the comparative lack of Christian references in *Audacht Morainn*, given its close associations with other texts so overtly religious in orientation. Moreover, it would hardly seem out of place for a wise sage or judge, even a mythical one like Morann, to counsel a king on appropriate pious behaviour when proffering advice. An explanation of the poem's lack of overt Christian references, therefore, must be sought elsewhere.

Part of the answer, I would argue, lies in the nature of the subject matter. The idea that the natural world might thrive or languish in direct relation to the behaviour of a secular ruler in what amounts to a kind of pathetic fallacy would seem, on the surface at least, to be a pre-Christian notion. What immediately comes to mind are the theories of kingship in early comparative mythological work and literary study of the sort beginning with Sir James Frazier and Jesse Weston (both now discredited) and continuing thereafter with the research of Georges Dumézil and others. To be sure, Irish literature is certainly replete with episodes in which the fertility of the land and the moral behaviour of a sacral king, whose acts may either bring prosperity or invoke cosmic disasters such as those

80 For a bibliographical and descriptive list of these texts see 'Appendix 2, List of Wisdom Texts', F. Kelly, *A Guide to Early Irish Law*, pp. 284–86.

81 Donahue, 'Beowulf, Ireland and the Natural Good', citing Thurneysen, 'Morands Fürstenspiegel'. I am sceptical of the precise biblical allusions the authors identify but, that said, *Audacht Morainn* would appear to have a close association with religious literature.

82 An exception which proves the rule is *Apgitir Chrábaid*. For an edition, see: Hull, '*Apgitir Chrábaid*', and for a translation, see Clancy and Márkus, *Iona*, pp. 195–207.

listed in the texts above, are related. An unambiguous example is found in the ninth-century text *Cath Maige Mucrama*.[83] There, a false judgement rendered by King Lugaid MacCon resulted in the immediate, supernatural destruction of part of his house and, '⟨b⟩líadain dó íar sain i rrígu i Temraig ⁊ ní thánic fér tria thalmain ná duil⟨l⟩e tre ḟidbuid ná gránni i n.-arbur' (after that he was a year in the kingship of Tara and no grass came through the earth, no leaf on tree, nor grain in corn).[84] Many such examples, too numerous to catalogue here, can be found throughout the corpus of Irish literature. In any case, negative repercussions in the natural world for unjust or improper behaviour on the part of a ruler are perhaps most fitting under the Law of Nature.

The Corroborative Value of the Law of Nature

Of interest to the present discussion is the fact that similar ideas found expression in early Irish law codes as well, beyond the examples already discussed. In the so-called 'Genuine' Prologue to the *Senchas Már*, for example, a direct link is made between natural disasters and human behaviour. Here, improper human behaviour (e.g., the dissolution of verbal contracts) was understood to have the potential to throw the world into chaos and, conversely, just deeds (e.g., the performance of pious religious duties such as tithing and alms-giving, not necessarily by a ruler in this case but, presumably, by members of society at large) could restore the natural order:

> § 7. Ataat téora aimsera imbi bailethach in bith: réchuaird duinebath, túarathliae coctho, fúaslucud cor mbél.
>
> § 8. Ataat a trí noda ícat: dechmada ⁊ prímiti ⁊ almsona ara-gairet réchuaird duinebath; tráethad cairde la ríg ⁊ túaith ara-gair túarathliae coctho; astud cáich inna ṡochur ⁊ inna dochur ara-gair bailiuth in betho.[85]
>
>> (§ 7. There are three occasions when the world becomes chaotic: an epidemic of plagues, a deluge of warfare, dissolution of contracts.
>>
>> § 8. There are three things which remedy them: tithes and first-fruits and alms which prevent an epidemic of plagues; the

83 The text and translation are from *Cath Maige Mucrama*, ed. and trans. by Daly. There (p. 18), Daly argues that some of the source material used in the text may date from as early as *c.* 700.

84 *Cath Maige Mucrama*, p. 58 (text); p. 59 (trans.).

85 Breatnach, *The Old Irish Law Tract 'Senchas Már'*, p. 6. Compare: *Corpus Iuris Hibernici*, 350.26–351.10; and compare also 1659.37-1660.8, 1897.27.

> imposition of treaties by king and people which prevents a deluge of warfare; holding everyone to their advantageous contract and their disadvantageous contract which prevents the chaos of the world).[86]

Here, the proper balance of human society is directly linked to virtuous behaviour. Immoral conduct had the potential to set the world, including human society, out of balance; and only pious actions could restore it.

Whatever the origins of this belief or its analogues in other early European and global ideologies, it was fully embraced by the early Irish Church, as the examples above demonstrate. From a distinctly ecclesiastical point of view, *Collectio canonum Hibernensis* and *De duodecim abusivis saeculi* directly relate balance in the natural world to a ruler's moral behaviour, while *Cáin Domnaig* and the *Epistil Ísu* transfer this relationship to the proper observance of the law, in this case, the Law of Sunday.[87] Although the belief itself may have pre-Christian origins, Irish clerics understood it within a Christian framework as an aspect of the Law of Nature. In this Christianized view, the cosmos was understood as a direct reflection of the creator, through which the Holy Spirit operated. Righteous behaviour, first and foremost by a ruler, but also by other authorities in some cases, and even society at large, maintained that balance, whereas injustice and impropriety led to chaos and disorder. By the time of the first written sources, this belief had been fully absorbed by the Church. What pagan Irish jurists understood as (*co*)*córus*, sometimes translated (in a legal context) merely as 'law', but here more accurately in its broadest sense as 'proper arrangement' in the universe,[88] was understood in Irish Christian legal doctrine as a feature of the Law of Nature, the first of the Four Laws in sacred history outlined above.

How did jurists understand the relationship between human justice and balance (or lack thereof) in the natural world? There is ample evidence in Irish legal texts attesting to the belief that violations of justice under the Law of Nature would result in chaos and disorder. In this way of thinking, the status of the natural world had corroborative value for assessing the validity of human jurisprudence: the proper function of the cosmos, including human society, was seen as a direct reflection of the righteousness of its ruler(s) and/or judge(s) and the propriety of their actions. This idea is explicitly stated in the law codes. For example, the 'Genuine' Prologue to the *Senchas Már* begins with a statement about the preservation and authority of the law:

86 Breatnach, *The Old Irish Law Tract 'Senchas Már'*, p. 7.
87 McLeod, 'The Concept of Law', p. 362.
88 See *eDIL*, s.v. *cocarus*, and McLeod, 'The Concept of Law', p. 360.

§ 1. Senchas fer nÉrenn, cid conid-roíter? Comchuimne dá ṡen, tindnacul clúaise di araili, díchetal filed, tórmach ó recht litre, nertad fri recht n-aicnid. Ar it é trénailig in sin frisa n-astaiter bretha in betho.[89]

> (§ 1. The tradition of the men of Ireland, what has preserved it? Joint recollection of two elders, transmission from one ear to another, chanting of poets, augmentation from the law of Scripture, reliance[90] on the law of nature. For those are the firm foundations on which the judgements of the world are fixed).[91]

The notion expressed here is that traditional lore (*senchas*), in this case legal lore, is passed down orally ('from ear to ear') by elders and poets. According to the text, that tradition later grew by the addition of *recht litre* and, most importantly for the present discussion, was reinforced and confirmed by the Law of Nature. In other words, the intrinsic justice of the ancient legal tradition, including Christian contributions to it, was verified and corroborated by the preservation of balance and order within the realm where it was applied.

Similar expression of the corroborative value of the Law of Nature, understood as maintenance of the cosmic balance, is found in the opening lines of *Uraicecht Becc*:

CID I NAGAR BREITHEMNUS BERLA FEINI .NĪ. I FIR ⁊ DLIGED ⁊ AIGNEAD [...] CONSUITER FIR FOR ROSCADAIB ⁊ FASAIGIB ⁊ TESDEMNAIB FIRAIB. [...] CONSUITER DLIGED FOR CORAIB BEL ⁊ AITIDEN. [...] **CONSUITER AICNED FOR LOGUD ⁊ COCORUS.**[92]

> (On what is the jurisprudence of the *Féni* bound? Not difficult: on truth and law[93] and nature. Truth is based on *roscada* ⟨legal verse⟩ and *fásaige* ⟨legal precedents that have become proverbial⟩ and true testimony ⟨or possibly 'written text' or 'scriptural quotation'⟩. Law

---

89 Breatnach, *The Early Irish Law Tract 'Senchas Már*, p. 4. Compare: *Corpus Iuris Hibernici*, 344.24–347.17 and 1657.10–165821, 1896.23–36.

90 See *DIL*, s.v. *nertad*, 'strengthening, [...] exhorting, urging'. It is the verbal noun of *nertaid* (see *eDIL*, s.v. *2 nertaid* (a): strengthens, confirms). It would appear that the basic sense is 'strengthening', but, in this context, 'confirmation', seems a better translation, especially given the context.

91 Breatnach, *The Early Irish Law Tract 'Senchas Már*, p. 5.

92 *Corpus Iuris Hibernici*, 1590.1–1592.24, and compare 634.11–635.1, 2256.13–35. See also, *A Companion to the Corpus Iuris Hibernici*, § 5.53, pp. 315–18. Compare McLeod's discussion of this passage in 'Concept of Law', p. 361. Emphasis my own, in both text and translation.

93 The term *dliged* has a wide semantic range. See *eDIL*, s.v. *dliged* and F. Kelly, *A Guide to Early Irish Law*, p. 309.

> is based on verbal contracts and legal acknowledgement.[94] **Nature is based on concession and proper arrangement**).[95]

The final phrase, *consuiter aicned for logud ⁊ cocorus* is problematic. First, the appropriate sense of *logud* (nominative *logad*, verbal noun of *logaid*, '(a) concedes, remits [...] (b) forgives [...] (c) [...] obtains, acquires [...]'),[96] which has a wide range of meaning, is unclear in this context. This fact is tacitly acknowledged by the editors of *eDIL* who tentatively translate the word in this context as 'concession', though cautiously, with a question mark.[97] This translation is unsatisfactory, since what must be conceded and by whom is unclear. At the same time, my translation of *cocórus* as 'proper arrangement'[98] requires some explanation: the proper arrangement of what? Etymologically, *cocórus* is a combination of *com-* + *córus*,[99] which may shed some light on this matter. The prefix *com-* can serve as an intensifier or it can signify mutual action. The word *córus* carried a sense of correct order or proper arrangement in the cosmos, of which human society was considered a vital element. So, perhaps an appropriate (very technical) translation of *cocórus* in this context might read something like this: 'the proper, mutual-ordering, or harmony between ⟨x⟩ and nature, where "x" is the behaviour (e.g., of a ruler or judge) of consequence to the natural order'.

Returning to the former question: what about signification of *logad*? Rendering it as 'concession' is unclear and leaves one to assume that the term bears some technical sense, now lost. Some light may be shed on the problem by the variant found in MS H. 3. 18 (*Corpus Iuris Hibernici*, 635.1), which differs slightly but significantly from the one given above in BB (*Corpus Iuris Hibernici*, 1591.24). Here, the text omits '⁊' (= *ocus*/ and), instead containing the variant reading *CONSUITER AIGNED FOR LOGAID CO CORUS* (nature is based on concession to proper arrangement), which is perhaps clearer. The underlying sense of the passage would appear to rely on the idea that nature itself (or 'the Law of Nature' as Eoin MacNeill suggests),[100] as one of the three pillars upon which the jurisprudence of the *Féni* relies, observably reflects the concord (or discord) between human judicial action and the cosmos. As such, nature has the power to corroborate (or, presumably, to discredit) law as handed down by humankind: where there is justice, there is harmony; and where there

---

94 Perhaps 'acknowledgement of or submission to legal procedure'.

95 The translation is my own.

96 See *eDIL*, s.v., 1 *logaid*.

97 See *eDIL*, s.v., *logad* (a): 'consuiter aicned for logud *is based upon concession*(?)'.

98 See *eDIL*, s.v., *cocarus*.

99 See John Strachan's comments in 'Review of Fled Bricrend', p. 419; McLeod, 'The Concepts of Law', p. 361, and *eDIL*, s.v. headword *cocarus*.

100 MacNeill, Eoin, 'Ancient Irish Law', p. 272.

is iniquity, chaos ensues. This last translation accords with the one offered by McLeod: 'Nature is established by conciliation and concordance with order'.[101]

A similar idea occurs in *Collectio canonum Hibernensis*, Liber XXI, *De iudicio* (Concerning judgement), where accordance with *natura* is listed as one of the three qualities that reflect a just judgement or truth itself:

> **Liber XXI, *De iudicio*, cap. 6, *De tribus modis, quibus debent iudices iudicare.***
> Augustinus: [...] III modis agnoscitur omne uerum: cum nemo ueniat contra naturam et uerbis scripturæ conueniat, et animis prudentium non desistet.[102]
>
> > **(Liber XXI, *Concerning judgement*, cap. 6, *Concerning the three ways in which judges ought to judge*).**
> > Augustine: [...] Every truth is recognized in three ways: When it does not contravene nature, and when it is consistent with the words of scripture, and when it does not depart from the opinions of the wise).[103]

The same passage is repeated nearly verbatim in the following book, i.e., Liber XXII, *De ueritate* (Concerning truth), cap. 4, *De III-bus modis quibus agnoscitur ueritas* (Concerning the three ways of identifying truth).[104]

These citations, drawn from a variety of law codes both secular and ecclesiastical in their primary orientation and written in both Latin and the vernacular, suggest that the idea expressed in Liber XXIV, *De regno*— that the just behaviour of the king is reflected in the balance of the natural world — had significantly wider currency in early Irish legal thought than previously realized. The notion that the processes of human jurisprudence directly impacted the order and balance of the cosmos not only seems to have survived Christianization but was employed actively and innovatively by ecclesiastically and secularly oriented jurists alike in pursuit of their agendas. Native belief in the causal relationship between human justice and the natural order, while likely pagan in origin, was recast by early Irish ecclesiastical jurists as an aspect of the Law of Nature, wherein divine justice operated through the forces of the universe itself, thereby passing sentence on human conduct by bringing peace and fertility or, alternatively, waste and desolation to the environment. In this way, a feature of native Irish legal thought was preserved, albeit adapted and contextualized within a larger Christian ideological framework. Thus, looking back to

101 MacLeod, 'Concepts of Law', p. 361.
102 *The Hibernensis*, B. I, p. 120.
103 *The Hibernensis*, Bk II, p. 562.
104 *The Hibernensis*, Bk I, p. 142 (text); Bk II, p. 578 (trans.).

Ireland before the coming of the faith, the heralds of the new religion could explain to their converts that this feature of their pre-Christian belief system — which, prior to their conversion they had understood in pagan terms — was, from the perspective of the new religion, a facet of the Law of Nature and, ultimately, an expression of divine will via the Holy Spirit. What is more, this conscious reframing of earlier pagan belief in Christian terms allowed the newly converted Irish to recontextualize their pagan past, without rejecting it, as merely the first stage in the unbroken progression of Christian history. Since Irish theologians adhering to Pelagian doctrine would have understood the Law of Nature, like the Law of Moses, to be a complete dispensation that was fulfilled rather than rescinded by the coming of the New Law, Irish converts could thus look back on their pre-conversion beliefs not with shame and regret, but with the understanding that it was a normal stage in Christian history, upon which the later covenants were built. Understood in this light, their ancient laws and traditions — not to mention their heathen forbears themselves — might be perceived as righteous and moral in Christian terms; not to be forgotten or condemned, but rather to be celebrated.

Despite the careful thought that must have gone into formulating such a detailed and carefully constructed understanding of Christian history, I do not mean to suggest that this accommodation was motivated by a conscious effort on the part of Irish jurists as a group, secular or ecclesiastical, to preserve a feature of native belief for its own sake. More probably, it was the product of devout reasoning by sincerely Christian jurists who perceived no inherent contradiction between pre-Christian Irish legal practice and the new faith, and who genuinely believed that the pagan Irish had lived, as all gentiles prior to their conversion, under the Law of Nature.

What did this theological position entail for the relationship between secular and ecclesiastical jurisprudence in early medieval Ireland? Above all, this Christian ideological framework preserved a place for at least one element of pre-Christian, native ideology which could continue to function with much the same significance as it had before. Given that the stability of society would be shaken if its traditional institutions were overturned wholesale, gestures such as this fostered a situation where the interests of elites with different interests aligned closely. Over time, they became indistinguishable.

This process is witnessed in the textual tradition. For example, the similarities between ecclesiastical texts written in Latin (*Collectio canonum Hibernensis* and *De duodecim abusivis saeculi*) and the vernacular (*Cáin Domnaig* and *Epistil Ísu*), with apparently secular-leaning sapiential literature like *Audacht Morainn* — all somewhat different in genre and orientation and, presumably addressing different audiences — would seem to have emerged out of a single, Christianized ideological tradition.[105] Moreover, similar ideas, for example about the corroborative value of the Law of Nature, as expressed in vernacular law codes often considered predominantly secular (the 'Genuine' Prologue to the *Senchas Már* and *Uraicecht Becc*) and Latin canon law (*Collectio canonum Hibernensis*) uphold the theory that early Irish law was the product of single class of intellectuals.[106] The predominantly Christian orientation of the texts they produced suggests that these individuals were clerics who, though devout in their faith, nonetheless maintained a deep respect for their native traditions. For such individuals, the continued relevance of pre-Christian customs after conversion was not a contradiction, but rather part of the natural process of cultural development for all gentile peoples after conversion.

Very significantly, they understood this Christianized view of Irish legal history as a manifestation of *naturale bonum* (natural good) an example of which, they believed, existed in Ireland before the coming of the faith and informed native practices. As such, they did not see their past as an endangered cultural heritage that had to be justified and self-consciously preserved. On the contrary, they understood their pagan past as a period that all gentile nations experienced prior to conversion. They understood their native customs, including their legal system, as a natural part of Creation and God's plan; something that was not inherently evil, but infused with innate goodness. As a result, traditional practices that did not stand in direct contradiction to Christian teachings, might continue to apply in the new order, though some explanation would be needed.

The doctrine of *naturale bonum* was central to this Irish Christianized worldview. Let us take a more in-depth look at how it was understood in early medieval Ireland. Whereas it would extend well beyond the scope of the present volume to examine this matter in detail throughout the corpus of Irish literature, one example will suffice to make the point. I shall begin by discussing a passage from what would seem to be a purely Christian statute preserved in an ostensibly ecclesiastical context that bears directly on an episode in what appears to be unambiguously secular literature. Take, for example the striking similarity between the punishment set down for killing a dog in *Canones Hibernenses* (Text VI), *De canibus sinodus sapientium* (A Synod of Wisemen Concerning Dogs) and Cú Chulainn's conduct after committing that very crime in a tale included among his

105 For a differing opinion, especially of the close relationship I posit between *Cáin Domnaig* and *Audacht Morainn*, see F. Kelly, *A Guide to Early Irish Law*, pp. 234–36.

106 See Ó Corráin, Breatnach, and Breen, 'The Laws of the Irish', p. 394.

macgnímartha (boyhood deeds) in *Táin Bó Cúailnge* (The Cattle Raid of Cooley):[107]

Comparison of *Canones Hibernenses* and *Táin Bó Cúailnge*[108]

I. from *Canones Hibernenses*, VI.3–4:
3. De his qui canem occident qui custodit peccora uel in domu manet prudentes dicunt: Qui occidit canem qui custodit peccora, .v. uacas reddat pro cane et canem de genere eius reddat, et quodcumque bestiae commedent de peccoribus usque ad caput anni.

4. Item statua prudentium: Qui canem .iiii. hostiorum, id est domus ubi habitat dominus eius et caule ouium et uitulorum et bouum, occidit, .x. uaccas reddat et canem de genere eius opera ipsius facientem, restituat.[109]

> (3. Concerning those who kill a dog that guards the flocks or stays in the house wise men say: He who kills a dog that guards the flocks shall pay five cows for the dog and supply a dog of the same breed and restore whatever wild animals eat from the flock until the end of the year.
>
> 4. Also, the constitutions of the wise: He who kills a dog of the four doors, namely, of the house where his master dwells, and of the fold of sheep, and of the byres of calves and of the oxen — shall pay ten cows and substitute a dog of the same breed that will do the dead one's services).[110]

II. from *Táin Bó Cúailnge* (Rec. I), *Aided con na cerda inso la Coin Culaind ⁊ aní día fil Cú Chulaind fair-seom* (The Killing of the Smith's Hound by Cú Chulainn and the Reason why he is Called Cú Chulainn):

> (⟨Cú Chulainn, until now known by the name Setanta, shows up late for a feast at the home of a smith named Culann, and is attacked by Culann's ferocious dog. Setanta, though only seven years old, kills the dog. When Culann finds out, he is distraught, lamenting aloud⟩:)

107 This correspondence is discussed by Breatnach, 'On the Glossing of the Early Irish Law-Texts'. See also, Ó Cathasaigh, '*Táin bó Cúailnge* and Early Irish Law', pp. 225–26 and Qiu, 'The Ulster Cycle in the Law Tracts'.

108 In O'Rahilly's volume, this section is entitled: *Aided con na cerda inso la Coin Culaind ⁊ aní día fil Cú Chulaind fair-seom* (The Killing of the Smith's Hound by Cú Chulainn and the Reason why he is Called Cú Chulainn).

109 Bieler, *The Irish Penitentials*, p. 174.

110 Bieler, *The Irish Penitentials*, p. 175.

'[...] Is bethu immudu mo bethu ⁊ is trebad immaig mo threbad i ndegaid mo chon. Conággaib ainech ⁊ anmain dam-sa', ol sé, 'in fer muintire ruccad úaim .i. mo chú. Robo dín ⁊ dítiu díar feib ⁊ ar n-indili. Ropo imdegail cacha slabra dún eter mag ⁊ tech'.

> ('[...] My livelihood is now a livelihood wasted, my husbandry a husbandry lost without my hound. The servant who has been taken from me, that is, my hound, maintained life and honour for me. He was defence and protection for my goods and cattle. He guarded all my beasts for me in the field and in house').

⟨Setanta responds, assuring him:⟩

'Ni mór bríg sin trá', ol in gilla. 'Ebéltair culén din chúani chétna lem-sa duit, ⁊ bíam cú-sa do imdegail do chethra ⁊ dot imdegail féin colléic cor ása in cú h-ísin ⁊ corop ingníma. Ocus imdíus-sa Mag Murthemne uile. Nocho mbérthar úaim-se éit ná h-alma ass manip aurderg lim-sa'.

> ('That is no great matter', said the boy. 'A whelp of the same litter will be reared by me for you, and until such time as that hound grows and is fit for action, I myself shall be a hound to protect your cattle and to protect yourself. And I shall protect all Mag Murthemne; neither flock nor herd shall be taken thence from me without my knowing it').[111]

In this passage, save for the payment of restitution, Cú Chulainn behaves, for the most part, according to the provisions stipulated in *Canones Hibernenses*.[112]

Certainly, this similarity could not have resulted by accident. On this general point, Elva Johnston observes:

> How was it possible and why was it desirable for Christian writers to create a secular literature based, to a large degree, on the continual elaboration of native traditions? What on earth does Cú Chulainn have to do with Christ? One answer is that the simple contrast between heroic *fabulae* and religious literature, imagined by Alcuin, or the gulf dividing the pagan classics from scripture, suggested by Jerome, are as rhetorically dramatic as they are psychologically and culturally false [...] Irish ecclesiastical writers seem to have believed that *scéla* and scripture were not necessarily competitors but had the potential to be complementary.[113]

---

111 *Táin bó Cúailnge: Recension I*, pp. 17–19 (text); pp. 140–42 (trans.).

112 For a discussion of the divergences and their potential significance, see Breatnach, 'Glossing of the Early Irish Law-Texts', pp. 19–20.

113 Johnston, *Literacy and Identity in Early Medieval Ireland*, p. 155.

Elsewhere in the same volume she states:

> It seem⟨s⟩ that ⟨Irish vernacular⟩ literature offered far more than the deception of *fabulae*. For some, it was part of the history of Irish salvation and this, in itself, invites further analysis. The good pagans of the pre-Christian past feature heavily in Irish literature and their significance has received detailed treatment in Kim McCone's influential monograph on the subject.[114] This makes a convincing case for the Christian contribution to the vernacular sagas and their conceptualisation as a type of Irish Old Testament.[115]

Furthermore, regarding the law tracts in particular, Robin Chapman Stacey has noticed such correspondences between the laws and the tales are not unusual:

> Even the tales occur almost always in legal contexts, either in actual law tracts or in collections that betray a considerable amount of legal knowledge on the part of their composers. Indeed, it is clear that a good proportion of these tales were actually used in the instruction of apprentice jurists, constituting such a standard item in the oral curriculum of the law schools that they could be referred to in shorthand form. Clearly, the presumption must have been that their general contours and characters would have been well known to all. In fact, storytelling would seem to have ⟨been⟩ an important educational technique for the Irish jurists generally. Law tracts of all traditions and regions made use of this tactic, drawing on characters from the literary realm like Finn, Cú Chulainn or Conchobar's jurist Sencha on the one hand, or characters from the Bible like Lucifer, Adam, or Cain and Abel on the other.[116]

Is it possible that the laws regarding dogs and dog-slaying were so tightly woven into the fabric of Irish society that these texts could have emerged independently, without having influenced one another directly? Discussing the *Canones Hibernenses*, Bieler pointed out that:

> One of the original tracts of the *Senchas Már* was called *Conṡlechta* 'Dog-classes' [...] Only some fragments of the text survive in later commentaries. One is tempted to regard the present section as derived from a latinized version of the lost tract, but there seems to be no correspondence between it and the surviving Irish fragments.[117]

---

114 That is, McCone, *Pagan Past and Christian Present*.
115 Johnston, *Literacy and Identity in Early Medieval Ireland*, p. 134.
116 Stacey, *Dark Speech*, pp. 9–10.
117 Bieler, *The Irish Penitentials*, pp. 8–9.

So, a tract on dog-laws constituted part of the *Senchas Már*,[118] and it is possible that it contained a vernacular version of the provisions contained in the *Canones Hibernenses*; though, if so, it has not survived.

What element of Irish society would have recorded such provisions? Bieler seems certain it emanated from elements outside the Church. He considers these canons to be '⟨a⟩ piece of purely secular legislation',[119] and deems it worthy of note that such non-ecclesiastical matters would have been prescribed by an assembly of apparent ecclesiastical purpose: 'One thing is certain: this is no piece of "ecclesiastical" legislation. All the same, these provisions, like those concerning tithes, are said to have been issued on the authority of a *sinodus sapientium*'.[120] Whatever their putative origins or contents, these provisions, meting out punishments for dog-related infractions, have survived only in a Latin document attributed to the proceedings of a *sinodus*. Is it impossible that such matters could have been adjudicated by the Church? Would these statutes, that essentially address disputes regarding livestock, seem terribly out of place, for example, among the regulations in the Pentateuch concerning cattle, oxen, and sheep?

The relationship between Cú Chulainn's apparently pious behaviour and these canons awaits definitive explanation. It seems improbable that the similarities between the two texts resulted from mere accident. More plausibly, one directly influenced the other, though it is difficult to say in what direction. According to Bieler, the *Canones Hibernenses* is early indeed, likely no later than the mid-seventh century.[121] The dating of the *Táin* episode, on the other hand, is more problematic. Suffice to say that, while the manuscript tradition dates no earlier than *c.* 1100, the extent of its prior history remains a matter of speculation. Certainly, its themes seem to be ancient, to the extent such matters can be assessed. McCone, for example, envisions a kind of totemic myth underlying the tale, arguing that '[t]he Cú Chulainn story clearly involves the permanent and beneficial fusion of the hound's attributes with those of its slayer to produce the perfect warrior [...]'.[122] If McCone's interpretation of the tale is correct, it likely dates back well into prehistoric antiquity; but his thesis, while not implausible, fails to meet the required burden of proof. In the extant written tradition, the Latin canon is at least four centuries earlier (though,

118 For a description, see Breatnach, *A Companion to the Corpus Iuris Hibernici*, pp. 301–02. Incidentally, there was also a legal text on cat laws, *Bretha for Catšlechtaib*, see Breatnach, *A Companion to the Corpus Iuris Hibernici*, p. 301. See also, Kelly, *Early Irish Farming*, index.

119 Bieler, *The Irish Penitentials*, p. 8.

120 Bieler, *The Irish Penitentials*, pp. 8–9.

121 Bieler, *The Irish Penitentials*, p. 9.

122 McCone, *Pagan Past and Christian Present*, p. 64.

admittedly, the *Táin* presumably had a long history prior to the form in which it survives). So, which came first?

I shall merely assert that I find it difficult to believe that there was not some degree of influence, in one direction or another, between these two texts or at least between the traditions they represent: directly or indirectly, either the canon helped shape tale, or it was derived from it. Despite the superficial plausibility of McCone's speculative totemic reading of the Cú Chulainn episode, there are other ways to understand the story, depending on the subject position of the reader. Even if McCone is correct about its mythical origins (though any such mythical origins — if they in fact existed — are so deeply buried in later narrative developments that they are rendered all but imperceptible in the text as it has survived), its synchronic reception by a later, Christian audience would likely have given rise to a different interpretation of the story. From this later perspective, Cú Chulainn's virtuous behaviour toward the smith he inadvertently wronged, for example, would likely have been understood as an *exemplum* of *naturale bonum* among the pagan Irish: a case where one of their celebrated ancient ancestors, living under the *lex naturae*, acted virtuously — analogous to the way a true Christian would behave — out of his own innate goodness prior to the coming of the Faith.

The idea of a pre-Christian *naturale bonum* had a great deal of currency in early Irish religious literature as well.[123] A few examples will suffice to make the point. Charles Donahue, whose two articles on the topic from the 1950s and 60s remain admirable landmarks, points to several early examples in the Irish tradition, including: (1) Murichú's description of Patrick's reception at Inber Sláne by an indentured swineherd in the service '[…] uiri natura boni, licet gentilis, cui nomen erat Díchu […]' ([…] of a man who was good by nature, although a pagan, whose name was Díchu […]);[124] (2) two instances in Adomnán's *Vita Sancti Columbae,* where St Columba baptizes innately virtuous pagans, the first described as '[…] quidam gentilis senex, naturale per totam bonam custodiens uitam' (a certain pagan old man, who has preserved natural goodness throughout his whole life),[125] and another who '[…] naturale bonum per totam uitam usque extremam senectutem conseruantem' ([…] has preserved natural goodness through his whole life, into extreme old age).[126]

From a different genre, I would add another example that sheds light on how the concept of *naturale bonum* was conceived of in early Ireland.

123 A good, basic introduction to the topic, which focuses heavily on Irish material, is Donahue, 'Beowulf, Ireland, and the Natural Good'. See also his follow-on article: 'Beowulf and Christian Tradition', pp. 55–116.

124 Bieler, *Patrician Texts*, p. 78 (text); p. 79 (trans.).

125 *Adomnán's Life of St. Columba*, I.33, p. 62.

126 *Adomnán's Life of St. Columba*, III.14, pp. 200–01.

It is found in the late seventh-century theological tract *Liber de ordine creaturarum*, Liber XII *De natura hominum post peccatum* (Concerning the nature of mankind after sin):

> **CAPUT XII.** *De natura hominum post peccatum*
>
> Sed huius interim orbis habitationi post originale peccatum homines distinati, non totum quod in conditione sua habuerunt **naturale bonum** perdiderunt, sed uitiatum primitus delicto parentis prauis insuper moribus corrumperant. Et ita fit ut, sicut cum labore terrae maledictae fructus percipiunt, sic et bonum naturale quod in se habent non absque laboriosa cura custodire possunt [...].
>
>> (**Chapter 12:** *On the nature of man after sin*
>>
>> But men who were destined to dwell temporarily on this orb after the original sin did not lose all the **natural goodness** they had at the time of their creation, but by their evil habits they further corrupted that goodness which had first been tainted by the sin of their parents. And thus, just as they have to toil to obtain the fruits of the cursed earth, it is only with the most assiduous efforts that they can preserve the natural goodness they have in them [...]).[127]

Expressed in this passage is the idea that at least some degree of natural goodness existed in postlapsarian humankind after the Fall, but prior to Christian redemption. According to this doctrine, humankind's sins debase them but, nonetheless, they possess the innate potential to retain a relict of the *naturale bonum* instilled in them at Creation.[128]

As these examples suggest, the idea of a *naturale bonum* would seem to have had wide currency in early Irish religious belief. In the case of the Cú Chulainn episode discussed above, I would speculate that an Irish intellectual (whether a jurist, a saga-writer, or both) saw the opportunity to portray Cú Chulainn in this light, i.e., as an innately virtuous pagan, acting with an inward light of virtue according to what was later revealed as Christian law. I would argue that the author intentionally shaped the text to that end, with the result that Cú Chulainn, whose general demeanor throughout the *Táin* could hardly be described as the paradigm of Christian rectitude, became in this instance a living model of primeval morality.

---

127 *Liber de ordine creaturarum*, p. 100 (text); p. 101 (trans.). Emphasis my own, in both text and translation.

128 This idea is quite similar to the Pelagian view. For example, Marina Smyth points out that: 'Pelagius devoted the beginning quarter of his Letter to Demetrias to his understanding of bonum naturale, that natural goodness which is part of man's created nature and which the patriarchs of the Old Testament were able to maintain [...]', 'The Seventh-Century Hiberno-Latin Treatise Liber de ordine creaturarum', p. 197 n. 151.

This point informs the question I raised above concerning the lack of religious allusions in *Audacht Morainn*. Given its close, verbal relationships with other overtly ecclesiastical texts (i.e., with *Cáin Domnaig, Epistil Ísu* and with the excerpts cited above from *Collectio canonum Hibernensis* and *De duodeim abusivis saeculi*), why does this text lack unambiguous, overt Christian references? Perhaps in *Audacht Morainn* we have another reflex of a literary gesture similar to the one I have argued motivated the author of the Cú Chulainn story. Morann, a mythical judge whose legend dates back into Celtic antiquity,[129] was a legendary pre-Christian jurist with numerous tracts attributed to his name,[130] and whose *bretha* (judgements) are included in the list of pre-Christian legal texts mentioned in the Pseudo-historical Prologue to the *Senchas Már*.[131] Perhaps, then, the author of his *Audacht* intentionally constructed the text so that it was spoken in a pre-Christian voice — that is, in the imagined, first-person voice of a virtuous, innately righteous pagan infused with *naturale bonum* proclaiming justice in pre-conversion Ireland.[132]

This theory is bolstered by the fact that elsewhere Morann is characterized as having received prognostic awareness of Christianity during the pagan period. Donnchadh Ó Corráin has described a series of excerpts dating from the Old and Middle Irish periods that narrate various means by which his conversion occurred. In one story, Morann received a magical collar directly from the apostle Paul, preventing him from uttering false judgements; in another, he receives a vision as an infant prodding him to sing a poem calling on everyone to praise the Christian God.[133] These tales point to a literary tradition in which the poet Morann obtained knowledge of Christianity preternaturally, before the advent of Christianity with the legendary coming of Patrick. Obviously, this tradition does not appear in *Audacht Morainn*. There, Morann's judgements are presented, without explanation, as the proverbs of an intrinsically righteous pre-Christian sage. Here, I would argue, an author deliberately cast Morann in this way in order to characterize him as an example of *naturale bonum* in pre-Christian Ireland, whose sapiential advice was fully in accordance with the Law of Nature, albeit unwittingly. Moreover, Christian scholars could point to the similarities between Morann's *Audacht* and canon law (as I have done in the comparisons above) — just as I have argued one could point to similarities between Cú Chulainn's behaviour and the *Canones Hibernenses* — to show that at least some pre-Christian Irish pagans could

---

129 See *Audacht Morainn*, pp. 22–23.

130 See Breatnach, *A Companon to the Corpus Iuris Hibernici*, p. 366.

131 See Carey, 'An Edition of the Pseudo-historical Prologue', pp. 13 and 19.

132 My speculative conclusion on this point differs starkly from Fergus Kelly's: see *A Guide to Early Irish Law*, p. 236.

133 Ó Corráin, 'Irish Vernacular Law and the Old Testament', pp. 286–87 and especially n. 5.

act by nature in accordance with divine precepts because of their innate goodness. Gestures of this sort (of which these are but two examples), though obviously contrived, served an agenda: they provided ecclesiastical Irish jurists with an opportunity to lay a solid ideological foundation for the legal system that recognized the superiority of church law while, at the same time, preserving the validity of certain pre-Christian, native practices. It is a strategy that could only have been deployed by scholars literate in more than one genre; or who — at the very least — frequently rubbed shoulders with colleagues expert in very different learned professions.

CHAPTER 5

Pseudo-history

Pseudo-history and Early Irish Law

The formation of a legendary 'synthetic' or 'pseudo' history to celebrate the origins of a nation is a feature common to many cultures worldwide.[1] With these stories, the imagined deeds of revered forbears in the ancient past serve to unite a people around a common mythology, to situate them within a historical teleology promising an idealized future, and/or to explain (or, just as often, to explain away) ideological problems or inconsistencies in the accepted narrative of a nation's history. As such, pseudo-history, while having little if any bearing on the real past, is a goldmine of information about the contemporary concerns of a culture. The tales that resonate with a culture when authors concoct its fictional origins and the issues they seek to address with these tales reveal much about its contemporary zeitgeist.

Composed from ancient times, Christian histories and chronologies by patristic authors such as Tertullian, Cyprian, Eusebius, Sulpicius Severus, Orosius, etc., laid the groundwork for national histories by authors such as Cassiodorus, Jordanes, Gregory of Tours, Isidore, Bede, Paul the Deacon, and others named, anonymous, and pseudonymously ascribed. In the earliest period and often thereafter, the authors of these pseudo-historical tales tended to harmonize, or at least synchronize, their narratives within the broader framework of Christian history. Over the course of the early Middle Ages, however, alternative sources emerged — legendary, mythological, and otherwise — from which various peoples derived their national origins. In the mid-seventh century, for example, the so-called 'Chronicle of Fredegarius' traced Frankish origins to Troy and the wanderings of individual heroes in the aftermath of the Trojan War, a surrogate for biblical chronology that became increasingly popular over the course of the Middle Ages.[2] The earliest Celtic example of this genre, the ninth-century *Historia Brittonum* pseudonymously ascribed to the

1 For recent scholarship on origin legends from Western Europe, See Brady and Wadden, eds, *Origin Legends in Early Medieval Western Europe*.

2 The two alternatives were not necessarily mutually exclusive. One finds numerous early medieval genealogies, for example, that trace noble lineage through both mythic (Trojan or otherwise) and biblical figures.

Welsh-speaking author Nennius (writing in Latin), similarly traced British descent from a Trojan lineage, a theme later picked up and elaborated by Geoffrey of Monmouth in his twelfth-century *De Gestis Brittonum*.[3]

In Ireland, and indeed throughout the early medieval Insular world, pseudo-history became an especially important and well-developed genre, as Lindy Brady has recently demonstrated.[4] The most famous example is the Middle Irish *Lebor Gabála Érenn* (The Book of the Taking of Ireland), an eleventh- and twelfth-century compilation of mythological and pseudo-historical lore, that brings together materials dating from as far back as the seventh century.[5] Lindy Brady describes it as such:

> The Lebor Gabála Érenn is a compilation of Irish origin material which was first put together in the eleventh century but which clearly drew on older literary traditions that no longer survive independently in addition to the known material that it incorporates. The Lebor Gabála incorporates a wide range of sources including classical and late antique geographical and encyclopaedic works, biblical texts, contemporaneous Irish material, and the other texts in the early insular corpus of historical and pseudohistorical works.[6]

This massive work is remarkable for its syncretism of widely divergent source material, harmonizing euhemerized pagan myth with biblical and patristic histories. As John Carey described it:

> Bringing together a heterogeneous body of legends and speculations regarding the ancient history and origins of its people, and fitting them into a single comprehensive framework, *Lebar Gabála* provided a narrative extending from the creation of the world to the coming of Christianity, and beyond — a national myth which sought to put Ireland on the same footing with Israel and Rome. In the centuries that followed, its doctrines served as foundation and backdrop for legend, historiography, poetry, and political thought.[7]

A full discussion of this vastly important work, including its sources and the traditions it represents, lies well beyond the scope of the present discussion.[8] For present purposes, suffice to say that, despite its eleventh-century date, *Lebor Gabála* is a compilation of significantly earlier mate-

3 See Summerfield, 'Filling the Gap', and Brady, *The Origin Legends*, p. 52.

4 Brady, *The Origin Legends*.

5 *Lebor Gabála Érenn*.

6 Brady, *The Origin Legends*, p. 60.

7 Carey, *The Irish National Origin-Legend*, p. 1.

8 Moreover, it has been expertly described elsewhere. See Carey, *Irish National Origin-Legend*, pp. 1–24 and Scowcroft, '*Leabhar Gabhála*, Part I' and his follow-on article: '*Leabhar Gabhála*, Part II'. See also Carey, 'Native Elements in Irish Pseudohistory'.

rial. As evidence, one finds, for example, that the *Historia Brittonum*,[9] composed roughly two centuries before the earliest surviving version of *Lebor Gabála*, nonetheless included two sections about Ireland, both of which bear close resemblance to episodes in *Lebor Gabála*.[10] At least one of these sections in the *Historia Brittonum*, ascribed there to *peritissimi Scottorum* (Irish scholars),[11] almost certainly draws on pre-existing Irish pseudo-historical lore. The existence of such parallels in a much earlier British text suggests that the core (at least) of some portions of *Lebor Gabála* circulated widely and attracted sufficient popularity to have survived exportation more than two centuries before the earliest manuscript witness.

Many early examples of Irish pseudo-history survive, and all evidence would seem to indicate that the Irish *literati* of various orientations maintained longstanding interest in this robust and thriving genre.[12] It is important to emphasize, however, that prior to *Lebor Gabála* no single version of events emerged as the canonical, generally accepted Irish origin legend (if, in fact, *Lebor Gabála* itself can be accorded that status). Even within this work, the author(s) and/or redactor(s) frequently included alternative and sometimes conflicting versions of a single event. The goal of individual stories, later gathered and stitched together into the more-or-less-continuous narrative we now call *Lebor Gabála*, would appear to have been aimed more at addressing specific ideological issues arising from particular events, rather than at crafting a complete, internally consistent account of Irish history. One gets the impression that, in the early period, tales were crafted to meet the needs of contemporary circumstances: some proportionately more derivative of biblical lore, some of euhemerized pagan myth, and some of legend, native or imported.

By any measure, *Lebor Gabála*'s complex interlace of narrative threads from multifarious sources warrants admiration. In what sense, however, did the authors expect it to be received as history? Individual episodes are often quite fantastical in nature, raising a host of questions about their intended truth-value. Indeed, certain tales within *Lebor Gabála* seem so gratuitous — for example, the story explaining how an early proto-Irish jurist named Caí Caínbrethach studied law under Moses during the Exodus (!) and subsequently brought it back to Ireland — that one cannot help but wonder if they were ever intended to be understood as historical, factual truth in literal terms. Reading certain portions of the text, I cannot help but wonder if they were crafted in a native tradition analogous to

9 See Nennius, *British History*.

10 See Carey, *Irish National Origin-Legend*, pp. 5–7.

11 See Nennius, *British History*, § 15, p. 62 (text); p. 21 (trans.).

12 Some of the earliest sources are discussed in Carney, 'The Dating of Archaic Irish Verse', especially pp. 52–53.

midrash,[13] i.e., as a kind of secular-homiletic narrative explaining canonical events with parable-like stories, not purporting to recount facts *per se* (or to be received as such), but rather to elucidate an underlying moral or cultural truth, or to address a contemporary ideological dilemma. The answer to this question, while certain to be elusive, has the potential to reveal much about the relationship between author and audience in early medieval Ireland. Addressing the truth-value of such stories, Donnchadh Ó Corráin observed:

> These ⟨pseudo-historical⟩ interpretations are expressed as dramatic narratives [...]. I do not hold that the scholars who wrote and re-wrote these narratives believed them to be literally true, to be what actually happened in the Rankean sense. Rather, the tales are discourses in symbolic form (like 'leading' cases in Irish law which explain the origin and purpose of some legal institutions) within a well-practised genre familiar to the intended readership or audience. They are narrative devices by which abstract ideas are conveyed and may be understood on a number of different levels, varying with the degree of understanding and intention the reader or hearer brings to the text. The level of authorial consciousness and the precise relationship of their scholarly creators to the tales are no doubt as complex as that of the modern historian to his interpretive hypotheses and pose problems of epistemological interest.[14]

How these pseudo-historical texts were understood by a contemporary audience is a topic that would benefit greatly from further research by narrative theorists. Clearly, there were multiple levels of interpretation at play beyond the literal, though it is by no means immediately obvious what these may be or how they functioned.[15]

---

13 Here, I am using the term 'midrash' not in its strict, technical sense, but in its less formal colloquial usage. See: *Oxford English Dictionary*, s.v. 'midrash', meaning 2: 'Usu. with lower-case initial. In extended use: this style of commentary ⟨i.e., from meaning 1, "[...] non-literal interpretation and legendary illustration [...]"⟩ applied to other literature [...]'. Martin McNamara has published two articles on midrash and its role in Irish literature, 'Midrash, Culture Medium and Development of Doctrine', and another, separate article confusingly with a similar title 'Midrash, Apocrypha, Culture Medium and Development of Doctrine'. Elizabeth Boyle's comments about 'truth without fidelity', regarding Irish storytelling in *History and Salvation*, p. 53 may also be apropos of this point.

14 Ó Corráin, 'Irish Vernacular Law and the Old Testament', p. 290. On the question of the truth-value of early Irish narratives, particularly the distinction between *historia* and *fabula*, see Sims-Williams and Poppe, 'Medieval Irish Literary Theory', pp. 302–07 and Poppe, *Of Cycles and Other Critical Matters*.

15 That said, at least some of these stories were regarded as literally true, a belief that persisted in some circles into the previous century. Carey, *Irish National Origin-Legend*, p. 2 and n. 4. See also: Binchy, 'The Pseudo-historical Prologue', p. 16.

Regardless of how they were received, the implications of these narratives for Irish legal history are important and far-reaching. Addressing the Irish legal pseudo-historical tradition as a whole, Donnchadh Ó Corráin made the following assessment:

> This extensive development of narrative materials is significant in a number of ways. No doubt it represents a defense of the Irish legal system as a whole in different times and circumstances and a justification of the practice of law, especially by clerics, but it is much more. It projects the Irish legal tradition backwards in time to venerable antiquity, to the very beginning of Irish history, and it provides a framework within which to justify legal practices which self-evidently did not derive from the authoritative source of law: revelation, and the interpretation of revelation by the Fathers and other Christian authorities. These texts of different date — some are much later than the Old Irish period, some early — bear witness to a lengthy concern (within an unbroken literary tradition stretching over many centuries) with the problem of the relationship of native law with natural law and the Mosaic law. The problem is approached consciously and in clearly defined terms, and somewhat varied solutions are proposed: native law is natural law in the Pauline sense, it is natural law as was the law of the pre-Mosaic period, it is essentially Mosaic law.[16]

Ó Corráin's analysis of the material is convincing. Above all, these narratives sought to ground Irish jurisprudence on solid ideological bedrock by formulating theologically innocuous explanations for the relationship between ecclesiastical and native law without compromising the basic tenets of either. In the early period most of all, early Irish historians preferred to situate the origin and development of their native judicial system within a Christian historical framework. However, at no time was a single version of events canonized. On the contrary, the imaginative construction of a theologically acceptable account of early Irish legal origins was an ongoing process: various strategies were employed over a long span of literary history, a fact which attests to a significant level of concern surrounding this important legal-theological dilemma in early Irish society. Given the high degree of variation, both diachronic and synchronic, within the tradition, is it possible to make any claims about the overall character of Irish legal pseudo-history that go beyond Ó Corráin's general assessment? Acknowledging that many difficulties exist, this is what I shall attempt to do in the remainder of section. To this end, I shall examine the strategies employed by early Irish lawyer-theologians and the implications of the narratives

16 Ó Corráin, 'Irish Vernacular Law and the Old Testament', p. 290.

they produced by conducting a detailed analysis first of the excerpt about Caí Caínbrethach (referred to above) and then, in the section that follows, of the Pseudo-historical Prologue to the *Senchas Már*.

Proceeding with caution, it is possible, I would argue, to make several descriptive claims about medieval Irish pseudo-history. First, albeit with some exceptions, early Irish historians seem to have preferred to situate, or at least synchronize, their imagined past within a biblical, as opposed to a Romano-Trojan framework. While examples of the latter can be found in later Irish literature, the predominant choice, especially in the early period, appears to have been biblical and specifically Old Testament. Second, pseudo-history seems to have been widely exploited in legal circles, particularly to address a variety of ideological dilemmas.

Let me turn to a story relating the adventures of Caí Caínbrethach and how he brought the Mosaic Law into Ireland prior to the conversion. The events of this episode are situated within the overall narrative framework of what eventually became the *Lebor Gabála*, though the story itself is not preserved there. Although found in a number of texts (with varying details), the fullest version of the story appears among a collection of legal materials related to the *Senchas Már* tradition in MS Trinity College Dublin 1336 (formerly H 3. 17).[17] Here, the story about Caí tops the list of famous early Irish jurists, itself situated between fragments of the Pseudo-historical Prologue to the *Senchas Már*.[18] The episode explains the origins of both Irish law and the Irish themselves simultaneously as part of the same overall narrative describing the Exodus of the Hebrews from Egypt and the events immediately preceding it. In this story, the Irish are portrayed as descendants of a marriage between Scot (elsewhere 'Scota'), Pharaoh's daughter (hence their later designation as *Scotti*), and Nél, son of Fénius Farsaid (an important ancestor credited, among other accomplishments, with the synthetic formulation of the Irish language).[19] To be sure, this short tale is by no means the sole, or even the most widespread, among the various Irish origin legends. Numerous stories in well-developed pseudo-historical narratives woven over the course of Irish literary history traced Irish national origins variously back to Scythia, Egypt, Israel, Spain, and other locations. The main interest of this particular story is that it posits an origin not only for the Irish themselves, but also

17 Other versions of the story exist dating back to the Old Irish period, suggesting that it had longstanding and wide currency in Irish circles. See: Ó Corráin, 'Irish Vernacular Law and the Old Testament', pp. 289–90 and n. 16.

18 See Carey, 'An Edition of the Pseudo-historical Prologue', pp. 1–2.

19 On the lineage of Fénius Farsaid, see: Carey, 'The Ancestry of Fénius Farsaid'. For the story relating Fénius's creation of the Irish language out of seventy-two separate languages after the biblical episode of the Tower of Babel, see Ahlqvist, *The Early Irish Linguist*, pp. 40–41 and 47–48. This is not the only version of the story.

for Irish law, at least for the persistent claim of direct Mosaic influence on pre-Christian Irish law.

I shall begin with the episode describing Caí's adventures:

> CETNA UGDUR *CET*AROBUIDH I NEIRINN AIMEIRGIN GLUINGEAL in file, dalt*a* cai cainbr*ethaig* eiside, in dala desci*pul* .lxx.*at* scoile feiniusa farrsaidh IS e in cae-isin forroglainn r*echt* muisi re taid*echt* anair, ⁊ it br*etha* r*ech*ta nob*er*et; ⁊ is aml*aid* in*n*ust*ar* sin: IN tan im̃ rofuidi feinius a da deiscip*ul* .uii.m*og*et do fogluim na nilb*erla* fon doman, cæ dan*o* as e rosiacht co eighipt, gerbo do eb*r*aidib a bunudus, ⁊ rofogluim a mb*er*la negebtacc*a*, ⁊ as e atcuaidh do *for*ann do rig egeptaca scæil*ed* na scoil*e* fon doman uile & la cai dochuadur na t*e*chta o forann do chuincidh feiniusa cuice; ⁊ ba si t*r*a fochc*r*ic tucc doib scot i*ngen* fo*r*uind do tabuirt do nel m*ac* feiniusa; innde dr̃ scuit o scotaib IAr t*echt* don scoil cuna naiti leo co forund, rofogluimestur a mb*erla* neg*eptach* la cai ISi-sin aimsir i ndenta na hairde mor*a* i negept .i. an ecplagh ⁊ ailia q*uae* in lege s*r*ipta ⟨sic.⟩ sunt ⁊ c̃c̃a O 'dconnuirc t*ra* feinius ⁊ na huile suid na br*eth*a mor donidis p*er* seruos dei, dotheghdis dia fogluim leo, ar doruirmenait*er* ba t*r*ia *for*c*raid* neolusa ⁊ frithgnama łsaruidhdis isr*e*ld*ai* na druidhe egept*acha* ⁊ dognidis ina airdhe imda ⁊rl- IN tan t*r*a rocuatar isr*eld*ai*d*aidh for teith*ed*, tainicc cæ la muisi IN sco*il*(?) olcena roecluidhsiut ar oman na nairde reimep*er*ta gin t*echt* isin sluaig*ed* la forund; et ar oman foruinn ⁊ aithb*ir* iar tiachtuin, doluid feinius for muir Robui t*r*a cai i caomnacht muisi f*r*isin ré-sin ⁊ robui ina gnais ac tuid*echt tar*sin dithrib, gur scarustur riu iar fogluim ⁊ r*ech*ta muisi; ⁊ ni do tir tairrngire son s̃ isin ng*r*eg co roibe i t*r*acia [...] Doluid dĩ cae laisin luinges doluidh a t*r*acia i nairrchis a muindt*iri* feisin, et rotaibein doib a gres o roscarsat .i. r*echt* de do dainib ⁊ a b*r*etha IAr sin t*r*a ba cai ba bre*ith*em laisin luinges uile [...].[20]
>
> (The first author that ever was in Ireland was Aimirgin Glúingeal the poet. He was a foster-son of Caí Caínbrethach, one of the 72 disciples of the school of Fénius Farsaid. It was that Caí who learned the Law of Moses before he came from the east and he gave judgements according to the Law ⟨of Moses⟩, and thus that matter is related. When Fénius sent his 72 disciples to learn the many languages throughout the world, it was Caí who went to Egypt, though he was a Hebrew by origin, and he learned the Egyptian language. He told Pharaoh about the dispersal of the school throughout the world and it was with Caí that the messengers came from Pharaoh asking Fénius to come to him. And the reward

20 The text is from *Corpus Iuris Hibernici*, 1653.16–39, 1654.5–7.

> he gave them was that Scot, daughter of Pharaoh, was given to Nél son of Fénius. Hence the Irish are called Scotti. When the school and their teacher had come to Pharaoh they learned Egyptian with Caí. This is the time when the great signs were wrought in Egypt i.e. the plague *et ailia quae in lege scripta sunt et cetera*. When Fénius and all the scholars saw the great judgements which were performed *per seruos Dei* they went to learn with them for they considered that it was through superior knowledge and application that the Israelites outdid the Egyptian druids and performed many signs. When the Israelites went in flight, Caí went with Moses. The school fled in terror of the signs already mentioned, did not go on the hosting with Pharaoh, and for fear of Pharaoh and his reproach on his return, Fénius put to sea. Caí remained in the company of Moses at this time and he was with him while crossing the desert and he parted from them ⟨the Israelites⟩ after he learned the Law of Moses. He did not go to the Promised Land but to Greece and he lived in Thrace [...]. Caí came with the fleet which came from Thrace to meet his own people and he showed them his achievement since they parted viz., the Law of God for men and His judgements. After that Caí was judge for the whole fleet).[21]

Although this is a Middle Irish account of the story, it is closely related to earlier versions, as Boyle points out.[22] A first point of interest is that, although a primary aim of this story was, apparently, to posit an organic connection between pre-Christian Irish law and the Law of Moses, there is no attempt to claim that the Irish are God's Chosen People, equivalent in any way (literally or metaphorically) to the Israelites.[23] Indeed, the author seems at pains to make clear that the Irish were not one and the same with the Israelites, and — especially — that they *did not* enter the Promised Land. True, in this version, Caí is referred to as a Hebrew (though in other versions of this story he is described as an Egyptian or of undetermined ethnic origin); but the *Scotti*, i.e., those who eventually became the Irish, are described as the offspring of the eponymous Scot, Pharaoh's daughter, and Nél, son of Fénius Farsaid (who was not a Hebrew). Though not stated in this text, Fénius had a biblical lineage, variously traced at

21 The translation is by Ó Corráin, 'Irish Vernacular Law and the Old Testament', pp. 288–89. See also: Boyle, History and Salvation, pp. 13–14.

22 Boyle, *History and Salvation*, p. 14.

23 See especially, O'Brien, 'The New Israel Motif', pp. 246–50. O'Brien discusses different versions of this story, ultimately concluding on p. 255 that: 'The Irish scholars who over long generations sought to bring their people's origin legend in line with the history they knew from the Old Testament, did so in an ad hoc manner which followed no set model of how to make the Gaels a New Israel'.

several removes (depending on the version) back to Noah's son Japheth.[24] Elsewhere, including the Irish *Sex Aetates Mundi* and Recension 1 of the *Lebor Gabála*, Fénius is identified as the primary ancestor of the Scythians,[25] reflecting a long pseudo-historical tradition that traces Gaelic origins to that region.[26] A second, notable point of interest is that the text explicitly states that the offspring of Scot and Nél, who we might call the 'pre-settlement' or 'proto-' Irish, *did not* accompany the Israelites on the Exodus or enter the Promised Land: Caí alone remained with Moses, studying the Law. Later, however, Caí too parted from the Israelites — significantly, and the text is explicit about this point — *before they entered the Promised Land.* He later rejoined the *Scotti* to become their chief judge.

Thus, although the Irish, by this account, believed they had received the Law of Moses nearly from the inception of their existence as a people — indeed, from before the time when their ancestors first set foot in Ireland — they *did not* claim to be God's Chosen People, i.e., they did not claim to be Hebrews in any literal sense, nor did any of their ancestors enter the Promised Land with the Israelites.[27] Apparently, they conceived of themselves as gentiles, albeit with a biblical lineage, clearly situated as such within biblical history, and took pains — as this narrative suggests — to emphasize that point. This fact has important implications in biblical law. The decision of the Synod of Jerusalem specified that gentiles were not subject to the Mosaic injunction in its entirety — that is, in the

---

24 See Carey, 'The Ancestry of Fénius Farsaid', pp. 104–12.

25 *The Irish Sex Aetates Mundi*, § 25, ll. 16–17, p. 74.

26 Carey, 'The Ancestry of Fénius Farsaid', p. 107.

27 In *History and Salvation*, p. 2, Elizabeth Boyle came to a very different conclusion about these stories: 'It is one of the contentions of the present study that the sources composed in early Christian Ireland, for all intents and purposes, reinvented Ireland: they fabricated a new historical narrative, new origin legends and new mythologies; produced an imagined pre-history for Ireland; and developed new social institutions and hierarchies, which fashioned Ireland according to predominantly Old Testament models and placed the Irish firmly within the scheme of salvation history as "God's chosen people"'. The disparity in our findings may result from two factors. First, that her study focuses primarily on literature while mine focuses on legal materials. Second, given the diversity of the views among the early Irish *literati*, it seems reasonable to expect that different views (about this matter and others) might exist simultaneously among various individuals and groups of the educated elite. Later in the same volume (p. 7), Boyle states: 'Medieval Irish views of the origins of the Gaelic-speaking population of Ireland were intensely complex and frequently contradictory, and the current state of scholarship is such that it is unclear whether these contradictions indicate that there were once entirely distinct origin legends, circulating in different parts of the island or amongst different parts of society'. Given the close relationship between early Irish origin legends and the way these stories constructed the role of the Irish in sacred history, I am inclined to read these passages together as evidence that Irish views on their relationship with the Divine as God's Chosen People — or not — varied among different segments of literate society. In legal milieux, however, my observations in this volume suggest that there was deeply held scepticism that the Irish held any such status.

post-conversion era. What about the pre-conversion era? This situation had no precedent: here, the Irish were cast in the unique position of being the only non-Jews to have received the Mosaic Law prior to the advent of Christianity.[28] Yet, neither Fénius, who departed with his people by sea before the Exodus, nor Caí, who accompanied Moses on part of the Exodus, entered the Promised Land, nor expressed any intention of doing so. While Fénius and the proto-Irish wandered for a period of time before reaching their eventual homeland — perhaps inviting some kind of loose analogy to the Israelites on the Exodus — this tacit comparison, if it was intended at all — is never expressed as an equivalence. While the *Scotti* may be similar to the Hebrews — perhaps more than any other non-Jewish people, given their direct, pre-conversion knowledge of the Mosaic Law — the relationship is one of analogy, not identity. The Irish were not literally Jews, and Ireland was not literally Canaan.

I wish to emphasize how the author of the story cited above specifically mentioned that, although Caí Caínbrethach accompanied Moses on the Exodus, he *did not* enter the Promised Land. This detail underscores an important theological point that, I would argue, early Irish legalists were keen to accentuate. Notice how, according to this story, the Irish had, in effect, received the Law of Moses without the Mosaic Covenant. In this way, they understood their place, at this point in sacred history, as pre-conversion gentiles under the dispensation of the Law of Nature; as a people who had received the letter, though not the spirit of the Mosaic Law. From this perspective, thus, the Irish remained — at this particular juncture in their imagined place in sacred history — subject to the equivalent (or perhaps an enhancement) of the Law of Nature, informed by Mosaic precepts but without becoming contractually bound by the Mosaic Covenant. So, this story allowed early Irish legalists to explain the influence of the Law of Moses on their own, pre-conversion law without adopting the theologically hazardous position that they were literally God's Chosen People or that Ireland was actually a New Israel.

In this way, they were able to emphasize the importance of the influence of Mosaic precepts on their pre-conversion laws without having to imagine that their pagan ancestors were therefore bound by the requirements of the Mosaic Law. This point is implicit in *Sanas Cormaic*, where the 'judgements of the law' (*bretha rechta*) are considered to be part of the overall native Irish legal system (*bérla*):

28 All indications suggest that they took the role quite seriously, establishing certain institutions described in the Old Testament throughout Irish society. See Ó Corráin, 'Irish Vernacular Law and the Old Testament', pp. 294–307.

[...] Cāí Cāínbrethach, dalta Feniusa, iss ē in deiscibul sin rosīacht Maccu Israheil fri fogloim n-ebra [...] is aire asberar Cāí Cāínbrethach de; fobīth it bretha rec[h]ta nobeired, ⁊ is aire it imda issin bērla.[29]

> ([...] Caí Caínbrethach, the fosterling of Fénius, he is that disciple who went with the Sons of Israel to study the Hebrew language [...] it for this he is called 'Caí Caínbrethach' ⟨i.e., Caí of the Just Judgements⟩, because they are judgements of the Law ⟨*recht*⟩[30] that he gave, and it is for this that they are abundant in the Irish legal system ⟨*bérla*⟩).[31]

Likewise, in a variant reading of the Pseudo-historical Prologue to the *Senchas Már*, the judge and poet Dubthach maccu Lugair described the nature of pre-Christian Irish law to Patrick in terms that deliberately — from the point of view of the text's clerical author, though, from Dubthach's point of view, unwittingly — echo the famous dictum from the Old Law requiring an eye for an eye:[32] 'is ed robai f*or*do cind i *n*dEiri*n*d breth rechta .i. indech*ad* eisidhi, cos i cois ⁊ suil i suil ⁊ ainm i n.-anm',[33] (what was before you in Ireland was judgement of law, that is retribution, a foot for a foot and an eye for an eye and a life for a life).[34] Ideologically, this pseudo-historical origin for the Irish legal system allowed jurists to posit a close relationship between pre-Christian, native law and the Law of Moses. Native Irish law, in this schema, was not merely the Law of Nature (in the Pauline or Pelagian sense) but, more than that, it was the Law of Nature infused with and enhanced by precepts drawn directly from the Law of Moses. From a purely legal perspective, therefore, the Irish were equivalent to Jews; within sacred history, however, they never entered into the Mosaic Covenant and therefore remained gentiles.

---

29 The text is from '*Sanas Cormaic*', p. 14.

30 As mentioned above, *recht* (law), has a wide range of meaning. Among these is the 'Law of Moses', though I have been cautious throughout not to translate *recht* with this more specific sense unless the context justifies it. In this particular context, *recht* clearly was intended to signify the 'Law of Moses'.

31 The translation is my own. Unmodified, *bérla* (= Old Irish *bélrae*) literally means 'speech, language'. See *eDIL*, s.v. *bélrae*. In the phrase *bélrae Féine*, it means 'the Language of the Féne', i.e., 'the language of the native laws'. Likewise, a *suí bérla* is 'a doctor of the "Bérla Féine"'. In this context *bérla* should be translated as 'the law of the Féne, native law, the native Irish legal system'.

32 Compare Exodus 21:23–27, Leviticus 24:17–21, Deuteronomy 19:21. Also, Christ refers to this precept in Matthew 5:38–39.

33 The text is from Carey, 'An Edition of the Pseudo-historical Prologue', p. 14 (in the notes to § 5). See also: McLeod, 'The Concept of Law', p. 366 and McCone, 'Dubthach maccu Lugair', p. 12. Note also that John Carey, in 'The Two Laws', p. 10, sees this passage as a later interpolation: 'it appears most reasonable to see this passage, and its ideology, as innovations extraneous to the original text'.

34 The translation is from McCone, 'Dubthach maccu Lugair', p. 12.

Thus, for the Irish at this stage of their self-conceived, pseudo-historical narrative, the Mosaic Law — received unsteeped in spiritual significance — might best be described as an enhanced equivalent of Law of Nature. This idea, that is, that the Mosaic Law is essentially Natural Law in a more perfect form, has precedent in patristic thought. Irenaeus (d. 202), for example, considered the Decalogue to be one and the same with the Law of Nature, and — further — claimed that God later imposed the full yoke of Mosaic Law on the Jews in order to bring them back in line with the Law of Nature, though God (according to Irenaeus) also added some special commandments at that time.[35] Ascetic Movement doctrine went even farther. For them, the (Mosaic) Law was inherent in nature; and, therefore, a reasoned understanding of the natural world ought to lead gentiles to both the Law and to knowledge of the Creator. Furthermore, Ascetic Movement doctrine held that the failure of gentiles to do so was a moral lapse tantamount to sin. Therefore, in this view, gentiles (who had no knowledge of the Law) were just as culpable for transgression as Jews (to whom God bestowed the Law directly), even prior to their conversion, since they were obliged to apply their reason actively to derive knowledge of the Creator and his Law from the nature of the cosmos itself. Pelagius expressed this idea most clearly in the Prologue to his commentary on the book of Romans in *Expositiones XIII Epistularum Pauli*, where he explained:

> [...] ambos uero populos et scienter et grauiter deliquisse, Iudaeos quod per praeuaricationem legis deum inhonorauerint, gentes uero quod, cum cognitum de creatura creatorem ut deum debuerint uenerari, gloriam eius in manu facta mutauerint simulacra.[36]
>
>> ([...] both peoples sinned knowingly and gravely, the Jews inasmuch as they dishonored God by transgression of the law, the Gentiles in that, although they ought to have worshipped God as the Creator revealed by the creation, they changed his glory into idols fashioned by hand).[37]

Augustine attributed similar views to Pelagius in *De gratia Christi et de peccato originali libri duo*, explicitly stating that Pelagius believed (1) that God imposed the Law of Moses to restore the Law of Nature, and (2) that gentiles were responsible for deriving not merely knowledge of the Creator — but knowledge of the Law as well — by applying their reason to nature:

> [...] ⟨Pelagius dicit⟩ 'primum uixisse iustos homines ex natura, deinde sub lege, tertio sub gratia — ex natura, scilicet ab Adam tam longe aetate, qua lex nondum erat data — tunc enim' [ille dicit] 'duce

35 See Irenaeus of Lyons, *Adversus Haereses*, 4.15.1.

36 The text is from Pelagius, *Expositions*, p. 7.

37 The translation is from Pelagius, *Commentary on St. Paul's Epistle to the Romans*, p. 58.

ratione cognoscebatur creator et quemadmodum uiuendum esset scriptum gerebatur in cordibus, non lege litterae, sed naturae. uerum uitiatis moribus,' ⟨Pelagius dicit⟩, 'ubi coepit non sufficere natura iam decolor, lex addita est, qua uelut l⟨i⟩ma fulgori pristino detrita rubigine redderetur'.[38]

(⟨Pelagius says⟩ that people first lived righteously by nature, then under the law, and thirdly under grace. By nature, that is, from Adam during the long period before the law had been given. ⟨He says⟩, Then the creator was known by the guidance of reason, and people carried how they should live inscribed on their hearts, not from written law, but from the law of nature. But, when nature was tarnished by corrupt morals and ceased to be sufficient, the law was added to it so that nature might be restored to its pristine brilliance with the rust scoured away as if by lime).[39]

Finally, a later Insular example of a similar vein of thought is found in Alcuin's *Quaestiones in Genesim*:

Inter. 14. Quare Deus in principio [humano generi] legem non dedit quam postea per Moysen tradidit? — *Resp.* Quia in hominibus primis diu lex bonae naturae servabatur; at ubi naturalis lex evanuit, oblata consuetudine peccandi, data est lex litterae per Moysen, ut bona quae sciebantur auctoritatem haberent, et quae latere coeperant, manifestarentur; et ut terror disciplinae corrigeret delinquentes, et fidem reformaret in Deum.[40]

(*Question.* 14. Why, in the beginning, did God not give the law to the race of men which he later handed down through Moses? — *Answer.* Because, for a while, the law of good nature was preserved among the first men; but when the law of nature failed, sacrificed by the habit of sin, written law was given through Moses, so that the good practices that were known would have authority, and those which had begun to fade might be made clear; and so that fear of chastisement would correct wrong-doers and restore faith in God).[41]

Thus, in all three of these examples — Irenaeus, Pelagius, and Alcuin — one sees slightly differing attestations of the idea that the Law of Moses should be understood as a perfected version, or enhancement, of the Law of Nature, imposed by God in writing to preserve or to restore the original

---

38 The text is from Augustine of Hippo, *De perfectione iustitiae hominis*, p. 190.

39 The translation is from Augustine of Hippo, *Answer to the Pelagians I*, pp. 449–50.

40 Alcuin, 'Quaestiones in Genesim', col. 517D.

41 The translation is my own.

state of justice inherent in nature that humankind's sinful behaviour had corrupted.

I posit that ideas similar to those contained in these patristic authors informed the Caí Caínbrethach episode discussed above, and that the primary innovation of the Irish legalist who composed the story was to create a narrative justification for a particular view of the pre-Christian, native legal system and its place within a broader Christian framework. As such, it was a brilliant gesture. It was one thing to assert that pre-Christian, native law was equivalent to the Law of Nature. That claim had precedent in Isidore,[42] was made by other medieval European cultures (often following Isidore), and was a strategy employed by Irish jurists in other texts. But what if the perfected version of the Law of Nature was defined as the equivalent of the Law of Moses, derivable from a reasoned, firsthand analysis of nature (as Pelagius believed) or imposed by God to restore the Law of Nature (as Irenaeus and Alcuin held)? If this was indeed their understanding of the relationship between the Law of Nature and the Law of Moses, Irish pseudo-historians might simply have claimed that righteous pre-conversion jurists, following the Pelagian injunction, derived the Mosaic Law from nature itself by fruitfully applying their inward light of reason. Or, even more palatably (from their perspective) — they could instead posit a historical, organic connection between native law (imagined as the Law of Nature) and the Law of Moses. This, I would argue, was the strategy employed by the author of the Caí Caínbrethach episode (discussed above). The advantage to this approach is that pre-Christian, native Irish law, it could be claimed, did not merely reflect Mosaic precepts derived by righteous pagan jurists from firsthand observation. Rather, with this narrative, Irish jurists could claim that pre-conversion Irish law incorporated Mosaic precepts without mediation or any imperfection that might arise if they had to deduce them from nature, because pre-Christian Irish jurists had received them directly from Moses himself. As such, the native legal system was placed on a significantly more solid ideological foundation. Finally, in this schema, native Irish law had a clear place in sacred history. It was the Law of Nature, to be sure, but it was also much more: it was the Law of Nature restored to its original, perfect state by the corrective imposition of the Mosaic Law. Likewise, the same methods of exegesis that applied to biblical law would, in light of this pseudo-historical explanation, apply to native Irish law, since — in this understanding — the two legal systems were both historically and organically one and the same thing.

42 See Isidore of Seville, *Etymologiarum*, I, V.iv.

The Pseudo-historical Prologue to the *Senchas Már*

The so-called Pseudo-historical Prologue to the *Senchas Már* stands out as among the most audacious treatises on legal ideology composed in the early medieval West. Its author applied legal, theological, and literary modes of expression with nothing less than creative genius. Though we know the author only from the text, their breadth of training is remarkable. Without doubt, their education represented the ideal paradigm of a well-rounded Irish scholar of the period: they were thoroughly versed in the Latin Christian tradition, both scriptural and patristic, while at the same time well steeped in native learning. We may assume they could move comfortably among both the secular and ecclesiastical *literati* (if indeed these two worlds were separate in any sense). The contents of the Pseudo-historical Prologue evince this fact: the text subtly and deliberatively engages with involved theological doctrine within the confines of a native poetic genre (i.e., the *rosc*),[43] artfully embedded in a traditional literary form reminiscent of an episode from the sagas, all concisely and elegantly set down in the vernacular. We might well imagine their role designated under various titles, its precise description depending on context: *iudex* or *brithem*; *clericus, monachus* or *scriba*; *ecnae* or *suí litre*; perhaps even *fili*. Whatever label(s) might best have fit the author (and in which situations), their composition has roots that reach into the intellectual traditions of both the Church and, at least symbolically, of native, pre-Christian Ireland.

Multiple, somewhat differing versions of the Pseudo-historical Prologue survive, suggesting that the story was worked and re-worked as it developed over time. These include: TCD MS 1337 (formerly H 3. 18)

---

43 Though native in some sense, the *rosc* was influenced by Latin Christian poetics as well. See Corthals, 'Zur Frage des Mündlichen', and Corthals, 'Early Irish *retoirics*'. Furthermore, in its legal sense, a *rosc* or *roscad* is a poem with which *filid* traditionally expressed their judgements in the native legal system. See *eDIL* s.v. *rosc* and *roscad*. According to F. Kelly, *A Guide to Early Irish Law*, p. 196, *roscad* (pl. *roscaid* or *roscada*) are 'found in both legal and non-legal material, and usually refer to a non-syllabic alliterative type of verse'. That said, as Stacey, *Dark Speech*, p. 100 notes, '⟨Scholars⟩ have now identified several instances in which sources composed in the classical Old Irish period — some of them Latin and ecclesiastical in nature and origin — were deliberately translated into *rosc*'. Johnston, *Literacy and Identity in Early Medieval Ireland*, p. 146, also points to Latin ecclesiastical influence on the *rosc*: '*Rosc* was an important part of the curriculum of the *filid*. The Middle Irish metrical tract on *filidecht* illustrates several types of *rosc* alongside the syllabic metres. The *retoiric* or *rosc* has been defined as a type of nonrhyming alliterative stress-counting verse form and as lying somewhere between poetry and prose, although it is not the same as either. It usually employs an archaic linguistic register, and it has been assumed that *rosc* is part of the Indo-European inheritance in Irish prosody. However, Johan Corthals has argued that this style is partly rooted in the theory and practice of Latin poetry and rhetoric as transmitted from the rhetorical schools of Late Antiquity'.

(**A**),[44] TCD MS 1336 (formerly H 3. 17) (**B**),[45] BL MS Harley 432 (**C**),[46] and a version known by the title *Comthóth Lóegaire co cretim ocus a aided* (The Conversion of Lóegaire to the Faith and his Death), among the so-called H-hand interpolations of the *Lebor na hUidre,*[47] RIA MS 23 E 25 (**D**).[48] There is also a short passage in the law tract *Córus Béscnai,* TCD MS 1316 (formerly H 2. 15a) (**H**),[49] that includes a portion of the tale, apparently at an early stage of its evolution.[50] Although these manuscripts date from a much later period — **A**, **B**, and **C** all date from sixteenth century, the H-hand in **D** from between the eleventh and thirteenth, and **H** from the fifteenth — the original text of the Pseudo-historical Prologue was, according to Liam Breatnach, part of the Old Irish Glossing of the *Senchas Már,* and thus can be dated to the middle of the eighth century.[51] The survival of several versions of the story in a number of manuscripts, alongside the fact that the central characters in the story, including the poet Dubthach maccu Lugair and king Loegaire mac Néill, appear elsewhere in Irish (specifically Patrician) literature, attests to its relatively widespread influence. The relationship between these different versions is complex and the subject of some debate (which goes beyond the scope of this chapter). For my present argument, I shall use John Carey's edition of the Pseudo-historical Prologue as opposed to the manuscript witnesses directly, except in the few cases where an alternative reading from a particular version is relevant to my discussion. Also, since Carey's edition does not include Dubthach's poetic judgement — the sole version of which survives in **C** — I shall use McCone's critical edition for that portion of the text.[52] Finally, aside from a few exceptional cases where I shall need to emphasize a particular nuance of the original text necessary for my argument, I shall use John Carey's translation of the Prologue,[53] including Dubthach's poetic judgement (which he included in an earlier article).[54]

44 *Corpus Iuris Hibernici*, 874.35–877.3.

45 *Corpus Iuris Hibernici*, 1650.1–1657.9.

46 *Corpus Iuris Hibernici*, 339.1–344.23.

47 *Lebor na hUidre.*

48 For a discussion of the manuscript evidence, see especially: Carey, 'An Edition of the Pseudo-historical Prologue', pp. 1–11. See also: Scowcroft, '*Recht Fáide*', pp. 143–46; McCone, 'Dubthach maccu Lugair', pp. 1–5; and Binchy, 'Pseudo-historical Prologue', pp. 16–17.

49 *Corpus Iuris Hibernici*, 528.17–29.

50 See: Breatnach, *Córus Bésgnai*, § 35–37 p. 34 (text); p. 35 (trans.).

51 Breatnach, *A Companion to the Corpus Iuris Hibernici*, p. 40, 874.35 and pp. 338–44.

52 McCone, 'Dubthach maccu Lugair'.

53 Carey published two translations, one in 'An Edition of the Pseudo-historical Prologue' and the other in *King of Mysteries*, pp. 139–44. Here, I am using the one in 'An Edition of the Pseudo-historical Prologue'.

54 John Carey's translation of Dubthach's poetic judgement is in 'The Two Laws', pp. 13–15.

Despite significant differences between the manuscript witnesses in details, the general outline of the narrative related in each version is more or less the same. The episode is set in Ireland in the period immediately after the conversion has begun, just after Patrick had defeated King Loegaire and his druids in a magico-religious duel recalling similar battles between the Old Testament prophets and the priests of Baal. King Loegaire, converted at least nominally thereafter, then commanded the leading men of Ireland to come together in a kind of proto-synod, expressly for the purpose of working out what impact their acceptance of new religion would have '[…] im chórus a mbéscnai ⁊ rechtgai'[55] ([…] concerning the proper relationship between their customs and their laws).[56] Patrick, too, was invited; but before he arrived, the king asked those gathered what feature of the new faith seemed most difficult for them to accept. They all replied unanimously that the doctrine of forgiveness was most difficult, since — in their opinion — it would undermine the native legal system and lead to unrestrained crime throughout the land. Loegaire then devised a plan to bring the crisis to a head, to test how Patrick's doctrine would function in actual practice, and to assess the fidelity of Patrick's adherence to his own belief. To this end, Loegaire charged one of his men (named Núadu Derg in **B** and **C**) to kill a member of Patrick's household so that they could gauge Patrick's response. As planned, Núadu killed Patrick's charioteer (named Odrán in **B** and **C**) with a cast of his spear. Led by Loegaire, all the men then promptly appealed to Patrick on Núadu's behalf to grant him forgiveness and absolution. Patrick, enraged at the heinous murder of his follower, lifted his hands to heaven and summoned down an earthquake upon the land, instilling terror among all who were present.

After some persuasion, Patrick's anger eventually relented, and he agreed to arbitration. Perhaps somewhat unexpectedly (certainly to a modern audience), he chose a native, pagan jurist, an apparently well-known judge named Dubthach maccu Lugair, described as a *rígfili* (king-poet, i.e., a royal poet)[57] and *lestar lán do rath in Spirta Naím*[58] (a vessel filled with the grace of the Holy Spirit).[59] Dubthach, upon being selected, immediately expressed reticence, balking openly at the profound difficulty of the case. Patrick, however, assured Dubthach that the Holy Spirit would guide him. Shortly thereafter, Dubthach uttered his pronouncement in verse, specifically in the archaic poetic genre known as a *rosc* (the text

55 The text is from Carey, 'An Edition of the Pseudo-historical Prologue', p. 11.

56 The translation is from Carey, 'An Edition of the Pseudo-historical Prologue', p. 17. The term *córus*, discussed above, is difficult to translate. Carey translated it 'proper ordering'. Given the context, I suggest a slightly nuanced alteration, to 'proper relationship'.

57 Carey, 'An Edition of the Pseudo-historical Prologue', p. 31 (text); p. 32 (trans.).

58 The text is from Carey, 'An Edition of the Pseudo-historical Prologue', p. 31. See also: Carey's discussion of this phrase in the same article, § 4.6–7 p. 22.

59 The translation is from Carey, 'An Edition of the Pseudo-historical Prologue', p. 32.

which is preserved uniquely in **C**). In essence, his decision stipulated that Núadu, the slayer, must suffer death for his crime, but Patrick must win forgiveness for his soul. In this way, the poet explains, 'ro-comallada in dá recht'[60] (the two laws were fulfilled).[61] Then, after Dubthach pronounced his judgement (and, presumably, the sentence was carried out), the men of the Ireland decided they had to reconcile their customary laws with the doctrines of the new religion. Patrick agreed, and this was done. In the end, we are told that virtually everything in the native system was, in Patrick's judgement, acceptable under the new faith, save only in those few cases (left unspecified) where overt contradictions with Christian belief as expressed in the scriptures arose. Effectively, the narrative ends with this decision, a decision of what might aptly be called a 'proto-synod'.

The Pseudo-historical Prologue has received a steady amount of scholarly attention in recent decades. Prior to this interest, Binchy's was the most prominent word on the subject. In a 1975 article, he dated the prose portion of the Prologue on historical grounds to the Middle Irish period (specifically *c.* 1100) and argued that the archaic verses containing Dubthach's judgement were a later interpolation, bearing no organic relationship to the prose narrative. Rather, he saw the poem as the hopelessly corrupted '[...] detritus of some ancient "leading case"'.[62] Brushing it aside with this declaration, he essentially ignored it.[63] Later scholarship has consistently rejected his conclusion, both regarding his date of the text and the relationship (or lack thereof) he proposed between the poem and the prose narrative. While his study provided a starting point for subsequent discussion of the Pseudo-historical Prologue and has contributed much to the current understanding of the text, the main points of his argument are no longer generally accepted.

Binchy's position has been questioned and substantially revised in a series of studies. First, Ó Corráin, Breatnach, and Breen in their milestone article, 'The Laws of the Irish',[64] while not explicitly challenging Binchy's dating of the prose, disagreed with his dismissive assessment of the poem. Instead, they argued that the poem is deeply religious and thematically consonant with the narrative that frames it. The main purpose of their relatively short treatment of the text, however, was not to offer a new, thoroughgoing interpretation of its main theme, but to draw attention to the poem's ecclesiastical orientation. Their brief but important discussion sparked a flurry of subsequent scholarship on the Psuedo-historical Prologue. Soon thereafter, Kim McCone proposed a comprehensive new

60 The text is from McCone, 'Dubthach maccu Lugair', § xx p. 30.
61 The translation is from Carey, 'The Two Laws', p. 15.
62 Binchy, 'The Pseudo-historical Prologue', p. 28.
63 Binchy, 'The Pseudo-historical Prologue', pp. 18–19, and p. 28.
64 Ó Corráin, Breatnach, and Breen, 'The Laws of the Irish', pp. 387–88.

analysis along with a critical edition of the poem (including a fresh translation). Significantly, he argued that the prose portion of the Pseudo-historical Prologue dated from the Old Irish period and was therefore equally as ancient as the poem, with both, in his view, dating from the mid-eighth century.[65] McCone's conclusion remains generally accepted today. Very significantly, McCone argued that the prose and the poem were organically part of the same original composition, and — further — he proposed a new interpretation of the text taking this position into account. For McCone, a primary purpose of the text was to justify the native practice requiring monetary compensation akin to the Germanic notion of *wergild* (Old Irish *éraic*) for capital offenses. More generally, he saw the whole narrative as a delicately woven and complex typological narrative in which Dubthach represented John the Baptist and Patrick represented Christ as bearer of the New Law.

Subsequently, John Carey questioned McCone's interpretation, though not his proposed date of the Prologue in two articles (the main purpose of the latter was to present a much-needed edition of the prose text). Carey strongly disagreed with McCone's thesis that a central concern of the narrative was to defend the native requirement for payment of monetary compensation in capital offences. As evidence, Carey demonstrated that McCone's conclusion was based on his idiosyncratic identification of **C** as the best manuscript witness.[66] As Carey pointed out, **B** and **C** are the only witnesses that mention *éraic*, and even there it contradicts what he identifies as the text's main theme, i.e., that capital punishment is not only acceptable, but the proper punishment for murder. Carey concludes, therefore, that the short discussion of *éraic* in **B** and **C** is most likely a later interpolation. Next, Carey challenged point-by-point McCone's interpretation of the Pseudo-historical Prologue as an extended scriptural conceit in which Dubthach stands as metaphor for John the Baptist and Patrick for Christ. Alternatively, Carey proposed a more literal, less typologically rigid interpretation of the text as a complex argument in support of capital punishment under the Law of Christ. As he saw it, the rationale provided in the text and parallelled in the Hiberno-Latin *De Mirabilibus Sacrae Scripturae*, is that a newly converted Christian, absolved and thus made perfect though baptism, cannot expect leniency for transgression any more than a demon who started out in just such an uncorrupted state. According to Carey's reading, the argument presented in the text is that, by this analogy, capital punishment befits a Christian who commits a crime after baptism and thereby debases himself. Even more significantly for the present discussion, Carey argues that the text 'situates the pagan

65 See also, Breatnach, *A Companion to the Corpus Iuris Hibernici*, p. 40, 874.35 and pp. 338–44.
66 Carey, 'The Two Laws', p. 5.

Irish within the broader context of Christian sacred history',[67] but does not equate them typologically or literally with the Israelites, nor their law with the Pentateuch (as did McCone). Rather, in his view, Dubthach's judgement accords with Noahide Law (though he does not use this term), rather than Mosaic Law. As Carey put it: 'The law which Dubthach invokes is that of Ararat, not Sinai: the Irish as descendants of Noah, have inherited his obligations'.[68] He continues, 'Pagans are bound by the covenant of Noah, Christians by the Gospel "preached to all nations": The laws of the Irish are an attempt to harmonize the two'.[69] Here, one might insert: 'Jews are bound by the Covenant of Moses'. Though Carey does not make this claim, these matters — specifically the relationship between biblical laws and their proper application to different peoples at different stages of sacred history — closely parallel those adjudicated by the apostles at the Synod of Jerusalem. As I shall argue below, these issues were in essence what was under debate in this early Irish proto-synod. Carey's reading provides the basis for my own, and I shall have more to say about it in what follows. Finally, Carey's 1994 edition, which includes a detailed analysis of the relationship between manuscript witnesses, is now standard.[70]

Since Carey, Damian Bracken has argued in several articles that a main goal of Dubthach's judgement was to present a highly technical, Christian defence of capital punishment.[71] Briefly summarizing his complex thesis, Bracken shows that the author of the Pseudo-historical Prologue drew heavily upon contemporary Hiberno-Latin theology concerning the Fall to make the case that, despite injunctions requiring forgiveness under the New Dispensation, the death penalty was still permitted:

> In ⟨the Pseudo-historical Prologue poet's⟩ typically subtle way, he shows that the Creator himself is an advocate of capital punishment, for the sentence of death is imposed on all humans. The gist of the poem's argument runs that humans must die before they can achieve perfection. Thus the Creator himself continues to be an advocate of capital punishment even after Christ's mission.[72]

What is more, Bracken argues that in the understanding of the Prologue's author, not just capital punishment, but talion law generally was permitted to enforce the law in both the Old and the New Testaments:

---

67 Carey, 'The Two Laws', p. 13.

68 Carey, 'The Two Laws', p. 17.

69 Carey, 'The Two Laws', p. 18.

70 Carey, 'An Edition of the Pseudo-historical Prologue'. See also Scowcroft, '*Recht Fáide*', where he proposes a minor emendation to Carey's text.

71 Bracken, 'The Fall and the Law', pp. 147–69 and Bracken, 'Immortality and Capital Punishment'.

72 Bracken, 'Immortality and Capital Punishment', p. 179.

> The composer of Dubthach's poem was [...] trying to provide a solution to the very real dilemma presented in the story of the execution of Patrick's would-be slayer. Dubthach, the christian synthesis of the old and new Laws, advocates capital punishment, a procedure characterized by retributive justice and associated with the Old Testament by the writers of Hiberno-Latin literature, literature which the composers of the introduction to the *Senchas Már* fully accepted and applied to their understanding of the native legal tradition. The poet [...] says that vengeance and retribution are found in the old and the new Laws.[73]

It was crucial, Bracken argued, for the Christian author of the Pseudo-historical Prologue to address what might have been perceived by his contemporaries as an abjuration of New Testament precepts. Since the enforcement of pre-Christian Irish law relied on a complex system of monetary compensation and obligatory vengeance (as opposed to capital punishment), Dubthach's imposition of the death sentence might have been understood as retributive justice, and therefore a violation of the Christian requirement to forgive. It was crucial, therefore, that Dubthach effectively make the case that both the Old and New Laws agreed on the propriety of capital punishment. Bracken supports his argument with an impressive collection of citations from patristic and Hiberno-Latin literature.

Bracken's argument has much to recommend it and has contributed much to our understanding of the place of the Pseudo-historical Prologue in the Irish intellectual tradition. In particular, he showed how profoundly well-versed the author of this text was in Hiberno-Latin learning, displaying knowledge consonant with ideas expressed in the *Reference Bible, Collectio canonum Hibernensis*, Augustinus Hibernicus, Pseudo-Bede, and others (or, at least, the theological principles that mutually informed them). Moreover, Bracken showed how nuanced and thoughtful this application of their ideas to practical legal matters could be. While I shall not challenge Bracken's identifications of parallels between ideas found in the Pseudo-historical Prologue and the broader corpus of Hiberno-Latin literature, it is possible, I shall argue, to show that the author of the Pseudo-historical Prologue drew on a specific source more proximate in both content and genre to the texts Bracken has noticed.

This scholarship, particularly the more recent work by McCone, Carey, and Bracken, has shaped our current understanding of Dubthach's judgement and its relationship to contemporaneous Irish legal doctrine, particularly Hiberno-Latin legal thought. That said, the immediate inspiration for the concepts expressed in his legal *rosc* has thus far been overlooked, and

73 Bracken, 'Immortality and Capital Punishment', pp. 180–81.

it will be necessary to examine this parallel in some detail — whether it be the source, directly or indirectly, or derived from an analogous tradition — before we can fully understand the force of Dubthach's judgement. The closest parallels to Dubthach's judgement appear spread over several chapters of *Collectio canonum Hibernensis,* including Liber XXVI, *De sceleribus et uindictis eorum* (Concerning offenses and their punishments),[74] which — as the title reveals — deals explicitly with the dilemma Dubthach confronted. These include:

1 cap. 8, *De uindicta non prohibenda in nouo, et de personis dignis ad uindictam*[75] (Concerning punishment not being prohibited in the New Testament and on those worthy of inflicting punishment)[76] which specifies, citing Jerome as authority, that '⟨h⟩omicidas et sacreligos punire non est effusio sanguinis, sed legum ministerium'[77] (Punishing killers and wicked men is not considered a shedding of blood, but serving the laws ⟨of God⟩).[78]

2 Any doubts about the severity of punishments intended in this provision are clarified fully in cap. 6, *De uindictis scelerum in nouo*[79] (Concerning punishments for offenses in the New Testament),[80] which lists a series of gruesome penalties selected from the Bible. These include crucifixion, dismemberment, and imprisonment, '[…] ut tenebris conclusus intereat'[81] ([…] so that ⟨the condemned⟩ might perish enveloped in darkness).[82]

3 Even closer to the ideas expressed in Dubthach's judgement is a citation attributed to Augustine in cap. 8 (immediately following the citation from Jerome, in (1) discussed above), which argues in favour of the death penalty. In this latter passage, there is no specific mention of capital punishment, but — as in Dubthach's judgement — concern is expressed that unpunished crimes may negatively affect the whole population: 'Quae est ista uanitas, uni parcere et omnes in discrimen adducer? Polluitur enim populus uno peccante'[83] (What is this vanity, to spare one and lead all others into danger? For the populace is polluted by a single sinner).[84] This concern closely parallels the sentiment expressed in the last part of Dubthach's poetic judgement: 'Iss

74 *The Hibernensis,* Bk I, pp. 162–84 (text); Bk II, pp. 593–608 (trans.).
75 *The Hibernensis,* Bk I, pp. 168–69.
76 *The Hibernensis,* Bk II, pp. 597–98.
77 *The Hibernensis,* Bk I, p. 168.
78 *The Hibernensis,* Bk II, p. 597.
79 *The Hibernensis,* Bk I, pp. 164–65.
80 *The Hibernensis,* Bk II, pp. 594–95.
81 *The Hibernensis,* Bk I, p. 165.
82 *The Hibernensis,* Bk II, p. 595.
83 *The Hibernensis,* Bk I, p. 169.
84 *The Hibernensis,* Bk II, p. 597.

ed im-deisid la firu Érenn: cách ina chinaid arnaro-foirbrea in peccad aithirriuch isin innsi-seo'[85] (This was established by the men of Ireland: everyone ⟨to die⟩ for his crime, so that sin might not increase in this island).[86] These two ideas — i.e., that capital punishment is permitted under New Testament Law and that it ought to be imposed to prevent the spread of sin among society at large — although interesting parallels and hardly commonplace, are not distinctive enough in and of themselves to indicate a direct connection between the two texts (though their close juxtaposition in both examples is certainly worthy of note). The fact that the same arguments were deployed by the author of the Pseudo-historical Prologue and the compilers of *Collectio canonum Hibernensis*, however, suggests that both shared a common ideological orientation and worked in the same (or a very similar) intellectual milieu.

4 The closest parallel between Dubthach's judgement and *Collectio canonum Hibernensis*, however, is found in cap. 9 of the book just mentioned, *De uindicata in novo*[87] (Concerning punishment in the New Testament).[88] This chapter consists of a long, substantially truncated[89] citation of Augustine's *De sermone Domini in monte*, I, 19.63–65.[90] Because the ideas expressed in it are so close to those in Dubthach's judgement, I shall cite the text in full before I discuss it:

Cap. 9, *De vindicta in novo*
Agustinus: Neque hic ea uindicta prohibetur, que uadit etiam ad correctionem. Ipsa enim pertinet ad misericordiam, nec inpedit illud propossitum, quo quisque paratus est ab eo, quem correctum esse uult, et plura perferre. Sed huic uindictæ referende non est idoneus, nisi qui odium, quo solent homines flagellare qui se uindicare desiderant, dilectionis magnitudine superauit. Non enim metuendum est, ne odisse paruulum filium parentes uideantur: cum ab eis uapuletur peccans, non peccet amplius. Et certe perfecte dilectionis ipsius Dei

85 McCone, 'Dubthach maccu Lugair', p. 30.
86 Carey, 'The Two Laws', p. 15.
87 *The Hibernensis*, Bk I, pp. 169–71.
88 *The Hibernensis*, Bk II, pp. 598–99.
89 The manner in which the text was reduced is itself a matter of interest. Here is one example: the decision to excise the phrase explaining that capital punishment of criminals is necessary so that crime should not increase in society at large *[...] peccatum, quod augeri posset si uiuerunt [...]* ([...] sin, which might be increased if they lived [...]) — assuming it was present in the scribe's exemplar — is curious, since it parallels the reasoning in the Pseudo-historical Prologue, and since the same basic idea is expressed via a citation from Jerome in the chapter immediately preceding this one in *Collectio canonum Hibernensis*.
90 Damian Bracken discusses the importance of Augustine's *De semone Domini in monte* for the ideas expressed in the Pseudo-historical Prologue but does not discuss the following excerpt of the text in *Collectio canonum Hibernensis*. See Bracken, 'The Fall and the Law', pp. 158–60.

patris imitatione nobis proponitur exemplum, cum in sequentibus dicit: Diligite inimicos uestros, et reliqua. Et tamen de ipso dicitur per prophetam: Quem enim diligit Deus, corripit et flagillat omnem filium, quem recipit. Magni etenim sancti uirii, qui iam optime scierunt mortem istam, que animam soluit a corpore, non esse formidandam, sed ⟨secundum⟩ eorum tamen animum, qui illam timent, nonnulla peccata morte punierunt, quo et uidentibus utilius metus incuteretur et illis, qui morte puniebantur non ipsa mors noceret.[91] ⟨Non temere illi iudicabant⟩ quibus tale iuditium donauerat Deus, id est quo Elias multos adfecit morte ex propria manu et igni diuinitus imperato. Cum et alii magni et diuini uiri, eodem spiritu consulentes, rebus humanis non temere fecerunt. Itaque posteaquam eos docuit quid est diligere proximum te ipsum. Infuso etiam spiritu sancto, quem misit, non defuerunt tales uindictae, quamuis multo rarius, quam in ueteri testamento. Nam et uerbis apostoli Petri Annanias et uxor eius exanimes ceciderunt. Et si huic libro heretici aduersantur et ueteri testamento nolunt credere, Paulum apostolum intueantur, dicentem de quondam peccatore, quem tradidit Satanæ in interitum carnis, ut anima salua sit. Et si nolunt mortem hic intellegere, fortasse enim incertum est, quamlibet uindictam per Satanan factam ab apostolo fateantur; quod non iam odio, sed amore fecisse manifestat illud adiectum: Vt anima salua sit. Aut in ipsis libris, quibus ipsi magnam tribuunt auctoritatem, animaduertant, quod, ubi scriptum est apostolum Tomam imprecatum cuidam, quod palma percussisset, atrocissime mortis supplicium, animam eius tamen commendat, ut in futuro ei saeculo parceretur. Cuius a leone occisi a cætero corpore discerptam manum canis tulit mensis, quibus conuiuebatur apostolus.[92]

⟨**Chapter 9, *Concerning punishment in the New Testament***
Augustine: Nor here is there a prohibition against that punishment, for it also leads toward correction. For it is an aspect of mercy. Nor does it impede that intention by which one is prepared to bear even more from him, whom he wants to be corrected. But no one is fit to administer punishment, except he who — through great love — has overcome hatred, by which men who wish to avenge themselves are accustomed to punish. For the following is not to be feared: that the parents should seem to hate their young son; let him be beaten by them when sinning, that he might not

91 It is at this point that the phrase *[…] peccatum, quod augeri posset si uiuerunt […]* (…sin, which might be increased if they lived […]) appears in Augustine's version of the text. Augustine's text, including the phrase in question, can be found in Augustine of Hippo, *Sancti Avrelii Avgvstini*, pp. 72–75.

92 *The Hibernensis*, Bk I, pp. 169–71.

> increase in sin. And certainly, through perfect imitation of the love of God the Father himself, an example is laid down to us, when he says in what follows: Love your enemies, etc. And nevertheless, concerning the same thing it is said through the prophet: For he whom the Lord loves he chastises, and he scourges every son whom he receives. For great and holy men who were already fully aware that this death, which releases the soul from the body is not to be feared, nevertheless punished many sins by death after the manner of those who fear it. By which he means fear was more effectively struck in the observers, while this death did not harm the ones who were being punished by death. They to whom God gave such judicial discretion did not decide rashly. By which discretion Elijah punished many by death, both by his own hand and by fire demanded from heaven. And also other great and divine men, being guided by the same Holy Spirit, did not act rashly in human affairs. Therefore, after that, he taught them what it means to love your neighbour as yourself. And after the Holy Spirit, which he sent, was poured out, such punishments did not desist, although they were much less frequent than in the Old Testament. For also Ananias and his wife fell lifeless by the words of Peter the apostle. And if the heretics deny this book, and also refuse to believe the Old Testament, let them observe Paul the apostle, saying of a certain heretic — whom he handed over to Satan for the destruction of the flesh — that his soul shall be saved. And if they refuse to understand death in this case — for perhaps it is uncertain — let them acknowledge that a punishment was inflicted by the apostle through Satan; which he did not do so much out of hatred, but out of love, is made clear by that addition: That his soul should be saved. Or let them turn their attention to the very same books, whose authority they themselves value greatly, for it is written there that Thomas the apostle wished a terrible death unto someone who slapped him; he nevertheless recommended that his soul be spared in the afterlife. A dog brought the palm, torn from the body of the dead man, who was killed by a lion, to the tables at which the apostle was feasting).[93]

Obviously, this chapter of *Collectio canonum Hibernensis* (quoted from Augustine) addresses legal-theological issues strikingly similar to those in Dubthach's judgement and draws similar conclusions about a central question: what, if any, is the proper role of capital punishment under the New Dispensation? Since the position expressed in *Collectio canonum Hibernensis* is much richer in detail than Dubthach's tersely aphoristic *rosc*,

93 *The Hibernensis*, Bk II, pp. 598–99.

much light can be shed on the poem's rationale by comparing the two texts. Let us consider this chapter from *Collectio canonum Hibernensis* in the context of the entire narrative of the Pseudo-historical Prologue.

Both texts, on the surface at least, take the position that capital punishment is not only permissible under the New Law, but both necessary and desirable to prevent the spread of sin. How can such a practice accord with the requirement that Christians should forgive all sins committed against them? Indeed, this apparent contradiction fomented quite a dilemma. The early Irish legal system, as in many other early societies particularly where centralized authority was weak, relied on a complex system of obligatory vengeance to enforce the law. Without the imminent threat of retribution from a victim's kin — who, for example in the case of murder, could either slay the perpetrator or collect a monetary fine (*éraic*) as compensation — there would be, in effect, no justice. This was the issue Loegaire summoned the men of Ireland together to discuss at the beginning of the Pseudo-historical Prologue; and they all declared that this legal issue, i.e., *cáin dílguda*[94] (the law of forgiveness),[95] posed the most difficult problem, and was the hardest part of the new religion for them to accept: 'ar ónd uair gébas cach duine céill for dílgud dó i nneoch dogéna di ulc, ní bia commus for foglaib ⁊ génaid ⁊ cach fer alaile, ar níba ecal leis a aithber fair'[96] (for as soon as every man expects to be forgiven for whatever evil things he does, there will be no restraint upon plundering, and every man will smite his fellow, for he will have no fear of being blamed for it).[97] In essence, then, the whole legal system — and the order in society it maintained — seemed to come under threat by the doctrines of the new faith; and the men of Ireland gathered at this synod-like assembly realized this important fact. Their decision to kill one of Patrick's followers constituted (at least as an imagined narrative) a clever strategy to test the new legal ideology in pragmatic terms: it was one thing for Patrick to preach forgiveness; quite another for him to practise it. So, by making a member Patrick's household the victim of a capital crime — and thereby making Patrick a litigant with both the right and obligation under customary Irish law to seek vengeance — they had devised the perfect plan to test how effectually Christian legal theory would operate when confronted with real-world crimes in Irish society.

Patrick's response, after a fit of righteous outrage in which he called down divine wrath in the form of an earthquake, was equally inspired. Specifically, his choice to call on a native Irish judge, Dubthach maccu Lugair, to adjudicate the dispute — besides asserting a right provided to

94 The text is from Carey, 'An Edition of the Pseudo-historical Prologue', p. 11.

95 The translation is from Carey, 'An Edition of the Pseudo-historical Prologue', p. 18.

96 The text is from Carey, 'An Edition of the Pseudo-historical Prologue', p. 11.

97 The translation is from Carey, 'An Edition of the Pseudo-historical Prologue', p. 17.

him as a foreigner under Irish law (or, perhaps, setting that precedent)[98] — underscored his absolute faith in the righteousness of his cause: for although Dubthach was a pagan (or perhaps a very recent convert to Christian belief),[99] Patrick knew him to be a righteous man.[100] As such, Dubthach was bound, not merely by the precepts of customary Irish law, but also (from Patrick's perspective, at least), by Christian law in a very real sense as well, since as a naturally good man infused with the Holy Spirit, he would judge justly in accordance with the Law of Nature. Moreover, Dubthach was bound to judge truthfully, since according to his pre-Christian, native belief (and later Christian belief, as discussed above) a false verdict could result in physical harm to himself and his *túath*. Dubthach explicitly acknowledged this potential outcome in his judgement by pointing out that, after he delivered his verdict, he did not develop the facial blemishes believed to mar the face of a judge who pronounced a false or unjust decision: 'Demnigur dim grúadaib, nad-goirfet gel míad, mída(i)r mesemnacht slá⟨i⟩n'[101] (I prove by my cheeks, which will not bring a blush to pure dignity, that I have judged a sound judgement).[102]

From a Christian perspective, everyone involved — Dubthach, Loegaire, the men of Ireland, and Patrick, etc. — were gentiles; and thus,

98 Carey, 'An Edition of the Pseudo-historical Prologue', p. 2 n. 4, points out that in **C** there is 'a brief statement concerning the selection of judges when the plaintiff is a foreigner (*Corpus Iuris Hibernici*, 340.11–13): *Is ann sin* [*ł is as* above the line] "gabthair, obus tar muir ticfa d'acra a dala, a roga breithemon i nEirinn do, ⁊ obus tar crich .u.id ticfa, a roga .b. isin .u. ed do" "Thence is derived (the ruling) that when he comes across the sea to plead his case, he has his choice of judge in Ireland; when he comes across the boundary of a province, he has his choice of judge in that province"'.

99 Although I do not intend to suggest that there is a textual connection between the two tales, an interesting analogue to this episode appears in the Old Icelandic *Íslendingabók* (*Book of the Icelanders*). Here, the question of whether or not to accept the Christian faith was decided in a legal procedure ultimately handed over to a pagan jurist named Þorgeirr for adjudication. When presented with the dispute, Þorgeirr — in what may represent some kind of shamanistic ritual — wraps himself up in a cloak for a day and a night and mumbles some unintelligible sounds before emerging to render his decision in favour of the new religion at the Law-Rock. For a text of the episode, see: *Íslendingabók*, pp. 16–17. For a translation, see: *Íslendingabók—Kristni Saga*, trans. by Grønlie, pp. 8–9. There is a fuller, parallel account in *Kristni Saga* (Saga of the Conversion), for which see: *Biskupa sögur I*, I, pp. 30–36 (text); *Íslendingabók—Kristni Saga*, trans. by Grønlie, pp. 47–50. For a discussion of the significance of this episode in the Scandinavian tradition, see Jón Hnefill Aðalsteinsson, *Under the Cloak*.

100 Also, in Muirchú's *Life of St. Patrick*, we are told: 'Hic, ut dixi, Dubthach solus ex gentibus in honorem sancti Patricii surrexit et benedixit ei sanctus crediditque primus in illa die Deo et repputatum est ei ad iustitiam' (This Dubthach, as I have said, alone among the pagans rose in honour of holy Patrick, and the holy man blessed him, and he was the first on that day to believe in God, and it was counted to him for righteousness). The text and translation are from Bieler, *Patrician Texts*, p. 92 (text); p. 93 (trans.).

101 The text is from McCone, 'Dubthach maccu Lugair', p. 29.

102 The translation is from Carey, 'The Two Laws', p. 14.

regardless of their religious beliefs, they all commonly acknowledged the Law of Nature (although they would have described it differently). That entailed, above all, the absolute virtue of truth and the destructive power of falsehood. For this reason, Dubthach was the perfect judge. Patrick, of course, imposed a Christian interpretation on these events. When, for example, Dubthach expressed concern over the difficulty of unravelling this apparent legal contradiction, Patrick, who had already described him as 'lestar lán do rath in Spirta Naím'[103] (a vessel full of the Holy Spirit),[104] reassured him, quoting Matthew 10:20 'a ndobera Dia for erlabrai, ráid amin. Non uos estis qui loquimini, sed spiritus patris uestris qui loquitur in uobis'[105] (Whatever God may give ⟨you⟩ to say, speak thus. *It is not you who speaks, but the spirit of your Father who speaks in you*).[106] At this point, Dubthach, acknowledged by Patrick as a voice both of the Law of Nature and of the Holy Spirit, recited his poetic judgement.

Dubthach's verdict, in which he condemned Núadu to death on the condition that Patrick win pardon for his soul postmortem, has often been regarded as somewhat of a hedge. It is clear from the text, however, that Dubthach — though not fully Christianized — nonetheless recognized the heart of the crux he was appointed to resolve: How could forgiveness be reconciled with capital punishment? Justice, in this case, seemed to demand both vengeance and pardon. Ultimately, his solution was to settle on both options at once. Yet, despite its superficial appearance as an attempt to save face, I would argue (with McCone, Carey, and Bracken) that Dubthach's judgement should not be understood as a cunning attempt to evade the point at hand, but rather as an inspired solution firmly grounded in early Irish theology. Admittedly, there is no overt allusion to the sources of his rationale in the text of the Pseudo-historical Prologue itself. Dubthach cited neither Augustine nor Jerome, nor did he knowingly quote directly from the Bible. He is, after all, characterized as a righteous pagan (or a new believer at the cusp of conversion), channelling the words of the Holy Spirit; so, it would have been remarkable if he could have invoked such authorities. In this sense, his voice is very much like that of Morann's (as I argued above): both pre-conversion figures are portrayed as expressing sound Christian theological concepts unwittingly, from the subject position of naturally good men who — though ignorant of the Faith — nonetheless pronounced justice drawn from their innate virtue under the Law of Nature. Thus, in the same way that Cú Chulainn's behaviour (in the story discussed above) seemed to imply a knowledge of penitential discipline before he could logically have had direct knowledge

---

103 The text is from Carey, 'An Edition of the Pseudo-historical Prologue', p. 11.
104 The translation is from Carey, 'An Edition of the Pseudo-historical Prologue', p. 18.
105 The text is from Carey, 'An Edition of the Pseudo-historical Prologue', p. 12.
106 The translation is from Carey, 'An Edition of the Pseudo-historical Prologue', p. 18.

of Christianity, Dubthach's judgement likewise reflects proleptic theological sophistication emanating from his innate goodness. All these episodes, I would argue — including *Audacht Morann*, the Cú Chulainn story, and the Pseudo-historical Prologue — represent an early Irish narrative motif in which famous, pre-conversion pagans are cast by Christian authors as innately virtuous proto-Christians, infused with *naturale bonum*. By crafting stories in which their ancestors acted naturally according to Christian principles, early Irish intellectuals could point to concrete examples of the inherent goodness of their pagan forbears behaving righteously in accordance with the Law of Nature. These texts could be held up as 'proof' of such goodness, both of the individuals involved and of the native legal system in general.

Similarly, Dubthach's judgement closely parallels the ideas in the passage from *Collectio canonum Hibernensis* that cites Augustine's *De sermone Domini in monte*. In this text, Augustine's purpose was to show that there was ample precedent in the New Testament for capital punishment, at least under certain conditions. Dubthach's judgement relies on similar reasoning. Thus — as the author of the Pseudo-historical Prologue could point out — Dubthach's verdict was ultimately based on Christian legal and theological principles, well before these ideas could have been known directly in Ireland by any other means.

In this citation, Augustine calls as evidence several biblical examples of capital punishment in order to make the case that the death penalty was permissible under the New Law. First, he pointed to the Old Testament example of Elijah, who called down death from heaven on many of his pagan opponents in numerous thaumaturgical duels. More to the point, he then related several episodes from the New Testament. First, he described the story in Acts 5:1–11, wherein a certain man named Ananias and his wife were both struck dead by God after Peter caught them lying about a sum of money they had collected. The biblical text, like the author of the Pseudo-historical Prologue, emphasizes the fear onlookers felt at witnessing the effects of divine wrath. As a result, Augustine explained, these onlookers would be less likely to transgress in similar fashion. The next two examples are especially significant because Augustine emphasizes that the perpetrators, while suffering death as a punishment in the temporal world, are nonetheless forgiven and redeemed in the afterlife, an idea closely parallelled in Dubthach's judgement. The first of these two examples is found in an episode from the apocryphal *Acts of Thomas*, a work well-known in medieval Ireland.[107] The specific portion to which

107 McNamara, *The Apocrypha in the Irish Church*, pp. 118–19.

Augustine referred narrates how the apostle Thomas,[108] while at a wedding feast, was unjustly struck by a cup-bearer. Outraged, Thomas retorted:

> 'Indulgeat tibi dominus in futuro iudicio, fili, in hoc vero saeculo protinus repraesentet dexterae illi quae me verberavit iniuste'. Erat autem iam imminens nox; epulantibus autem illis subito defecit aqua ministeriis nuptialibus. Euntibus autem multis ad hauriendum et tardantibus ipse quoque pincerna cucurrit, et accedente eo ad fontem affuit leo magnus qui apprehensum puerum confregit et in frusta discerpsit. Cuius dexteram apprehensam canis qui aderat detulit ad domum et portabit per convivia epulantium, requirentibus autem illis quis deesset ex famulis cognoscunt pincernam interemptum esse ad fontem, quem cum leo devoraret huius dexteram a cane fuisse correptam convivioque delatam.[109]
>
> ('May the Lord forgive you in his future judgement, boy; however, let him soon recompense in this world that right-hand which struck me unjustly'. It was already approaching night. In a short space of time the water began to run short for those wedding guests in attendance. With many waiting to draw water, the cup-bearer himself ran after some. When he was approaching the fountain, a great lion appeared. It seized the boy, devoured him, and tore him to bits. A nearby dog snatched up the boy's right hand, carried it to the house, and brought it through the dinner party to the feasters. These feasters, then, inquired which of the servants was absent. They soon learned that the cupbearer had been killed at the fountain; that a lion had devoured him, and that his right hand had been snatched up by a dog and carried to the feast).[110]

To the amazement of all the guests, the dog carried the offending right hand to the very spot at the feast where Thomas was seated. Here — just like Núadu in the Pseudo-historical Prologue — the cupbearer suffered death for his transgression but (we may assume from Thomas's invocation) was granted forgiveness in the world to come.

Immediately preceding the reference to Thomas in Liber XIV, chapter 9 of *Collectio canonum Hibernensius*, Augustine (from whose *De sermone Domini in monte* the text is quoted), cites an example from Corinthians that bears a close resemblance to Dubthach's judgement.[111] Here, Augustine

108 In the text he is referred as 'Judas Thomas', reflecting a complicated tradition of the apostle's name.

109 The text is from *Die Alten Lateinischen Thomasakten*, pp. 47–48.

110 The translation is my own.

111 As this book was going to press, I was made aware of a master's thesis that linked 1 Corinthians 5:5 and its use by Augustine in *De sermone Domini in monte* as cited in *Collection canonum Hibernensis* to Dubthach's judgement in the Pseudo-historical Prologue.

refers to 1 Corinthians 5:1–8, where the apostle Paul wrote to convey his judgement on those individuals among the Corinthians who have committed fornication, pronouncing his decision in 1 Corinthians 5:5 'tradere huius modi Satanae in interitum carnis ut spiritus salvus sit in die Domini Iesu' (To deliver such a one to Satan for the destruction of the flesh, that the spirit may be saved in the day of our Lord Jesus Christ). The sentence Dubthach recommends for Núadu echoes these sentiments closely:[112] 'Ro-hort(a) in bibdu ina chinaid ⁊ do-roilged dia hanmain'[113] (the culprit was killed for his crime, and it ⟨his crime⟩ was pardoned to his soul).[114] I would suggest that 1 Corinthians 5:5, if not indeed this particular citation of the verse from Augustine's *De sermone Domini in monte* excerpted by the compilers of *Collectio canonum Hibernensis*, is the immediate source for Dubthach's judgement. It would have been perfectly natural for an Irish jurist in the mid-eighth century to consult a source like *Collectio canonum Hibernensis* and render the legal-theological concepts expressed there in a vernacular narrative like the Pseudo-historical Prologue, designed to elucidate perceived conflicts or contradictions between secular and ecclesiastical jurisprudence. That, I would argue, is the situation out of which this text emerged.

There remains a great deal more to say about this text. Consider the character of Dubthach, for instance. Portrayed by the author of the Pseudo-historical Prologue in the role of a righteous pagan (or new convert), Dubthach does not (and, in the role he was cast, presumably could not) identify his source. As a man intrinsically virtuous, however, he nonetheless judged truthfully and justly in full accordance with the Law of Nature, unwittingly channelling the will of the Holy Spirit. It is

---

See O'Sullivan, 'Let deaths be died', especially pp. 48–58. Please note that I had access only to photographic images of a small number of pages in O'Sullivan's thesis (graciously provided by the author himself), so I was not able to consult the entire document. From what I can tell, O'Sullivan and I have independently identified many of the same textual connections and generally appear to agree on their significance, even if we differ on minor points. O'Sullivan, however, discusses this episode and the place of capital punishment in early Irish theology more extensively than I do here. Particularly important is O'Sullivan's discussion of the treatment of 1 Corinthians 5:5 in patristic writings, including authors often cited in early medieval Ireland. See especially pp. 51–55. While elements of our conclusions differ, O'Sullivan's argument has much to contribute to our understanding of Dubthach's judgement, the sources that underlay it, and its significance for early Irish law and theology.

112 Augustine, in the passage cited above, acknowledged that the phrase in 1 Corinthians 5:5, 'tradere huiusmodi Satanae' (to deliver such a one to Satan), might not imply a death sentence (though he obviously thought it did). At the very least, he argued, it signified a severe punishment of some sort, equivalent, for all intents and purposes, to destruction. He cites the example from the *Acts of Thomas* immediately after it as an unambiguous example of the death penalty.

113 The text is from McCone, 'Dubthach maccu Lugair', p. 30.

114 The translation is from Carey, 'The Two Laws', p. 15.

worth considering, in this instance, if the author had Pelagian doctrine in mind, specifically the notion expressed in the Prologue to his commentary on Romans, where Pelagius accused all non-Jews of transgressing the will of God by failing to derive the Law from close observation of the creation as, in his opinion, all gentiles were obliged to have done. If so, we might be invited to understand Dubthach as an example of the perfect pre-Christian gentile who achieved the Pelagian ideal by deducing the Law from nature itself; and, by extension, we might likewise be invited to assume the same about pre-Christian Irish law in general. Whether they regarded the story as literally true or not, later Irish jurists could point to the sound virtue of his judgement as witness to the sanctity and rectitude of pre-Christian Irish jurisprudence: if Dubthach was a righteous Irish gentile who could judge justly according to the Law of Nature prior to the conversion, then presumably other pagan Irish jurists, like but not limited to Moran and Fíthal, could have done so as well; and therefore much, if not all, pre-Christian, native Irish law (including the mechanisms that produced it) might be regarded as virtuous jurisprudence enacted under the Law of Nature. As such, its continued application would be acceptable in the new Christian order. In fact, this is the conclusion reached in the Pseudo-historical Prologue after Dubthach and Patrick together reviewed the full corpus of pre-Christian, native following Núadu's death:

> Ina bretha fíraicnid trá didiu ro labrastar in Spirut Naem tre ginu breithemon ⁊ filed fíréon fer nÉrenn ó congbad in insi-seo co cretem anall, dosairfen Dubthach uili do Pátraic. Ní didiu nád tudchaid fri bréthir nDé i recht litre ⁊ núḟiadnaise ⁊ fri cuibse na crésion, conairged i n.-ord brethemnachta la Pátraic ⁊ ecailsi ⁊ flaithi Érenn do neoch. Roba dír recht aicnid uile inge cretem ⁊ a cóir ⁊ a comuaim n-eclaise fri tuaith.[115]
>
> > (As for the judgements of true nature which the Holy Spirit uttered through the mouths of righteous judges and poets of the men of Ireland, from the time when this island was settled until the coming of the faith: Dubthach revealed them all to Patrick. Whatever did not go against God's word in the law of scripture and in the New Testament, or against the consciences of the faithful, was fixed in the system of judgement by Patrick and the churches and the princes of Ireland severally. The whole law of nature was acceptable, save ⟨in what concerns⟩ the faith, and its proper dues, and the knitting together of church and kingdom).[116]

115 The text is from Carey, 'An Edition of the Pseudo-historical Prologue', p. 12.
116 The translation is from Carey, 'An Edition of the Pseudo-historical Prologue', pp. 18–19.

This passage, I would argue, expresses the main theme of the Pseudo-historical Prologue. Pre-Christian, native law, though ultimately subject to the Church's review is, in the view of the text's author, generally in accordance with ecclesiastical law, and so remains fully in effect. As Robin Chapman Stacey described it,

> Particularly striking is the way in which the text of ⟨Dubhtach's⟩ judgement itself juxtaposes native and Christian notions of authority in a manner designed to underscore the fundamental compatibility of each with the other. There can be no doubt as to its essential orientation: the text is overtly Christian in tenor and content throughout. But the new dispensation is portrayed as building on rather than rejecting the past.[117]

To be sure, the emphasis is on the consonance and joint utility of two systems of law, not their differences; but there is more going on in this passage.

The statement declaring that 'Roba dír recht aicnid uile' (the whole law of nature was acceptable), has further implications. More than merely positing that the Pre-Christian native legal system was based on the Law of Nature, the author of the Pseudo-historical Prologue situated pre-Christian Irish law within a contemporaneous understanding of Christian history in a very particular way. According to the view expressed in the text, pre-Christian Irish law was, essentially, the Law of Nature, though not straightforwardly in the Pauline sense: that is, it was not simply the law of intrinsically virtuous, but ignorant pagans. Rather, as John Carey has noticed, Dubthach's judgement invokes Noahide Law: 'Sinu aithrib, aithrib Nae, nert nad- cláen -coicert Coimdiu cona- forcraid -fobair for fuilechair fer'[118] (Older than the fathers, the fathers of Noah, is the power which God did not deem wicked, so that the bloodshed of men does not swell to excess).[119] In the same vein elsewhere in the text, the pre-Christian jurists of Ireland are compared to the prophets and patriarchs of the Old Testament:

> Ar in Spirut Naem ro labrastar ⁊ doaircechain tria ginu na fer fíréon ceta-rabatar i n.-inis Érenn amail donaircechain tria ginu inna prímḟáide ⁊ inna n-uasalaithre i recht petarlaice [...].[120]

> (For the Holy Spirit spoke and prophesied though the mouths of the righteous men who were first in the island of Ireland, as He

117 Stacey, *Dark Speech*, p. 84.
118 The text is from McCone, 'Dubthach maccu Lugair', p. 29.
119 The translation is by Carey, 'The Two Laws', p. 13.
120 The text is from Carey, 'An Edition of the Pseudo-historical Prologue', p. 12.

> prophesied though the mouths of the chief prophets and patriarchs of the Old Testament [...]).[121]

These allusions to Noah and the Patriarchs were carefully chosen. In the first quotation, neither Noah nor Noahide law is directly referenced; rather it is those 'older than the Fathers of Noah', who are mentioned. Who was Dubthach referring to with this statement? Following Damian Bracken, I would argue that the poet intended to signify Adam, and the death that Adam received as a punishment for his transgression in Eden. As Bracken has demonstrated, Hiberno-Latin ideas about Adam's fall inform much of the imagery in the poem.[122]

That said, it is noteworthy that in the first citation the poet refers to Noah and his predecessors as 'fathers', in effect tracing the descent of the Irish to Adam expressly via Noah, thus situating them as gentiles within a Christianized framework of sacred history. The second quotation likens the pre-Christian Irish to the patriarchs of the Old Testament, albeit with a simile (*amail*, 'as, just as, like'; i.e., not a metaphor). This conceptualization of Irish ancestral history accords with the view recounted in the Caí Caínbrethach episode (described above), where the Irish are portrayed as the progeny of the Egyptian princess Scot and Nél, son of Fénius Farsaid, himself a descendent of Japheth, Noah's son. Though variations occur, Irish pseudo-historical texts (and other kinds of texts) are relatively consistent in tracing their decent back to Noah via Japheth, thereby situating themselves within sacred history as gentile descendants of Noah, who were thus subject to the Law of Nature as expressed in the Noahide Law until the coming of Christianity.

Moreover, the proto-Irish descendants of Scot and Nél, who were resident in Egypt at the time of Moses and sympathetic to his cause, did not accompany Moses *en masse* on the Exodus, but rather sent one of their number — Caí Caínbrethach — to study law directly from him. Even so, neither Caí nor any of the proto-Irish entered the Promised Land, and thus they never received the Mosaic Covenant. This collective genealogy casts the Irish as Noahide gentiles — not as God's Chosen People literally or metaphorically — despite the fact that they had access to the Mosaic Law. This is the understanding of Irish descent expressed in the Pseudo-historical Prologue, specifically in the stipulations of Dubthach's judgement (as John Carey has noted).[123] Both the Caí Caínbrethach episode and the Pseudo-historical Prologue attest to the belief that the Irish understood themselves to be gentiles who hailed from a Noachic line.

---

121 The translation is from Carey, 'An Edition of the Pseudo-historical Prologue', p. 18.

122 See Bracken, 'Immortality and Capital Punishment', pp. 147–63, and Bracken, 'The Fall and the Law', pp. 147–56.

123 Carey, 'The Two Laws', p. 17.

This perception of Irish ethnic history has important legal-theological implications in biblical law. Without question, Irish pseudo-historians did not consider their pre-Christian ancestors to be Israelites in any sense, literal or otherwise, at least in the literature under consideration.[124] Rather, they understood them to be gentiles, but gentiles with a particular biblical genealogy; namely, they understood themselves to be descendants of Noah via Japheth. The Irish shared this pseudo-historical view of their ethnic past with any number of other Christian peoples in Europe and beyond. The Irish differed from most of their counterparts, however, in how they understood what this lineage meant for them and their pre-Christian, native system of jurisprudence within biblical law.

For the early Christian Irish, positing this biblical genealogy meant that, prior to conversion, Irish pseudo-historians understood their ancestors to be gentiles under the dispensation of the Law of Nature. However, as both texts also suggest, the Irish were gentiles with special access to the Law of Moses. Very importantly, however, this foreknowledge did not render them recipients of — or in any way contractual parties to — the Mosaic Covenant. In effect, they believed themselves to have had literal access to the Mosaic Law without the spiritual obligations of those who received it with the Covenant (i.e., Jews). From their perspective, therefore, Irish pre-Christian law could be described as the innately righteous jurisprudence of virtuous legalists subject to the Law of Nature, confirmed and informed by Noahide Law, and — very significantly — with proleptic Mosaic influence.

In terms of biblical law, this meant that, prior to conversion, the Irish would have come under the particular expression of the Law of Nature established when God made his Covenant with Noah on Mount Ararat after the Great Flood. In the Jewish tradition, this body of law — called Noahide law — though appearing in various formulations, most commonly consists of seven precepts including those given to Adam in the Garden of Eden and those given to Noah after the flood.[125] Theological scholarship on the Noahide laws, their precise contents, their applicability, and their role in sacred history, is a highly technical topic both in Jewish and Christian exegesis, ancient and modern, extending well beyond the scope of the present discussion. For the purpose of the present argument, suffice to say that, for the Irish, Noahide law consisted of biblical precepts handed down to mankind beginning with Adam and continuing thereafter

124 See O'Brien, 'The New Israel Motif', pp. 246–50 and p. 255.

125 These include injunctions against idolatry, murder, theft, fornication, blasphemy, avoidance of eating blood, and just legal practice. As has often been noticed (and variously interpreted by Jewish and Christian exegetes), this basic set of commandments, though slightly broader in scope, generally parallels the legal stipulations required of new Christian converts decided at the Synod of Jerusalem, as described in Acts 15.

until Moses's epiphany on Mount Sinai. The most significant moment during this period occurred when God established his postdiluvian Covenant with Noah, in Genesis 9:1–17. At this time on Mount Ararat, God laid down several commandments explicitly: (1) that mankind should be fruitful and multiply (Genesis 9:1,7), (2) that no-one should eat meat with blood (Genesis 9:4),[126] and (3) that murderers must receive capital punishment (Genesis 9:6).[127] In whatever way the Irish conceptualized the legal requirements of the Noahide Covenant (for it is not explicitly addressed in surviving literature),[128] they would have understood it, at the very least, to contain these three precepts.

As both Donnchadh Ó Corráin and John Carey have remarked,[129] the wording of Dubthach's judgement closely parallels the Noahide injunction requiring that murders be punished with death, as stated in Genesis 9:6:

> **Pseudo-historical Prologue**
> Baad cach óen oirges duine deilb ríg roda- slúagaid –sert. Saigid éc elgnas ⟨n⟩derg diambi marb nech de [...].[130]
>
> > (Let everyone die who kills a man in the image of the King who arrayed them in multitudes. Death pursues bloodshed, if someone dies of it [...]).[131]
>
> **Genesis 9:6**
> quicumque effuderit humanum sanguinem fundetur sanguis illius ad imaginem quippe Dei factus est homo.
>
> > (Whosoever shall shed man's blood, his blood shall be shed: for man was made in the image of God).

---

126 Carey, 'The Two Laws', p. 17 and n. 80 notes that the first fourteen canons in the *Canones Adomnani* 'appear to be a dietary code based on God's commandment to Noah not to eat meat with blood in it [...] rather than on the restrictions revealed to Moses'. See also: Ó Néill and Dumville, *Cáin Adomnáin and Canones Adomnani.*

127 As Ó Corráin notes, Genesis 9:6 is cited in *Collectio canonum Hibernensis*, Liber LXVI, *De contrariis causis* (Concerning contrary sources), cap. 4, *De seueritate uindicte, et contra, indulgentia* (Concerning the severity of punishment and, on the contrary, clemency), albeit truncated, and in non-standard form: 'Qui effunderit sanguinem innocentis, sanguis ejus effundetur' (He who sheds the blood of an innocent person, let his blood be shed). See *The Hibernensis*, Bk I, p. 471, l. 4 and note to l. 4 (text); Bk II, p. 829 (trans.).

128 That said, Noah had special significance in the Irish tradition. As Carey, 'The Two Laws', p. 17, n. 80, has noted: 'Noah seems to have had special significance for the Irish as an apical ancestor whom they shared with the Chosen People; thus in *Lebor Gabála* he is called "the second Adam" (*in tAdam dedenach, Book of Leinster*, I, l. 33), and the arcane word *noe* "human being, person", is presumably his name used as a substantive (*eDIL*, s.v. 1 *noe*)'.

129 Ó Corráin, Breatnach, and Breen, 'Laws of the Irish', pp. 388–89; Carey, 'The Two Laws', p. 17.

130 The text is from McCone, 'Dubthach maccu Lugair', p. 29.

131 The translation is from Carey, 'The Two Laws', p. 14.

At its foundation, then, Dubthach's judgement is based on Noahide law. That Dubthach could make such a judgement certainly aligns with contemporary Irish pseudo-history: Irish pseudo-historians, believing themselves to be descendants of Japheth would, presumably, have imagined their pre-Christian ancestors to have inherited these pre-Mosaic legal precepts. The author of the Pseudo-historical Prologue seems to have equated this Noahide heritage with the Law of Nature.[132] Later, for instance, when Patrick and Dubthach are examining native Irish law to decide what they can keep and what must be discarded, pre-Christian, native law is specifically and repeatedly referred to as *recht aicnid* (the Law of Nature):

> Is ann ro herbad do Dubthach taisbénad breithemnusa ⁊ uile filidechta Érenn ⁊ nach rechta ro fallnasat la firu Érenn i recht aicnid ⁊ i recht fáide, i mbrethaib indse Érenn ⁊ i filedaib doaircechnatar donicfad bélra mbán mbiait .i. recht litre. Ar in Spirut Naem ro labrastar ⁊ doaircechain tria ginu na fer fíréon ceta-rabatar i n.-inis Érenn amail donaircechain tria ginu inna prímfáide ⁊ inna n-uasalaithre i recht petarlaice; ar rosiacht recht aicnid már nád roacht recht litre. Ina bretha fíraicnid trá didiu ro labrastar in Spirut Naem tre ginu breithemon ⁊ filed fíréon fer nÉrenn ó congbad in insi-seo co cretem anall, dosairfen Dubthach uili do Pátraic. Ní didiu nád tudchaid fri bréthir nDé i recht litre ⁊ núfiadnaise ⁊ fri cuibse na crésion, conairged i n.-ord brethemnachta la Pátraic ⁊ ecailsi ⁊ flaithi Érenn do neoch. Roba dír recht aicnid uile inge cretem ⁊ a cóir ⁊ a comuaim n-eclaise fri tuaith. Conid é Senchus Már in sin.[133]
>
> > (Then it was entrusted to Dubthach to exhibit judgement, and all the poetry of Ireland, and every law which held sway among the men of Ireland, in the law of nature and the law of the prophets, in the judgements of the island of Ireland and among the poets who had prophesied that the white language of the *Beati* would come, i.e. the law of scripture. For the Holy Spirit spoke and prophesied through the mouths of the righteous men who were first in the island of Ireland, as He prophesied though the mouths of the chief prophets and patriarchs of the Old Testament; for the law of nature reached many things which the law of scripture did not reach. As for the judgements of true nature which the Holy Spirit uttered through the mouths of the righteous judges and poets of the men of Ireland, from the time when this island was settled until the coming of the faith: Dubthach revealed them all to Patrick. Whatever did

---

132 This identification of Noahide Law with Natural Law, incidentally, was raised by theologians of a much later era. The scholarship on the subject is quite involved but, for a good discussion of the topic, see Bleich, 'Judaism and Natural Law'.

133 The text is from Carey, 'An Edition of the Pseudo-historical Prologue', p. 12.

> not go against God's word in the law of scripture and in the New Testament, or against the consciousness of the faithful, was fixed in the system of judgement by Patrick and the churches and the princes of Ireland severally. The whole law of nature was acceptable, save (in what concerns) the faith, and its proper dues, and the knitting together of church and kingdom. So, this is the *Senchas Már*).[134]

It would seem, therefore, that from the standpoint of the Prologue's author, pre-conversion Irish law was the equivalent of the Law of Nature, though not straightforwardly in the Pauline sense. Rather, it appears that he believed it to be a native outcrop founded ultimately upon Noahide Law, which the Irish understood themselves to have inherited directly as descendants of Japheth. Furthermore, they believed that those elements of the native legal system beyond the Noahide core arose, by analogy, just as they did for the Patriarchs (as stated in the passage above), that is, by the voice of the Holy Spirit speaking through righteous men. So, in this view, Irish law is Noahide Law; as such, it is also the Law of Nature, but with a distinct biblical lineage. In this way, the composer of the Pseudo-historical Prologue situated the pre-conversion Irish within sacred history as gentiles, but of a very special sort. They were gentiles who had received the Noahide Covenant and its laws; and therefore everything in their legal system beyond the precepts of Ararat (and beyond their precocious foreknowledge of Mosaic Law, thanks to Caí Caínbrethach) — that is, everything that might be attributed to the Law of Nature — did not arise merely from the minds of the naturally good jurists *ex nihilo* (as it did elsewhere), but from the hearts of naturally good, pre-Christian Irish legalists whose native jurisprudence had a theologically defined place in Judeo-Christian history. What is more, the later developments of their native legal system might be attributed directly to the prophetic guidance of the Holy Spirit.

Dubthach's judgement, however, is even more firmly grounded in the early Irish conception of biblical law. Portrayed in the text as a fatidic, pre-conversion channeller of divine will, it is perhaps not surprising that Dubthach's verdict accorded neatly with biblical law on each of the four levels recognized in early medieval Ireland, though Dubthach himself, characterized as a righteous pagan on the verge of receiving the Christian faith, could not have realized it. A perceptive, Christianized audience on the other hand — who may or may not have regarded this story as literal history — would certainly not have missed this important fact. Like the decision of the Synod of Jerusalem discussed above, Dubthach's decision that Núadu should die while his soul should be saved found scriptural

134 The translation is from Carey, 'An Edition of the Pseudo-historical Prologue', pp. 18–19.

authority in biblical law at every stage of sacred history (from a medieval Irish Christian perspective). Specifically, early Irish Christians, at least those who subscribed to this position, believed that capital punishment was permitted, even required, under Noahide Law (which is to be understood as the equivalent, in this case, of the Law of Nature), the Law of Moses, the Law of the Prophets, and the Law of Christ.

That at least some early Irish Christians believed there was scriptural authority in all four levels of biblical law is clear implicitly in the passages from *Collectio canonum Hibernensis* cited earlier in this chapter (the chapters from Liber XXVI, *De sceleribus et uindictis eorum* and is overtly stated in Liber LXVI, *De contrariis causis*[135] (Concerning contrary sources),[136] cap. 4, *De seueritate uindictae et eius indulgentia*[137] (Concerning the severity of punishment and, on the contrary, clemency):[138]

> **Cap. 4 *De seueritate uindictae et eius indulgentia***
> Lex: Qui effunderit sanguinem innocentis, sanguis eius effundetur. Dauid): Deus ultionum, Dominus Deus; usque: Qui iudicas terram. Item: Letabitur iustus cum uiderit uindictam; usque: Ad peccatoris. Hieremias: Maledictus homo, qui prohibet gladium suum a sanguine. In nouo: Verbis Phetri Annaniam et Saphira exanimes cadunt. Hironimus: Dum parcunt peccatoribus sacerdotes, æcclesie moliuntur interitum. Item: Qui non occidit latronem, ipse perdit inopem. Mortificat animas, que non moriuntur, et uiuificat animas, quae non uiuunt. Item: Non morientem quippe mortificat, qui injustum uiuificare nititur et qui reum a supplicio soluere conatur. Item: Qui occidit in gladio, oportet eum in gladio occidi. Augustinus: Que est ista uanitas, uni parcere et omnes in discrimine adducere? Pulluitur enim populus uno peccante. Lex, e contra: Ne memor sis iniurię ciuium tuorum. Dauid: Misericors et miserator Dominus, patiens et multę misericordiae. Item: Si dereliquerint fili eius legem meam; usque: non dispergam ab eis. Christus: Diligite inimicos uestros. Item: Si non remiseritis hominibus peccata eorum, non remitet uobis pater uester cælestis, qui in caelis est. Item): Superexaltat misericordia iuditio. Phetrus: interrogauit: Si peccauerit in me frater meus, quoties dimitam ei, usque septies? Veritas respondit: Non dico usque septies, sed septies et septuagies. Dominus orauit pro Iudeis: Pater ignosce illis. Sic et Stiphanus dixit: Domine Ihesu, ne statuas illis hoc in peccatum; nesciunt {seruiens} enim, quid faciunt.[139]

---

135 The full text of Liber LXVI can be found in *The Hibernensis*, Bk I, pp. 466–74.

136 The full translation of Liber LXVI can be found in *The Hibernensis*, Bk II, pp. 825–31.

137 The texts of cap. 4 is from *The Hibernsnsis*, Bk I, pp. 471–72.

138 The translation of cap. 4 is from *The Hibernensis*, Bk II, p. 829.

139 The text is from *The Hibernensis* Bk I, pp. 471–72.

> (**Chapter 4** ***Concerning the severity of punishment and, on the contrary, clemency***
> The Law: Whoever will shed innocent blood, his own blood shall also be shed. David: God the Lord God of revenge; as far as: You who judge the earth. Likewise: The just man will rejoice when he shall see the punishment; as far as: Of the sinner. Jeremiah: Cursed be he who withholds his sword from blood. In the New Testament: Ananias and Saphira fall lifeless at Peter's words. Jerome: So long as *sacerdotes* spare sinners, churches bring about death. Likewise: He who does not kill a thief, himself destroys the helpless. He puts to death the souls that do not die, and revives the souls that do not live. Likewise: He who strives to revive the unjust and tries to release a criminal from punishment puts the one who is not dying to death. Likewise: He who kills by the sword, ought to be killed by the sword. Augustine: What is this vanity, to spare one and lead all others into danger? For the people are polluted by a single sinner. The Law, on the contrary: Be not mindful of the injury of your citizens. David: The Lord is gracious and merciful, patient and plenteous in mercy. Likewise: And if his children forsake my law; as far as: I shall not move away from them. Christ: Love your enemies. Likewise: If you will not forgive men their sins, your heavenly father, who is in heaven, shall not forgive you. Likewise: Mercy exalts itself above judgement. Peter asked: If my brother offend against me, how many times shall I forgive him? Up to seven times? The truth responded: I say not unto you, up to seven times, but up to seventy-seven times. The Lord pleaded on behalf of the Jews: Father, forgive them. So Stephen also said: Lord Jesus, do not reckon this as their sin, for they know not what they do).[140]

Here, reference to the Noahide stipulation (taken to be equivalent to the Law of Nature) that homicide must be punished with death (Genesis 9:6) tops the list. This passage likewise references sentiments expressed in the Law of Moses, as expressed in Deuteronomy 21:7–8. It is followed by Old Testament citations from David in the Psalms and Jeremiah, the latter representing the Law of Prophecy, and finally, reference to the story of Ananias from the New Testament (Acts 5) representing the Law of Christ. In this way, the Irish notion that a just judgement accords with biblical law on all relevant levels is elegantly achieved;[141] and thus Dubthach's judgement, albeit unwittingly to him, agreed with the Law of Nature/Noahide

140 The translation is from *The Hibernensis*, Bk II, p. 829.

141 Obviously, the purpose of this chapter is to cite authorities on both sides of the argument: hence following the citations from authorities representing multiple levels of biblical law in support of capital punishment, the compilers present an equivalent (apparently contradictory) list of citations expressing the opposite point of view in favour of forgiveness.

Law, the Law of Moses, the Law of the Prophets, and the Law of Christ, as exemplified by these scriptural passages.[142]

Conspicuously missing is the Mosaic *locus classicus* in support of capital punishment, Exodus 21:23–25 (compare, Deuteronomy 19:21). What explains the absence of any reference to this verse? A number of possibilities emerge: perhaps this passage was considered so obvious as to hardly warrant notice. Liber XXVI of *Collectio canonum Hibernensis, De sceleribus et uindictis eorum* (Concerning offenses and their punishment), for example, includes two chapters asserting that capital punishment is not prohibited in the New Testament and explaining the reasons why it is allowed, but makes no mention of the Old Testament position in favour of it. So, quite possibly, the compliers of *Collectio canonum Hibernensis* felt the Mosaic requirement for capital punishment was sufficiently well-known to obviate any need for its mention. That said, the redactor of the **C**-text of the Pseudo-historical Prologue included some reference to this precept of Mosaic Law, and so added the following statement to Dubthach's reluctant acceptance of Patrick's request that he stand as judge: 'is ed robai f*or*do cind i *n*dEiri*n*d breth rechta .i. indech*ad* eisidhi, cos i cois ⁊ suil a suil ⁊ ainm i n.-anm'[143] (it is this which was before you in Ireland, that is vengeance, a foot for a foot, an eye for an eye, a life for a life).[144] This is such an overt allusion to the renowned Mosaic precept that it can hardly be mistaken for anything else. For the redactor of **C**, then, Dubthach had knowledge both of Noahide and (presciently) of Mosaic Law. I have already discussed Irish belief about pre-conversion foreknowledge of the Noahide Code, but what about the Law of Moses? In this case, I would argue that the redactor was acquainted with the pseudo-historical tradition (discussed above) in which Caí Caínbrethach studied law under Moses on the Exodus and brought it back to Ireland. It is also possible that the redactor subscribed to the Pelagian belief that pre-conversion gentiles possessed both the ability and the responsibility to derive the Law by close observation of the Creation, and thus naturally good Irish jurists would have deduced this from their own experiences.

The evidence considered so far supports the notion that at least some early Irish Christians believed that capital punishment for certain offences was not only permitted in all four biblical laws, but even that it was required it in some cases. The text of the Pseudo-historical Prologue

142 The fact that text of *Collection canonum Hibernensis* here also provides scriptural *loci* advising against capital punishment does not undermine Dubthach's judgement, since the point of the exercise is to find appropriate authorities in support of a particular decision, whether or not one might also find authorities advising differently. It was the role of the judge to decide which authorities apply best to a given case.

143 The text is from Carey, 'An Edition of the Pseudo-historical Prologue', p. 14 (in the notes to § 5).

144 The translation is from McCone, 'Dubthach maccu Lugair', p. 12.

in its most ancient form (that can be reconstructed, i.e., the version in Carey's edition) presents, at least superficially, a neatly packaged, internally consistent argument in favour of capital punishment, elegantly consonant with Irish law, both Christian and pre-Christian. And yet, there are a number of issues, reflected in the textual tradition of the Pseudo-historical Prologue and elsewhere, suggesting that the use of capital punishment was not so straightforwardly clear-cut in all segments of early Irish society. In fact, the above cited chapter of *Collectio canonum Hibernensis,* Liber LXVI, *De contrariis causis* (Concerning contrary sources), cap. 4, *De seueritate uindictae et, e contra, indulgentia* (Concerning the severity of punishment and, on the contrary, clemency) consonant with its title, gives voice to just such a controversy: first, it lists a series of scriptural and patristic quotations seemingly in favour of capital punishment followed immediately by a comparable, apparently contradictory list, calling for mercy and forgiveness. Like the other topics considered in this Book of *Collectio canonum Hibernensis,* citations were compiled expressing both sides of the argument, with no attempt at reconciliation.

What are we to make of this apparent ambiguity, if indeed it is not doctrinal conflict outright? Despite the strong case made for capital punishment in the Pseudo-historical Prologue, all evidence suggests that the pre-Christian, native legal system allowing monetary compensation for homicide (*éraic*), paid under threat of retributive vengeance obligatorily carried out by the victim's kin group, continued well after conversion and certainly long after the composition of the Pseudo-historical Prologue. If the purpose of the Prologue was to root out the native system, and the endless internecine feuding it precipitated between *fini* (kin groups) and *túatha* (peoples) in favour of ecclesiastically sanctioned executions, it would seem to have failed. In fact, **B** and **C** contain what McCone has referred to as a 'rider on *éraic*',[145] which may suggest that the native system usually won out:

> ISs ed tuicther triasin mbreith-sea anuas rofaillsigh dia do dubth*ach* .i. tiachtain it*er* dilgud ⁊ indech*ad*, uair indech*ad* robi ria pat*raic* i neirind ⁊ dilgud tuc pat*raic* lais .i. nuada do marb*ad* ina chinaidh ⁊ nem o pat*raic* do; s̄ ata dilgudh isin mbr*eith*-se*n* ⁊ ata indech*ad* IS e tiachtain it*er* dilgud ⁊ indech*ad* donither inniu, uair nach fuil comus nime ac neoch inniu am*ail* roboi in la-sin: cen duine do marb*ad* ina cintaib comraiti a*n* cein fogaba eiric, ⁊ cach uair na fuigbe eric, a marb*ad* ina cintaib comraiti, ⁊ a chur ar muir in chintaib anfoit ⁊ indeithb*ire* torbu, ⁊ fogn*am* uad ina chor ⁊ in chundr*ad*.[146]

145 See: McCone, 'Dubthach maccu Lugair', p. 2–3.
146 The text is from **C**, *Corpus Iuris Hibernici*, 341.24–32.

> (What is understood by this judgement above that God revealed to Dubthach is a compromise between forgiveness and retribution, since it is retribution that was in Ireland before Patrick and (it is) forgiveness that Patrick brought with him, that is the killing of Núadu for his crime and heaven from Patrick to him. This is the compromise between forgiveness and retribution that is made today, since the power of (bestowing) heaven belongs to no one today as it did in those days: a person is not killed for his intentional crimes as long as he procures wergild, and whenever he should not procure wergild he is killed for his intentional crimes, and he is put out to sea for his inadvertent crimes and criminal negligence, and service from him in his contract and in his covenant).[147]

McCone reads this provision as the Church's reluctant acceptance of native tradition,[148] while Carey sees it as a later interpolation, at odds with the overall pro-capital punishment theme of the text:

> The principle thrust of this passage is to *undermine the judgement itself*: Dubthach's sentence of death for murder is replaced by the normal system of *éraic*. Nothing in the judgement itself, or in the rest of the prose, gives any indication that this watering down of the divinely inspired verdict was any part of *PHP*'s doctrine: it is at least as likely that the paragraph is an attempt at rationalization as that it reflects an 'original core'.[149]

Here, I am inclined to agree with Carey's assessment, but go further and see this attempted rationalization as indicative of a larger ideological conflict within the Irish Church concerning this thorny legal matter.

There is more evidence that such a controversy existed. As mentioned above, clear indication of the Church's ambivalence on the topic is found in *Collectio canonum Hibernensis*, Liber LXVI, *De contrariis causis* (Concerning contrary sources), cap. 4, *De seueritate uindictae et ejus indulgentia* (Concerning the severity of punishment and, on the contrary, clemency) which compiles scriptural evidence both for and against capital punishment without offering resolution. Interesting in this light as well is the context of the citation from Augustine's *De sermone Domini in monte* that constitutes nearly the entirety of Liber XXVI, cap. 9 (cited above), which the compliers of *Collectio canonum Hibernensis* provided as evidence that capital punishment is allowed under New Testament law. Noteworthy in particular is that the sentiment expressed in Augustine's *De sermo Domini*

---

147 The translation is from McCone, 'Dubthach maccu Lugair', p. 8.

148 McCone, 'Dubthach maccu Lugair', p. 18.

149 Carey, 'The Two Laws', p. 7.

in monte immediately preceding the portion excerpted in *Collectio canonum Hibernensis* specifically discusses the issue of compensation and vengeance as redress for certain crimes, and condemns it:

> Namque omnia in quibus inprobitatem aliquam patimur in duo genera diuiduntur; quorum alterum est quod restitui non potest, alterum quod potest. Sed in illo quod restitui non potest uindictae solatium quaeri solet. Quid enim prodest quod percussus repercutis? numquid propterea illud quod in corpore laesum est restituitur in integrum? Sed tumidus animus talia fomenta desiderat; sanum autem firmum que ista non iuuant, quin potius misericorditer perferendam alterius infirmitatem iudicat, quam alieno supplicio suam mitigandam, quae nulla est.[150]
>
>> (For all cases in which we suffer some kind of evil deed are divided into two categories, of which the one is where restitution is not possible, and the other is where it is possible. But in that case in which restitution is not possible, usually people seek revenge as compensation. But what does it benefit you, having been struck, that you strike back? Surely, the wound that was inflicted on your body is not healed, on that account? A person full of anger, however, wants that kind of solace. Such things as that, however, please no-one who is healthy or mature; nay, such a ⟨healthy and mature person⟩ judges that the weakness of another is better endured mercifully than that his own ⟨suffering⟩, which is nothing, be alleviated by another person's punishment).[151]

Collectio canonum Hibernensis picks up immediately after this passage, beginning with, 'Neque hic ea uindicta prohibitor, que audit etiam as correctionem [...]',[152] (⟨n⟩or here is there a prohibition against that punishment, for it leads also to correction [...]),[153] which expresses a justification for vengeance that Augustine seems to have regarded as a less-than-ideal exception. Did the compiler who excerpted this portion of *De sermo Domini in monte* consider this context too controversial to include? Might it have undercut or mollified his stated purpose, i.e., to provide scriptural evidence that capital punishment was permitted in the New Testament? Admittedly, this is speculation from silence, since it is impossible to know if the compilers' failure to include Augustine's context for this passage reflected an agenda or not, assuming it even existed in their exemplar.

150 Augustine of Hippo, *De Sermone Domini in Monte*, I.62, ll. 1558–68 pp. 71–72.
151 The translation is my own.
152 The text is from *The Hibernensis*, Bk I, p. 169.
153 The translation is from *The Hibernensis*, Bk II, p. 598.

Noteworthy, in any case, is the treatment of Corinthians 5:5, which underscores the culmination of Augustine's reasoning in that portion of his *De sermo Domini in monte* supporting capital punishment that is cited in *Collectio canonum Hibernensis*, Liber XVI, cap. 9. 1 Corinthians 5:4–5 reads as follows (with my own emphasis):

> (4) in nomine Domini nostri Iesu Christi congregatis vobis et meo spiritu cum virtute Domine Iesu 5 **tradere** huiusmodi **Satanae** in interitum carnis ut spiritus salvus in die Domini Iesu.
>
> > ((4) In the name of our Lord Jesus Christ, you being gathered together, and my spirit with the power of our Lord Jesus; 5 **to deliver such a one to Satan** for the destruction of the flesh, that the spirit may be saved in the day of our Lord Jesus Christ).

At stake is what the phrase *tradere [...]Satanae* means. Does it signify capital punishment, or something else? Below is the passage as it is cited from Augustine's *De sermo Domini in monte* in Liber XXVI of *Collectio canonum Hibernensis, De sceleribus et uindictis eorum* (Concerning offenses and their punishment), cap. 9, *De uindicto in nouo* (Concerning punishment in the New Testament):

> Et si huic libro heretici aduersantur et ueteri testamento nolunt credere, Paulum apostolum intueantur, dicentem de quodam peccatore, quem **tradidit Satanæ** in interitum carnis, ut anima salua sit. Et si nolunt mortem hic intellegere, fortasse enim incertum est, quamlibet uindictam per Satanan factam ab apostolo fateantur; quod non iam odio, sed amore fecisse manifestat illud adiectum: Vt anima salua sit.[154]
>
> > (And if the heretics deny this book, and also refuse to believe the Old Testament, let them observe Paul the apostle, saying of a certain heretic — whom he **handed over to Satan** for the destruction of the flesh — that his should be saved. And if they refuse to understand death in this case — for perhaps it is uncertain — let them acknowledge that it was a punishment inflicted through Satan; which he did not do so much out of hatred, but out of love, is made clear by the addition: That his should be saved).[155]

Here, Augustine — and presumably the compilator of *Collectio canonum Hibernensis* citing him — is at pains to emphasize that, in this scriptural passage, Paul's phrase *tradere* [...] *Satanae* signified a judgement of death. As such, he took it as a straightforward justification of capital punishment.

---

154 The text is from *The Hibernensis*, Bk I, p. 170. Emphasis is my own, in both text and translation.

155 The translation is from *The Hibernensis*, Bk II, p. 599.

The precise meaning of this phrase and the punishment it stipulated, however, would appear to have been a matter of some controversy in the Hiberno-Latin tradition. The Würzburg glossator, for example, understood it very differently. For him, the phrase *tradere [...] Satanae* apparently indicated the performance of penance, not capital punishment. Thus, *Satanae* is glossed 'satanae .i. donfresndid .i. pænitentiæ .i. iscotarsne dondúalig insualig darahési' (to Satan, i.e. to the adversary, i.e., *poenitentiae* (to penance), i.e., opposed to the vice is the virtue which takes its place), and, in the margin: '[...] Aliter isdo dásact asberar athindnaculsa istresodin bidslán á animsom in die domini rl' (otherwise to madness it is said that he is given up: through this will his soul be saved *in die Domini* (on the day of the Lord), etc.).[156] The same sentiments are echoed in the gloss on 1 Timothy 1:20, where the same phrase *tradere [...] Satanae* describes judgement on a blasphemer. Here, the phrase '[...] quos tradidi Satanae' ([...] whom I have handed over to Satan), was glossed '.i. pænitentiæ ł dodásacht [...]' (i.e., to penance, or to madness [...]).[157] Consistently, therefore, the Würzburg glossator understood the phrase *tradere [...] Satanae* (to hand over to Satan) figuratively as 'tradere penitentiae' (to hand over to, i.e., = to require to perform penance). He did not take it literally to mean capital punishment. In fact, penance — not capital punishment — is frequently prescribed as remediation for homicide in the Irish penitentials, both for offending clerics and laymen alike.[158]

This contradictory evidence points to a dispute within the early Irish Church concerning the proper treatment of heinous crimes. At least some clerics fervently advocated in favour of capital punishment (as has often been claimed),[159] though that position was not universally held, and may indeed have met with significant resistance in some quarters. We may safely conclude, in any case, that the ecclesiastical jurist who composed the Pseudo-historical Prologue subscribed to the pro-capital punishment point of view. On the other hand, others within the Christian community, perhaps the majority, seem to have favoured penance — albeit very harsh

156 The text and translation are from, *Thesaurus Palaeohibernicus*, I, p. 551.

157 The text and translation are from *Thesaurus Palaeohibernicus*, I, p. 680. It is interesting that both glosses take madness as a form of (divinely imposed?) penance. I find it likely that this tradition is related to the well-known Irish literary genre of the *buile*, a word which as a common noun is defined in *eDIL*, s.v. *baile* as 'vision; frenzy, madness (originally arising out of supernatural revelations)', but also defines a 'class of tales' in which a man, often referred to as a *geilt*, suffers such a condition.

158 See Bieler, *The Irish Penitentials*, p. 311. A number of examples are listed under '*homicidium*' in the '*Index rerum uerborum locutionum*'. Many of the penances prescribed involve acts which might well lead to the death of the offender, such as unarmed exile. Execution, however, regardless of the eventual state of the perpetrator's soul, is clearly not preferred in these documents.

159 See especially: Bracken, 'Immortality and Capital Punishment'.

penance — as the appropriate punishment for murder, even in some of its more atrocious forms.[160] At the same time, secular society apparently continued unabated the pre-Christian practice of paying *éraic* to the kin group of the slain, under peril of vengeance should the offender fail to render compensation.

What are we to make of this complex, varied, and at times seemingly contradictory approach to justice within early the early Irish Church and society at large? First and foremost, I would argue that differences between the prescribed mechanisms of justice reflect the reality that early Irish jurisprudence was anything but monolithic. Certain legal principles and practices were more or less widely accepted throughout Ireland but, in general, I strongly suspect that justice was almost exclusively a local affair with all practical matters, both secular and ecclesiastical, conducted on the level of the *túath* or *provincia*. This high degree of decentralization accounts for much of the variation in particular legal customs and procedures apparent in the surviving documents. Beyond that, I speculate that the predominant methods of law enforcement were penance (imposed by the Church), the payment of *éraic* (imposed by the victim's kin group, both threatening — and carrying out — vengeance, if it was not paid), and royal prerogative which, presumably, was stronger or weaker depending on the merits of the ruler who applied it. Ideally — and perhaps in times of stress and out of pure necessity — these various mechanisms functioned conjointly, with each institution reinforcing the others: payment of *éraic* to a homicide victim's kin group, for example, would not necessarily have relieved a Christian transgressor of the religious obligation to perform penance, and vice versa; both, therefore, would be necessary for the redemption of the slayer.

Further, as has often been argued (and frequently overstated), I suspect that at least some of the complexities we find in the law codes can be accurately attributed to the reflex of certain well-intentioned jurists toward hyper-systematized, scholastic idealizations of a reality that was — of practical necessity — more likely to be austerely straightforward and pragmatic.[161] As D. A. Binchy famously proclaimed about the glosses and

160 For example, the *Penitential of Finnian*: 'Si qui⟨s⟩ autem clericorum ruina maxima ciciderit et genuerit filium et ipsum occiderit, magnum est crimen fornicatio et homicidium, sed redimi potest per penitentiam et misericordiam Dei [...]' (But if one of the clerical order falls to the depths of ruin and begets a son and kills him, great is the crime of fornication with homicide, but it can be expiated through penance and God's mercy [...]), Bieler, *The Irish Penitentials*, p. 76 (text); p. 77 (trans).

161 For an example of how scholasticism can present an artificial, idealized picture of reality, consider the statements in *Críth Gablach* and *Uraicecht na Ríar* that poets and laymen are divided into seven grades, explicitly cast as a parallel to the seven-fold division of ecclesiastical grades. See *Críth Gablach*, § 2, p. 1 and *Uraicecht na Ríar*, § 1, p. 103. See also Breatnach's discussion of the topic in the introduction to the same work, pp. 85–86.

commentary on the Old Irish law tracts: '[...] they weave a crazy pattern of rabbinical distinctions, schematic constructions, academic casuistry, and arithmetical calculations, none of which has any value for the student of Irish legal history'.[162] Here, caution is warranted, lest we reject valuable evidence as irrelevant when, to medieval sensibilities, it may not have seemed so. It is hardly dismissive, however, to suggest that ecclesiastical scholars may have crafted narratives like those I have discussed here, not for real-world procedural guidance or to shape actual legal practice, but primarily to exemplify points of doctrine regarding the ideological foundations of early Irish law. I suspect that both the Caí Caínbrethach episode and the Pseudo-historical Prologue fall into this category. I find it quite likely that the view of capital punishment advocated in the latter text represents an idealized, rather than a practical reality, fuelled by a highly intellectualized, clerical reading of texts such as Augustine's *De sermone Domini in monte*. More than anything else, I suspect that the author of the Pseudo-historical Prologue set out to create a kind of homiletic *exemplum* or dramatic midrash intended to explicate his view concerning a complicated point of legal theology regarding the place of the Irish in sacred history and the ideological foundations of their laws. At the same time, I would argue that, while the principal aim of the Pseudo-historical Prologue was not to stipulate pragmatic points of law, it sought to explicate a vein of contemporary doctrine concerning the proper relationship of the various biblical laws within sacred history (from an Irish perspective). To accomplish their goal, the author focused on the adjudication of a particular case at a crucial moment — the very cusp of Ireland's conversion — when law, understood in the broadest sense, was in a state of flux. By choosing a superficially problematic case at this momentous juncture, the author was able to raise an important ideological question (which, ultimately, would have practical implications): 'What law applies?' For the author's purpose, I would argue, the details of the case were largely irrelevant. The issue of capital punishment, while theologically significant, merely presented a convenient case-in-point. Rather, the specific legal procedure — and its theological implications — were his real matter of concern.

As the narrative sought to demonstrate, procedurally, a just legal pronouncement relied on scriptural authority, and should ideally agree with biblical law on all four levels (or, at least as many as possible): the Law of Nature/Noahide Law, the Law of the Prophets, the Law of Moses, and the Law of Christ. From the author's point of view, none of the successive laws in the medieval Irish view of sacred history displaced its precursor(s), but rather fulfilled them. Thus, just as the decision of the Synod of Jerusalem

162 Binchy, 'The Linguistic and Historical Value', pp. 225–26.

agreed (from a medieval Irish perspective) with biblical law on its four levels, so must any theologically significant decision of Irish courts. Minor decisions could rely on different kinds of authorities and fewer agreements between them, but important cases required agreement between all the four levels of biblical law. Expressing this point of doctrine, I would argue, was the main purpose of the Pseudo-historical Prologue. I do not know whether the author had the Synod of Jerusalem specifically in mind — after all, there is no reference to it in the text — but, in effect, the Irish document adjudicates a very similar question. In essence, it asks what law applies, to what extent, and how it should be administered to a newly converted people at a unique point in their sacred history. Intentionally or not, therefore, the Pseudo-historical Prologue constitutes an Irish Synod of Jerusalem.

CHAPTER 6

Conclusions

In early medieval Ireland, there never emerged a single, monolithically 'Irish' model to describe the relationship between pre-Christian, native Irish law and ecclesiastical law. The arrival of the new faith fomented a legal-theological dilemma that threatened some of the fundamental pillars of Irish society, and which (as I have shown) left its mark on early Irish legal literature. In different ways, at different times, and in different genres, Irish intellectuals of various specialties and intellectual orientations addressed this crucial question: how could one reconcile the disparate jurisprudential orientations that existed in early medieval Ireland in a way that satisfied the multifarious seats of power in society without undermining its ideological foundations? Though highly intellectualized, the discussion had practical implications: a society without clearly established, generally accepted ideas about justice risks falling into chaos. How, for example, could a legal system that relied on obligatory vengeance for crimes like murder function in a framework that mandated forgiveness? Stability between vastly differing cultural worldviews, some of which possessed significant power in early Irish society, depended on generally accepted answers to such questions. For that reason, a primary, ongoing endeavour among the early Irish *literati* involved various attempts to describe the relationship between the pre-Christian, native and the ecclesiastical legal systems in a manner that rested on solid, ideological bedrock. No single one of their 'solutions' ever achieved general acceptance, although common themes are identifiable. While it is clear from the written record that the Church's interests loomed largest in this debate, other interests, for example pre-Christian, native notions of jurisprudence ultimately rooted in Ireland's pagan past, left their mark as well.

A basic element of virtually all attempts to reconcile these discrete legal ideologies was biblical law. More specifically, fundamental to the Irish understanding of their own legal history was that it was inextricably tied to — even one and the same with — sacred history, that is, the Christian notion that humanity passed through a series of 'dispensations' or 'revelations', in which they entered into a series of 'covenants' with God promising to obey his law in return for a greater understanding of the divine plan. As such, early Irish attempts to reconcile pre-Christian, native, and ecclesiastical law relied on theological and pseudo-historical arguments at least as much as jurisprudence. Indeed, it is impossible to understand early Irish law outside of Irish Christian views of sacred history and biblical law.

Typically, though not ubiquitously, Irish Christians believed there were four dispensations over the span of sacred history. As I have shown, these consisted of the Law of Nature (which often included the so-called Law of Noah), the Law of Moses, the Law of the Prophets, and the Law of Christ, the first often described as 'ante legem', the second two as 'sub lege', and the fourth as 'sub gratia'. To be sure, this view of history cast humanity on a trajectory culminating in Christian law. That said — and this is an especially important point — many early Irish theologians adhered to the idea, expressed by Pelagius and others, that none of these covenants or laws was ever revoked. Rather, they adhered to the notion expressed in Matthew 5:17, i.e., that each law 'fulfills' or 'expands upon' those that came before, but does not abrogate them. As such, each law at every stage of sacred history was considered 'perfect' in its own right. The implications of this belief varied among the Irish *literati,* but — at its most basic level — this idea upheld the notion that the jurisprudence of each era was legitimate within a Christian ideological framework and — even more significantly — might continue to remain in force. In fact, one key method of determining the validity of a given precept, as expressed in *Collectio canonum Hibernensis,* was whether or not it found support in scriptural passages representing the various stages of sacred history.

The 'Law of Nature', the first stage within the Christian framework of sacred history, provided a convenient means to describe pre-Christian Irish jurisprudence. This gesture had the advantage of acknowledging the fundamental importance of pre-Christian, native law, while placing it on a narrative arc culminating with Christianity. The early Irish version of this belief contained some notable and unique features. First, early Irish legal-theological ideology emphasized the idea, expressed by Pelagius and others, of a *naturale bonum,* that is, the 'natural goodness' of individuals living (and legislating) *ante legem*. As such, major legalists in early Irish law, Dubthach maccu Lugair for example, were described in this manner, thus infusing their judgements with special importance and continued significance, even in later Irish law *sub gratia*. Thus, in the Pseudo-historical Prologue to the *Senchas Már,* Dubthach's review of Irish law with St. Patrick — in which the body of it was declared acceptable by the Saint, minus a few precepts which contradicted Christian beliefs — had the effect of justifying customary practice in Christian terms. At the same time, however, it made clear that Christianity — and, presumably, Christian jurists — held superior authority.

Very importantly, Irish ecclesiastical jurists did not think of themselves as Levites in the Old Testament sense, as has been argued and is now generally held. Both early Irish theological and pseudo-historical writings make clear that early Irish Christian intellectuals understood their place within sacred history as gentiles who lived under the Law of Nature (and, in some circles, the Law of Nature as expressed by the Law of Noah) prior to their conversion. Irish exegesis, for example on the Pauline epistles where the question of Judaizing is a frequent topic, consistently makes this point clear. What is more, while some Irish pseudo-historical texts, as I have described, make the case that pre-Christian, native Irish jurists had access to the Law of Moses, they are at pains to emphasize that the Irish never entered into the Mosaic Covenant. That said, they believed that the Law of Nature and the Law of Moses were perfect and continued to hold sway under the Law of Christ, and thus early Irish law as well.

Throughout the early period in Ireland, pseudo-history — particularly regarding legal matters — was an especially important method for describing and clarifying legal-theological issues. One gets the sense that this genre allowed for a degree of creative exploration of these dilemmas. Ultimately, it remains unclear how much truth-value these stories held for the educated classes; but, in any case, it is clear that a great deal of early Irish legal ideology was developed within the narrative genre of pseudo-history. For example, I discussed different versions of the story of Caí Caínbrethach who studied law under Moses on the Exodus, while those who eventually became the Irish were migrating from their homeland on a course that took them through many lands, including Egypt, before they eventually settled in Ireland. In one version of this story, Caí Caínbrethach learns the entirety of the Mosaic Law, but — and this is a subtle but crucial point — departs from the Israelites before entering the Promised Land and rejoining the Irish. The implications of this final point allowed Irish jurists who believed this story to claim knowledge not just of the Law of Nature before their conversion to Christianity, but also of the Law of Moses, without committing themselves (and their ancestors) to the reciprocal obligations of the Mosaic Covenant. In this view, therefore, pre-Christian, native Irish law was informed both by the Law of Nature and the Law of Moses before ever coming into contact with the Church or the Christian religion. What wonder, then, that that this body of pre-Christian, native law was acceptable to St Patrick, as narrated in the Pseudo-historical Prologue?

So, what were the ideological foundations of early Irish law? To be sure, the details varied over time and from text to text. Very basically, though, they consisted of a view of sacred history in which the Irish played a special role as the gentile recipients of the Law of Nature and — more specifically — the Law of Noah. In some circles, too, their jurisprudence emerged with special knowledge of the Law of Moses, which they believe they acquired before the coming of the faith (unlike other gentile peoples), and — in their case in particular — without their having entered into the mutual obligations of the Mosaic Covenant. As such, pre-Christian, native Irish law was imbued with authority that derived from its practitioners' self-perceived place in sacred history, and which — very significantly — justified the continued existence of many customary practices post Conversion. That said, the authority of customary practices relied on an understanding of Christian history that culminated in the Law of Christ and ecclesiastical law. Christian jurisprudence, therefore, had the final say. In the end, the picture that emerges is one of an ongoing discussion that continued through the Middle Ages without achieving generally accepted resolution, though with consistent, robust development over the full course of the early period. From the broadest perspective, one gets the sense that, generally speaking, this was a friendly, constructive discussion, even if its implications for individual stakeholders at specific times and locales might have been more political and ideologically impactful. That, however, would need to be the topic of another volume.

Part Two

Anglo-Saxon Law

CHAPTER 7

Background

Having discussed the ideological foundations of early Irish law, it remains to consider how and to what extent, if at all, these ideas — the conceptual bedrock upon which early Irish law rested — were received in Anglo-Saxon England. From the outset, it is important to establish that intercultural transmission of ideological frameworks, wholesale or in part, should not be considered unusual or improbable. The ideas of 'democracy' and 'republic' that emerged in ancient Athens and Rome eventually spread around the globe, with multifarious realizations of 'democracy' and 'republic' developing idiosyncratically at any number of removes. The Roman Republic differed in substantial ways from the republican governments that later arose, for example, in India and the United States; nonetheless, both are recognizable as such and can be traced back, ultimately, to a common ancestor.

In similar fashion, it should not be surprising that fundamental legal ideologies might have spread between early Ireland and Anglo-Saxon England, especially given what these two cultures had in common: both were Christianized (or, at least, Christianizing) peoples situated outside the erstwhile boundaries of the old Roman Empire at the time when their first written laws emerged,[1] both shared a common language (Latin) and an ecclesiastical culture, both developed vernacular written traditions relatively early, and both possessed extensive systems of pre-Christian, native law that survived in the collective memory. Moreover, they had extensive contact during Late Antiquity and the early Middle Ages due, above all, to ongoing Irish missions aimed at converting their Germanic-speaking neighbours. At least initially, these efforts bore more fruit than simultaneous attempts by Rome. Quite possibly, the relative success of the Irish missions resulted from a similar cultural perspective they shared with their English converts; a perspective that necessarily entailed concerns with which Roman Christians could not so readily empathize or address effectively. Thus, despite superficial differences, the early Irish and Anglo-Saxons held more in common with each other than either had in common

1 This statement is true of the Anglo-Saxons in the sense that the various peoples they consisted of originally migrated to the formerly imperial province of Britannia from unincorporated northern Germania. Culturally, therefore, they were never officially part of the erstwhile Empire.

with their neighbours on the European Continent, regardless of other linguistic, genetic, or cultural affinities.

Across the channel in regions formerly under the aegis of the now the dilapidated Western Empire, remnants of Roman infrastructure, both civil and material, persisted into Late Antiquity, though only to some waning extent that varied by locale. In some areas, a sense of continuity with late Roman institutions and cultural practices persevered into the early Middle Ages, laying the groundwork for what became the Holy Roman Empire. Nothing directly comparable existed in early Ireland or Anglo-Saxon England. For these Insular cultures outside the administrative structures of the old Empire, the new religion marked a stark break with the past. Neither culture experienced the relatively gradual changes that occurred to institutions (legal, religious, and otherwise) within the Empire as it Christianized and thereafter. Rather, in both Ireland and Anglo-Saxon England, conversion happened more abruptly and without close precedent. Early on, therefore, these cultures would have to address certain questions, including: to what extent were pre-Christian native legal practices still applicable? And, no less important, what status did they, as gentile Christian peoples, hold both historically and presently within the Christian understanding of sacred history? Although ultimately ideological in nature, answers to such questions had consequential implications for real-world legal affairs that could disrupt society, even long after paganism as a living belief system had obsolesced and disappeared. Stability mattered; and the purpose of law, at its base, is to provide stability. It should not be surprising, therefore that the early Irish legal tract *Córus Bésgnai* begins by expressing apprehension about the dissolution of human society:

> § 1. *Córus Bésgnai co háragar? I coraib bél, ar is bailedach in bith mani astaitis cuir bél.*[2]
>
> > (§ 1. The arrangement of discipline, how is it secured? By contracts, for it would indeed be a chaotic world if contracts were not held fast).[3]

Indeed, a notable feature of the earliest Irish laws is their attempt to describe normatively, as a first order of business, the proper functioning of society and the relations of individuals within it, rather than to enumerate various misdeeds and to prescribe sanctions for them. This gesture, I posit, arose from anxiety about certain implications of Christian belief and the potential they had to destabilize society and any number of ingrained cultural practices.

---

2 The text is from Breatnach, *Córus Bésgnai*, p. 26.
3 The translation is from Breatnach, *Córus Bésgnai*, p. 27.

Given the similarities and close contact between early Irish and English jurists throughout the early period, it should not be surprising that they would borrow from each other when addressing similar dilemmas. And indeed, there are clear avenues through which such transmission could — and did — occur.[4] From the earliest period, Irish missionaries played a fundamental role in converting the English, especially in the north of the country. That, and the fact that the Irish were converted roughly a century and a half before the English (and were thus chronologically first to address the ideological dilemmas that provide the central focus of this volume, foremost among them how to justify the continued practice of certain pre-Christian, native legal practices in a new, Christian milieu) has led me to surmise, albeit cautiously, that the primary direction of influence flowed from Ireland to Anglo-Saxon England. My inference on this point is bulwarked by the fact that the Irish texts I focus on most heavily tend to predate the English texts I shall discuss, though this is a kind of evidence that must be carefully scrutinized, since the date of a surviving witness often reveals little about a possible textual history that underlies it. Also, it is important to recognize that influence could, and sometimes did, flow in the other direction; a fact I remain cognizant of throughout and mention where appropriate.

Before going any further, it is important to mention that I am not the first to compare early Irish and Anglo-Saxon law. Robin Chapman Stacey, for example, addressed this matter in a 1991 article entitled 'Law and Order in the Very Old West: England and Ireland in the Early Middle Ages'.[5] There, Stacey was concerned primarily with how early medieval Irish and Anglo-Saxon jurists (among others) used lawbooks:

> Lawbooks were viewed in the early middle ages as sources of principles, old and new, in which legal decisions might be grounded; they were consulted not for specific rules that would be applied to every case that arose, but rather for a general understanding of how things ought to be. Deliberately elastic concepts like duty and the neglect of duty, status and the absence of status, could be continually reinterpreted in the light of contemporary standards and expectations.[6]

Although she expands upon his claims significantly, Stacey acknowledges that her view owes much to Dafydd Jenkins, who argued that the Anglo-Saxon laws, like their medieval Welsh counterparts, should be understood as records of royal judgements:

4 I shall elaborate on this claim below.

5 Stacey, 'Law and Order in the Very Old West', pp. 39–60.

6 Stacey, 'Law and Order in the Very Old West', p. 54.

> The king's declaration would be a judgement, a *brawd*, a *dom*, on the particular problem before him; the decision of a court of law or the opinion of a learned man of law would have the same character; hence every book which contained rules for particular circumstances would be a *brawdlyfr* or *domboc* [...]. A judgement might be a private note of the custom of the country, and the judge (or the doomsmen) to whom it was cited would be glad of its help in deciding the instant case, without being much concerned with its origin if it provided relief from the painful responsibility of decision. Laymen seldom realise how intensely lawyers prefer outside authority to personal responsibility as a basis for decision.[7]

Here, Jenkins is concerned with how the lawbooks were used; and in many ways, this passage could just as well describe the use and function of the early Irish laws, as evinced by the heavy glossing and commentary that accompanies them in many manuscript witnesses. It is more difficult to make the same case for the Anglo-Saxon law codes, however, since (for example) they typically lack anything like the glossing (or other symptoms of regular use) found in their Irish counterparts. Jenkins himself admits the potential tenuousness of this claim when applied to the Anglo-Saxon law codes when he says:

> [...] ⟨I⟩f the doombooks, as we may surely now call them, were private collections, could we not expect some of them to have survived? The argument just propounded would certainly be strengthened if a manuscript could surface in Leningrad or the Vatican which bore unmistakable signs of being a book used by a lawyer in tenth- or eleventh-century England, as we believe some of the Welsh law manuscripts to have been used by thirteenth-century practitioners.[8]

Jenkins's comparison between the Welsh and Anglo-Saxon laws has much in common with what Stacey later claimed about similarities between the Irish and Anglo-Saxon legal materials. While the idea that the law books were private collections for practical use by jurists is compelling as a model describing the practical function of the laws — and convincing as regards both the Irish and Welsh legal materials — it lacks the support of textual evidence where the Anglo-Saxon laws are concerned. Thus, while intriguing as a possible point of contact, all such theories remain speculative until more evidence is forthcoming. What method, then, can we use to investigate possible points of contact between early Irish and Anglo-Saxon legal ideology which — given the abstract quality of all 'ideologies', not to mention the difficulties involved in comparing them across cultures —

---

7 Jenkins, 'The Medieval Welsh Idea of Law', p. 345.
8 Jenkins, 'The Medieval Welsh Idea of Law', pp. 345–46.

presents a dilemma arguably even more fraught than the more practical question Stacey raises?

To examine the question of whether Irish legal ideologies might have been transmitted to Anglo-Saxon England, I have proceeded with the following, very general principles: first, I sought to identify broad, ideological trends, that is, the fundamental ideas that shaped the laws. I did not seek to catalogue minor, isolated similarities between individual precepts that might be attributable to anything ranging from analogous responses to a similar legal problem in both cultures, their common Indo-European heritage, or even anomalous direct borrowing (in either direction), unless those similarities pointed to a broader trend. My goal was not to inventory similar details shared by both bodies of law (regardless of their origin), but rather to examine the bedrock upon which their respective notions of jurisprudence rested. Overall, thus, I sought to identify influences of a higher order, for example, fundamental legal ideas and their underlying ideologies, or common patterns of thought that might be detectable. Thus, I focused on the ideological foundations of the laws in both cultures rather than on seeking to ferret out broadly similar *comparanda* between their statutory content. Second, I concerned myself primarily with texts that framed, justified, and explained the law codes, instead of on the statutes (or otherwise culturally normative material) in the codes themselves. The differences between what was considered 'legal' in these two cultures — indeed, between what was even considered 'law' at all — is so pronounced that stepping back to look at the bigger picture in this manner seemed most fruitful as a first gesture, and a vantage point that might provide a context for more tightly focused research on statutory details in future studies. Third, I looked hardest at Latin, ecclesiastical points of contact since, I hypothesized, that was the channel through which ideas were most likely to be shared in the first instance, given a common language and, to a certain extent, a common religious culture. Of course, I did not limit myself to Latin materials since legal ideologies would likely be reflected in vernacular texts as well. I hypothesized, however, that transmission would more likely occur via a lingua franca; and in the early medieval Insular realms, Latin filled that role.

In what follows, I shall consider two major cases that I have identified where early Irish legal ideologies appears to have influenced Anglo-Saxon jurists. These include: (1) the method used to cite authorities in eighth-century Northumbrian legal texts, and (2) the use of biblical pseudo-history to contextualize, explain, and justify English legal practices in the late ninth-century laws of King Alfred (and certain other texts, including genealogies, that emanated from his royal court). To be sure, Irish influences on Anglo-Saxon law were never profound or formative. At the same time, it is likely that none of the contemporary legalists involved — whether Irish or English — ever thought of the matters I am about to discuss as distinctively 'Irish'. What I have detected is the influence of certain ecclesiastical ideas apropos of converted gentile peoples that situate ultimately pre-Christian, native legal systems within a Christian framework. These ideas, I posit, spread from Irish ecclesiastical circles (where they first developed and were cultivated by Irish clerical jurists) to Anglo-Saxon England, where they appear to have informed and inspired analogous reflexes. For both the Irish and the English alike, these gestures involved situating their respective, pre-conversion myths of ethnogenesis within a more expansive, universalizing context of scared history. Moreover, these gestures aimed to explain and justify the continued use of certain, pre-Christian, native legal mechanisms after conversion, albeit within a Christian framework. As such, what evidence I have found of Irish influence on Anglo-Saxon law is primarily theological in nature, and 'legal' only to the extent that theology provided a context for the law.

Below, I shall discuss my evidence for Irish influence first on early Northumbrian legal practices, and second on certain documents that emanated from the court of King Alfred. As I shall demonstrate, early Northumbrian law shows distinctively Irish influence on the way jurists evoked authoritative sources in legal argumentation. Indeed, these texts seem to follow the order of precedence laid out explicitly in *Collectio canonum Hibernensis*.[9] Next, I shall discuss how Alfredian legal ideology rested upon a carefully crafted, pseudo-historical narrative of the Anglo-Saxon ethnogenesis that situated the English and their native legal practices within a Christian understanding of sacred history. This reimagined narrative cast the English as a gentile *gens* within sacred history in a manner similar to and, I would argue, ultimately inspired by Irish reflexes of the same gesture. I shall consider each of these points in turn.

---

9 Several manuscripts of *Collectio canonum Hibernensis* that ended up in England made their way there via Brittany, were the texts were glossed. We should not, therefore, rule out the possibility of Breton influence as well. Given, however, that *Collectio canonum Hibernensis* was compiled within Irish cultural milieux and given the early date of the Irish missions to Northumbria, I regard parallels between Anglo-Saxon laws and *Collectio canonum Hibernensis* to reflect primarily Irish influence, though we must be cautious not to rule out Breton contributions as well.

CHAPTER 8

Eighth-Century Northumbrian Law

The Authorities of Early Northumbrian Law

The extensive contacts between early Ireland (including areas under its cultural influence in northern Britain) and the Anglian kingdom of Northumbria have been well documented. Since these contacts have been described elsewhere both recently and far better than I could recount them myself, I shall not attempt to summarize them here.[1] Suffice to say that mutual influences between these areas were multifaceted, continuous, and wide-ranging. That said, there has been little-to-no discussion of legal points of contact, perhaps because, until recently, it was commonly held that no law survived from early Northumbria beyond a small number of Latin, ecclesiastical tracts, the importance of which has been underappreciated for a variety of reasons. Recently, Gilbert Markús somewhat optimistically described the extant corpus of legal materials from early medieval Northumbria as follows:

> No early Anglo-Saxon law survives from ⟨what later became⟩ Scotland, but a good deal of material survives from Northumbria and other parts of England, and there is no good reason to believe that the laws in Northumbrian southern Scotland differed radically from the laws in English Northumbria.[2]

I concur with Gilbert Markús that 'material survives from ⟨early medieval⟩ Northumbria', though I remain sceptical that it amounts to 'a good deal' of material. From before 900, there exist only a handful of surviving texts connected with Anglo-Saxon Northumbria that can be considered 'legal', none of which were written in the vernacular nor attached to the name of a king like the southern codes.

That said, the ecclesiastical laws that survive are more important than scholars have previously recognized. Arguing for the importance of these texts as witnesses to early Northumbrian jurisprudence, I have made a

1 See, for example, Edmonds, *Gaelic Influence in the Northumbrian Kingdom*; McCann, 'Bede's "Plures De Scottorum Regione"'; Whitelock, McKitterick, and Dumille, eds, *Ireland in Early Mediaeval Europe*; Ní Chatháin and Richter, *Irland und Europa im früheren Mittelalter*, and Flechner and Meeder, *The Irish in Early Medieval Europe*.

2 Markús, *Conceiving a Nation*.

case in several recent articles that two texts in particular — the so-called *Dialogue of Ecgberht* and the *Legatine Capitulary of 786* — preserve a tradition of Northumbrian law.[3] The *Dialogue of Ecgberht*, on the one hand, stands as a witness to Northumbrian law not only because it specifically addresses matters of clerical malfeasance, but also because it often adapts and applies secular legal practices to ecclesiastical situations. The *Legatine Capitulary*, on the other hand, stands as a witness to Northumbrian law not only because it was composed on site, in Northumbria specifically to address local affairs but, even more significantly, because it was composed by Alcuin, a native-born Northumbrian, drafting legislation in his homeland for his own people.[4] From these two texts, I argue, it is possible to distill a sense of early Northumbrian legal practices both secular and ecclesiastical. The full extent of that discussion, however, extends beyond my present argument.[5] Important for my present purpose is that both of these documents should be regarded as witnesses to early Northumbrian legal ideology and practice, and that the way both texts cite authorities derives ultimately from Irish methods. In fact, one will notice similarities with the method Columbanus used to cite authorities which I discussed in the introduction to this volume.

Historical and Textual Background of the Northumbrian Sources: The *Dialogue of Ecgberht* and the *Legatine Capitulary* of 786

The Dialogue of Ecgberht

Very little has been written about the *Dialogue of Ecgberht*, a document attributed to Archbishop Ecgberht of York (*c.* 732–766). Although other texts attributed to Ecgberht have been determined to be pseudonymous, his *Dialogus* would appear to be genuine.[6] The text is preserved in its entirety only in a single manuscript, BL, Cotton Vitellius A.xii, which also contains a number of Hiberno-Latin texts including, for example, Cummian's *Epistola de controuersia paschali*. Several fragments also bear

3 See K. Carella, 'Northumbrian Law before the Vikings'; B. Carella, 'The Earliest Expression for Outlawry'; and B. Carella, 'Alcuin and the Legatine Capitulary of 786'.

4 B. Carella, 'Alcuin and the Legatine Capitulary of 786'.

5 I shall explore the evidence for law north of the Humber more fully in my forthcoming E. C. Quiggin Memorial Lecture, entitled *Northumbrian Law before the Vikings*.

6 Both Henry Mayr-Harting and Barbara Yorke include the *Dialogue of Ecgberht* in recent discussions Anglo-Saxon history without qualification. See Mayr-Harting, *The Coming of Christianity*, pp. 251–52 and Yorke, *Kings and Kingdoms*, p. 74.

witness to the text.[7] The most recent edition is in Haddan and Stubbs' late nineteenth-century *Councils and Ecclesiastical Documents Related to Great Britain and Ireland*.[8] The *Dialogus* was translated in full only once, in an eighteenth-century volume by John Johnson.[9] More recently, a few excerpts of it have been translated by McNeill and Gamer in *Medieval Handbooks of Penance*.[10]

The Legatine Capitulary *of 786*

The *Legatine Capitulary* will require more substantial discussion. It is preserved in only one fragmentary medieval witness, Wolfenbüttel, Herzog-August Bibliothek, Cod. Guelf. 454 Helmstedt (dated to *c.* 1000[11]) and in full by the Magdeburg Centuriators, in a sixteenth-century transcription that appears to have been meticulously faithful to its exemplar.[12] It has been translated two times, once in full by John Johnson (save for the scriptural passages) in the mid-eighteenth-century,[13] and in part (i.e., a few short excerpts) by Dorothy Whitelock in *English Historical Documents*, I, no. 191.[14]

The *capitula* survive in the form of a letter sent by George of Ostia — the head of a delegation sent by Pope Hadrian to address certain, unspecified abuses in England — to report on the status of the mission. The legation also included Theophylact of Todi, a former head of the papal library and an abbot named Wigbod. As Bishop George's summary report makes clear, the *capitula* contained in the letter were not written to correct the abuses which the legation had been dispatched specifically to address. Those are lost to history. Rather, the *capitula* recounted in George's letter addressed matters which the mission learned about when

7 Fragments occur in Cambridge, CCC, 265 and Oxford, Bodl., Barlow 37.

8 The standard edition, which I use here, is Haddan and Stubbs, *Councils and Ecclesiastical Documents*, III, pp. 403–13. This edition is based on the only complete copy, preserved in BL, Cotton Vitellius A.xii.

9 The *Dialogue of Ecgberht* has been translated in its entirety only once, by John Johnson in his mid-eighteenth-century *Collection of the Laws and Canons of the Church of England*, pp. 159–80.

10 McNeill and Gamer, *Medieval Handbooks of Penance*, pp. 239–43.

11 Bullough, 'Albinus deliciosus Caroli Regis', p. 80 n. 24, citing an unpublished lecture of H. J. Schuffels, argued that the manuscript was associated with Hildesheim and dated from *c.* 1000. See also, Levison, *England and the Continent*, p. 128 n. 9, who attributed the preservation of the document to abbot Wigbod; and see Sdralek, *Wolfenbüttler Fragmente*, I.2, pp. 87–89.

12 *Ecclesiastica Historia*, VIII–IX, pp. 575–81; see B. Carella, 'The Earliest Expression for Outlawry', pp. 122–27.

13 The *Legatine Capitulary of 786* has been translated in its entirety only once, namely, by Johnson, *Collection of the Laws and Canons of the Church of England*, pp. 266–85.

14 *English Historical Documents*, pp. 836–40.

one leg of it arrived in Northumbria.[15] In the North, so the text of the *Legatine Capitulary* explains, the legation proper was joined by Alcuin and Pyttel, two native Northumbrians who served in a capacity described in the text as *lectores* (the precise responsibilities of which are unclear). Soon after they joined the mission, the *Legatine Capitulary* was drafted explicitly in response to abuses the legation learned about while they were present in Northumbria. The *capitula* they formulated to correct these abuses, the text explains, were read aloud both in a Northumbrian council and then later in a second council convened south of the Humber in Mercia, attended by King Offa of Mercia among other magnates.

While it was formerly held that George of Ostia authored this document, more recent arguments by Catherine Cubitt and I have shown that the substance of the *Legatine Capitulary* was drafted, or at least heavily influenced on textual level, by Alcuin. As a document composed by a prominent Northumbrian legislating in his homeland for his own people, I posit, it should be regarded as a witness to Northumbrian legal practices. What is more, the document's adherence to Anglo-Saxon diplomatic and synodal practice, as Joanna Story has demonstrated,[16] make clear that this document was carefully crafted to address a local audience in terms they would recognize and understand. In sum, the *Legatine Capitulary* of 786 stands as the most substantial extant witness to early Northumbrian law, secular or ecclesiastical.

The Authorities of Law in the *Legatine Capitulary* of 786

As I mentioned in the introduction to this volume and discussed in part one, Irish ecclesiastical jurists ensconced in canon law a systematic order for invoking authorities in matters of legal and theological argumentation. The first and most basic authority according to this method was scripture, though it too had to be cited according to a specific order of precedence. Ideally, a jurist could point to more than one authoritative citation supporting their case. As other early Irish texts make clear (and as I discussed in part one), a jurist should show how their case was upheld by citations from successive sections of the bible representing the 'four laws' of sacred history recognized by the Irish, that is, the Law of Nature (probably considered equivalent to the Law of Noah; thus, Genesis), the Law of Moses

15 After holding an initial meeting with magnates in the south of England, the legation split up, with Theophylact heading into *Britannię partes* (meaning, presumably, the British-speaking parts of the island), while the others went North to meet with King Ælfwald of Northumbria.

16 Story, *Carolingian Connections*, p. 77 and n. 65.

(i.e., the Pentateuch), the Law of Prophets (i.e., the prophetic books), and the Law of Christ (i.e., the New Testament). In many if not most cases, finding authoritative citations representing all four laws was not possible; and so fewer would be invoked. Moreover, if no scriptural authority could be found (or, in order to bulwark scriptural evidence), other kinds of authorities could be adduced as well, for example, patristic writings, papal decrees, the *exempla* of saints, conciliar and synodal decisions, etc., as I explained in part one. That said, scripture, as represented and reinforced in the four laws, stood out as the first and most basic authority of early Irish ecclesiastical law; and Irish jurists and ecclesiastical scholars relied on it heavily. The question I shall explore presently is whether any reflex of this methodological gesture existed, possibly as a borrowing, in Anglo-Saxon law? To address this matter, let me begin with the *Legatine Capitulary* of 786, which cites scripture copiously.

The **Legatine Capitulary** *of 786*

Catherine Cubitt aptly described the *Legatine Capitulary* as '[...] a mosaic of biblical citations'.[17] Without question, the importance of scripture in the text can hardly be overstated. A few numbers will underscore her point and reveal just how important a role scripture plays in supporting these *capitula*. In the document, I count eighty-five allusions to scripture, cited in whole, in part, or invoked by a clear allusion. Of these, three occur in the epistolary prologue to the *capitula* and function unambiguously as literary embellishment.[18] The remaining eighty-two are packed tightly into the *capitula* themselves and serve in one way or another to bolster them. This latter group will be the subject of the present study. The density of these citations is striking: all occur within the roughly 3800 words that comprise the *Legatine Capitulary* proper (that is, among the *capitula* themselves, minus its prologue and epilogue), amounting to an average of about one biblical citation for every forty-six words of text. The precise function of the eighty-two citations in the latter group warrants closer examination. While I intend to make some progress toward that goal here, more focused work on this topic remains to be done. For my present purpose, I consider all eighty-two biblical citations in the *capitula* to function as referential authorities since all of them appear to be intended either to bulwark the provisions straightforwardly by echoing them in literal terms, for example:

---

17 Cubitt, *Anglo-Saxon Church Councils*, p. 180.

18 Matthew 13:25–30, Alcuin, 'The Legatine Capitulary', p. 220, ll. 12–13; Matthew 4:1, Alcuin, 'The Legatine Capitulary', l. 16, p. 20; Psalms 88:10, Alcuin, 'The Legatine Capitulary', l. 17, p. 20.

> Decimo capitulo, ut ne quislibet ex ministris altaris nudis cruribus ad missam celebrandam accedere audeat, ne turpitudo eius appareat et offendatur Deus: scientes, quod si hoc in lege prohibitum est [...].[19]
>
> > (In the tenth *capitulum*: that no minister of the altar presume to come forth for celebrating mass with naked legs, lest his unsightliness should appear and God should be offended ⟨Ex. 20:26⟩: since, given that we know this was prohibited in the Mosaic Law [...]).[20]

or by providing an *exemplum* legitimizing the various provisions laid down in the text, for example:

> In necem regis nemo communicare audeat, quia christus Domini est: et si quis tali sceleri adhaeserit, si episcopus est, aut ullus ex sacerdotali gradu, ex ipso detrudatur, et a sancta hereditate deiciatur, sicut Iudas ab apostolico gradu eiectus est: et omnis quisquis tali sacrilegio assenserit, aeterno anathematis vinculo interibit, et Iudae traditori sociatus, sempiternis cremabitur incediis, ut scriptum est: 'Non solum qui faciunt, sed et qui consentiunt facientibus, iudicium Dei non effugiunt.'[21]
>
> > (Let no one dare to conspire in the death of the king, because he is the Lord's anointed: and, if anyone consents to such a crime, if he is a bishop or any of the priestly grades, let him be thrust out from it and cast down from the holy inheritance, just as Judas was cast down from the apostolic order — and all who assent to such a sacrilege will perish in the bond of eternal anathema, and as a comrade of Judas the Traitor, will burn in eternal fire, as it is written: 'Not only they who do them, but they also who consent to those who do them, will not escape the judgement of God' ⟨Romans 1:32⟩).[22]

or, finally, by providing a hortatory injunction urging compliance with the legal provision in question by citing or referring to a scriptural locus that echoes either the wording or the spirit of the provision, for example:

> [...] episcopi, abbates et abbatissae subiectis sibi in omnibus exemplum bonum prebeant, ut Petrus ait: 'Estote forma facti gregis secundum Deum', et. cet.[23]

---

19 Alcuin, 'The Legatine Capitulary', ll. 5–7, p. 23.

20 The translation is my own.

21 Alcuin, 'The Legatine Capitulary', ll. 15–21, p. 24.

22 The translation is my own.

23 Alcuin, 'The Legatine Capitulary', ll. 18–20, p. 22.

> ([...] let bishops, abbots, and abbesses give good example to their subjects in all things, as Peter said: 'Be made a pattern of the flock after God,' etc., ⟨1 Peter 5:3⟩).[24]

As these examples demonstrate, the author(s) of the *Legatine Capitulary* drew on scripture for a variety of purposes. Despite this diversity of usage, however, the most basic function of the eighty-two allusions to scripture in the *capitula* is to lend greater authority to the provisions under which they are marshalled.

Scripture represents, by far, the most common authority cited in the text. The authors cite other authorities, to be sure, but much less frequently and usually in less specific terms. I count only eighteen non-scriptural authoritative citations (or references), ranging from direct quotations, sometimes identified by name, for example: 'Augustinus quoque ait: "Quia habet iniustum lucrum sine iusto damno. Ubi lucrum, ibi damnum: lucrum in arca, damnum in conscientia"',[25] (Likewise, Augustine says: 'How can one have unjust profit without just loss? Where there is profit, there is loss: profit in the coffers, loss in the conscience').[26] There are four such direct quotations in the *capitula*, including another reference to Augustine (or a pseudonymous intermediary),[27] one attributed to a certain *sapiens* for which I can identify no source, and one idiosyncratic quotation of Prudentius's *Diptychon* 1.3 (for which I can find no exact parallel). A thoroughgoing source analysis of the *Legatine Capitulary* has never been carried out; and while I suspect such a study might uncover a few more quotations of this sort, I doubt the number would grow significantly; certainly not in relation to the overwhelming weight of scriptural citations.

The remaining non-scriptural invocations of authorities in support of the various provisions in the text are extremely vague in nature. They include, for example, such instances as one non-specific reference to the Nicene Council (admonishing that it be upheld),[28] to similarly imprecise allusions to the six ecumenical councils,[29] and even more generalized appeals to authorities attributed with phrases such as: 'secundum canonica statuta' (in accordance with canonical statutes, in the pl.),[30] 'secundum canonicas institutiones' (in accordance with canonical teachings),[31] 'synodalia edicta universalium sex conciliorum cum decretis pontificum

---

24 The translation is my own.
25 Alcuin, 'The Legatine Capitulary', ll. 4–6, p. 26.
26 The translation is my own.
27 Alcuin, 'The Legatine Capitulary', ll. 39–41, p. 23.
28 Alcuin, 'The Legatine Capitulary', l. 10, p. 21.
29 Alcuin, 'The Legatine Capitulary', ll. 20–21, p. 22 and Alcuin, 'The Legatine Capitulary', ll. 14 and 16, p. 23.
30 Alcuin, 'The Legatine Capitulary', l. 18, p. 21.
31 Alcuin, 'The Legatine Capitulary', l. 27, p. 21.

Romanorum' (the synodal edicts of the six universal councils along with the decrees of the Roman pontiffs),[32] 'auctoritate apostolica' (by Apostolic authority),[33] and 'in canone vel in evangelica doctrina et decretis apostolicorum dogmatum' (in canon law or in the doctrine of the gospels and in the decrees of apostolic teachings),[34] etc. Overall, the non-specific, generalized nature of these attributions suggests that the author(s) of the *capitula* expected their audience neither to know these texts intimately, nor perhaps to hold them unequivocally authoritative in and of themselves. Rather, the author(s) of the *Legatine Capitulary* clearly considered scripture to be the most basic, most fundamental authority by which law should be justified. Given this fact, several questions immediately arise: what are we to make of this practice? Is it typically Northumbrian? And most directly to my point here: were the Northumbrian authors of the *Legatine Capitulary* influenced by the prescribed Irish method for citing authorities which, as I have already discussed, relied heavily on scripture as a fundamental basis of jurisprudence?

The Authorities of Law in the *Admonitio Generalis* of 789

To answer these questions, it will first be necessary for me to discuss a closely related Carolinigian document, the so-called *Admonitio Generalis* of 789. For many reasons — not all immediately bearing on my present argument — the *Legatine Capitulary* makes for an informative comparison with the *Admonitio Generalis,* a legal text very similar in nature and purpose. Like the papal legates who promulgated the *Legatine Capitulary* in England in 786, the authors of the *Admonitio Generalis* of 789 inaugurated a thoroughgoing reform agenda for Carolingian society by laying down a set of directives aimed at various segments of the population, including those both secular and ecclesiastical. Very significantly, Alcuin played a substantial role in both efforts: in fact — like the *Legatine Capitulary* composed three years earlier, the second half of the *Admonitio Generalis* has been securely attributed to him.[35]

Even a cursory inspection of the *Admonitio Generalis* reveals marked differences between the first, non-Alcuinian section of the document (§ 1–

32 Alcuin, 'The Legatine Capitulary', ll. 20–21, p. 22.

33 Alcuin, 'The Legatine Capitulary', l. 17, p. 25.

34 Alcuin, 'The Legatine Capitulary', ll. 33–34, p. 25.

35 The case for Alcuin's involvement in composing the second portion of the *Admonitio Gemeralis* of 789, that is, sections sixty through eighty, is now well-established. For a discussion of this matter see B. Carella, 'Alcuin and the Legatine Capitulary of 786', pp. 231–38.

59) and the second portion which is firmly ascribed to him (§ 60–80). Since the character of the Alcuinian portion is important for my present argument, I shall first describe the differences between these two sections before going any further. A brief sample from each section of the *Admonitio Generalis* will suffice to illustrate the overtly contrasting nature of the two sections:

From the *Admonitio Generalis* of 789 (section I, not attributed to Alcuin)
1. Omnibus. Sunt enim aliqui, qui culpis exigentibus *ab episcopo proprio excommunicantur* et *ab aliis* ecclesiasticis vel *laicis* praesumptiose in *communionem accipiuntur,* quod omnino sanctum **Nicenum concilium** simul et **Calcidonense** necnon et **Antiochenum** atque **Sardicense** fieri prohibent.

2. Episcopis. Item enim habet **in eodem concilio,** ut eorum qui ad ordinandum veniunt fides et vita prius ab episcopo diligenter *discutiatur,* et sic ordinentur.

3. Omnibus. Item **in eodem concilio** necnon et in **Antiocheno** simul et **in Calcidonense,** ut fugitivi clerici et *peregrini* a nullo *recipiantur* nec ordinentur sine *commendaticiis litteris* et *sui episcopi* vel abbatis licentia.[36]

> (1. To all. There are some who are excommunicated by their own bishop by reason of their faults and are presumably received in communion by other ecclesiastics or by laymen. It is utterly forbidden by the **Holy Council of Nicea,** as well as by that of **Chalcedon** and also by those of **Antioch** and **Sardica,** that this should happen.
>
> 2. To bishops. Further, **in the same council** it is maintained that the faith and life of those who come to be ordained are to be diligently examined by the bishop before they are ordained.
>
> 3. To all. Further, **in the same council,** and also in that of **Antioch** as well as that of **Chalcedon**: that fugitive clerics and *peregrini* are not to be received or ordained by anyone without a letter of commendation, or authorisation, from their bishop or abbot).[37]

From the *Admonitio Generalis* of 789 (section II, attributed to Alcuin)
65. Omnibus. Item praedicari necesse est, quantum malum sit odium vel invidia, quia **in lege** scriptum est: *Non oderis fratrem tuum in*

36 *Die Admonitio Generalis,* pp. 184 and 186. Emphasis is my own, in both text and translation.
37 *Charlemagne. Translated Sources,* pp. 210.

> *corde tuo, sed publice argues eum* ⟨**Leviticus 19:17**⟩. Item **Iohannes evangelista**: *Qui odit fratrem suum, homicida est* ⟨**1 John 3:15**⟩. Item **in evangelio:** *Si peccaverit in te frater tuus, vade et corripe eum inter te et ipsum solum,* et cetera, quae ibi leguntur ⟨**Matthew 18:15**⟩. De avaritia autem **apostolum** legimus dicentem: *Avaritia, quae est idolorum servitus,* cavenda ⟨**Ephesians 5:5, Colossians 3:5; cf. Luke 12:15**⟩. Item de concupiscentia legitur, quod *radix* sit *omnium malorum* ⟨**1 Timothy 6:10**⟩. Et **in lege**: Non concupisces rem proximi tui ⟨**cf. Exodus 20:17**⟩.[38]

> (6⟨5⟩. To all. Further, it is necessary to preach how great an evil is hatred or malice, for it is written **in the Law**: 'You shall not hate your brother in your heart but shall reproach him openly' ⟨**Leviticus 19:17**⟩; further, **John the evangelist**: 'He who hates his brother is a killer' ⟨**1 John 3:15**⟩; further, in **the Gospel**: 'If your brother sins against you, go and rebuke him with no one else present' ⟨**Matthew 18:15**⟩, and other passages which are read there. As regards avarice, however, we read the words of **the Apostle**: 'It is necessary to beware of avarice, which is idolatry' ⟨**Ephesians 5:5, Colossians 3:5; cf. Luke 12:15**⟩. Further, we read concerning cupidity that it is the root of all evils ⟨**1 Timothy 6:10**⟩, and **in the Law**: 'You shall not covet your neighbour's property' ⟨**compare Exodus 20:17**⟩).[39]

Most notably, the use of authorities in these separate sections of the document stand in stark contrast to one another. In the first, non-Alcuinian section, tersely worded injunctions seek to regulate or prohibit specific ecclesiastical procedures and behaviours (for example, administering the eucharist to excommunicants, or ordaining fugitive clerics). Moreover, only the ecumenical councils are invoked as authorities (i.e., Nicea, Chalcedon, Antioch, etc.) without direct quotation.[40] The second, Alcuinian section is quite different. The *captiula* in this latter section tend rather to address general issues of morality (for example, hatred and malice), with reference (in this example) solely to scriptural authorities that are enumerated, one after the other, from various sections of the Bible and almost always quoted directly, in whole or impart. Thus, not only do the sources of authority differ between the non-Alcuinin and the Alcuinian sections of the *Admonitio Generalis,* but also their style and content as well. Indeed, the concern with fundamental moral rectitude imbues the Alcuinian section, at times, with a hortatory, homiletic tone.[41]

---

38 *Die Admonitio Generalis*, p. 218.
39 *Charlemagne. Translated Sources*, p. 216.
40 That is, if one includes the Council of Serdica.
41 See: K. Carella, 'The Historical and Literary Context', pp. 144–50.

This latter portion of the *Admonitio Generalis* is similar in just about every mode of comparison with the *Legatine Capitulary* (a fact that is perhaps not all that surprising given their similar aims and common authorship): the overall concerns of the *Admonitio Generalis*, many of the topics it addresses, occasionally its wording, and its hortatory focus on general morality at times echoing an almost homiletic tone, all recall the 786 document.[42] Above all else, the heavy reliance on scriptural authority in this latter, Alcuinian portion is a prominently distinguishing feature of the text. A few numbers will suffice to make the point: the Alcuinian portion of the *Admonitio Generalis* consists of approximately 2240 words, containing forty-three direct quotations of, and twenty-five allusions to scripture. This tally amounts to one scriptural reference for every thirty-four words of text (in comparison with the *Legatine Capitulary*, which refers to scripture in a similarly high volume, that is, once every forty-six words). On the other hand, invocations of authorities other than scripture in this second portion of the *Admonitio Generalis* are correspondingly rare. While the authorities cited are more specific and wide-ranging than in the *Legatine Capitulary*, the number of such citations pales in comparison with scriptural references: I count only eleven non-scriptural citations, ranging from patristic authorities such as Prudentius, Gennadius, Benedict of Nursia, and Isidore of Seville to the Irish collection of canon law known as *Collectio canonum Hibernensis*, Creeds of the Church, and prayers of the Divine Office. In these ways, then, the Alcuinian section of the *Admonitio Generalis* has much in common with the *Legatine Capitulary*, particularly in the way authorities are cited with heavy reliance on scripture as the most fundamental authority.

However significant these similarities may be, the differences between the first, non-Alcuinian section of the *Admonitio Generalis* and the *Legatine Capitulary* are also instructive. While the last twenty sections of the *Admonitio Generalis* are marked by their close resonance with the *Legatine Capitulary*, the first fifty-nine sections are quite distinct from those that follow, not only in tone, but also in the kinds of authorities they invoke. So great are the differences in these two portions of the *Admonitio Generalis*, that one cannot help but get the impression that two very different, ideologically consonant but methodologically distinct textual endeavours were grafted together into a loosely bound, hybrid document, broadly addressing the same concerns, to be sure, but in very different ways. In the first, non-Alcuinian portion, each injunction is substantially shorter than in the second — indeed, almost terse at times — and relies far less heavily on scripture. In fact, I count only five direct citations of, and three allusions to scripture in this first, non-Alcuinian portion of the *Admonitio*

---

42 For a survey of this question, see B. Carella, 'Alcuin and the Legatine Capitulary of 786', pp. 231–38 and K. Carella, 'The Historical and Literary Context'.

Generalis. In contrast, the second, Alcuinian portion contains a virtual flood of scripture that dominates the latter half of the text. What is more, Alcuin artfully embeds these scriptural citations into his arguments, often in support of hortatory (as opposed to punitive) points of law, such that at times the text reads almost like a homily.

As it turns out, the first fifty-nine sections of the *Admonitio Generalis* derive mostly from the *Dionysio-Hadriana* and justify their legislation by reference to a mix of mostly post-scriptural authorities ranging (first and foremost) from ecumenical and provincial councils and earlier Carolingian capitularies to papal decrees and patristic writings, among an array of other sources. Moreover, invocations of these authorities in the first fifty-nine sections of the *Admonitio Generalis* are much more precise than those in the *Legatine Capitulary*. In the first section of the *Admonitio Generalis* for example, the author(s) usually justify their edicts by reference to a specific church council (albeit typically without citing the text), quite unlike the vague, imprecise references to conciliar, pontifical, or canonical authority generally, which — virtually without exception — typify such references in the *Legatine Capitulary*.

What explains the affinities and differences between these documents? More specifically, what explains the similarity between the authorities of law and the way they are cited in both the *Legatine Capitulary* and the Alcuinian portion of the *Admonitio Generalis* on the one hand, in contrast to the first portion of the *Admonitio Generalis* on the other? Two factors bear on this question. First, each text addressed different audiences: the *Legatine Capitulary* was intended to address Anglo-Saxons, while the *Admonitio Generalis* was intended to address Franks; needless to say, these are two very different audiences. Second, Alcuin — who drafted or formatively influenced both the *Legatine Capitulary* and the second portion of the *Admonitio Generalis* — was guided by his Insular, Northumbrian education. This is an especially important point for my current argument. While Alcuin's method of citing authorities clearly was not antithetical to a Carolingian audience's sensibilities (as the overall impact of the document attests), other methods were possible, perhaps even preferred; as is shown by the first fifty-nine sections of the *Admonitio Generalis*, which rely almost exclusively on post-scriptural ecclesiastical legislation. The differences, in any case, are telling: where we find a heavy reliance on scripture in relation to other kinds of authorities, we find a connection to Northumbria, attributable, in both cases I discuss here, to Alcuin. So, the question arises: is this heavy reliance on scripture as the most basic, fundamental authority of law distinctively Northumbrian? And, if so, what are its sources?

The Authorities of Law in *Collectio canonum Hibernensis*

The closest parallel I have identified to the methods for citing the authorities of law in the *Legatine Capitulary* and the Alcuinian portion of the *Admonitio Generalis* is *Collectio canonum Hibernensis*. One example will suffice to make the point: consider the following except from *Collectio canonum Hibernensis*. Note that, in these comparisons, I am not focusing on their content, but rather the types of authorities that are invoked and the way those authorities are cited in support of the various *dicta*. I have placed the names of the authorities in bold for emphasis. Note also that, here and throughout, I am choosing passages that best exemplify the point I wish to make. To be sure, not every section of *Collectio canonum Hibernensis* (or, for that matter, the other texts I discuss in this section) are as straightforward in the types of authorities they cite as the examples I quote here. That said, these passages I cite show a pattern most clearly that appears consistently throughout the texts in question.

> **From: Liber LXVI *De Contrariis Causis*, cap. 4, *De seueritate uindicte et, e contra, indulgentia***
>
> **Lex**: Qui effunderit sanguinem innocentis, sanguis eius effundetur ⟨**Genesis 9:6; Deuteronomy 21:7–8**⟩.
> **Dauid**: Deus ultionum Dominus Deus; usque: Qui iudicas terram ⟨**Psalms 93:1–2**⟩.
> **Item**: Letabitur iustus cum uiderit uindictam; usque: Ad peccatoris ⟨**Psalms 57:11**⟩.
> **Heremias**: Maledictus homo, qui prohibet gladium suum a sanguine ⟨**Jeremiah 48:10**⟩.
> **In novo**: Verbis Phetri Annaniam et Saphira exanimes cadunt ⟨**Acts 5:5, 10**⟩.
> **Hironimus**: Dum parcunt peccatoribus sacerdotes, æclesiae moliuntur interitum.
> **Item**: Qui non occidit latronem, ipse perdit inopem. Mortificat animas, que non moriuntur, et uiuificat animas, quae non uiuunt ⟨**Ezekiel 13:19**⟩.
> **Item**: Non morientem quippe mortificat, qui iniustum uiuificare nititur et qui reum a supplicio soluere conatur ⟨**Gregorius, *Hom. In Evang.* 25.5**⟩.
> **Item**: Qui occidit in gladio, oportet eum in gladio occidi ⟨**Revelation 13:10**⟩.
> **Augustinus**: Que est ista uanitas, uni parcere et omnes in discrimine adducere? Pulluitur enim populus uno peccante ⟨**Caesarius, *Epist. de Concilio Massiliense***⟩.
> **Lex**, e contra: Ne memor sis injurię ciuium tuorum ⟨**Leviticus 19:18**⟩.

David: Misericors et miserator Dominus, patiens et multę misericordiae ⟨**Psalms 85:15**⟩.
Item: Si dereliquerint filii eius legem meam; usque: Non dispergam ab eis ⟨**Psalms 88:31, 34**⟩.
Christus: Dilegite inimicos uestros ⟨**Matthew 5:44**⟩.
Item: Si non remiseritis hominibus peccata eorum, non remitet uobis pater uester cælestis, qui in caelis es ⟨**Matthew 6:14; cf. John 20:23**⟩.
Item: Superexaltat misericordia iuditio ⟨**James 2:13**⟩.
Petrus interrogavit: Si peccauerit in me frater meus, quoties dimitam ei, usque septies? **Veritas** respondit: Non dico usque septies, sed septies et septuagies ⟨**Matthew 18:1–22**⟩.
Dominus: orauit pro Iudeis: Pater ignosce illis ⟨**Luke 23:34**⟩.
Sic et **Stiphanus** dixit: Domine Ihesu, ne statuas illis hoc in peccatum; nesciunt {seruiens} enim, quid faciunt ⟨**Acts 7:59, cf. Luke 23:34**⟩.[43]

(From Liber LXVI, *Concerning contrary sources*, cap. 4, *Concerning the severity of punishment and, on the contrary, clemency*

The Law: Whoever will shed innocent blood, his own blood shall also be shed ⟨**Genesis 9:6; Deuteronomy 21:7–8**⟩. **David**: God, the Lord God of revenge; as far as: You who judge the earth. ⟨**Psalms 93:1–2**⟩. **Likewise**: The just man shall rejoice when he shall see the punishment; as far as: Of the sinner ⟨**Psalms 57:11**⟩.
Jeremiah: Cursed be he who withholds his sword from blood ⟨**Jerermiah 48:10**⟩.
In the New Testament: Ananias and Sapphira fall lifeless at Peter's words ⟨**Acts 5:5, 10**⟩. **Jerome**: So long as *sacerdotes* spare sinners, churches bring about death.
Likewise: He who does not kill a thief, himself destroys the helpless. He puts to death the souls that do not die, and revives the souls that do not live ⟨**Ezekiel 13:19**⟩.
Likewise: He who strives to revive the unjust and tries to release a criminal from punishment puts the one who is not dying to death ⟨**Gregorius, *Hom. In Evang.* 25.5**⟩.
Likewise: He who kills by the sword ought to be killed by the sword ⟨**Revelation 13:10**⟩.
Augustine: What is this vanity, to spare one and lead all others into danger? For the people are polluted by a single sinner ⟨**Caesarius, *Epist. de Concilio Massiliense***⟩.
The Law of Moses on the contrary: Be nor mindful of the injury of your citizens ⟨**Leviticus 19:18**⟩. **David**: The Lord is gracious and merciful, patient and plenteous in mercy ⟨**Psalms 85:15**⟩. **Likewise**:

43 *The Hibernensis*, Bk I, p. 471–72.

And if his children forsake my law; as far as: I shall not move away from them ⟨**Psalms 88:31, 34**⟩.
Christ: Love your enemies ⟨**Matthew 5:44**⟩.
Likewise: If you do not forgive men their sins, your heavenly father, who is in heaven, shall not forgive your ⟨**Matthew 6:14; cf. John 20:23**⟩.
Likewise: Mercy exalts itself above judgement ⟨**James 2:13**⟩.
Peter asked: If my brother offend against me, how many times shall I forgive him? Up to seven times? **The truth** replied: I say not to you, up to seven times, but up to seventy seven times ⟨**Luke 23:34**⟩.
The Lord pleaded on behalf of the Jews: Father, forgive them ⟨**Luke 23:34**⟩.
So **Stephen** also said: Lord Jesus, do not reckon this as their sin, for they know not what they do ⟨**Acts 7:59, cf. Luke 23:34**⟩).[44]

This chapter is one of the very last in *Collectio canonum Hibernensis*, in a book that provides authoritative citations in support of both sides of a *quaestio* or *causa*. Given the apparent contradictory nature of equivalent authorities, perhaps the matter remained in dispute, or perhaps it was a matter wherein a judge would need to consider the facts of a particular incident in light of these differing opinions to determine which best pertain to the case at hand? Ultimately, the purpose of enumerating opinions representing both sides of a dispute is not clear.

What is apparent however, is (1) the heavy reliance on scripture as the most basic and by far the most frequently cited authority, and (2) the canonist's adherence to the method prescribed in Liber XIX, *De ordine inquisitionis causarum* (Concerning the order of invoking authoritative sources), described above. Notice, for instance, how this chapter begins with a citation of Genesis 9:6, that is, expressing the Law of Noah (perhaps considered an expression of the Law of Nature). Citations from later in the Bible follow, including, for example, excerpts from Jeremiah (the Law of the Prophets) and then Acts (the Law of Christ), showing that the precept in question is supported on several levels of biblical law before other kinds of authorities, scriptural and non-scriptural, are invoked. To be sure, scriptural authorities are not always cited in order, nor was it always possible to find authorities representing every one of the four laws in sacred history. The goal was merely to identify and enumerate as much confirmation as possible. In this case, the canonist follows the same procedure in the second half of the canon citing authorities who express an opposing opinion.

---

44 The translation is from *The Hibernensis*, Bk II, p. 829.

Now, compare the manner in which authorities are cited in *Collectio canonum Hibernensis* to the way they are cited in this excerpt from the *Legatine Capitulary*:

From the *Legatine Capitulary*, capitulum XVII:
Decimum septimum caput. De decimis dandis, sicut **in lege** scriptum est: 'Decimam partem ex omnibus frugibus tuis seu primitiis deferas in domum domini Dei tui' ⟨**Exodus 22.29, Deuteronomy 14.22**⟩. **Rursum per prophetam**: 'Adferte, inquit, omnem decimam in horreum meum, ut sit cibus in domo mea, et probate me super hoc, si non aperuero vobis cataractas caeli et effudero benedictionem usque ad abundantiam, et increpabo pro vobis devorantem, qui comedit et corrumpit fructum terrae vestrae et non erit ultra vinea sterilis in agro', dicit Dominus ⟨**Malachi 3.10–11**⟩. Sicut **sapiens ait**: 'Nemo iustam elemosynam de his quae possidet facere valet, nisi prius separaverit Domino, quod a primordio ipse sibi reddere delegavit. Ac per hoc plerumque contingit, ut qui decimam non tribuit, ad decimam revertitur' ⟨**source unknown**⟩. Unde etiam cum obtestatione praecipimus, ut omnes studeant de omnibus quae possident decimas dare, quia speciale domini Dei est, et de novem partibus sibi vivat elemosynas tribuat et magis eas in absconditis facere suasimus, quia scriptum est: 'Cum facis elemosynam, noli tuba canere ante te' ⟨**Matthew 6.2**⟩. Usuras quoque prohibuimus, dicente Domino ad David: 'Dignum fore habitatorem tabernaculi sui, qui pecuniam suam non dederit ad usuram' ⟨**Psalms 14.1, 5**⟩. **Augustinus** quoque ait: 'Quia habet iniustum lucrum sine iusto damno. Ubi lucrum, ibi damnum: lucrum in arca, damnum in conscientia' ⟨**Sermo VIII, de decem plagis et praeceptis, ch. 7**⟩. Statuimus etiam, ut mensuras aequas et pondera aequalia statuant omnibus, dicente Salomone: 'Pondus et pondus, mensuram et mensuram odit Deus' ⟨**Proverbs 20.10**⟩: id est ne alio quis vendat pondere vel mensura, alia emat: 'quia ubique Deus iusticiam diligit, et aequitatem videt vultus eius' ⟨**Psalms 10.8**⟩.[45]

(XVII. The seventeenth chapter: concerning giving tithes, thus in the **Law** it is written: 'The tenth part of all your produce or first fruits, bring them into the house of the Lord your God' ⟨**Exodus 22.29, Deuteronomy 14.22**⟩. **Again, by the prophet**: 'Bring', he said, 'all the tithes into my storehouse, so that there may be food in my house, and examine me in this, if I do not open unto you the floodgates of heaven, and pour out a blessing even to abundance, and I will rebuke for your sakes the devourer who consumes and

---

45 Alcuin, 'The Legatine Capitulary', l. 37, p. 25 — l. 9, p. 26. Emphasis is my own, in both text and translation.

> spoils the fruit of your land: and the vine in the field will also not be barren, says the Lord' ⟨**Malachi 3.10–11**⟩. As a wise man says: 'No-one can justly give alms from those things which he possesses unless he has first separated for the Lord what from the beginning, he had set aside to be paid to him. And it happens quite commonly in these situations, that he who does not give a tenth is himself reduced to a tenth' ⟨**source unknown**⟩. Wherefore also, we advise with earnest entreaty, that all should endeavour to pay a tenth from those things which they possess, because that in particular belongs to the Lord God, and from his nine parts let a man live and give alms. And we urge even more that alms be made in secret, as it is written: 'When you give alms, do not sound a trumpet before you' ⟨**Matthew 6.2**⟩. We also prohibited usury, as God said to David: 'He will be worthy to dwell in the tabernacle, he who has not put out his money to usury' ⟨**Psalms 14.1, 5**⟩. **Augustine** also says): 'How can one have unjust profit without just loss? Where there is profit, there is loss: profit in the coffers, loss in the conscience' ⟨**Sermo VIII, de decem plagis et praeceptis, ch. 7**⟩. We also established that equal measures and equal weights should measure in all cases, as Solomon said: 'The Lord hates diverse weights and diverse measures' ⟨**Proverbs 20.10**⟩. That is, no-one who buys by one weight or measure should sell by another, 'For God everywhere loves justice, and his countenance beheld righteousness' ⟨**Psalms 10.8**⟩).[46]

Just as in *Collectio canonum Hibernensis*, scripture is by far the most commonly cited authority, and it is cited in a manner that suggests adherence to the same method and order as prescribed in the Irish canons. Notice, for instance, how in this *capitulum* Exodus/Deuteronomy is cited first (the Law of Moses), followed by a citation from Malachi (the Law of the Prophets) and then Matthew (the Law of Christ) before other kinds of sources, non-scriptural and scriptural, are invoked. To be sure, there is no expression of the Law of Nature/Law of Noah; but the general procedure is followed, as closely as possible, just as it is laid out in *Collectio canonum Hibernensis*, Liber XIX, *De ordine inquisitionis causarum* (Concerning the order of invoking authoritative sources) and exemplified in the canons throughout that collection.

Next, compare also this example from the Alcuinian portion of the *Admonitio Generalis*:

From the *Admonitio Generalis* (part II, attributed to Alcuin)

46 The translation is my own.

63. Omnibus. Item habemus **in lege** domino praecipiente: *Non periurabis in nomine meo nec pollues nomen domini dei tui* ⟨**Leviticus 19:12**⟩. Et: *Nec adsumes nomen domini dei tui in vanum* ⟨**Leviticus 19:12**⟩. Ideo omnino ammonendi sunt omnes diligenter, ut caveant periurium non solum in sancto evangelio vel in altare seu in sanctorum reliquiis, sed et in communi loquella, quia sunt aliqui, qui per caritatem et veritatem iurant et cavent se a iuramento nominis dei et nesciunt, quia idem est deus, quod est caritas et veritas, dicente **Iohanne apostolo**, quia *deus caritas est* ⟨**1 John 4:16**⟩. Item ipse dominus in evangelio: *Ego sum via et veritas* ⟨**John 14:6**⟩. Ideo, qui in veritate et caritate iurat, in deo iurat. Item cavendum est, ne farisiaca superstitione aliquis plus aurum honoret quam altare, ne dicat ei **dominus**: *Stulte et caeca, quid est maius? Aurum* vel *altare, quod sanctificat aurum* ⟨**Matthew 23:17, 18, 19**⟩? Sed et nobis honestum videtur, ut, qui in sanctis habeat iurare, hoc ieiunus faciat cum omni honestate et timore dei et sciat se rationem redditurm deo uniuscuiusque iuramenti ubicumque sit, sive intra ecclesiam, sive extra ecclesiam. Et ut parvuli, qui sine rationabili aetate sunt, non cogantur iurare, sicut Guntbodingi faciunt. Et qui semel periuratus fuerit, nec testis sit posthaec nec ad sacramentum accedat nec in sua causa vel alterius iurator existat.[47]

> (6⟨3⟩. To all. Further, we have **in the law** the Lord's commandment: 'You shall not swear falsely in My name; neither shall you profane the name of the Lord your God' ⟨**Leviticus 19:12**⟩, and 'You shall not take the name of the Lord your God in vain' ⟨**Exodus 20:7**⟩. For this reason let everyone be diligently admonished, in absolute terms, to beware perjury, not only on the holy gospel or on the alter or on saint's relics but also in everyday speech, for there are some who swear by love and truth, taking care to avoid an oath in God's name, and do not know that God is the same thing as love and truth, the apostle John saying that 'God is love' ⟨**1 John 4:16**⟩, and the Lord Himself, in the gospel, 'I am the way and the truth' ⟨**John 14:6**⟩. Whoever swears by truth and love, therefore, swears by God. Further, care is to be taken lest, with pharisaical superstition, anyone honours gold more highly than the altar, that the Lord may not say to him: 'You fools and blind: which is greater, the gold or the altar that sanctifies the gold?' ⟨**Matthew 23: 17, 18, 19**⟩. But this too seems proper to us, that whoever has to swear on the saints does this while fasting and with all respect and fear for God; and he is to realize that he will render an account to God for each single oath, wherever it may occur, within a church or outside it. And that children who have not reached

47 *Die Admonitio Generalis*, pp. 214–15. Emphasis is my own, in both text and translation.

> the age of reason are not to be forces to swear, as is the practice among the Burgundians. And whoever shall have once committed perjury is thereafter neither to be a witness not to enter upon sworn obligations not to take an oath in his own or someone else's legal case).[48]

Here too, as throughout the Alcuinian section of the *Admonitio Generalis,* scripture is the predominant — indeed, in this case, the only — authority invoked. Also, the same method for citing authorities would appear to be the same as what is prescribed in chapter XIX of *Collectio canonum Hibernensis* and reflected in the *Legatine Capitulary*. In this passage, the first authorities cited are from Exodus and Leviticus (representing the Law of Moses), after which follow three New Testament quotations, from 1 John, the gospel of John, and the gospel of Matthew (representing the Law of Christ). Thus, this same order for invoking authorities is found in the *Admonitio Generalis* as well, a fact that is significant for the present argument because its author — Alcuin — was a native-born Northumbrian whose method (at least in this case) differs markedly from the prior section of the document, presumably because this method was a deeply ingrained part of his Northumbrian education.

The Authorities of Law in the *Dialogue of Ecgberht*

So far, I have shown how the method for invoking authoritative sources prescribed in *Collectio canonum Hibernensis* was apparently followed in two texts connected to Northumbria, that is, the *Legatine Capitulary* and the second portion of the *Admonitio Generalis*. Since both documents were authored by Alcuin, however, it is possible that his utilization of this method was merely a stylistic choice idiosyncratic to him and therefore not a feature of his Northumbrian education generally. Thus, it is conceivable that it could have been something Alcuin observed in Irish texts and chose, for whatever reason, to replicate. Are there other examples of this method in Northumbrian legal texts not authored by Alcuin, that would show it was more widespread than a single individual?

While few legal documents from early Northumbria survive for comparison, one additional witness to local legal practice is the *Dialogue of Ecgberht,* a document authored by Archbishop Ecgberht of York sometime in the middle of the eighth century. Although many of the chapters are quite short, addressing practical matters directly, in several of the longer chapters the method for invoking authorities prescribed in *Collectio canonum Hibernensis* is, in fact, apparent. To be sure, Ecgberht's use of

48 *Charlemagne. Translated Sources,* p. 215.

authoritative sources is more varied than in either the *Legatine Capitulary* or the Alcuinian section of the *Admonitio Generalis*. Though Ecgberht tends not to identify his sources by name and often echoes their wording only vaguely, references (both clearly identified and likely) include the most commonly cited canon law texts of the period, a wide array of papal letters and decretals, as well as other texts such as sermons in the Eusebius Gallicanus collection and the *Regula Sancti Benedicti*.[49] A full study of the authorities to which Ecgberht appeals remains to be conducted and is beyond the scope of the present study. Noteworthy for my purpose, however, is that, as Martin J. Ryan points out, '[...] it seems most probable that the *Dialogus* was intended for an insular Anglo-Saxon audience',[50] and — very significantly — though his work may have entered into dialogue with the broader, transnational concerns of the Church, '⟨f⟩or answers that relate specifically to the Anglo-Saxon situation, Ecgberht's borrowing from other sources is far less extensive and tends to be limited to biblical references, both direct and indirect'.[51] Thus, when addressing a native English audience, Ecgberht does so in a way distinct from when he addresses international matters, tending in the former case to refrain from citing far-flung authorities, and instead relying primarily on the Bible itself, just like the *Legatine Capitulary* and the Alcuinian section of the *Admonitio Generalis*. Moreover, when Ecgberht cites scripture, it is apparent that he tries to pair references to the Old Testament with analogous authorities in the New Testament, thus expressing the same confirmation of successive authorities on multiple levels of biblical law, as I have shown to exist in the other Irish and Northumbrian sources. One example will suffice to make the point:

> **From the *Dialogue of Ecgberht* Interrogatio XVI**
> De secundo Jejunio. Secundum jejunium quarti mensis a veteri lege exortum est, quando lex ⟨data⟩ est Moysi in Monte Sinai, et præceptum est a Domino ut sit populus paratus ad audiendam vocem in diem tercium, et ne adpropinquent uxoribus suis ⟨**cf. Exodus 19:11, 15**⟩. Et iterum Dominus ad Moysen: 'Tolletis de cuntis frugibus vestris primitias, et offeretis ea Domino Deo vestro' ⟨**Exodus 23:19**⟩. Quod et in Novo Testamento constitutum est, juxta id quod Dominus ait: 'Non possunt filii sponsi jejunare quandiu cum illis est sponsus', et reliqua ⟨**Matthew 9:15**⟩. Quod juxta congruentiam temporum post ascensionem Domini ad cœlos, præsentia corporali subtracta, tunc indictum est jejunium quarti mensis secundo sabbato. Hoc

49 For a discussion of Archbishop Ecgberht's sources, see Ryan, 'Archbishop Ecgberht and His *Dialogus*'.

50 Ryan, 'Archbishop Ecgberht and His *Dialogus*', p. 48.

51 Ryan, 'Archbishop Ecgberht and His *Dialogus*', p. 52.

> autem jejunium idem beatus Gregorius, per præfatum legatum, in Antiphonario suo et Missali, in plena epdomada post Pentecosten Anglorum æcclesiæ celebrandum destinavit. Quod non solum nostra testantur Antiphonaria, sed et ipsa quæ cum Missalibus suis conspeximus apud apostolurum Petri et Pauli limina.[52]
>
> (Of the second fast. — The second fast of the fourth month took its rise from the ⟨O⟩ld Law, when the Law was given to Moses on Mount Sinai, and it was commanded by the Lord that the people should be prepared to hear his voice on the third day and that they should not come near their wives ⟨**cf. Exodus 19:11, 15**⟩. And again, the Lord saith to Moses: 'Take the first fruits of all your corn and offer them to the Lord thy God' ⟨**Exodus 23:19**⟩. which is also established in the New Testament according to that which the Lord saith: 'The children of the bridegroom fast while the bridegroom is with them', and so forth ⟨**Matthew 9:15**⟩. And according to the convenience of the seasons, after the ascension of the Lord to the skies, his bodily presence being withdrawn, this was then announced as the fast of the fourth month on the second Saturday. However, through the aforesaid legate, the Blessed Gregory, in his Antiphonary and Missal, ordained this same fast, to be celebrated in the Church of the English during the whole week after Pentecost. This is not only attested by our antiphonaries, but also by those very things which we have seen with his missals, at the thresholds of the Apostles Peter and Paul).[53]

Here, too, although the overall quantity of scriptural citations is smaller than we have seen in other sources, a pattern comparable to the other texts I have discussed is apparent. First, in passages aimed at an Anglo-Saxon audience (as Martin J. Ryan noted),[54] scripture is the primary authority. To be sure, the Antiphonary and Missal of Pope Gregory the Great are mentioned, but only as vague allusions, without acknowledgement, in a manner similar to non-scriptural allusions to authorities in the *Legatine Capitulary* and the Alcuinian section of the *Admonitio Generalis*. Rather, in this passage and elsewhere, Ecgberht builds his argument around scriptural *loci*. Second, Ecgberht makes his case initially by invoking the Law of Moses (Exodus 19:11, 15; Exodus 23:19), and then shows how the same principle is upheld in the Law of Christ (Matthew 9:15). Thus, the same two features of legal practice evident in *Collectio canonum Hibernensis*, the *Legatine Capitulary*, and the Alcuinian portion of the *Admonition Generalis* are identifiable in the *Dialogue of Ecgberht* as well. These include: (1)

---

52 *Councils and Ecclesiastical Documents*, III, pp. 411–12.

53 *Medieval Handbooks of Penance*, pp. 241–42.

54 Ryan, 'Archbishop Ecgberht and His *Dialogus*', p. 52.

reliance on scripture as the most fundamental authority, and (2) the practice of building evidence for a case by showing how a given principle is supported by scripture on multiple levels representing successive laws in sacred history.

Very significantly, this evidence demonstrates that the full corpus of extant witnesses to early Northumbrian law (though it is small) all rely on a method of citing scriptural authorities widely attested in early Irish legal practice. Let me summarize that method here. The procedure for citing the authorities of law is made explicit in *Collectio canonum Hibernensis*, Liber XIX *De ordine inquisitionis causarum* (Concerning the order of invoking authoritative sources), as I discussed at length in part one. The relevant portion reads:

> [...] de causis in quibus soluendi ligandique auctoritas est: XXII librorum ueteris testamenti, IIII evangeliorum cum totis apostolorum scriptis. Si non appareat, ad diuina recurrito scripta, que grece agiographa dicuntur [...].[55]
>
> > ([...] concerning sources in which there is authority to loose and bind: The twenty-two books of the Old Testament, and the four gospels together with all the writings of the apostles. Should an answer not present itself, turn to the divine texts that are called *hagiographa* in Greek [...]).[56]

What follows is a series of ecclesiastical authorities other than scripture. Importantly however, scripture is the first and the most basic of the authorities, underlying all the others. It is not equivalent to other sources; it is fundamental.

Moreover, it was ideal that scriptural authorities on various levels agree with one another, as I described in the introduction to this volume. Columbanus emphasized this very point in his *Epistula II* addressing the Gaulish bishops:

> [...] quaeso vos, amantissimi patres ac fratres, et videamus qualis verior sit traditio — vestra an fratrum vestrorum in Occidente. Omnes enim ecclesiae totius Occidentis [...] non respiciunt fieri debere resurrectionem ante passionem, id est ante aequinoctium

55 *The Hibernensis*, Bk I, p. 111.

56 The translation is from *The Hibernensis*, Bk II, p. 556. Also note: not 'hagiography' in the modern sense, but rather 'sacred writings'. These are defined by Isidore of Seville in *Etymologiarum*, VI.i.7, as containing nine books, including Job, the Psalms, Proverbs, Ecclesiastes, Song of Songs, Daniel, Paralipomenon, Ezra, and Esther. See also *The Hibernensis*, Bk II, p. 848 n. 151.

Pascha, et vigesimam lunam non excedunt, **ne sine auctoritate Veteris Testamenti sacramentum Novi Testamenti agant.**[57]

> (I beseech you, my most loving fathers and brethren, and let us see which be the more true tradition — yours, or that of your brethren in the West. For [...] all the churches of the entire West do not consider that the resurrection should take place before the passion, that is Easter before the equinox, and they do not wait beyond the twentieth moon, **lest they should hold a sacrament of the New Testament without authority of the Old**).[58]

Similarly, later:

> Absit ergo ut ego contra vos contendam congrediendum [...] alioquin aliter inter nos potest convenire, ut *aut unusquisque in quo vocatus est in eo permaneat apud Deum* ⟨**1 Corinthians 7:20**⟩, si utraque bona est traditio, aut cum pace et humilitate sine ulla contentio libri legantur utrique, et **quae plus Veteri et Novo Testamento concordant, sine ullius invidia serventur.**[59]

> (Far be it then that I should maintain the need to quarrel with you [...] ⟨W⟩e may agree in some other way, so that either *each should remain before God* in the condition in which he was called ⟨**1 Corinthians 7:20**⟩, if both traditions are good, or else both books should be read over in peace and humility without any argument, and **what agrees better with the Old and New Testament should be maintained without any ill-will at any**).[60]

And, very importantly, as I discussed in part one, this goal of finding agreement between scriptural authorities on all its various levels — that is, between the four biblical laws, or periods which early Irish Christians understood as the progression of sacred history, i.e., the Law of Nature (sometimes equated with the Law of Noah), the Law of Moses, the Law of the Prophets, and the Law of Christ — was a basic tenet of early Irish legal ideology. A judgement supported by scriptural authorities representing each of the four laws was an indication of its truth and righteousness,

---

57 Columbanus, *Sancti Columbani Opera*, 'Epistula II', ll. 10–13 and 14–17, p. 16. Emphasis is my own, in both text and translation.

58 Columbanus, *Sancti Columbani Opera*, 'Epistula II', ll. 10–18, p. 17. I have used Walker's translation of Columbanus's *Epistulae*, though with caution since their accuracy has been seriously called into question. See Esposito, 'On the New Edition', and Bieler, 'Editing Saint Columbanus'.

59 Columbanus, *Sancti Columbani Opera*, 'Epistula II', ll. 17–18 and 20–24, p. 18. Emphasis is my own, in both text and translation.

60 Columbanus, *Sancti Columbani Opera*, 'Epistula II', ll. 21–29, p. 19.

as we see, for example, in Dubthach maccu Lugair's judgement in the Pseudo-historical Prologue to the *Senchas Már*.

Now, in practice, rarely — even in Irish sources — was this procedure followed step-by-step, in order; nor was it common for authorities representing all four laws to be cited in support of any given statute. Clearly, that ideal was not always, or even often achieved. Nonetheless, the more authoritative citations from as many levels of scripture as could be identified, the better, it would appear. Usually, the complex nature of legal questions — *causae*, if you prefer — meant that any individual question, with its constituent parts and sub-questions, would direct a jurist to apply this procedure in composite and sometimes incomplete ways; and, not infrequently, biblical excerpts were cited out of order. That said, scripture was by any measure the most basic authority underlying all other authorities in the order-of-operations prescribed in *Collectio canonum Hibernensis*. Scripture was in all cases the first place to look for guidance and precedence. This order for citing authoritative sources was used throughout *Collectio canonum Hibernensis* and elsewhere in Irish ecclesiastical sources, such as Cummian's letter on the paschal controversy, Colmán's testimony in the Synod of Whitby, etc.; but describing the widespread use of this procedure extends beyond the purpose of this volume. Most important for my current argument is that use of this order of operations for citing the authorities of law is also apparent in the corpus of early Northumbrian legal texts.

Taken together, what does this evidence indicate? I posit that this originally Irish method for invoking authorities — where scripture is the most fundamental source and where, ideally, multiple scriptural passages are marshalled in support of a given premise, each from different sections of the Bible, representing successive covenants between humanity and God over the course of sacred history — was borrowed from Irish sources into early Northumbrian law. This method for legal and theological argumentation — detectable in Irish legal and theological argumentation at least as early as Columbanus's writings in the late sixth century, then Cummian's letter on the paschal controversy and Colmán's testimony in the Synod of Whitby in the seventh century and, most importantly, laid out explicitly as much as a century later in *Collectio canonum Hibernensis* in the eighth century — is what underlay the similar, heavy reliance on scripture as the single most fundamental authority in the *Legatine Capitulary*. Likewise, we see similar examples of this same reflex in the Alcuinian portion of the *Admonitio Generalis* and the *Dialogue of Ecgberht*. I posit that this method for invoking authoritative sources was transmitted to early medieval Northumbria from early medieval Ireland, most likely via Iona and the Irish bishops of Lindisfarne who filled that office through much of the early seventh century, and that it remained, residually, the standard method for citing the authorities of law as late as the end of the eighth century. This claim, I would argue, best explains the heavy, nearly exclusive reliance on scripture as the basic authority of law in the *Legatine Capitulary*, the Alcuinian section of the *Admonitio Generalis*, and the portions of the *Dialogue of Ecgberht* that address English concerns.

The implications of this claim go substantially further (and beyond the scope of this volume). Most significantly, the commonly held view that no Anglo-Saxon law from early Northumbria survives must be revised. The current historical model of Anglo-Saxon law is based almost exclusively on materials that emanated from south of the Humber, all of which were written in vernacular Old English and promulgated primarily by secular authority. What I am suggesting, in contrast, is that not only was there a thriving legal culture in eighth-century, Anglian Northumbria, but also that it was somewhat different from the legal culture we find in the predominantly Saxon south of the country.[61] If my argument that the *Legatine Capitulary* and the *Dialogue of Ecgberht* should properly be regarded as witnesses to a Northumbrian legal tradition is accepted, then it is possible to draw some conclusions about their character and how they differed from other documents that comprise the currently accepted canon of early English law. In particular, in the north of England: (1) law could be written in Latin, whereas south of the Humber it was typically written in vernacular Old English, (2) in the North, law could be written and projected (if not enforced) primarily by ecclesiastical prerogative (as, for example, was the case with the two texts I discussed in this section), whereas south of the Humber it was almost always royally sanctioned, and (3) as I have demonstrated here, Northumbrian law was formatively influenced by early Irish ideas and legal ideology, namely, by the manner scripture was invoked as an authoritative source. This claim breaks fundamentally from some of the currently accepted ideas regarding the origins and development of Anglo-Saxon law.

61 I have discussed this matter more thoroughly in K. Carella, 'Northumbrian Law before the Vikings' and in my forthcoming Quiggin pamphlet, entitled *Northumbrian Law before the Vikings*.

CHAPTER 9

The Court of King Alfred

The Prologue to the Laws of Alfred

When Alfred acceded to the West-Saxon throne in the spring of 871, the world as he knew it was on the verge of collapse. Scandinavian attacks throughout Britain, which had begun almost a century earlier with yearly raiding campaigns targeting coastal monasteries and other poorly defended sources of easy plunder, had escalated to organized invasions aimed at the subjugation or displacement of the English and the establishment of permanent settlements. When, upon the death of his predecessor (the last of his elder brothers) in April of 871, Alfred was poised to assume royal authority, all the English kingdoms in Britain had succumbed to the seafaring invaders, save Wessex. Their Celtic-speaking neighbours inhabiting the less arable uplands to the north and west and across the sea in Brittany and Ireland suffered constant raids and incursions into their territories as well.[1] At this particular moment, it must have seemed as if the glorious period following the early fifth-century *Adventus Saxonum* had run its course, and that hegemony over Britain would now pass inevitably to these new Scandinavian overlords. We cannot know to what extent the remarks of the Welshman Asser, Alfred's chief advisor and biographer, can be taken at face value when he reported in *De rebus gestis Ælfredi* that Alfred received the royal dignity

> [...] quasi invitus [...] nimirum enim non putabat se, nisi divino fultum auxilio, tantam paganorum unquam posse solum sufferre austeritatem [...]..[2]

> > ([...] almost unwillingly [...] for he did not consider himself at all capable to bear the great severity of the vikings, unless supported by divine help [...]).[3]

1 For an excellent introduction to Alfred's Celtic contemporaries, see W. Davies, 'Alfred's Contemporaries'. On the viking raids into their territories during the late ninth century, see pp. 333–37.

2 Asser, *Life of King Alfred*, § 42, ll. 11–15, p. 32. All citations of Asser's text are from this edition.

3 The translation is my own.

Although, given the dire circumstances, it might be more difficult to imagine that he lacked any reluctance to undertake this awesome and seemingly hopeless responsibility.[4]

I describe the events surrounding Alfred's accession not to dramatize the situation for its own sake, but rather to emphasize the gravity of the challenges Alfred faced from the onset of his reign. Immediate military exigencies aside, Alfred apparently was farsighted enough to understand that the long-term survival of his culture — if indeed it could be preserved at all — depended on substantially more than victory in battle. With an insight uncommon among leaders of any era, Alfred realized that enduring success required the formation of a unified and unifying English identity, a common mythology extending beyond the vague and dimly conceived sense(s) of common ancestry and common history shared by Angles, Saxons, Jutes, Frisians (and others) whose primary allegiance was to ethnicity, locale, and kin group rather than to a unified English identity. Much has been written on this topic, and it lies well beyond the scope of my present argument to fully recount prior scholarship on the subject here.[5] For present purposes, suffice to say that the idea of English national identity — though a latent notion incipiently present in the writings of authors such as Theodore, Gregory, and Bede[6] — firmly took root in the English collective consciousness at least in part due to its active promotion by Alfred and his royal circle.[7] As Sarah Foot has explained:

> What Alfred can be seen to have recognised is the potential for his own purpose of the model invented by Pope Gregory and promoted by Bede: one Church, one people and one faith could prefigure a political unity, an ideal which might be made real by a king with sufficient power and ideological energy to promote it.[8]

4 Janet L. Nelson's point in her 'Presidential Address', that viking barbarism has been overstated by medieval and modern authors alike, and that the decline of intellectual culture in Britain (and elsewhere) attributed them was underway well before their invasions began, is well taken. That said, the political reality of Alfred's reign was that the continued existence of Anglo-Saxon culture free of Scandinavian hegemony was under significant threat.

5 Whitelock, 'The Old English Bede', pp. 57–90; Dumville, 'Kingship, Genealogies, and Regnal Lists'; Wormald, 'Bede, the *Bretwaldas* and the Origins of the *Gens Anglorum*'; Reynolds, 'What Do We Mean by "Anglo-Saxon"?'; Foot, 'The Making of *Angelcynn*'; K. Davis, 'National Writing in the Ninth Century'; Harris, 'The Alfredian *World History*'; Molyneaux, 'The *Old English Bede*'; Molyneaux, 'Did the English Really Think They Were God's Elect?'.

6 See especially: Wormald, 'Bede, the *Bretwaldas* and the Origins of the *Gens Anglorum*', pp. 99–129 and Reynolds, 'What Do We Mean [...]?', p. 404.

7 See especially: Foot, 'The Making of *Angelcynn*'; K. Davis, 'National Writing in the Ninth Century'; and Harris, *Race and Ethnicity*, pp. 83–106.

8 Foot, 'The Making of the *Angelcynn*', p. 41.

Foot's comments on this point, which represent a vein of argumentation championed by Patrick Wormald and others, must be weighed against George Molyneaux's comments about important differences between the Latin text of Bede's *Historica Ecclesiastica Gentis Angorum* and the Old English translation of it:

> The translator ⟨of the Old English Bede⟩ appears to have regarded the *H⟨istorica⟩ E⟨cclesiastica⟩* as valuable primarily as a store of examples to inculcate Christian behaviour, not as an account of a single *gens Anglorum* with a special relationship with God. Since it is likely that the *O⟨ld⟩ E⟨nglish⟩ B⟨ede⟩* was more widely known than the *H⟨istorica⟩ E⟨cclesiastica⟩* in England during the first half of the tenth century, this analysis undermines Wormald's interpretation of the role of Bede in the political developments of this period.[9]

Molyneaux's cautions on this matter, while well-taken, focus on the role of the *Old English Bede* and what it can reveal about Alfred's political agenda as a single witness, not about Alfred's agenda writ large. What we can see by looking at the whole picture is that Alfred's agenda overall aimed at creating and promoting a perception by the various and diverse Germanic-speaking peoples over whom Alfred came to hold sway of themselves as a single people with a common ethnogenesis, cultural mythology, history, and future. This process was no doubt accelerated by the viking conquest of every English kingdom save his own (thus simplifying internecine polity) and became a central feature of Alfred's ideological agenda.

Let me begin with a brief overview of Alfred's plan to reform English culture before turning to the question of his reliance on certain Irish legal ideas for part of that plan. Foremost on this agenda was Alfred's strategy to foster a renewed intellectual culture among his countrymen. As he explains most fully in the prologue to his vernacular rendering of Pope Gregory's *Cura Pastoralis*, this effort commenced with a programme to translate from Latin into Old English a series of works he considered essential reading (here expressed in the often-cited phrase, '[…] suma bec, ða ðe niedbeðearfosta sien eallum monnun to wiotonne […]' ([…] certain books which are most necessary for everyone to know […]).[10] What is more, his programme mandated the training of English youths not occupied with more immediately pressing military affairs to read and write in Old English and, further, those who showed exceptional talent, to be taught Latin letters. As a result, Alfred has been credited (rightly or not), among his other achievements, as the 'father of English prose'.

Alfred's overall success notwithstanding, scholarly assessment of the surviving textual evidence of his educational programme has raised doubts

9 Molyneaux, 'The Old English Bede', p. 1316.
10 King Alfred, *Alfredian Prologues and Epilogues*, p. 72 (text); p. 73 (trans.).

about the extent of his personal contribution. Above all, questions surrounding two issues have led to sustained controversy.[11] These include: (1) which works were translated as part of Alfred's programme (and which were not)? And (2), was the king himself responsible for any of them personally? Suffice to say that, over time, the size of the accepted corpus of his work has steadily declined as has general acceptance that Alfred translated any of the texts alone, independent of his advisors. Despite scepticism concerning Alfred's personal involvement, however, few disbelieve that at least some subset of those texts commonly attributed to him were the product of his royal initiative.[12] Whether he actively participated in the technical process of rendering Latin into Old English is an open question. In whatever way the debate resolves, Alfred's main achievement was to bring together a diverse group of intellectuals who, without obvious precedent, collectively developed what amounts to a theory of translation, and who subsequently produced a series of texts rendered in the vernacular specifically chosen to promote his ideological agenda. My view is that the Alfredian translations were drafted more or less independently by individuals (or parties) among the diverse group of international scholars Alfred sponsored at his court. While the texts they produced at times seem to adhere to a common, overarching plan as a result of their collective thinking, at the same time they reflect notable variations in details (due, among other factors, to the varied background of their authors) in areas ranging from dialectal and other linguistic features to underlying political and theological ideas secondary to the main Alfredian agenda.[13] It is not my purpose here to add my voice to the more-than-a-century-old body of scholarship on the question of precisely how and by whom these texts were drafted. For my present argument, I merely assert that these translations emanated from Alfred's royal circle — at least those texts important for my present argument, including the Prologue to his Old English translation of the *Cura Pastoralis* and the Prologue to his law code, as well as certain royal genealogies I shall discuss below — and

11 These questions have a long history in scholarship. See especially: Sisam, 'The Authorship of the Verse Translation of Boethius'; Whitelock, 'The Prose of Alfred's Reign'; Clement, 'The Production of the *Pastoral Care*'; Wormald, *The Making of English Law*, pp. 272–77; Bately, 'The Old English Orosius'; Bately, 'King Alfred and the Old English Translation of Orosius'; Bately, 'Compilation of the Anglo-Saxon Chronicle'; *The Old English Orosius*; Bately, 'Lexical Evidence for the Authorship of the Prose Psalms'; Bately, *The Literary Prose of King Alfred's Reign*; Bately, 'Old English Prose'; Bately, 'The Alfredian Canon Revisited'; *Alfred the Great*; Godden, 'Wærferth and King Alfred'; Gill, Swartz, and Treschow, 'A Stylometric Analysis of King Alfred's Literary Works'; Godden, 'Did King Alfred Write Anything?'; Gill, Swartz, and Treschow, 'King Alfred's Scholarly Writings'.

12 Alfred's translation of Augustine's *Soliloquies* is a possible exception. See Godden, 'Did King Alfred Write Anything?'.

13 For convenience, I shall at times refer to Alfred as author of these texts, fully aware that they may well have been composed by others in his royal circle.

that they were formatively influenced by distinctively Alfredian ideological concerns, including an emergent myth of a unified English identity.

Of particular interest for the present argument is the apparently liberal approach toward translation in the Alfredian circle. Even though almost all of the works attributed to Alfred's circle are translations of Latin originals, one must be cautious not to dismiss them as slavish recapitulations of their exemplars, devoid of innovation. Quite the contrary: as has often been discussed, the translations produced by Alfred's circle were typified by interpolations and modifications — sometimes striking modifications — of the Latin originals. Examples of this practice, too numerous to catalogue here, have been the subject of much scholarly interest. Though evidence of this practice can be found throughout the Alfredian corpus (even the biblical text in the Prologue to his law code was not immune from substantive alteration) these features are most prominent in the Old English translation of Orosius's *Historiae adversum paganos libri VII* and Boethius's *De consolatione philosophiae*.[14] Elsewhere, for example in the Old English Bede, the translator tended to follow the Latin text closely, though excising substantial portions in a way that may reflect a broader agenda.[15] To be sure, the translators in Alfred's royal circle often did not merely render their base texts in rote fashion by, for example, closely adhering to the often-cited Alfredian dictum 'hwilum word be worde, hwilum andgit fram andgiete' (sometimes word for word, sometimes sense ⟨from⟩ sense).[16] Rather, in many instances, they engaged with their Latin

14 One might add Alfred's translation of Augustine's *Soliloquies* to the list, though its inclusion in the Alfredian corpus has recently been seriously challenged by Godden, 'Did King Alfred Write Anything?'.

15 See Molyneaux, 'The Old English Bede', pp. 1291–92: '[...] the *OEB* is not a full translation: substantial chunks of the Latin are omitted or abridged. The translator worked carefully, deleting cross-references to omitted sections, adding clarification where earlier omissions made this appropriate and showing consistency in the kinds of material left out. Many of the documents that Bede quoted are excluded. Doctrinal disputes are much less prominent: Pelagianism is cut entirely and, although several brief references to the dating of Easter are retained, Bede's lengthy discussions of the issue are generally omitted or abridged and it therefore ceases to be a major theme of the text. Indeed, a reader of the *OEB* would not learn that there had been a Synod of Whitby. Historical narrative without a clear moral purpose is often condensed or omitted; this is particularly seen in the very significant abridgement of the Roman history in book one. A lack of interest in the chronology of narrative is reflected in the omission of Bede's chronological summary and of some dates. Digressions on matters of intellectual interest, such as etymology, terminology, topography and natural phenomena, are usually neatly excised: examples include the observation that the lengths of days and nights vary with latitude, a discussion of the difference between *murus* and *uallum* and a description of the tides at Lindisfarne'.

16 *Alfredian Prologues and Epilogues*, p. 72 (text); p. 73 (trans.). Note that I have altered Irvine's translation slightly. As Albert S. Cook first noticed in 'Alfred's "Word for Word" Translation', p. 108, Alfred's phrasing in this instance was ultimately based on Jerome's (variously construed) description of his translation style 'uel uerbum e uerbo, uel sensum de

exemplars actively, often interpreting them, reshaping them, and crafting them into distinctly reimagined narratives that, in places at least, seem more like novel compositions in their own right.

What motivated this effort? That is — other than to foster a unified sense of English identity that might help galvanize Alfred's diverse subjects during a period of crisis — what, more specifically, were the ideological aims of Alfred's translation programme? Why were the works translated in Alfred's circle the ones 'most necessary for all men to know'? Considered fully, these questions — while important for understanding Alfred's goals — lie beyond the scope of what I shall be able to consider here. At this time, I shall venture only a few generalizations relevant to my present purpose. The works translated as part of the Alfredian programme can be classified as either Christian didactic or Christian (pseudo-)historical in nature, or both. The practice of altering such texts in translation, to the extensive degree witnessed in the Alfredian corpus, is unprecedented. Presumably, these texts were not perceived as works of fiction, but documents that contained some sort of historical verity. Reconstruing such works — i.e., works with a high degree of what reception theorists call 'truth-value' — by selectively modifying them or interpolating material into them, strongly suggests that their translators, beyond merely attempting to render the meaning of the Latin original into Old English as accurately as possible, instead set out with self-conscious intent to interpose an agenda.[17] Most probably, this practice was carried out with more than a single aim. For present purposes, I posit only that among these goals, the translators in Alfred's royal circle sought to promote a pseudo-historical version of an Anglo-Saxon past ensconced within a particular understanding of Christian history wherein they played a special role. The nature of this special role, however, has not been properly understood, I would argue, due at least in part to a consistent failure to grasp the themes in the Prologue to Alfred's law code and certain other texts associated with his royal initiative. In essence, what the Alfredian translators accomplished with the Prologue to his law code (and in certain other texts that I shall discuss) was to write pseudo-history; not, for the most part, by composing whole narratives *ex nihilo* (which, as we have seen, was common practice in Ireland), but rather by modifying and interpolating material into pre-existing historical

---

sensu, uel ex utroque commixtum' (either word from word, or sense from sense, or out of both combined). See also Discenza, 'Wise Wealhstodas', p. 492 and n. 12.

17 Translation theorists would point out that, on the most basic level, all translation relies on interpretation. While I do not disagree, my argument here is that the translators in Alfred's circle set out from the beginning to alter these texts consciously and with a specific agenda in mind. Thus, their 'interpretation' affects their work on (at least) two levels, one guided by a premeditated ideological endeavour (which I am addressing here), and the other by the at least partly unconscious interpretive choices any translator must make when rendering culturally unique ideas from one semantic system into another.

and theological works and remoulding them to fit Alfred's agenda. By doing so, they shifted emphasis onto matters of Germanic and, more precisely, English historical interest. More importantly, where they deemed it necessary, they re-crafted their exemplars to create an ideologically prominent place for their ancestors — both historical and mythological — within a broader framework of Christian history.[18]

Those familiar with scholarship on the Alfredian translations will find little new or groundbreaking in what I have said thus far. What has not been properly understood, however, is the way in which Alfred's law code — specifically the sophisticated legal-theological treatise that functions as a prologue to his laws — fits within the broader context of his overall ideological plan. Most scholars would agree that it is simply not true, as Attenborough pronounced in the early years of the twentieth century, that Alfred's Prologue '[...] has no bearing on Anglo-Saxon law'.[19] That said, scholars since Attenborough have nonetheless failed to appreciate the essential details of Alfred's argument, misguidedly focusing on the Mosaic preface in isolation from the rest of the Prologue, or seeking to identify Hincmarian sources and analogues to the extent that they have missed the proverbial forest for the trees. As a result, no one has yet fully grasped the ideological purpose of the text.[20] In the rest of this section, I shall explicate Alfred's ideological aims in this Prologue and, in particular, show how it reflects a distinctively Alfredian pseudo-historical view of early English jurisprudence designed to situate customary Germanic legal practice within a biblical (and biblically derived) narrative of sacred history. Understood in this way, the Prologue to Alfred's laws is as much an expression of historical and theological ideology as it is a treatise on

18 Pseudo-historical narratives and pseudo-historically inspired interpretations of the English past (though the term 'pseudo-history' is not often used in the scholarship to describe them) were not uncommon in England throughout the early Middle Ages, as has been expertly described. See, for example, Howe, *Migration and Mythmaking* and Scheil, *The Footsteps of Israel*. I shall have more to say about their work below.

19 *The Laws of the Earliest English Kings*, p. 35.

20 Note Allen Frantzen's comment on prior scholarship relating to the Prologue to Alfred's law code in 'The Form and Function', p. 123: 'The most conspicuous victim of prefatory ambiguity is, of course, the preface to his law-code. Attenborough omitted most of it because it "had no bearing on Anglo-Saxon Law". Only small sections of the introduction have been translated by Whitelock and by Keynes and Lapidge. Hence, as Wormald has demonstrated, readers have missed almost entirely the ideological significance of the king's legislation as literature'. Later, on p. 136 in the same work, Frantzen adds: 'It would also be a mistake to form these texts into a complete picture of educational reform with Alfred at its nexus, a gesture that merely echoes the king's claim in the prose preface to the *Pastoral Care*. It would, I think, be more profitable to speculate on these prefaces as performances, trying to imagine how the double prefaces and the complex preface to the law-code were received and enacted in public'. The whole of the Prologue to Alfred's law code is translated in *An Introduction to Early English Law*, pp. 44–56.

the closely related topic of legal theory. As such, the Prologue to Alfred's laws functions in a manner similar to certain Irish analogues and, as I shall suggest, was ultimately inspired by Irish legal-theological ideologies. These are the matters I shall examine in what follows. Since, however, this document has received relatively scant attention in comparison with the other works associated with Alfred's royal circle, I shall begin with a brief description of its contents and prior scholarship on the text.

Description of the Prologue to the Laws of Alfred and Prior Scholarship[21]

Of the works attributed to King Alfred, the Prologue to his laws has drawn some of the least scholarly attention. Such neglect could not be more unwarranted: it stands out as one of the most sophisticated examples of legal theory composed in England before the Norman Conquest (and for some time thereafter), a fact all the more remarkable considering its attribution to a secular ruler. Although a tradition of Anglo-Saxon vernacular law seems to have existed from the earliest period,[22] nothing prior in Old English can be classified unambiguously as an expression of 'legal theory'. What negligible discussion of theoretical matters can be found in early Anglo-Saxon legal texts at all — if in fact any of it fits that description — appear scattered throughout the Latin writings of clerical authors such as Alcuin, though such texts are almost always wholly derivative of, if not outright excerpts from, earlier patristic writers. The Prologue to the Laws of Alfred, on the other hand, stands out as one of the more ideologically daring legal texts of its era.[23] Like other works in the Alfredian corpus, it is presented as a translation (in this case from Exodus), though it includes other, presumably original material. In this case, even his translation of scripture — which, as has often been pointed out, departs from the original in significant and loaded ways[24] — cannot be described accurately

21 For prior scholarship on the Prologue to the Laws of Alfred, see especially: Wormald, '*Lex Scripta et Verbum Regis*', p. 134; Frantzen, *King Alfred*, pp. 11–21; Wormald, *The Making of English Law*, pp. 264–85 and 419–30; Treschow, 'The Prologue to Alfred's Law Code'; Pratt, *The Political Thought of King Alfred the Great*, pp. 214–41 and Jurasinski, 'Slavery, Learning, and the Law of Marriage'.

22 Prior to Alfred's *Domboc*, the most recent laws were those attributed to Wihtred of Kent (reigned *c.* 690–725) and Ine of Wessex (reigned 688–726), the latter surviving only as an appendix to Alfred's own code. Both documents are difficult to date, but — roughly speaking — were probably issued sometime *c.* 700.

23 I consider this point to be true despite the often-repeated (and I think mistaken) claims that Carolingian and, specifically, Hincmarian ideas were the primary influences on Alfred's text. I have argued against these claims in B. Carella, 'Evidence for Hiberno-Latin Thought'. I shall have more to say about this matter in what follows.

24 See B. Carella, 'The Source for the Prologue to the Laws of Alfred'.

as simply a rendered text. As such, the Prologue to Alfred's laws bears resemblance to his other prologues. Alfred typically framed his translations with original, prefatory frames that interact discursively with his main text and invite his audience to understand the translated document in a particularly Alfredian way. The result is a body of documents that, although translations in part, nonetheless project a distinctively Alfredian worldview.

This approach is especially apparent in the Prologue to the Laws of Alfred. Besides containing the earliest translation of the Bible into English of any significant length (indeed, into any northwestern European vernacular), it situates Anglo-Saxon customary law within the broader narrative of sacred history with a distinct ideological purpose, i.e., to equate (or equivocate) the customary Germanic legislation of Anglo-Saxon kings with the decrees of ecclesiastical synods, as I shall demonstrate.[25] Yet, despite its importance, two main factors have led to persistent misunderstanding of this document on the part of modern scholars, namely, the economy of its style and misguided scholarly theories about its sources. I shall discuss each in turn.

The first reason that the Prologue to the Laws of Alfred has been misunderstood results from its concise economy of style. Here, the author of the text (and we can say 'author' rather than 'translator' since this is the only document emanating from the Alfredian royal circle not 'a reworking of classical or patristic sources')[26] stitched together a series of biblical excerpts and other prefatory material with only a bare minimum of transitional cues or authorial commentary that might provide a sense of the overall structure and purpose of the implicit argument. The text consists of a series of juxtaposed ideas presented largely without explicit guidance as to how those ideas, taken together, should be understood. Nowhere, for example, does the author (whom I shall at times refer to as Alfred for convenience, though it may have been a member of his royal circle) state a thesis or otherwise explain their overall purpose. Rather, the reader is left to work out the implications of the text largely for themselves. In my view, this lack of overt transparency reflects the King's awareness of how novel his ideas might be understood to be, particularly by churchmen. For the same reason, almost nowhere in this Prologue — certainly not until the end — does Alfred speak unambiguously in his own voice. The austerity of his prose combined with his lack of authorial intrusion serves, I would argue, to foster the impression that the series of scriptural passages he quotes speaks for itself. The text begins with 'DRYHTEN WÆS SPRECENde ðas word to Moyse ⁊ þus cwæð: Ic eom dryhten ðin god [...]' (The

25 Compare the discussion in Pratt, *The Political Thought of King Alfred the Great*, pp. 226–28. The conclusions he drew from this observation, however, differ significantly from my own.

26 Frantzen, *King Alfred*, p. 11.

Lord was speaking these words to Moses and thus said 'I am the Lord your God' [...] ⟨*El.* Pro.⟩),[27] and shifts imperceptibly at some point near the end to 'Ic ða Ælfred cyning þas togædere gegaderode [...]' (Then I, Alfred, King of the West-Saxons, commanded those to be gathered together [...] ⟨*El.* 49.9⟩).[28] The overall effect is to give the audience the impression that it is the revealed word of God — not Alfred — who narrates the content of the document.

Before considering the second reason why the Prologue to Alfred's laws has often been misunderstood, it will first be necessary for me to describe the contents of the Prologue to the Laws of Alfred. The text begins abruptly,[29] with an extended Old English translation of Exodus chapters 20:1 through 23:13 ⟨*El.* Pro.–48⟩.[30] For the most part, the translator rendered the text in a manner best described as 'word by word', though they did occasionally alter or omit portions of the biblical text liberally.[31] These changes are sometimes parallelled in the exemplar, sometimes not.[32] Immediately after the Mosaic Prologue there follows, with virtually no transitional guidance to aid the reader, what I shall refer to as an 'explanatory bridge' ⟨*El.* 49–49.10⟩. This second part contains a series of New Testament scriptural references, including a paraphrase of Matthew 5:17, where Christ states that he came to fulfill the law, not to abrogate it, a passage which — as I discussed in Part One — is a biblical *locus classicus* defining the relationship between the Old Law of Moses and the New Law of Christ. Next, Alfred cited the decision of the 'Synod of Jerusalem', recounted in Acts 15 — also a *locus classicus* defining the relationship between the Old and New Laws — where (as I likewise discussed in Part One) the early Christians formally decided that gentiles newly converted

27 All citations of the Prologue (*Einleitung* = *El.*) to the Laws of Alfred are from *Die Gesetze der Angelsachsen* and are cited parenthetically in the text by section number (Pro.–49.10). I have used the E-text (i.e., Cambridge, Corpus Christi College 173 — the so-called Parker Chronicle and Laws). All translations of the Prologue to the Laws of Alfred are my own unless otherwise stated. This citation is from I, p. 26.

28 *Die Gesetze der Angelsachsen*, I, p. 46.

29 The abrupt beginning of Alfred's text closely parallels that of the *Liber ex lege Moysi* in the manuscript tradition. Though the latter begins with Exodus 20:2 (as opposed to Alfred's Prologue, which begins with Exodus 20:1), both texts present the Mosaic Law without providing an explanation or context for it.

30 *Die Gesetze der Angelsachsen*, I, pp. 26–42.

31 See especially, Jurasinski, 'Slavery, Learning, and the Law of Marriage'; Carella, 'Asser's Bible and the Prologue to the Laws of Alfred', and B. Carella, 'The Source for the Prologue'.

32 It is now generally accepted that Alfred relied not on a text of the Bible directly, but rather on a version of a Hiberno-Latin collection of excerpts from the Pentateuch known as the *Liber ex lege Moysi* for his base text. I shall have more to say about this text and Alfred's use of it below. Since none of the four surviving witnesses of the *Liber ex lege Mosyi* could have been the one used by Alfred, and since there are small-but-significant differences between each of them, it is impossible to be certain in all cases which departures from the biblical text appeared in the Alfred's exemplar, and which should be attributed to Alfred himself.

to the faith would not be subject to the full sanction of the Mosaic injunction as Jews were. Finally, the biblical portion of the Prologue to the Laws of Alfred ends with a non-standard, negatively construed citation of the Golden Rule that occurs as a variant in some biblical texts (i.e., this is a variant reading of Matthew 7:12):[33] 'þæt ge willen, þæt oðre men eow ne don, ne doð ge ðæt oþrum monnum' [*El.* 49.5][34] (What you ⟨pl.⟩ might wish that other men do not to you ⟨pl.⟩, do not do that to other men). Immediately thereafter, Alfred recasts this statement to emphasize the act of judgement, transforming Christ's statement to make it more applicable to a legal context:

> Of ðissum anu*m* dome mon mæg geðencean, þæt he æghwelcne on ryht gedemeð; ne ðearf he nanra domboca oþerra. Geðence he, þæt he nanum men ne deme þæt he nolde ðæt he him demde, gif he ðone dom ofer hine sohte ⟨*El.* 49.6⟩.[35]
>
> > (From this one judgement, one can consider that he judges everyone justly; he does not need any other law books. Let him consider, that he not judge any man ⟨in such a way⟩ that he ⟨i.e., the first man⟩ would not wish that he ⟨i.e., that man judged by the first man⟩ judged him, if he had pursued judgement on him).

Here, Alfred was thinking about how biblical principles might apply to English jurisprudence and, more specifically, how the requirements of the Law of Christ (as expressed in Matthew 5:17 and the Golden Rule) might function in actual practice. Thus, the notion of 'do not *do* onto others as you would not have them do unto you', expressed from the point of view of a participant in the action, shifts to 'do not *judge* others as you would not have them judge you', this time expressed from a third-party perspective of one rendering judgement (perhaps in a legal suit).

After this series of scriptural citations, Alfred proceeds with the following statement, apparently intended to provide some degree of clarification regarding the significance of his prior argument:

> Siððan ðæt þa gelamp, þæt monega ðeoda Cristes geleafan onfengon, þa wurdon monega seonoðas geond ealne middangeard gegaderode, ⁊ eac swa geond Angelcyn, siððan hie Cristes geleafan onfengon, halegra biscepa ⁊ eac oðerra geðungenra witena; hie ða gesetton, for ðære

33 *Councils and Synods*, I.i, p. 17; Wormald, *The Making of English Law*, p. 423 and n. 28; Pratt, *Political Thought*, pp. 229 and n. 128. This variant is attested in the Book of Armagh, a distinctive Insular text with mixed Vulgate and Old Latin readings. On at least one occasion, Asser cites a variant attested in this text as well. On the possible significance of this fact, see B. Carella, 'Asser's Bible', p. 201 (especially).

34 *Die Gesetze der Angelsachsen*, I, p. 44.

35 *Die Gesetze der Angelsachsen*, I, p. 44.

> mildheortnesse þe Crist lærde, æt mæstra hwelcre misdæde þætte ða weoruldhlafordas moston mid hiora leafan buton synne æt þam forman gylte þære fiohbote onfon, þe hie þa gesettan […] Hie ða on monegum senoðum monegra menniscra misdæda bote gesetton, ⁊ on monega senoðbec hie writan, hwær anne dom hwær oþerne [*El.* 49.7–8].[36]
>
> (Thereafter it happened that many nations received belief in Christ. Then there were many synods convened throughout all the world, and, likewise, among the English after they received belief in Christ, of holy bishops and of other distinguished wise men. They then set down, on account of the mercy that Christ taught, that secular lords (*weoruldhlafordas*) could, with their permission and without sin, collect monetary fines (*fiohbot*) for almost every crime at the first offense, which they then established […] Then, in many synods they set down compensation for many human crimes, and in many a synod-book they wrote down here one decision, there another).

Finally, Alfred closed with a short, customary statement explaining how he, with the consent of his advisors, selected for inclusion in his own code those statutes from the laws of his ancestors and other prior Anglo-Saxon kings that seemed best (adding some minor improvements). Among the laws of his forbears, Alfred included the laws composed: '[…] on Ines dæge, mines mæges, oððe on Offan Mercna cyninges oððe on Æþelbryhtes, þe ærest fulluhte onfeng on Angelcynne […]' ⟨*El.* 49.9⟩[37] ([…] in Ine's day, my kinsman, or in Offa's, King of the Mercians, or in Æðelbehrt's (who first among the English people received baptism) […]). Among these individuals, Ine alone was a West-Saxon. Presumably, Alfred's enumeration of his legal predecessors reflected his desire to include all his English subjects. He asserts, thus, that his laws derived not only from his West-Saxon predecessors, but also from the edicts of the preeminent Mercian and Kentish kings of the past whose realms, having fallen to the vikings, had lost their independence and whose inhabitants, we may assume, now looked to Alfred for leadership.[38] With this statement, Alfred tacitly implied that, as the giver of their laws, he was their king.

---

36 *Die Gesetze der Angelsachsen*, I, p. 46.

37 *Die Gesetze der Angelsachsen*, Bd. 1, p. 44.

38 Reynolds, 'What Do We Mean by "Anglo-Saxon"?', p. 406. Likewise, Asser reports that, in 886 after Alfred liberated and restored London, 'Ad quem regem omnes Angli et Saxones, qui prius ubique dispersi fuerant aut cum paganis sub captivitate erant, voluntarie converterunt, et suo dominio se subdiderunt' (All the Angles and Saxons — those who had formerly been scattered everywhere and were not in captivity with the Vikings — turned willingly to Alfred and submitted themselves to his lordship). The text is from Stevenson, *Asser's Life*, § 83, p. 69. I have used the translation in *Alfred the Great*, p. 98, and I have

This gesture was a move toward establishing a pan-English identity: Alfred (the audience was to understand), though king of the West-Saxons, was not merely that, but — far more — he was king of all the Anglo-Saxon inhabitants of Britain, regardless of ethnic affiliation: he was king of the *Angelcynn*. As has often been remarked on (and sometimes used as a criterion for proposing an early date for the text's promulgation),[39] Alfred, at the end of the Prologue to his laws, still referred to himself as *West-seaxna cyning* (king of the West-Saxons) ⟨*El.* 49.9, 49.10⟩. This designation, however, must be measured against his use of the term *Angelcynn* in the second citation above. Here, Alfred — having just listed some of the famous royal predecessors of his Mercian and Kentish subjects alongside his West-Saxon ancestors — described Æðelberht (King of Kent, d. 616) as the first to become a Christian, and referred to them all collectively with the unifying term *Angelcynn* ('[...] Æðelbryht [...] þe ærest fulluhte onfeng on Angelcynne ⟨*El.* 49.9⟩';[40] [...] Æðelbehrt, who first received baptism among the English). He also used the same word to describe all the English earlier in this same text: 'Siððan ðæt þa gelamp, þæt monega ðeoda Cristes geleafan onfengon, þa wurdon monega seonoðas geond ealne middangeard gegaderode, ⁊ eac swa geond **Angelcyn**, siððan hie Cristes geleafan onfengon [...]' ⟨*El.* 49.7⟩[41] (Thereafter it happened that many nations received belief in Christ. Then there were many synods convened throughout all the world, and, likewise, among the **English** after they received belief in Christ [...]). Likewise, as Patrick Wormald noted,[42] several times in his Prologue to the *Cura Pastoralis*, Alfred referred to all the Anglo-Saxons, regardless of their ethnic affiliations, with the word *Angelcynn* and their language as *Englisc*.[43] We should understand these rhetorical gestures as early moves on Alfred's part toward establishing a unified English identity. Perhaps Alfred was not sufficiently confident and well-established at the time when he issued his law code, especially among his non-Saxon subjects, to credibly fashion himself (as he did later in

---

accepted Keynes and Lapidge's correction of Stevenson's text (restoring the manuscript reading) described in n. 199.

39 Whether the Prologue to the Laws of Alfred was released early or late in his reign has been the matter of some disagreement. On this question see Frantzen, *King Alfred*, p. 11, and *Alfred the Great*, pp. 39 and 163. For a dissenting opinion, see Whitelock, *English Historical Documents*, p. 372.

40 *Die Gesetze der Angelsachsen*, I, p. 46.

41 *Die Gesetze der Angelsachsen*, I, p. 44.

42 Wormald, 'Bede, the *Bretwaldas* and the Origins of the *Gens Anglorum*', pp. 103–04.

43 The use of the term *Englisc* to describe the language of the multi-ethnic Anglo-Saxons is curious, especially given the existence of a more general, non-ethnically-affiliated alternative. For example, in the *Legatine Capitulary of 786*, we are told that the individual *capitula* were read out, '[...] tam latine quam theodisc [...]' (in both Latin and the vernacular [...]). The word used for the vernacular is *theodiscę* (in the ablative), obviously a Latinized form of Old English *þeodisc*, Alcuin, 'The Legatine Capitulary', l. 15, p. 28.

his reign) as *rex Anglo-Saxonicum* or *rex Anglorum et Saxonicum* without seeming to appropriate a dignity not due to him.[44] So, instead, he chose a potentially less presumptuous alternative, referring to his people collectively as *Angelcynn* without openly claiming the title of their collective leader. Later in his reign, he described himself with designations that asserted his claim to lordship over all the English more aggressively.[45] If his law code was indeed a text produced early in his programme, then we might see it as representing an early stage in Alfred's move toward thinking of himself as king of all the English. I shall set discussion on these matters aside for now. At this juncture, the Prologue to his Laws concluded, and thereafter followed the mostly traditional collection of statutes that constitute Alfred's law code proper, with the law code of his West-Saxon ancestor Ine also appended.

With this Prologue — consisting of the Mosaic preface, the short narrative account of Anglo-Saxon legal history, including a series of scriptural quotations — and the law code that followed it, Alfred laid out an ideologically loaded conceptualization of the relationship, in his view, between various kinds of law, including (1) the Law of Moses, as expressed in Exodus, (2) the Law of Christ, as expressed in the gospels and the Acts of the Apostles, (3) all subsequent ecclesiastical legislation, as promulgated by ecclesiastical councils and synods throughout all Christendom, including England and, finally, (4) the mostly traditional collection of statutes that comprised the main body of his law code. Including the fourth of these categories — customary Anglo-Saxon law — in this series of relationships stands out as a particularly innovative gesture.

With these juxtapositions tacitly implying a continuous narrative, Alfred promoted a conception of both English and Christian legal history expressing how, in his view, Anglo-Saxon jurisprudence fit within the broader framework of sacred history. Specifically, with the Prologue to his laws, he cast English customary law — i.e., the legacy of his pre-Christian (and incompletely Christianized), Germanic forbears — as one and the same with the decrees of provincial synods of the Church. According to this proposition, Anglo-Saxon secular jurisprudence differed in no way from canon law.[46] In Alfred's view, the traditional, royal assemblies of the early English *witenagemot* from which these laws emanated, amounted to nothing less than ecclesiastically sanctioned, provincial councils.[47] To be sure, the *witenagemot* typically included strong ecclesiastical representation, but it was not an ecclesiastical gathering; certainly not a 'synod'. And

---

44 Nelson, 'The Political Ideas of Alfred of Wessex', p. 131 and n. 42.

45 See, for example, Nelson, 'The Political Ideas of King Alfred of Wessex', pp. 134–35.

46 Compare Pratt, *The Political Thought of King Alfred the Great*, p. 228. Pratt's assertion is similar to mine, though his conclusions differ from my own.

47 The *witenagemot* typically included strong ecclesiastical representation.

yet, Alfred seems to assert implicitly that the laws that emanated from these gatherings were tantamount to synodal decrees. I shall have more to say about this claim presently.

Before proceeding, however, let me turn now to the second reason why scholars have misunderstood the Prologue to Alfred's laws, that is, incorrect theories about its sources. Generally speaking, received opinion holds that Alfred likely relied on a Hiberno-Latin collection of excerpts from the Pentateuch known as the *Liber ex lege Moysi* as a base text for his translation of Exodus,[48] and that he almost certainly relied on the political thought of Hincmar of Rheims for the explanatory bridge that follows it.[49] Ironically, the former claim, although typically regarded as less certain, is supported by textual evidence, while the latter is based, for the most part, solely on perceived thematic parallels. In a series of articles, I have investigated these claims.[50] First, I conducted a close textual comparison of the *Liber ex lege Mosyi* against Alfred's translation of Exodus, confirming that Alfred relied on this Hiberno-Latin text as his exemplar.[51] Next, I assessed the case for Frankish (particularly Hincmarian) influence on the Prologue to Alfred's laws, examining the textual comparisons proposed by Patrick Wormald and Michael Treschow as evidence of Alfred's reliance on Hincmar's thought. I concluded that none of it proved a likely source. Instead, I suggested that Alfred probably drew on material he found in the Hiberno-Latin collection of canon law known as *Collectio canonum Hibernensis*, a text for which the *Liber ex lege Moysi* served as an introduction in the manuscript tradition.[52] Additionally, I rejected the thesis that Alfred was guided by a letter from Archbishop Fulk, Hincmar's successor at Rheims (a point generally accepted in Alfredian scholarship), arguing instead that the Prologue to his Laws should be understood as a pointed response to it.[53]

---

48 The similarities between the *Liber ex lege Moysi* and Alfred's Old English translation of Exodus were first noticed by Fournier, 'Le *Liber ex lege Moysi*', pp. 230–31. See also: Kottje, 'Der *Liber ex lege Moysis*'.

49 Frankish influence on the non-Mosaic portion of the Prologue to the Laws of Alfred, particularly of the writings of Archbishop Hincmar of Rheims, has gone mostly unquestioned. I remain highly sceptical (as I shall discuss). See especially: Wallace-Hadrill, *Early Medieval History*, p. 209; Treschow, 'The Prologue to Alfred's Law Code', pp. 102–07; Patrick Wormald discusses this matter on a number of occasions, but most fully in *The Making of English Law*, pp. 423–27; Pratt, *The Political Thought of King Alfred the Great*, pp. 214–38.

50 B. Carella, 'The Source for the Prologue'; 'Evidence for *Hiberno*-Latin Thought'; and 'Asser's Bible and the Prologue to the Laws of Alfred'.

51 B. Carella, 'The Source for the Prologue'.

52 B. Carella, 'Evidence for Hiberno-Latin Thought'.

53 Dorothy Whitelock commented on what she interpreted as the letter's '[…] arrogant and patronizing tone […]'. See *English Historical Documents*, p. 814. Janet L. Nelson, however, has disagreed with Whitelock's reading, asserting that '[…] what has sounded "patronising"

As a result of this mistaken attribution of the second half of Alfred's Prologue to Hincmarian influence, scholarly assessments of the text have tended to regard it less of a whole than as a sum of its parts. Taken together, these separate theories about Alfred's use of sources — i.e., that he relied on a Hiberno-Latin source for the Mosaic preface and drew on Hincmar for the rest — amount to a rather unlikely scenario: to reconcile these conclusions, one would have to believe that Alfred relied on a Hiberno-Latin text, i.e., the *Liber ex lege Moysi,* without respect for its broader context, as an exemplar for his translation of Exodus, and then subsequently put it down without drawing from anything else in the codex. This seems unlikely from an author and king whose prologues suggest, if nothing else, that he cared about and deeply appreciated the rhetorical power of framing and context. One would have to believe as well that, immediately after using the *Liber ex lege Moysi,* Alfred turned abruptly to Hincmar — picking up we do not know what text (or perhaps he took dictation from Grimbald, verbally professing Hincmarian ideas?) as his inspiration for the rest of the narrative.

Prima facie, such a course of events seems unlikely. Instead, I see this Prologue as primarily an Alfredian innovation, inspired in some of its details by texts from the Hiberno-Latin tradition available to Alfred in a single manuscript, i.e., a manuscript that included the *Liber ex lege Moysi* in its context as an introduction to *Collectio canonum Hibernensis.* I am inclined, therefore, to regard this Prologue not as a patchwork of diverse sources, but rather as a thoughtfully constructed and unified narrative, based loosely on a single source, that makes a thoughtfully conceived argument about the relationship between ecclesiastical and traditional English jurisprudence, and — more specifically — about the place of the English and their laws in sacred history. This belief underlies the rest of my argument in this section.

The Prologue to the Laws of Alfred and Sacred History

In his Prologue to Pope Gregory's *Cura Pastoralis,* Alfred famously explained his plan to revive learning among the English and laid out his

---

in modern ears may have simply represented the rhetoric of respectable, and respectful, *patrocinium* — rhetoric that may well echo Alfred's own', in Nelson, '...*sicut olim gens Francorum*', p. 141. David Pratt also sees the Prologue to Alfred's laws as a response to Fulk's letter, although he understands the nature of this response differently than I do: Pratt, *The Political Thought of King Alfred the Great,* pp. 228–29.

translation programme.[54] This text is extremely important for Alfredian studies and has received a great deal of scholarly attention. Of present interest, however, is Alfred's ostensible reference to legal matters. Here (with hindsight or anticipation — it is not clear which), Alfred seems to have had his *Domboc* foremost in mind, at least the excerpt from the Mosaic Law that prefaces it:

> Ða gemunde ic hu sio æ wæs ærest on Ebrisc geðiode funden, & eft, þa hie Crecas geleornodon, þa wendon hi hie on hiora agen geðiode ealle, & eac ealle oðre bec. And eft Lædenware swa same, siððan hi hie geleornodon, he hie wendon ealla ðurh wise wealhstodas on hiora agen geðeode. & eac ealla oðra Cristena ðioda sumne dæl hiora on hiora agen geðiode wendon.[55]
>
> > (I remembered how the law ⟨Old English *æ*, here meaning 'Law of Moses'⟩ was first discovered in the Hebrew language, and thereafter, when the Greeks learned it, they translated it all ⟨i.e., all of the Law of Moses⟩ into their own language, and also all other books ⟨i.e., all the other books of the Bible⟩. And thereafter the Romans did the same: after they studied them, they translated them all ⟨i.e., all the books of the Bible⟩. ⟨And all other Christian nations translated some portion of them⟩ ⟨i.e., books of the Bible⟩ into their own language).[56]

Besides its significance as a likely allusion to his translation of Exodus that begins the Prologue to his law code, it is curious that Alfred apparently considered *æ*, here likely signifying 'Law of Moses', as the starting point for biblical study and translation among newly Christianized nations. Why the Mosaic law? Would Genesis 9 (as an expression of the Law of Nature = the Law of Noah, i.e., the law that applied to Gentiles) or Matthew (as the first of the gospels) not make a more fitting choice?

I would argue that the rationale behind Alfred's view of the Mosaic Law as the fundamental scriptural *locus* where newly Christianized nations began their study and translation of the Bible can be explained by his conceptualization of the place of converted gentiles (including the English) in sacred history. This insight provides a key for interpreting his argument in the Prologue to his laws. Before considering this issue further, however, we must make sure we know precisely what Alfred intended to signify with

54 Discenza has argued that Alfred's introduction to the *Cura Pastoralis* owes a debt to the introduction to Sirach found in some Old Latin and Vulgate manuscripts. See Discenza, 'Wise Wealhstodas', pp. 488–99.

55 *King Alfred's West-Saxon Version of Gregory's Pastoral Care*, pp. 5–6.

56 The translation is my own.

the word *æ* in this particular context.[57] Although *æ* has a relatively wide range of meaning, covering secular, ecclesiastical, and divine law, in this context it appears to bear the specialized sense of the 'Law of Moses'.[58] It is possible, however, that Alfred intended to signify something even more precise, if in fact his account of nations that successively translated the Law of Moses — first the Greeks, then the Romans, and thereafter 'ealla oðra Cristena ðioda' (all other Christian nations), presumably including the English — does in fact allude to the Mosaic preface in the Prologue to his law code. Significantly, Alfred did not translate the entire Pentateuch, but limited himself to a small portion of it (Exodus 20:1-23:13), despite the fact that his exemplar, the Hiberno-Latin *Liber ex lege Moysi*, included excerpts from the whole book of Exodus — i.e., without a break at verse 23:13 or skipping a large number of verses immediately thereafter — and continued with excerpts from Leviticus, Numbers, and Deuteronomy. What motivated Alfred to translate only this portion of the Mosaic Law?

His choice to include Exodus 20:1-21, i.e., the Ten Commandments (or 'ethical Decalogue')[59] is obvious enough: these verses encapsulate the most basic statement of the Old Law, handed down by God to Moses at the epiphany on Mount Sinai. Why, then, did Alfred also choose to include the sundry provisions contained immediately following in Exodus 21:22-23:13, many of which stand in marked contrast to customary English legal practice? I would posit that, far from a haphazard selection, Alfred's decision to translate this specific portion of the Mosaic Law attests to his sophisticated understanding of the Pentateuch. These verses immediately following the ethical Decalogue constitute the so-called 'Book of the Covenant' (or 'Covenant Code'), traditionally including Exodus 20:22-23:19.[60] The name derives from Exodus 24:7: 'adsumensque **volumen foederis** legit audiente populo qui dixerunt omnia quae locutus est Dominus faciemus et erimus oboedientes' (And taking the **book of the covenant**, he [i.e., Moses] read it in the hearing of the people; and they said: All things that the Lord has spoken we will do, we will be obedient). The position of this first written law code is important in sacred history: by accepting this code, the Jews entered into a special covenant with God, whereby they became his Chosen People. What is more, in return for their

---

57 *The Dictionary of Old English*, s.v. 1. *æ* defines *æ* as 'law (divine and secular), statement of law (written or customary), code of behaviour; also figurative'.

58 I take *æ* to mean 'Law of Moses' in this context, since in the phrase '[...] hi **hie** on hiora agen geðiode **ealle** [...]' (explaining what the Greeks translated), 'hie [...] ealle' (both, in this case, acc. sing. fem.) appears to refer back to $\overline{æ}$ (nominative singular feminine) as its antecedent. I see no other possible candidate for an antecedent.

59 The laws of the 'ethical Decalogue' are contained in Exodus 20:1–17 and Deuteronomy 5:6–21.

60 Alfred omits the very specific dietary and sacrificial provisions in the last six verses of the Covenant Code, Exodus 23:14–19.

obedience to his law, God vowed to lead them into the Promised Land. This portion of Exodus, therefore, contains the first, most basic, and most secularly oriented portion of the Pentateuch. In choosing to translate this selection, thus, Alfred may have been inspired by later references to the *volumen foederis* in II Kings 23:2, 3, and 21,[61] where the story is related how King Josiah found the Book of the Covenant in the temple and read it aloud to his people, thereby renewing their covenant with God.[62] Could Alfred have intended to signify the Book of the Covenant (as opposed to the whole of the Mosaic law), with his use of *æ* in the excerpt from the Prologue to the *Cura Pastoralis* cited above? It is impossible to know for certain — his description of biblical translation does not yield any clues — though it is noteworthy (as I mentioned earlier) that Alfred's likely exemplar (i.e., the *Liber ex lege Moysi*) continued without break after Exodus 23:13, including excerpts (albeit with increasing sparsity) from the remainder of Exodus and the three remaining books of the Pentateuch.

Keeping this question in mind, it is tempting to wonder if Alfred's decision to include this specific range of verses stemmed from knowledge — direct or, more likely, indirect — of Sulpicius Severus's *Chronicorum*.[63] This work, little-known outside of Ireland (particularly the monastery at Iona),[64] recounts in greatly abridged summary the major events in the Bible (excluding the gospels and Acts of the Apostles) and sacred history up until Sulpicius Severus's own time (i.e., *c*. 363-*c*. 425). Of great interest for present purposes, chapters seventeen and eighteen of the *Chronicorum* contain a summary in relatively high detail of the Decalogue and the Code of the Covenant covering almost exactly the same range of verses as Alfred's Prologue, i.e., Exodus 20:1-23:12. Only Exodus 23:13 is present in Alfred's translation but absent in the *Chronicorum*, perhaps because it repeats the prohibition against idolatry (here expressed as an injunction against making oaths in the name of strange gods); and in keeping with his practice throughout, Sulpicius Severus reduces and summarizes the scriptural text, among other means by omitting redundant (and very

61 It is possible that the reference in II Kings 23:2, 3, and 21 do not signify the Book of the Covenant (= Exodus 20:22–23.19), but rather the so-called Deuteronomic Code (= Deuteronomy 12–26). See Doorly, *The Laws of Yahweh*, pp. 28–30.

62 II Kings 23:2, 'verba libri foederis' (the words of the Book of the Covenant); 23.3 'verba foederis huius quae scripta erant in libro illo' (the words of this Covenant, which were written in that book); 23.21 'quod scriptum est in libro foederis huius' (what is written in the book of this Covenant). Rosamond McKitterick sees a comparison between Charlemagne and Josiah in the *Admonitio Generalis* (789). See McKitterick, *The Frankish Church*, p. 1–2. If Alfred was influenced by that Continental gesture, he makes no reference to it here.

63 For a text of the *Chronicorum* see Sulpicius Severus, *Chronicorum*. For a translation, see Sulpicius Severus, *Works*.

64 *Iona*, p. 216. See also: O'Loughlin, 'The Library of Iona', p. 41; Brüning, 'Adamnans Vita Columbae', pp. 247–48.

similar) provisions. Another similarity between Alfred's translation and this portion of the *Chronicorum* worthy of mention is the attitude both authors have toward the biblical text, specifically their willingness to alter it. Although it is clear that Alfred's base text for translation was the *Liber ex lege Moysi* (not the *Chronicorum*), his practice of reworking details of the Mosaic Law (perhaps to conform with contemporary early English practice or perhaps for some other purpose)[65] finds a methodological and stylistic parallel in the *Chronicorum*. While the details Sulpicius Severus modified text do not seem to have inspired Alfred directly in any instance, both authors would appear to have deliberately revised scripture with an extraordinary sense of freedom, specifically to make it applicable in their own time. I am not suggesting that Alfred knew the *Chronicorum* firsthand; and yet, it is tempting to wonder if someone in his circle did. In any case, the relationship between the *Chronicorum*, the *Liber ex lege Moysi*, and the Prologue to the Laws of Alfred warrants further examination. Whatever Alfred's rationale for choosing this segment of Exodus, it was not random or indiscriminate: he selected the oldest and most fundamental statement of the Mosaic Law — indeed, the first instance of written law in sacred history — with which to begin his Prologue.

Leaving the problem of sources behind and returning to the original question: why, instead of Genesis 9 or the gospels, did Alfred consider the Law of Moses to be an apposite starting point for biblical study and translation (as he expressed in his Prologue to the *Cura Pastoralis*)? To answer this question, it is necessary to understand Alfred's conception of sacred history and — more specifically — his ideas about the role of the English within it. Unsurprisingly, his views concerning these matters were quite sophisticated. Yet, his position on the subject has been consistently misrepresented by scholars due, I would argue, to the mistaken belief that, with this preface, Alfred sought to represent the English, literally or metaphorically, as God's Chosen People, perhaps inspired by analogues of this theme prevalent in the writings of Gildas, Bede, Alcuin, and some of the writings that emanated from Alfred's circle.[66]

Let me begin by discussing scholarship on this topic. As has been widely claimed, prominent within Anglo-Saxon (pseudo-)historical ideology was a belief in their inherent role as God's Chosen People, a feature of early medieval thought (not exclusively English) sometimes referred to

65 See *English Historical Documents*, p. 332, where Whitelock speculatively asserts: '[...] the additions and changes show that the king was seriously considering the law of Exodus with a view to its applicability to the conditions of his own time [...]'.

66 Molyneaux, in 'The Old English Bede', argues convincingly that the weight of evidence, at least from the Old English translation of Bede's *Historica Ecclesiastica Gentis Anglorum*, does not support the position that Alfred envisioned the English as God's Chosen People, at least not in the sense of the English as a New Israel.

in modern scholarship as the *populus Israhel* tradition. While a full exploration of this topic would extend well beyond the scope of the present argument, some brief discussion is necessary for what follows. In Anglo-Saxon England, expressions of this idea were anything but monolithic, varying from author to author over the course of the period between the early fifth-century *Adventus Saxonum* and the Norman Conquest. Seeds of the notion, planted by the fifth-century British historian Gildas (applied, in that case, to his Welsh countrymen), emerged fully formed, it has been argued, in Bede's *Historia Ecclesiastica Gentis Anglorum* (adopted and applied to the English), and quickly became pervasive throughout Old English and Anglo-Latin literature of all genres. As Andrew Scheil described it in his extensive study of the topic:

> The enduring image of the *populus Israhel* — the Jews conceived as a 'tribe', a 'race', a 'nation' — and the related narratives concerning their history bound together by patterns of repeated motifs and images and assembled into a rough unity by the parameters of Christian historiography — all these elements form the outlines of a complex representational nexus [...]. As metaphor, image, and exemplum, the 'people of Israel' function as a foundational *mythos* [...].[67]

He continues later in the same work:

> [...] ⟨this⟩ 'mythos', or perhaps the 'Matter of Israel', also bears all the features of an ideological 'master narrative'. To use the *populus Israhel* as a metaphor, an image, or an exemplum, while its inner dynamics are in essence literary, is to deploy an ideology, a founding narrative for societies in the Christian West.[68]

Here, Scheil defines the *populus Israhel* tradition and lays the groundwork for describing how it gained momentum in the Anglo-Saxon consciousness. This notion, which was originally 'in essence literary', soon gained significantly more ideological gravity as a 'founding narrative'.

Most influentially, Patrick Wormald has argued in favour of this view. Claims to this effect can be found throughout his scholarship, including (most recently) in *The Making of English Law*, where he stated:

> [...] Alfred's lawbook was above all an ideological statement. He gave Mosaic Law more prominence and more sophisticated handling than any other early medieval legislator. He thereby showed that West Saxon law — and implicitly Mercian and Kentish law too — belonged from the outset to the history of divine legislation for humanity. The

67 Scheil, *The Footsteps of Israel*, p. 104.
68 Scheil, *The Footsteps of Israel*, p. 190.

> emergent kingdom of the English was thus invited, even obliged, to live as a new Chosen People.[69]

All but the last sentence evokes no objection. What however, does Wormald mean to signify with the phrase 'a new Chosen People'? He expressed this idea somewhat more fully in an earlier article, perhaps shedding more light on his meaning:

> A single people may not need a single ruler. But a people of the Covenant does. Israel, after all, was the archetype of the 'Kingdom divided against itself', and of its lamentable results. By directly tracing English destinies to God's plan, Bede lent the campaign for a united 'English' kingdom an urgency that *soi-disant* kings of Tara might well envy. Alfred's sketch in his *Pastoral Rule* preface of 'happy times', when 'kings were obedient to God and his messengers, and upheld peace and morals and authority at home, and also extended their territory abroad, and prospered both in warfare and in wisdom', was clearly drawn from Bede's picture of the seventh-century 'Golden Age' of the English Church. In stressing 'what temporal punishments [i.e. Vikings] came upon us when we possessed only the name of Christians, and few possessed the virtues', he implicitly invoked the English Covenant. His lawbook opens with another remarkable preface: a translation of nearly three chapters of Mosaic law from the Book of Exodus, followed up by the story of how the Church had modified and transmitted this law 'throughout the whole world, and also to the *Angelcynn*'. This had the effect of showing Anglo-Saxons how similar were their laws to those of Ancient Israel. It also invited them to remodel themselves as a new Chosen People.[70]

Here, Wormald offered a few more details to help explain precisely what he meant by 'Chosen People' in Alfred's ideology. Apparently, he based this interpretation on his understanding of Alfred's reading of Bede's *Historica Ecclesiastica Gentis Anglorum* and from that concluded that Alfred, like Bede (indeed, directly inspired by him) believed that the English were a party to some kind of spiritual covenant, analogous to the Mosaic Covenant God made with the Jews, thereby promoting them to a new status (in some never fully defined sense) as God's Chosen People. In very similar language (though going a bit farther with his claims), Wormald emphasized the role of Bede's thought for the development of Alfred's ideology elsewhere:

> ⟨According to Bede's view, t⟩he 'Gens Anglorum' too was a people of the Covenant. Its destiny was indissolubly bound up with its duty

69 Wormald, *The Making of English Law*, p. 426.
70 Wormald, 'The Venerable Bede', pp. 24–25.

> to its Maker. In presenting the Anglo-Saxons with such an image of their past and future, Bede gave their would-be unifiers an impetus that *soi-disant* kings of Tara could only envy [...]. It is no surprise, then, that Bede's *History* was among the works translated into the vernacular at King Alfred's court. Alfred's own account, when introducing his educational programme, of 'happy times' when 'kings were obedient to God and his messengers, and upheld peace and morals and authority at home, and also extended their territory abroad, and prospered both in warfare and wisdom', was obviously drawn from Bede's story of the English Church in the in its seventh-century Golden Age. His stress on 'what temporal punishments came upon us when we possessed only the name of Christians, and few of the virtues' pointed the moral. Further, his lawbook went farther than Charlemagne. It begins with a translation of three whole chapters of the Law of God as given to Moses in the Book of Exodus, before going on to describe how this had been modified by the Christian Church and transmitted 'throughout the world, also to the *Angelcynn*'. On the one hand this showed Anglo-Saxons how like their own law was to that given by God himself. On the other, it invited them to remodel themselves in Israel's image. This was to be a kingdom not just of bodies but of souls.[71]

It is not entirely clear whether Wormald believed that the notion of the English as God's Chosen People was a feature of Bede's historiographical typology, or an idea that, for Bede and Alfred both, carried real spiritual substance. I suspect Wormald intended to argue in favour of the former, though he does not elaborate.

At the very least, Wormald seems to suggest that, with the Prologue to his law code, Alfred was urging the English to aspire toward Chosen status; to remake themselves as a 'People of a Covenant'. Even in this light, however, it remains unclear how literally Wormald believed Alfred and his lawyers took this idea: Was this equivocation between the English and God's Chosen People merely a useful simile or, to a greater or lesser extent, real theology? Figurative or not, clerical lawyers (and others, no doubt) could not have overlooked such a doctrinally loaded claim as merely an innocuous literary conceit: allegations of this sort had real-world (and real-heavenly) legal and theological repercussions. Certainly, it is significant that Alfred nowhere asserts Chosen status for the *Angelcynn* outright. Although Wormald's position on this matter has often been repeated in scholarship (albeit typically with little development), it is based purely on his own interpretation of Alfred's text based on his misapplication (in my view) of Bede's philosophy to it.

---

71 Wormald, '*Engla Lond*', pp. 376–77.

In a similar vein, David Pratt has envisioned a notably more sophisticated conceptualization of Alfred's views concerning the English as God's Chosen People, emphasizing the role of existing West-Saxon practices in addition to Bedan and Frankish influences:

> The 'divine' character of royal law has emerged as a central fact of the tenth-century 'English' polity, exploited to the full by archbishop Wulfstan under renewed Viking pressures. Its Alfredian emergence has generally been attributed to the impact of Frankish models, over a biblical agenda borrowed from Bede. Yet its precise formulation, subtly recasting Hincmarian theory, strengthens the significance of internal practices whose operation received such learned defence. The reception of Frankish learning must be judged against the existing character of West Saxon kingship, already harnessing 'chosen' status in a distinctive blend of devotional ritual. Mechanisms of covenant and divine aid gave service to West Saxon dynastic triumph, symbolically renewed by royal anointing and specifically related to the operation of justice and divine law. Solomonic posturing, the role for ealdormen in the transmission of the royal scepter, the 'three precepts' issued by ⟨the⟩ new king to his subject people: all elements combined to express the existing status of West Saxon royal justice, specifically devoted to the forbidding of 'thefts' and the upholding of God's 'equity and mercy'. Rather than Frankish or Bedan borrowing in this respect, the *Domboc* emerges as a further 'strengthening' of West Saxon kingship, the textual extension of 'chosen' status within a single framework of royal and divine justice.[72]

Later he continues, linking the notion of 'Chosen' status specifically to the English as a Christian people:

> Every aspect of the comparison ⟨between Mosaic Law as expressed in Alfred's prologue and his own statutes⟩ asserted 'chosen' status under royal justice. The role of mercy was integral to this status, as the additional property of the *populus Christianus*, as was kingship, exclusively informed by synodal norms.[73]

Thus, although scholars vary on the details, the idea that the Anglo-Saxons viewed themselves as 'God's Chosen People' and as a 'New Israel' has enjoyed wide acceptance.

More recently, however, George Molyneaux has challenged these arguments. In separate articles, he has argued convincingly against the claim

---

72 Pratt, *The Political Thought of King Alfred the Great*, pp. 228–29. See also pp. 63–78 on the devotional rituals to which he refers.

73 Pratt, *The Political Thought of King Alfred the Great*, p. 232.

that the Anglo-Saxons envisioned themselves as 'God's Chosen People' or as a 'New Israel':

> It is often stated that the English regarded themselves as 'a new Israel', or even 'the new Israel', but I am not aware that any text from Anglo-Saxon England labels the English novus Israel. I therefore find it hard to see the benefit of using the term 'new Israel' when discussing the Anglo-Saxon period; if it is to be used, it should be carefully defined, for it is imprecise but evocative. To me, it suggests a belief in divine election above all other peoples, but there is little or no evidence of such a belief. Some people who now use the expression may, however, intend a weaker meaning: it could refer to the English as one of many gentile nations who had converted to Christianity, all of whom thereby received God's grace and became successors to the Old Testament Israel. These ideas should not be conflated: the less particularist the claim to divine favour, the less politically potent it becomes.[74]

Elsewhere, he concludes that,

> [a]s Christians, the English could see themselves as among the chosen, along with every other Christian people. This, however, is fundamentally different from the notion that they were the peculiar successors to the Old Testament Israel, and thus 'an elect nation enjoying God's special favour'. The contention that this more potent claim was already prevalent in the Anglo-Saxon period should be treated with the deepest of scepticism, and probably rejected entirely.[75]

Molyneaux's points are well taken. Given these arguments, therefore, it is necessary to reassess Wormald's views about Alfred's laws — and especially their Prologue — as an expression of the *populus Israhel* ideology.

Assuming that the intellectuals in Alfred's royal circle considered these matters thoroughly — and all indications are that they did — they may have felt that such ideas, when unambiguously recognized as metaphors or as purely literary *topoi*, might be harmless. If, for example, all parties involved understood that attributing the status of a 'New Israel' and 'God's Chosen People' to the English implied no direct, spiritual connection with their Old Testament precursors, few if any doctrinal problems would arise. Outside of a legal-theological context (in literature, for example), beliefs of this sort might well have been perceived to have utility, perhaps for promoting a unifying ideology. That said, the technicalities of Christian jurisprudence could not easily abide such a blatantly unorthodox claim. What is more, such ideas, when taken to their logical conclusions, might necessarily carry repercussions that Alfred's clerical jurists must have felt

74 Molyneaux, 'Old English Bede', p. 1319.

75 Molyneaux, 'Did the English Really Think They Were God's Elect?', p. 737.

were best avoided. This point would seem to find support in the fact that, despite claims to the contrary, the notion of the English as God's Chosen People is absent in Alfred's legal writings. As Molyneaux points out regarding the Prologue to Alfred's Laws, and especially the Mosaic preface:

> Wormald thought that ⟨Alfred's Mosaic Preface⟩ invited the English 'to remodel themselves as a new Chosen People', on the grounds that it begins with the Ten Commandments and excerpts from the next three books of Exodus, sometimes modified to suit contemporary circumstances. This interpretation is, however, undermined by what comes next. After noting that Christ came to augment rather than break the commandments of the Old Testament, the text describes how the Apostles taught 'throughout all the earth' ('geond ealle eorðan') and converted 'many heathen peoples' ('monega hæðena ðeoda'), who were only required to adhere to basic Christian precepts. It then explains that, once 'many peoples' ('monega ðeoda') had received the faith, synods were assembled 'throughout all the world' ('geond ealne middangeard'), including among the English, and that these synods mercifully permitted that most types of wrongdoing could be emended through payments. The text then moves explicitly into Alfred's voice: he states that he had reviewed the decrees of earlier kings, accepting some and rejecting others, and proceeds to declare his ordinances, many of which prescribe fines or compensation payments for various misdeeds. As in the Pastoral care preface, the English are here treated as but one of numerous gentile nations: nothing is said to imply that their position in relation to God or Israel was different from that of others of the 'many peoples' converted to Christianity 'throughout all the earth'.[76]

Molyneaux, however, has little else to say about Alfred's legislation and how it bears on this question. While I concur with Molyneaux, there is more to say on this matter.

Literary assessments aside, treatment of the *populus Israhel* myth was substantially more cautious in legal literature than in other kinds of texts. Indeed, in Part One, I argued that Irish clerical jurists similarly avoided such claims. In matters of law, such attestations — even if they were not received as literally true — carried with them weighty implications; a fact unlikely to be lost on ecclesiastically trained jurists such as those who advised Alfred about the Prologue to his laws. Most importantly, the claim to 'Chosen' status would, of necessity, situate a people within sacred history in a position equivalent to Jews and — very significantly —

76 Molyneaux, 'Did the English Really Think They Were God's Elect?', p. 735.

necessarily bear along with it a full load of concomitant legal-theological obligations. Above all, as Acts 15 makes clear (and, presumably, as Alfred wished to emphasize by quoting it), converted gentiles were released from the full measure of the Mosaic injunction. Christianized Jews, however, were still fully subject to the Old Law, albeit in a different way, namely, as it was fulfilled by the New.[77] This passage from Acts is arguably the portion of the Prologue to Alfred's laws most important for understanding his fundamental claim about the place of the English in sacred history. Very significantly, Alfred quoted the decision of the Synod of Jerusalem in Acts 15 at length in an especially meaningful context and provides an explanation regarding its importance. After the Mosaic preface, Alfred continued:

> **Based on Matthew 5:17**
> Þis sindan ða domas þe se ælmihtiga God self sprecende wæs to Moyse ⁊ him bebead to healdanne; ⁊ siððan se ancenneda Dryhtnes sunu, ure God þæt is hælend Crist, on middangeard cwom, he cwæð, ðæt he ne come no ðas bebodu to brecanne ne to forbeodanne, ac mid eallum godu*m* to ecanne; ⁊ mildheortnesse ⁊ eaðmodnesse he lærde ⟨*El.* 49⟩.[78]
>
> **Based on Acts 15:23–29**
> Ða æfter his ðrowunge, ær þam þe his apostolas tofarene wæron geond ealle eorðan to læranne, ⁊ þa giet ða hie ætgædere wæron, monega hæðena ðeoda hie to Gode gecerdon. Þa hie ealle ætsomne wæron, hie sendan ærendwrecan to Antiohhia ⁊ Syrie, Cristes æ to lærenne. ⟨El. 49.1⟩ Þa hie ða ongeaton, þæt him ne speow, ða sendon hie ærendgewrit to him. Þis is ðonne þæt ærendgewrit þe ða apostolas senden ealle to Antiohhia ⁊ to Syria ⁊ to Cilicia, ða sint nu of hæðenum ðeodu*m* to Criste gecirde: ⟨El. 49.2⟩ Ða apostolas ⁊ þa eldran broðor hælo eow wyscað; ⁊ we eow cyðað, þæt we geascodon, þæt ure geferan sume mid uru*m* wordum to eow comon ⁊ eow hefigran ⟨wisan budon⟩ to healdanne þonne we him budon, ⁊ eow to swiðe gedwealdon mid ðam mannigfealdum gebodum, ⁊ eowra sawla ma forhwerfdon þonne hio geryhton. Ða gesomnodon we us ymb ðæt, ⁊ us eallum gelicode ða, þæt we sendon Paulus ⁊ Barnaban; ða men wilniað hiora sawla sellan for Dryhtnes nama. ⟨El. 49.3⟩ Mid him we sendon Iudam ⁊ Silam, þæt eow þæt ilce secgen ⟨El. 49.4⟩. Þæm halgan Gaste wæs geðuht ⁊ us, þæt we nane byrðenne on eow settan noldon ofer þæt ðe eow neddðearf wæs to healdanne: þæt ⟨is⟩ ðon*ne*, þæt ge forberen, þæt

77 Precisely what this concept meant and what implications it carried have been the matter of involved theological discussion that go well beyond the scope of the present argument. For my purposes here, suffice to say that the obligations of Christianized Jews in biblical law were more onerous than for converted gentiles.

78 *Die Gesetze der Angelsachsen*, I, p. 42.

ge deofolgeld ne weorðien, ne blod ne ðicggen ne asmorod, ⁊ from diernum geligerum [...] ⟨El. 49.5⟩.[79]

Based on Matthew 7:12
[...] ⁊ þæt ge willen, þæt oðre men eow ne don, ne doð ðæt oþrum monnum [...] ⟨El. 49.5⟩.[80]

(**Based on Matthew 5:17**
These are the commands that Almighty God himself spoke to Moses and ordered him to uphold; and when the only son of the Lord our God, that is Christ the Savior, came to middle-earth, he said that he did not come to violate or repeal these commands, but to increase them with all goodness; and he taught mercy and benevolence.[81]

Based on Acts 15:23–29
Then, after his passion, before his apostles had gone all over the world to teach, but were still together, many pagan nations converted to Christianity. While ⟨the apostles⟩ were all together, they sent messengers to Antioch and Syria to teach the Law of Christ. When they perceived it was not going well for them, they send a letter to them. This is the letter that the apostles sent to Antioch, Syria, and Cilicia, which are now converted from pagan nations to Christian [nations]. 'The apostles and the elder brothers [of the Church] wish you health and we are letting you know that we have learned that some of our companions have reached you with our instructions and have ordered you to maintain a stricter set of rules than we ordered them [to teach], and have greatly led you astray with complex rules, and have more perverted your souls than set them aright. So, we gathered together regarding this matter, and it seemed good to all of us that we send Paul and Barnabas, men who would give their lives for God's name. With them we sent Judas and Silas so that they might say the same to you. It seemed to the Holy Spirit and to us that we should not wish to impose upon you any burden beyond what was necessary for you to bear, namely, that you refrain from worshipping idols, consuming blood or suffocated offerings, illicit fornication [...].[82]

Based on Matthew 7:12

79 *Die Gesetze der Angelsachsen*, I, pp. 42, 44.
80 *Die Gesetze der Angelsachsen*, I, p. 44.
81 The translation is my own.
82 The translation is my own.

> [...] and what you wish that other men do not do to you, do not to that to other men [...]).[83]

Alfred's intent here is clear, albeit implicit. For Alfred, the English, like the Christian peoples of Antioch and Syria, were gentile converts to the faith. Like them, the English too were bound by the Law of Moses: Christ, after all, did not come to rescind the Old Law, but rather to fulfill it. By invoking Matthew 5:17 in this context, Alfred emphasized the continuity between the Law of Moses (as represented by his extended translation from Exodus) and the Law of Christ. Then, by referring to Acts 15, Alfred explained precisely what this understanding of their place in sacred history as converted gentiles meant for the English in practical terms: They were bound by the Law of Moses only in the sense explicitly decided by the Synod of Jerusalem. That decision forbade just three behaviours, i.e., idol worship, consuming blood and strangled offerings, and fornication. Finally, Alfred concluded with a fundamental statement of moral responsibility for all Christians under the Law of Christ, i.e., Matthew 7:12. Central to Alfred's argument is the idea that the English were converted gentiles and that, as such, they were expressly not God's Chosen People with an injunction to uphold the Law of Moses in its fullness. Rather, as converted gentiles, the English were only responsible for upholding the reduced injunction as expressed in Acts 15.

Bede would appear to have understood the significance of the Synod of Jerusalem in a manner similar to Alfred. For example, in his description of the Synod of Whitby, Bede describes how Wilfrid, defending the Roman method for calculating the date of Easter, argued that Colmán's defence of the Irish method was, in effect, based on Old Testament practices that — like circumcision — were no longer lawful given the decision of Synod of Jerusalem (Book iii, chapter 25):

> At Uilfridus 'Absit' inquit 'ut Iohannem stultitiae reprehendamus, cum scita legis Mosaicae iuxta litteram seruaret, iudaizante adhuc in multis ecclesia, nec subito ualentibus apostolis omnem legis obseruantiam, quae a Deo instituta est, abdicare, quomodo simulacra, quae a daemonibus inuenta sunt, repudiare omnes, qui ad fidem ueniunt, necesse est; uidelicet ne scandalum facerent eis qui inter gentes erant Iudaeis. Hinc est enim quod Paulus Timotheum circumcidit, quod hostias in Templo immolauit, quod cum Aquila et Priscilla caput Chorinti totondit, ad nihil uidelicet utile, nisi ad scandalum uitandum Iudaeorum; hinc quod eidem Paulo Iacobus ait: "Vides, frater, quot milia sunt in Iudaeis qui crediderunt, et omnes hi aemulatores sunt legis". Nec tamen hodie clarescente per mundum euangelio necesse est,

83 The translation is my own.

immo nec licitum, fidelibus uel cicumcidi uel hostias Deo uictimarum offere carnalium.'[84]

> (Wilfrid replied ⟨to Colmán ⟩, 'Far be it from me to charge John ⟨the Apostle⟩ with foolishness: he literally observed the decrees of the Mosaic law when the Church was still Jewish in many respects, at a time when the apostles were unable to bring to a sudden end the entire observance of that law which God ordained in the same way as, for instance, they made it compulsory on all new converts to abandon their idols which are of devilish origin. They feared, of course, that they might make a stumbling-block for the Jewish proselytes dispersed among the Gentiles. This was the reason why Paul circumcised Timothy, why he offered sacrifices in the temple, and why he shaved his head at Corinth in company with Aquila and Priscilla; all this was of no use except to avoid scandalizing the Jews. Hence James said to Paul, "Thou seest, brother, how many thousands there are among the Jews of them which have believed; and they are all zealous for the law". But in these days when the light of the Gospel is spreading throughout the world, it is not necessary, it is not even lawful for believers to be circumcised or to offer God sacrifices of flesh and blood').[85]

As this passage shows, Bede — like Wilfrid and Alfred — would appear to have envisioned the Anglo-Saxon people as converted gentiles, not as 'God's Chosen People' or a 'New Israel', at least not in any literal sense.

But there is another point to consider. For the English, the pagan practices of their forbears — lost neither to sentiment nor memory in late ninth-century England — would, if they were subject to the Law of Moses as God's Chosen People, have amounted to apostasy, leaving their ancestors in hell, unredeemed and unredeemable.[86] Given these ramifications, advisors in Alfred's circle, no doubt aware of the potential legal and theological repercussions, apparently decided that any analogy between the English and God's Chosen People should be avoided, at least where legal matters were concerned. Thus, while such a claim may or may not have enjoyed creative development in other genres — literary, historical, or otherwise — it received significantly more wary and precise treatment by legalists, particularly clerical jurists, who understood fully what was at stake. Such caution, I would argue, informed the composition of the Prologue to Alfred's laws.

---

84 Bede, *Ecclesiastical History*, pp. 300, 302.

85 Bede, *Ecclesiastical History*, pp. 301, 303.

86 This point is especially ripe for comparison with contemporary Old English literary and homiletic texts.

Andrew Scheil and Nicholas Howe, both of whom have argued in favour of the claim that the Anglo-Saxons viewed themselves as God's Chosen People, must have realized the problematic nature of the evidence presented by the Prologue to the Laws of Alfred (and, perhaps also, by the Alfredian corpus in general). Scheil, whose stated goal was to trace the 'footsteps of Israel' in the Anglo-Saxon tradition, has nothing to say about Alfred's extended translation of the Mosaic law, nor the Prologue to his law code at all. Similarly, Howe — whose expressed purpose was to examine the so-called 'migration myth' in Anglo-Saxon literature, an idea that quickly led him to examine comparisons between the English and the Israelites — likewise, has little to offer on the subject, deferring his opinion on Alfred's Mosaic preface for the most part to Dorothy Whitelock's decades-earlier assessment of the text in *English Historical Documents*:

> [...] the chapters from Exodus devoted to law provided King Alfred with a model to transform the law code from a list of individual offenses into an incipient theory of justice. As Dorothy Whitelock notes, Alfred's code 'was seriously considering the law of Exodus in relation to the conditions of his own time'.[87]

Both Scheil and Howe, thus, leave the topic of Alfred's legislation essentially undiscussed.

Following Molyneaux's arguments, I posit that any attempt to understand the Prologue to the Laws of Alfred as a reflex of the *populus Israhel* myth would be misleading. Instead, I would argue that, with this text, Alfred set out to propose an entirely different ideological conceptualization of English history. His choice to begin the Prologue to his laws with the Decalogue and Code of the Covenant, while in the first instance based on his observation that the *Liber ex lege Moysi* served as an introduction to *Collectio canonum Hibernensis*,[88] equally derives from (or perhaps sparked) his careful consideration of the place of English lawgiving within sacred history. At least where matters of law hung in the balance, Alfred made no attempt to develop the metaphor of the English as *populus Israhel*; quite the contrary, in legal contexts at least, Alfred consistently — indeed, it would appear, without exception — asserted the status of the English as a converted gentile nation. An overt example of this gesture appears in the Old English Prologue to the *Cura Pastoralis*, cited above. There, perhaps as anticipatory justification for his own plans to do likewise, Alfred enumerated the various peoples who had translated the Law of Moses into their own tongue. Notice how all the peoples on his list are gentile nations:

---

87 Howe, *Migration and Mythmaking*, p. 103. Howe refers to *English Historical Documents*, pp. 362–63 in the 2nd edn (1979). In the previous edition, see pp. 331–32.

88 See B. Carella, 'The Source for the Prologue', pp. 115–18 and Bradshaw, *The Early Collection of Canons*, p. 25.

First he mentions the Greeks, then the Romans, and finally '[...] ealla oðra Cristna ðioda [...]' ([...] all other Christian peoples [...]).[89]

Though presumably gentiles (the Jews obviously would not have back-translated the Law of Moses), what people did Alfred have in mind with this last, vague designation, '[...] ealla oðra Cristna ðioda [...]'? What other people translated the Bible, or at least the Law of Moses, about which Alfred could reasonably have known? Apparently, the only scholar to address this question in depth was Francis P. Magoun, who — despite his acknowledgement that Alfred's statement about 'all other Christian nations' translating the Bible '[...] is the most uncertain to interpret' — nonetheless optimistically posits that

> ⟨t⟩hrough travelers and emissaries it is by no means inconceivable that he knew some of the Oriental translations of the Septuagint (in Syriac, Coptic, Ethiopian, and Arabic) and of the New Testament (Syriac in the Gospel harmony or *Diatessaron* of the Mesopotamian Christian Tatianus, Coptic, Ethiopian, and Arabic). From the West he may have heard of the missionary activities and the Macedonian-Slavic translations of the brothers Constantine (died in Rome in 869, having assumed the monastic name Cyril) and Methodius, busy in Moravia after 863, also he may have known of the Gothic version of Bishop Wulfila. The Gothic language and Gothic traditions, including Arianism, lived on in Visigothic Spain into the tenth century and the Wulfilan Bible was the Bible of the Germanic peoples of Southern Europe; it is not impossible that the great Codex Argenteus came to Werden on the Ruhr late in the eighth century thanks to the Visigoth Theodolfus, bishop of Orleans; the abbot and founder of Werden was one Liudger, pupil of Alcuin of York. Various Old High German items, too, might be taken into account: fragments of the Psalms, the fairish-good Monsee-Vienna translation of parts of the *Gospel according to St Matthew*, and the slavish, often outlandish translation of a Latin translation of Tatian's *Diatesseron* mentioned above. It would seem that Alfred did not reckon here the OE versifications of Bible stories.[90]

Prima facie, Magoun's suggestions, while not technically impossible, seem unlikely. To this list of speculative possibilities (if, indeed, any additions are necessary), one might add the many biblically based narratives in the Irish and Hiberno-Latin traditions; though, I hasten to say, I find it just as unlikely that Alfred would have known about or relied on any of these texts as those that Magoun suggests. For example, the author (or redac-

89 *Alfredian Prologues and Epilogues*, p. 72 (text); p. 73 (translation). See also Molyneaux's comments in 'Did the English Really Think They Were God's Elect?', p. 735.
90 Magoun, 'Some Notes on King Alfred's Circular Letter', pp. 100–01.

tor) of the Irish *Sex aetates mundi*[91] — a late tenth- or eleventh-century compilation of biblical stories and biblical lore, possibly representative of earlier attitudes toward biblical translation — went so far as to call their work a 'translation' of the Bible, asserting this status for the text in the incipit to the work:

> Panechte INcipit .i. **tintúd**[92] Duiblitrech huí hUathgaile forsin Pandecht Cirine tria Goédeilg in so sís.[93]
>
> (⟨Here⟩ begins the Pandicept, i.e., Dublitter Ua hUathgaile's **translation** into Irish of Jerome's Pandicept ⟨ = Vulgate⟩ ⟨follows⟩ below).[94]

More likely to have been known to Alfred, though admittedly stretching the definition of 'translation', are partial versions of the Latin Bible glossed in different vernaculars, of the sort that have survived on the European Continent.[95] Among these would be the *Liber ex lege Moysi* (discussed above; a text which Alfred apparently knew firsthand), which consists of Latin excerpts from the Pentateuch glossed in Old Irish and Old Breton (in addition to Latin) in several manuscript witnesses. I must emphasize again, however, that I find it no more likely that Alfred had any of these documents in mind when he composed his Prologue to the *Cura Pastoralis* than any of the translations enumerated by Magoun.

Rather, the most likely candidates to have inspired Alfred among those that Magoun mentions — i.e., the various Germanic verse renditions of biblical episodes — he dismisses unconvincingly in a footnote. Here, Magoun explained his reasons for rejecting the possibility that Alfred may have had in mind Old English verse renderings of biblical material (and their Old Saxon counterparts, which he groups in the same category) as follows:

> [...] ⟨T⟩he OE *Genesis A* and *B, Exodus, Daniel,* and the Old-Low-German *Hêliand* and *Genesis,* were the latter known to him [...] such pleasing poems, stemming from a fine old tradition of Latin Biblical poetry, ⟨these⟩ he would surely have regarded [...] more or less as Sunday-school retellings and paraphrases [...].[96]

---

91 This is a vernacular work with a Latin title. See, *The Irish Sex Aetates Mundi.*

92 Old Irish. *tintúd* is the verbal noun of *do·intaí.* See *eDIL*, s.v. *tintúd*: '(c) act of translating: translation, version'.

93 The text is from *The Irish Sex Aetates Mundi*, p. 64.

94 The translation is from *The Irish Sex Aetates Mundi*, p. 109.

95 Several examples of this sort, such as the Würzburg glosses on the Pauline Epistles and the Milan glosses on the Psalms (those glosses in Old Irish, though not the ones in Latin) can be found edited and translated in *Thesaurus Palaeohibernicus.*

96 Magoun, 'Some Notes on King Alfred's Circular Letter', p. 101 n. 35.

Magoun's trivializing assessment of these poems would likely not meet with general acceptance today. Since his time, close scholarly examination of these 'translations' has revealed a high degree of technical awareness and careful theological sensibilities in these retellings. These works, or similar were by far more likely to have been known to Alfred than the various other possible candidates — Coptic, Ethiopian, Gothic, Slavic, etc. — that Magoun mentioned, or the equally improbable Irish and Breton addenda to his list that I have dubiously posited. All speculation aside — and the proceeding paragraphs have been rife with that — it seems most likely that Alfred had no particular translation of the Bible in mind. His argument, in this case, did not depend on specifics. His crucial point was merely that great nations, after their conversion, translate the Bible (or at least some portion of it) into their own language; the English, as a great nation, will do the same; in this instance, by his own pen.

Notice that Alfred chose to align the English with the Greeks and the Romans as another people in the succession of great gentile nations converted to the faith. Significantly, he did not compare — and he certainly did not equate — the English to the Jews as God's Chosen People, literally or figuratively. This point is necessary for understanding the Prologue to his laws. The English were not, in his view, a people who made a special covenant with the God of Moses. Rather, they were gentiles who inherited the Mosaic Law as a result of their conversion as it was fulfilled in the Law of Christ and as it was limited by the Synod of Jerusalem as recounted in Acts 15.

How does this fact explain his decision to begin the Prologue to his laws with a translation of the Decalogue and the Code of the Covenant? To explain his decision, it is necessary to understand the place of the Mosaic Law in sacred history which, from a Christian perspective, is different for Jews than for gentiles. As I discussed in part one, for Christianized Jews, sacred history evolved gradually through a series of dispensations or revelations. At the beginning of each new dispensation, God made a covenant with his people, revealing more of his plan in return for their obedience to his law. To summarize the most basic Christian conceptualization of sacred history briefly: at the moment of creation, all mankind was under the Law of Nature. Next, after God destroyed the world in the Great Flood, he made a covenant with Noah, laying down a set of provisions in Genesis, chapter nine, known as the Noahide (or Noachide, or Noachic) Law (which is often, in various traditions, equated with the Law of Nature). Then, speaking to Moses on Mount Sinai, God established a special covenant with the Jews, wherein they became his Chosen People. God would lead the Jews to the Promised Land in return for their compliance with his Law (i.e., the Mosaic Law), by which, in this context, is signified — specifically — the Decalogue and the Code of the Covenant (and eventually the rest of the Pentateuch). With the coming of Christ, the Law of Moses was not understood to be revoked or abrogated but rather 'fulfilled' (a difficult theological concept variously conceived) as Christ stated in Matthew 5:17. Thus, for Christianized Jews, each of the dispensations was handed down one after the other, in stages over the course of sacred history, as God chose to reveal increasingly more of his plan.

For Christianized gentiles, on the other hand, the process was somewhat different. Gentiles who converted to Christianity skipped a distinct period wherein they were subject to the Mosaic Law apart from the Law of Christ. Rather, at the point of conversion, they inherited the Old Law *as it was already fulfilled by the New*. In effect, gentiles were never subject to the Law of Moses in and of itself: viewed from a Christian perspective, they proceeded directly from the Law of Nature (perhaps understood as the equivalent to Noahide law) to the Law of Christ. Since the Law of Christ was understood as a fulfillment of the Law of Moses, gentiles technically did not avoid the requirements of the Mosaic Law; it applied to them, at least in theory, just as it did to Christianized Jews. This notion of one law fulfilling another, however, led to confusion among early Christians about the practical applicability of Mosaic precepts to converted gentiles. The matter was settled by the Synod of Jerusalem (as recounted in Acts 15) which remitted gentiles from the obligation to live under the full weight of the Law of Moses. As I discussed in Part One, the Synod of Jerusalem determined that gentile converts would not be required to undergo circumcision nor, by analogy, would they be accountable to any other injunctions of the Law of Moses beyond a few basic stipulations.

Nonetheless, for Christianized gentiles, the Decalogue and the Code of the Covenant provided a starting point: legally, they became subject to these precepts at the point of their conversion, albeit only as they were understood in light of the Christian dispensation that completed and expanded it; i.e., that 'fulfilled' it. From the perspective of gentiles within sacred history — despite the subsequent dispensation of the Law of Christ — the significance of the Decalogue and Code of the Covenant cannot be overstated: Though indisputably the most fundamental expression of the Law of Moses, these documents marked the beginning of their legal history as Christians, even if they were not subject to them straightforwardly. The moment was significant enough that Sulpicius Severus in his *Chronicorum* summarized it in great detail. Likewise, it was significant enough that the question might be raised without irony in a seventh-century, Hiberno-Latin biblical commentary (here discussing the Decalogue): 'Cum initium legis[97] est decem uerba, cur non a decalogo incipit Moyses scribere legem?'

97 The word *lex* has a wide semantic range in Hiberno-Latin. In this context, it seems to have the sense listed under meaning (5) in the *Dictionary of Medieval Latin from British Sources*, s.v. 5 *lex*, '(w. ref. to the Bible) scripture, testament'. As the supporting citations in the

(Since the beginning of the scriptures is the 'ten words' Decalogue⟩, why does Moses not begin to write the scriptures with the Decalogue?),[98] to which the answer is given:

> Ideo — tribus causis: ut qui uoluit ducere filios Israel ad terram repromissionis prius cognouisset quia ipse est potens qui 'fecit caelum et terram'; et qui uoluit liberare illos de manu Pharaonis, — hic potens est qui liberauit Noe de diluuio et Abraham de Ur Caldeorum; et qui uoluit delere xii genera Cannaneorum coram illis, — ille est potens qui deleuit gigantes et omnes peccatores in diluuio. Ideo praedixit eis Moyses, 'In principio fecit deus', reliqua; item de diluuio; item de genere Abraham; et postea legem dictauit eis, id est, decalogum et que secuntur.[99]
>
>> (For these three reasons: so that he who wished to lead the sons of Israel to the Promised land would have known beforehand that he ⟨i.e., God⟩ is the powerful one who 'created heaven and earth', and he who intended to free them from the hand of Pharaoh, that he is the powerful one who freed Noah from the Flood and Abraham from Ur of the Chaldeans; and who wished to destroy twelve generations of Canaanites in their presence. He is the powerful one who destroyed the giants and all the sinners in the Flood. Therefore, Moses told them first, 'In the beginning, God created', etc. Likewise concerning the Flood; likewise concerning the generations of Abraham; and thereafter he pronounced the law to them, that is, the decalogue and what follows ⟨e.g., the Code of the Covenant?⟩).[100]

I do not intend to suggest that Alfred had either the *Chronicorum* or Hiberno-Latin exegesis in mind, was inspired by them, or even that he knew about them. Rather, I only mean to show how important this particular scriptural expression of law was in the minds of converted gentiles concerned with jurisprudence: The Decalogue and the Code of the Covenant marked the beginning of their legal history as a Christian people, inherited — albeit with certain, practical limitations — at the moment of their conversion.

We must understand the purpose of the Prologue to the Laws of Alfred in this light. With this treatise Alfred set out to situate Anglo-Saxon

---

Dictionary suggest, this specialized sense is more common in early works (i.e., before the ninth century).

98 The text is from *Pauca problesmata de enigmatibus ex tomis canonicis*, § 367, ll. 1–2, p. 162. The translation is my own.

99 This passage is from the so-called 'Reference Bible'. The text is from *Pauca problesmata de enigmatibus ex tomis canonicis*, § 367, ll. 2–11, p. 162.

100 The translation is my own.

jurisprudence within sacred history, and he accomplished this goal in a manner that, as I shall describe, projected a clear ideological agenda. Before addressing this point, however, it is necessary for me to summarize my earlier analysis of Alfred's sources and his motivations for organizing the Prologue to his laws as he did. As I argued elsewhere, Alfred was influenced by *Collectio canonum Hibernensis*, a text he likely knew about given his use of the *Liber ex lege Moysi*, and which appears to have functioned as an introduction to *Collectio canonum Hibernensis* in some manuscript witnesses.[101] In particular, I posit that Alfred was influenced by the order of precedence prescribed in *Collectio canonum Hibernensis* by which the authorities of law were to be consulted in legal proceedings. This order is laid out in Liber XIX, *De ordine inquisitionis causarum* (Concerning the order of invoking authoritative sources), which I cited above and in part one, and will include here again for convenience of comparison:

> Innocentius dicit de causis in quibus soluendi ligandique auctoritas est: XXII librorum ueteris testamenti, iiii quoque euangeliorum cum totis apostolorum scriptis. Si non appareat, ad diuina recurrito scripta, que grece agiographa dicuntur. Si nec inuenies in illis, ad catholicę æclesiae historias catholicas doctoribus catholicis scriptas manum mitte. Si nec in his, canones apostolicæ sedis intuere. Si nec in istis, sanctorum exempla perspicaciter explorata inspice. Quod si his omnibus inspectis huius questionis qualitas non lucide inuestigatur, seniores prouinciae congrega et eos interroga. Facilius namque inuenitur, quod a plurimis in unum sentientibus queritur. Verus enim repromissor Dominus ait: Si duo ex uobis conueniant super terram in nomine meo de omni re quamcumque petierint fiet illis.[102]
>
> > (Innocent says concerning sources in which there is authority to loose and bind: the twenty-two books of the Old Testament, and the four gospels together with all the writings of the apostles. Should an answer not present itself, turn to the divine texts that are called *hagiographa* in Greek. If you do not find the answer in them, reach for the catholic histories of the catholic church written by catholic doctors ⟨*æclesiae historias catholicas doctoribus catholicis scriptas*⟩. If they do not have it, examine the canons of the apostolic see. If they do not have it, consult examples of the saints ⟨*sanctorum exempla*⟩, which have been acutely examined. But if, after consulting all of these, the essence of the matter is not clearly revealed, convene the elders of the province ⟨*seniors provinciae*⟩ and

101 B. Carella, 'The Source for the Prologue', pp. 115–18 and Bradshaw, *The Early Collection of Canons*, p. 25.

102 This is the complete text of *Collectio canonum Hibernensis*, Liber XIX, *The Hibernensis*, Bk I, p. 111.

> ask them. For that which is sought by many giving an opinion on one issue is more easily found. For the true surety, the Lord, said: Should two of you come together upon the earth in my name, concerning any thing whatsoever they shall ask, it shall be done for them ⟨Matthew 18:20–19⟩).[103]

Alfred's adherence to this order of precedence in the organization of the Prologue to his law code can be summarized as follows:

Outline of the plan for Prologue to the Laws of Alfred

Sources of Authority in Alfred's Prologue	Order of Precedence in CCH
(1) Exodus 20:1–23:13 (*El.* 0–48)	Decalogue, Law of Moses
(2) Matthew 5:17 (*El.* 49.0)	Law of Christ
(Matthew 7:12)[104] (*El.* 49.6)	
(3) Acts 15 (*El.* 49–1–49.6)	Apostolic Writings,
	Ecumenical Councils
(4) *seonoðas* (*El.* 49.7–8)	provincial synods
(5) *weoruldhlafordas* (*El.* 49.7)	cf. *seniores provinciae*
witan (*El.* 49.9)	

Furthermore, it is possible (again, given Alfred's use of the *Liber ex lege Moysi*) to reconstruct, at least in part, the contents of the manuscript he likely had on hand when composing the Prologue to his laws.[105] The core group of texts included:

a the *Liber ex lege Moysi*
b the A-text of *Collectio canonum Hibernensis*
c the *Excerpta de libris Romanorum et Francorum* (formerly the *Canones Wallici*)
d the *Canones Adamnani*

There was a programmatic relationship between these texts, as I have argued elsewhere,[106] that influenced Alfred's organization of his *Domboc*. Most importantly, I suggested that Alfred may have been inspired by the

103 The translation is from *The Hibernensis*, Bk 1, p. 556.
104 See above — I include mention of Matthew 7:12 since most commentators refer to it, though in the Prologue to Alfred's Laws this reference is likely to be a variant of Acts 15, not a direct reference to Matthew 7:12.
105 B. Carella, 'Evidence for Hiberno-Latin Thought', pp. 17–18.
106 B. Carella, 'Evidence for Hiberno-Latin Thought'.

placement of the *Excerpta de libris Romanorum et Francorum*, a largely secular collection of statutes immediately following *Collectio canonum Hibernensis*, to situate his own law code at the pinnacle of what is essentially a narrative recounting the development of ecclesiastical law over the course of sacred history. As I stated in my conclusion:

> [...] in his putative source document, ⟨Alfred⟩ would have found a basic statement of the Law of Moses (expressed in the *Liber ex lege Moysi*) introducing the *Collectio canonum Hibernensis* where, by the hierarchy of precedence outlined above, the relationship between Mosaic law and the various mechanisms of Christian law (including the New Testament, patristic writings, conciliar legislation, etc.) was elucidated. Finally, in the *Excerpta*, Alfred would have come across an ostensibly secular collection of laws, whose primary purpose was to assign compositions and monetary fines to a wide variety of crimes. Alfred may well have understood the *Excerpta* as the final element in this core group of texts reflecting the historical development of Christian legislation: While the Decalogue remained the basic statement of the law, it could be modified by New Testament provisions, clarified and illuminated by the church fathers, and expanded by ecumenical and provincial synods which inform and shape secular (or, in this case quasi-secular) legislation.[107]

On the most basic level, then, the Prologue to the Laws of Alfred is an attempt to redefine the customary processes of early English law, not as the inheritance of pre-Christian tradition, but rather as ecclesiastical (or at least ecclesiastically sanctioned) legislation promulgated canonically (in Alfred's view) by Anglo-Saxon jurisprudential bodies such as the *witenagemot* to which he attributed the status of provincial synods.[108]

At the same time, Alfred's account of the development of English law had the effect of situating the English within the broader narrative of sacred history unequivocally as gentiles. For Alfred — at least in this technical legal context (as opposed to more literary expressions) — the English were not the *populus Israhel*, literally or metaphorically. Above all, they were not a 'People of a Covenant', at least not in literal, Mosaic terms. Thus, despite persistent claims to the contrary in prior scholarship, the long excerpt with which Alfred begins his Prologue was not so placed in order that its readers would understand it (at least not straightforwardly) as living law, any more than it was for any other Christian community. Yes, Alfred understood that the Law of Moses remained fully in effect under the New Law, but only as it was fulfilled in the Law of Christ as expressed in Matthew 5:17 and elucidated and limited by Acts 15, as

107 B. Carella, 'Evidence for Hiberno-Latin Thought', pp. 24–25.

108 Compare: Pratt, *The Political Thought of King Alfred the Great*, pp. 226–29.

is clear from the 'explanatory bridge' that follows his translation of the Mosaic law. The *populus Israhel* tradition should best be understood as a purely literary *topos*. Deploying this idea in a technical legal context would have born with it unintended (and apparently undesirable) implications within biblical law. Alfred realized this potential problem, and so, at least in the case of the Prologue to his laws, he chose a different course. Instead, he opted to posit a narrative of English history in which the *Angelcynn*, as a converted gentile nation, acceded to the same dignity formerly held by Greece and Rome. This, ultimately, was the ideological core of the common English identity Alfred sought to create, as he expressed it in both the Prologue to the *Cura Pastoralis* and the Prologue to his law code. This, moreover, was the identity with which he sought to unify his diverse subjects: they, collectively the *Angelcynn*, were invited at Alfred's urging to think of themselves as a great Christian nation, successors and inheritors both historically and figuratively to the most illustrious bygone empires of Christendom.[109]

109 For an excellent discussion of the importance of the idea of Christendom in Alfredian thought, particularly as it is expressed in his translation of Orosius's *Historiae adversum paganos*, libri VII, see Harris, 'The Alfredian *World History*', pp. 482–510.

CHAPTER 10

The Alfredian Pseudo-historical Genealogies

Further evidence that intellectuals in Alfred's royal court conceived of the English as a special subclass of gentiles can be found in the pseudo-historical genealogies developed and re-worked during his reign.[1] These understudied texts have the potential to shed a great deal of light on numerous aspects of the Alfredian ideological programme. Unfortunately, it lies beyond the scope of this volume to examine them fully here. For my present purpose, I wish to ask only one, very specific question: what can these genealogies reveal about Alfred's understanding of the English as a gentile people and their role in sacred history? Very significantly, these documents underwent substantial revisions during the late ninth century, the most significant of these being (1) the recontextualization of traditional English genealogies (often including the names of euhemerized pagan deities such as 'Woden') within a broader context of biblical lineages reaching back to Adam and, most extraordinarily, (2) the reimagination of Sceaf, a mythological ancestor of various Germanic peoples, as an ark-born, fourth son of Noah. As David Anlezark has shown, these changes should be understood not only as belonging to Alfred's reign, but — more importantly — as part of his larger ideological agenda:

> Genesis provided no explicit account of the origins of the Anglo-Saxons, or of any Germanic tribe, and this silence presented a gap which an imaginative genealogist could fill. The key figure in this integrating strategy in Wessex is the elusive Sceaf, who appears in the genealogies as the ark-born son of Noah. This singular Anglo-Saxon invention is found in regnal lists and genealogies tracing Anglo-Saxon royal descent back to Adam [...]. ⟨The⟩ evidence suggests that the incorporation of Sceaf into the genealogies is a West Saxon innovation and draws on West Saxon tradition, and that his transformation into the ark-born son is the product of Alfred's reign.[2]

1 A foundational study of the genealogies is Sisam, 'Anglo-Saxon Royal Genealogies'. See also: Dumville, 'The Anglian Collection of Royal Genealogies'; Dumville, 'The West Saxon Genealogical Regnal List'; Moisl, 'Anglo-Saxon Royal Genealogies'; C. R. Davis, 'Cultural Assimilation in the Anglo-Saxon Royal Genealogies', and Anlezark, 'Sceaf, Japheth and the Origins of the Anglo-Saxons'.

2 Anlezark, 'Sceaf, Japheth and the Origins of the Anglo-Saxons', p. 18.

Later he adds:

> The shift back to the biblical patriarchs through the ark-born son is not a cultural development associated with the conversion, but rather with the ideological programme of the reign of Alfred, when biblical names first appear in the genealogies.[3]

Finally, Anlezark addresses Alfred's motivation for crafting such a story, explaining (at least in part) how these genealogical developments fit into Alfred's larger ideological purpose:

> The fusion of the heroic Germanic past with the world of the biblical patriarchs which the invention of Sceaf as the fourth son of Noah suggests is certainly an ideological innovation appropriate to the reign of Alfred [...] this genealogical creation suggests that at least the West Saxon genealogists desired to create for their kings — and implicitly for the Anglo-Saxons and all those who shared their common origin — a unique relationship with Noah, the second father of the human race. The implicit extension of this sense of uniqueness includes their Germanic cousins, who like the Anglo-Saxons themselves are not accounted for by the 'true' version of early world history found in Genesis, claimed for the West Saxons a privileged place among the northern peoples.[4]

Like the other texts in the Alfredian programme, these genealogies underwent modification as new material was interpolated into them for specific ideological purposes. Though not translated, they were certainly transformed: the lineages of pagan ancestors, tracing the descent of both gods and heroes, were not wholly jettisoned but rather euhemerized and reconfigured within a Christian framework that provided new signification. This gesture, I would argue, is ideologically consonant with the Prologue to Alfred's laws. There, too, Alfred did not abandon ancient tradition (in this case customary law) in favour of adopting foreign statutes from Rome or from broader Christendom but, like the traditional matter in the genealogies, he situated them within a Christian framework wherein the old laws, kept more-or-less unchanged, drew greater legitimacy from a new ideological perspective.

Returning to the question I asked above: what do the genealogies reveal about Alfred's view of English in sacred history? Whether or not a more formally conceived narrative of Sceaf's Noachic ancestry was ever set to vellum, his insinuation into West-Saxon genealogies implies an underlying pseudo-historical account of the English ethnogenesis carefully ensconced within a biblical framework. Positing Sceaf, the founder of their

3 Anlezark, 'Sceaf, Japheth and the Origins of the Anglo-Saxons', p. 32.
4 Anlezark, 'Sceaf, Japheth and the Origins of the Anglo-Saxons', p. 35.

ethnic line, as a son of Noah had the effect of situating the English within sacred history unambiguously as gentiles. As such, the English, prior to their conversion, would have partaken in the Noahide Covenant and would thus be subject to Noahide law. It seems reasonable to posit that, for the Alfredian genealogists, Noahide law was the equivalent of the Law of Nature, though nowhere is this idea stated overtly. Either way, it would appear that — according to the understanding of sacred history implicit in the genealogies produced, or at least revised, during Alfred's reign — the English people were, in origin, gentiles who lived under the Noachic dispensation and were subject to its injunction until their conversion. In this view, the English were never subject to the Law of Moses directly, save only as it was fulfilled in the Law of Christ and clarified in the Synod of Jerusalem, as Alfred laid out in the Prologue to his Law Code.

By positing a fourth, ark-born son of Noah, the author of this genealogical account showed a willingness to bend the scriptural version of events to a degree parallelled by the Irish author of the Caí Caínbrethach story.[5] Very significantly, however, neither story — i.e., neither the West Saxon account of Sceaf nor the early Irish story of Caí Caínbrethach — claimed direct descent from God's Chosen People; indeed, quite the contrary. To do so would have had profound implications in biblical law, entailing their own and their ancestors' responsibility to uphold Mosaic Law in its entirety. While the idea of the English as 'God's Chosen People' might have seemed harmless enough as a trope in certain literary and political genres, for ecclesiastical jurists who knew keenly what was at stake, the significance of such a metaphor in a legal-theological context was too consequential to be overlooked. If the pre-Christian Anglo-Saxons had been subject to the Law of Moses, both they and their ancestors would have been responsible for living according to its precepts to the letter; not the reduced injunction expressed in Acts 15. For the Christianized English, that would mean that their pagan ancestors were in hell, since they would have been responsible for upholding to the Pentateuch in its fullness, just like Jews. Instead, like their Irish counterparts independently confronting a

5 It is certainly significant that a fourth son of Noah, in this case named Bith, appears in the Irish pseudo-historical transition as well. It is difficult, however, to identify any direct connection between the Irish account of Bith and the English account of Sceaf. The two stories differ in both their content and, apparently, in their ideological resonances. That said, it is notable that such a gesture was possible in both cultures — i.e., the interpolation of personages with local ethnic connections into the biblical narrative (in both cases, a non-biblical, fourth son of Noah). See especially *Lebor Gabála Érenn*, II, pp. 200–09 (for an extensive version of the story). On the origin of the story, see Carey, 'The Origin and Development of the Cesair Legend'.

similar dilemma,[6] the West Saxon genealogists who interpolated Sceaf into biblical history avoided making any such comparison between the English and God's Chosen People in favour of a gentile, Noachic ethnogenesis. From this perspective, the pre-Christian English would have lived under the Law of Nature, explicitly equated with the Law of Noah (given the biblicalization of the Sceaf story), and then, upon their conversion, under the Law of Christ.

Although I am not suggesting that it was intended as a companion piece to the genealogies, the underlying ideological agenda of the Prologue to the Laws of Alfred is consonant with the implied pseudo-historical narrative of Sceaf in the genealogies. According to the Alfredian understanding of sacred history, pre-Christian English law was conceived of as unwritten Noahide law. Later, post conversion, English law was considered to be part of the Law of Christ. This belief was based on a subtle equivocation. For Alfred, English laws promulgated by Christian kings and their *witenagemot* were tantamount to the edicts of provincial synods acting in the same tradition — and with the same authority — as the Synod of Jerusalem.

Let me explain how these various parts fit together as a unified argument. In the Prologue to his law code, one of Alfred's main purposes was to narrate the role of the English within sacred history from a legal perspective. With this text, Alfred tacitly suggested that the English, as a newly Christianized gentile people, inherited the Law of Moses, albeit as it was fulfilled in the Law of Christ (as described in Matthew 5:17 and Acts 15). For Alfred, however, Christianization did not mean that the Law of Moses was abrogated, as he makes clear with his translation of Matthew 5:17 (emphasis my own):

> Vulgate: nolite putare quoniam veni solvere legem aut prophetas non veni solvere sed **adimplere**.
>
> > (Do not think that I am come to destroy the law, or the prophets. I am not come to destroy, but to **fulfill**).
>
> Alfred: *Crist [...] cwæð, ðæt he ne come no ðas bebodu to brecanne ne forbeodanne, ac mid eallum godum to* ***ecanne*** ⟨*El.* 49⟩.[7]

6 I should emphasize that I am not suggesting any direct influence from the Irish tradition. Rather, it seems most likely in this case that legalists in both traditions independently proposed analogous solutions to similar problems.

7 *Die Gesetze der Angelsachsen*, I, p. 42.

> (Christ said that he did not come to break or repeal the laws,[8] but with all goodness, to **increase** ⟨them⟩).[9]

In this passage — significantly — Alfred used the verb *eacan* 'to increase' to translate Latin *adimplere* '(1) to fill up (with); (2) to fulfill, carry out (an obligation, promise, etc.)'.[10] With this word choice, it would seem, Alfred wished to emphasize the addition of new legal obligations rather than to express the more theologically complex notion of fulfillment. At the same time, he did not intend to suggest that the Mosaic Law still applied literally in his own time, unmediated by the Law of Christ.[11] Rather, he makes it abundantly clear in his 'explanatory bridge' that the Law of Moses was fulfilled by the Law of Christ (Matthew 5:17). Moreover, he understood that this basic explanation of the relationship between the Old and New Laws in the gospels underwent further adjudication at the Synod of Jerusalem as described in Acts 15, particularly regarding how the obligations of the Mosaic Law were reduced for gentiles. Alfred cites the decision of the Synod of Jerusalem (Acts 15:23–29) at great length, as I described above, because he considered it of great importance and especially apropos to English sacred history. For him, this passage served two purposes: (1) it explained the practical application of the Law of Moses to a converted gentile people, including the English, and (2) as the first ecclesiastical synod, it created a precedent for other provincial synods to make decisions under the Law of Christ; and, for Alfred, post-Conversion English law was the product of such synods.

Throughout his legal writings, the placement of the English within sacred history as a converted, gentile nation stands out as central to Alfred's agenda. Above all, he sought to explain how God's law applied to gentiles. Never in a legal context did he ever allege (even figuratively) the status of God's Chosen People for the English. Quite the contrary: to have done so would have undercut the main theme of the Prologue to his law code — which sought to elucidate the relationship between the Old and New Laws

8 OE *bebod*, here probably in its special sense of the 'Ten Commandments', which, by synecdoche, implies the whole of the Mosaic Law. See: *The Dictionary of Old English*, s.v. A.1.b *be-bod*, 'specifically: (one of the) Ten Commandments'. In this case, however, *bebodu* is nominative plural, confirmed but the modifying demonstrative adjective '*ðas*'.

9 The translation is my own.

10 This is the definition in the *Oxford Latin Dictionary*. The semantic range is apparently quite similar in medieval British uses. Compare in the *Dictionary of Medieval Latin from British Sources*, s.v. 1 *adimplere*, '1 to fill up. b to complete (an amount or period). c to make good, fill (a role). d to fill the role of [...] 2 to fulfil a a task. b a desire or impulse. c a promise. d a prophecy. e a command or request'.

11 Here, I agree with David Pratt, *The Political Thought of King Alfred the Great*, p. 231, that 'There can be no question of the Mosaic excerpts actually applying in Alfred's kingdom', although — here again — my reasons for drawing this conclusion differ from his.

in a way that could be practically applied to Anglo-Saxon jurisprudence — rendering everything following his translation from Exodus meaningless.

In the last section of this Prologue, Alfred completed his tersely construed narration of English sacred history, bringing it up to his present day. There, he made his most unique and audacious claim. Applying a rationale for which no clear source has yet been identified (and which I believe is likely an Alfredian innovation), he described how the various converted gentile nations, throughout Christendom and including the English, began to participate in the promulgation of ecclesiastical law, modelled on the procedure laid down at the Synod of Jerusalem as related in Acts 15:

> Siððan ðæt þa gelamp, þæt monega ðeoda Cristes geleafan onfengon, þa wurdon monega seonoðas geond ealne middangeard gegaderode, ⁊ eac swa geond Angelcyn, siððan hie Cristes geleafan onfengon [...] Hie ða on monegum senoðum monegra menniscra misdæda bote gesetton, ⁊ on monega senoðbéc hie writan, hwær anne dom hwær oþerne ⟨*El.* 49.7–8⟩.[12]
>
> (Thereafter it happened that many nations received belief in Christ. Then there were many synods convened throughout all the world, and, likewise, among the English after they received belief in Christ [...]. Then, in many synods they set down compensation for many human crimes, and in many a synod-book they wrote down here one decision, there another).[13]

Presented in these terms, there is little that even the most devoutly anti-secular cleric might find objectionable. Next, however — without overtly calling attention to the gesture — Alfred shifted the topic immediately to his own laws and those of his forbears, among whom (as we have seen) he included Ine, Offa, and Æðelbehrt. He concluded by introducing his own law code, which can only be described as an essentially traditional collection of English customary law, consisting of mainly secular statutes. In this way, thus, Alfred equated English customary law — not just his own, but those of his predecessors since the time of conversion — with legislation promulgated by ecclesiastical synods, a process which, he tacitly suggested, began with the Synod of Jerusalem, and continued uninterrupted to his day. English law, therefore, was and had been since conversion (in his view) ecclesiastical law.[14]

I have discussed the details of this gesture in a previous article.[15] Here, however, my purpose is to examine what this claim reveals about

---

12 *Die Gesetze der Angelsachsen*, I, pp. 44, 46.

13 The translation is my own.

14 Compare Pratt, *The Political Thought of King Alfred the Great*, pp. 226–29.

15 B. Carella, 'Evidence for Hiberno-Latin Thought'.

Alfred's view of Anglo-Saxon Christian identity and the overall ideological aim of the Prologue to his laws. Understood in the context of sacred history, Alfred's strategy in the Prologue to his laws is unique — I know of nothing parallel to it in early medieval law. Various strategies were employed by different cultures in early medieval Europe to justify the continued existence of their customary, pre-Christian legal systems, often expressed in prefaces to statutory legal codes. We have seen examples of Irish reflexes of this gesture in part one. The Germanic peoples on the Continent likewise deployed a series of arguments to this end, expressed in a wide variety of documents.[16] None of which I am aware, however — other the Prologue to the Laws of Alfred — went so far as to claim that the inherited mechanisms of their native, ultimately pre-Christian legal systems should be regarded as provincial ecclesiastical synods.

At this point, it is possible to summarize the ideological goal of the Prologue to the Laws of Alfred. As we have already seen in his Prologue to the *Cura Pastoralis*, the English were, for him, a nation of converted gentiles, who — like the Greeks and the Romans — successively discovered the Law of Moses and translated it into their own language. They were God's Chosen People in no sense beyond this. Specifically, in matters of law, Alfred made the argument, albeit by implication rather than with an overt statement, that Anglo-Saxon jurisprudence introduced nothing novel nor innovative, but merely legislated according to the procedure established by the first apostolic synod, subsequently employed throughout all Christendom, including England. Thus, as the product of a legitimate and well-precedented mechanism of Christian jurisprudence, post-conversion English law was, in his view, tantamount to ecclesiastical law: the *witenagemot* (populated by ecclesiastical as well as secular magnates) was, for him, the English manifestation of a provincial synod, carrying with it the same authority and sanction. According to Alfred's view, therefore, the English possessed no written secular law separate from the vernacular codes he tacitly (re)defined as 'ecclesiastical' law. Significantly, his equivocating understanding of the relationship between English secular and ecclesiastical jurisprudence depended on a particular conceptualization of the place of the English in sacred history. It can be summarized as follows: From the Prologue to his laws and the royal genealogies reimagined during his reign, we see that, for Alfred, the English, like all gentile nations prior to conversion, were beneficiaries of the Noahide Covenant and likewise subject to its injunction. This law, of course, was (mostly) unwritten;[17] it was, for all intents and purposes, the Law of Nature (though Alfred never uses this term). Later, upon conversion, the English (like all other nations at

16 A very interesting example is the Prologue to the *Lex Baiwariorum*. The text is available in *Lex Baiwariorum*.

17 That is, beyond the handful of injunctions outlined in Genesis 9.

the moment of their Christianization), inherited the entirety of Christian law (which is written), including the Law of Moses, the Law of Christ, and the laws promulgated by the synodal procedures of the Church. Moreover, like all Christian nations, Alfred asserted, the English conducted their own 'synods' and produced their own written laws which, for him, were tantamount to ecclesiastical law. In this way, Alfred fundamentally (re)interpreted English customary law as Christian law, preserving both his own statutes and those of his English forbears essentially unchanged in most of their particulars, justifying their continued application in purely ecclesiastical terms.

It is in this context that we must understand the unifying identity with which Alfred sought to galvanize his subjects to face the viking threat. For Alfred, the English were not a 'People of a Covenant', chosen by God to inherit the Promised Land. Alfred, I think, was too practically minded for such a poorly grounded literary flourish, especially when such serious (and dire) political matters were at stake. Rather, the English were, in his conception, a new preeminent Christian people, successively acceding to that status after the Greeks and Romans, in turn. More specifically, the English were — as descendants of Noah, via his son Sceaf — the great people of Germanic Christendom. With the Prologue to his law code, Alfred provided more than one of early medieval Western Europe's most innovative treatises on legal theory. Beyond that, he created for his war-tattered subjects a narrative of their ethnic history that glorified their learned past and urged them to press onward to assume what was, in his view, their rightful place among the great Christian nations.

CHAPTER 11

Conclusions

What can be said in general about the reception of Irish legal ideologies in Anglo-Saxon England? From the outset, it must be acknowledged that such influence was neither profound nor widespread. English borrowing from Irish models occurred at specific times and places; not as a typical or common *modus operandi*. What influences are apparent primarily involved matters of ecclesiastical interest and, presumably, were transmitted via Latin, ecclesiastical channels. Indeed, all evidence for the transmission of legal ideologies from early medieval Ireland to England points to the Church as the primary if not sole conduit, even though the effects of the borrowing may have secondarily affected vernacular documents and those with more worldly concerns. Even so, the body of surviving evidence is scant. Generally speaking, Irish ideological influence on Anglo-Saxon law occurred at two main junctures: (1) mid-to late eighth-century Northumbria, and (2) late ninth-century Wessex, during the reign of King Alfred the Great. I shall summarize each of these cases in turn.

A distinguishing feature of early Northumbrian legal methodology is its use of authorities, including both the kinds of sources that were invoked and how those citations were deployed as part of a larger argument in support of a given legal case. Northumbrian legalists apparently considered scripture to be the most fundamental authority and relied on it far more heavily than any other kind of authority. While they also cited other, non-biblical sources, they did so with much less frequency and with a tendency to identify them only by vague, non-specific allusions (e.g., 'the ecumenical councils'). More than merely foregrounding scripture as an authority, however, Northumbrian legalists, like their Irish counterparts sought, where possible, to build their cases with multiple citations of scripture reflecting the successive stages or 'Laws' of sacred history. Though it was not always possible, a given precept would ideally be supported by citations representing the Law of Nature, the Law of Moses, and the Law of Christ.[1] While the number of surviving legal documents from early Northumbria available for comparison is quite small — I discussed two texts connected with Alcuin (the *Legatine Capitulary of 786* and the

1 Perhaps also citations representing the 'Law of the Prophets' would ideally also be included, but the evidence is too scant to suggest that this 'Law' was recognized as such in early medieval Northumbria.

Admonitio Generalis of 789) and one with Archbishop Ecgberht of York (the *Dialogue of Ecgberht*) — these features are apparent throughout.

Notably, this method for citing authorities is made explicit in the early Irish canon law collection known as *Collectio canonum Hibernensis*, Liber XIX, *De ordine inquisitionis causarum* (Concerning the order of invoking authoritative sources), and it is utilized throughout the text. Other examples appear in many early Irish texts, including the letters of Columbanus (which I discussed in the introduction to this volume), Cummian's *De Controversia Paschali*, etc. Although the exact route of transmission is unclear, contacts between the early Irish and the Northumbrian Churches, not to mention between areas under Irish cultural influence in northern Britain and the Northumbrian royal court, were robust throughout the early medieval period. None of the parties involved would likely have considered this method of citing authoritative sources to have been distinctively Irish, but merely as part of a typical Christian education. This method of invoking authorities and building an argument with citations drawn mostly from scripture as the most fundamental authority and representing it on various levels, took root in Ireland in Late Antiquity and became standard procedure. Eventually, this method was described explicitly in *Collectio canonum Hibernensis*. Later, by at least the mid-eighth century, it was transmitted via ecclesiastical channels to early medieval Northumbria, possibly via Iona (or possibly via Brittany from which *Collectio canonum Hibernensis* was, in several later cases, most proximately transmitted to Anglo-Saxon England), and where it remained in use until that kingdom fell to the vikings.

The next time we see Irish ideological influence on early English law is during the late ninth century, in the court of King Alfred. Clerical intellectuals in Alfred's court were deeply interested in the ethnogenesis of the English people, their place within sacred history, and their relationship with God in the divine plan. Indeed, medieval Irish and English jurists were both concerned with these questions. As was common practice in Ireland, these ideas were typically expressed via biblical pseudo-history. Perhaps surprisingly, ecclesiastical lawyers in both Ireland and Anglo-Saxon England understood themselves and their peoples to be converted gentiles who lived under the Law of Nature prior to their conversion, after which they lived under the Law of Christ. I say 'surprisingly', because it has long been held that both Irish and the English intellectuals thought of themselves, to a greater or lesser extent literally, in Old Testament terms. It is commonly held, for example, that English *literati* thought of themselves as 'God's Chosen People', that Irish jurists thought of themselves as 'Levites' and that both understood the Law of Moses to be living law. The evidence I have presented here challenges these widely held claims.

Whereas Old Testament comparisons such as these may have held currency in other genres, my evidence demonstrates that they were generally avoided in legal-theological circles. Why? For ecclesiastical jurists, the legal implications of such beliefs were highly problematic. They would mean, for example, that their ancestors were subject to the Law of Moses before Christianization and thus damned forever. Furthermore, even to clerical jurists, such beliefs might be taken to mean that even after conversion, they too remained subject to the letter of the Law of Moses in the same way as Christianized Jews, rather than to the reduced injunction settled upon in the Synod of Jerusalem. Instead, what we see consistently in legal-theological documents from both early Ireland and the court of King Alfred is that Christian jurists conceived of themselves and their peoples as gentiles who lived under the dispensation of the Law of Nature until the point of conversion, where they became subject to the Law of Christ. As such, they were subject to the Law of Moses, too, but only as it was fulfilled in the Law of Christ; and the Synod of Jerusalem made clear that, practically speaking, that entailed only three prohibitions, that is, to avoid consuming blood and offerings, idolatry, and fornication. This point above all — their place in sacred history as converted gentiles, with its concomitant legal obligations, and limits — was of central importance to jurists in both cultures.

Variously, also, both early medieval Irish and Alfredian jurists understood their customary law within the context of sacred history. For the Irish, the Pseudo-historical Prologue to the *Senchas Már* explained their pre-Christian, native law as an expression of *naturale bonum* under the Law of Nature. It was ultimately approved by St Patrick himself in a kind of proto-synod (of the sort, perhaps, that Columbanus was referring to in his *Epistula III*). For the English on the other hand, the Prologue to the Laws of Alfred makes the case that Anglo-Saxon customary law should be understood as one and the same as the edicts of ecclesiastical synods. In both cultures, therefore, traditional, pre-Christian law was situated in a Christian context that imbued it with authority and allowed it to remain in force virtually unchanged. In neither culture was the Law of Moses accepted straightforwardly as living law, nor did ecclesiastical lawyers think of themselves as Old Testament jurists. On the contrary, their understanding of the progression of sacred history and their place within it as converted gentiles was repeatedly made clear, for example, in various biblical commentaries, especially exegesis on the Pauline Epistles where this question provides a main topic for discussion, as well as other texts I have discussed here.

Since this use of pseudo-history was widespread in early Irish literature but occurs in England almost exclusively in texts associated with the court of King Alfred, it seems reasonable to posit that the direction of influence was east across the Irish Sea to Anglo-Saxon England. How were these ideas transmitted? While there is no direct textual evidence to bear witness, this situation is not without precedent. Elsewhere, too,

Alfred relied on Hiberno-Latin thought of a more ideological kind. As I discussed above, Alfred's sophisticated use of the *Liber ex lege Moysi* as an exemplar for the Mosaic preface of the Prologue to his laws — which shows an awareness of how it was used in an Irish legal context, that is, as a prologue to *Collectio canonum Hibernensis* — demonstrates that he was willing to rely on the Hiberno-Latin tradition for guidance. Also, we know from Asser that Alfred was willing to look to foreigners for instruction on ecclesiastical matters.[2] Finally, as Patrick O'Neill has demonstrated, Alfred applied a distinctly Irish exegetical method in his introductions to the *Prose Psalms*, emphasizing 'concrete and historical (Old Testament)' interpretations above allegorical or Christological readings.[3]

Overall, the evidence I have adduced in this volume suggests that early Irish ideological influence on English law was limited and mostly technical in nature, having to do with the proper methods for citing authorities in jurisprudential argumentation and the legal implications of a people's place in sacred history. As such, the Irish influence on Anglo-Saxon legal ideology for which there is evidence is thoroughly Christian in nature and likely to have been transmitted through Latin, ecclesiastical channels, though it is not entirely clear precisely what those channels were. There is no direct, textual evidence for transmission; just the co-occurrence of distinctive ideas and the similar application of those ideas to legal texts. In the end, I suspect that none of the parties involved thought of the points of contact I have identified here as particularly 'Irish', but merely as part of a typical Christian education. Twentieth- and twenty-first-century scholars might identify certain, distinctive features of legal and theological ideology as 'Irish' (or even 'Celtic'), but I doubt early Irish or Anglo-Saxon jurists would have thought of them in that way. Future research into the question of possible Irish influence on early English law may well unearth more details. I believe, though, that those details will be isolated, and that what I have laid out in this volume aptly summarizes the Irish ideological influence on Anglo-Saxon law.

2 See *King Alfred's Old English Prose Translation of the First Fifty Psalms*, p. 44 and n. 60, citing the following: Asser, *Life of King Alfred*, §§76, 91, and 102, pp. 60, 76–77, and 89; *Alfred the Great*, pp. 92, 101, 107, and 302; and Hughes, 'Evidence for Contacts', pp. 58 and 66.

3 O'Neill, *King Alfred's Old English Prose Translation of the First Fifty Psalms*, p. 44.

Works Cited

Manuscripts

Cambridge, Corpus Christi College, MS 173
Cambridge, Corpus Christi College, MS 265
Dublin, Royal Irish Academy, MS 23 E 25
Dublin, Trinity College, MS 1316 (H 2. 15a)
Dublin, Trinity College, MS 1336 (H 3. 17)
Dublin, Trinity College, MS 1337 (H. 3. 18)
London, British Library, MS Cotton Otho E. xiii
London, British Library, MS Cotton Vitellius A.xii
London, British Library, MS Harley 432
Munich, Bayerische Staatsbibliothek, MS Clm. 1476
Munich, Bayerische Staatsbibliothek, MS Clm. 1477
Orléans, Médiathèque, MS 221
Oxford, Bodleian Library, MS Barlow 37
Oxford, Bodleian Library, MS Rawlinson B 502
Paris, Bibliothèque nationale de France, MS lat. 3182
Paris, Bibliothèque nationale de France, MS lat. 11561
Città della Vaticano, Biblioteca Apostolica Vaticana, MS Vat. Reg. lat. 49

Primary Sources

Adomnán, *Life of St Columba*, ed. and trans. by Alan Orr Anderson and M. O. Anderson, 2nd edn (Oxford: Clarendon, 1991)

Alcuin, 'Quaestiones in Genesim', in *Opera Omnia*, ed. by Jacques-Paul Migne, Patrologiae cursus completus: series latina, 100–01, 2 vols (Paris: Garnier, 1851–1863), I, cols 515A–570B

———, 'The Legatine Capitulary of 786' (= *Epistula III*), in *Alcuini Epistolae*, ed. by Ernst Dümmler, Monumenta Germaniae Historica: Epistolae Karolini Aevi, IV (Berlin: Weidman, 1895), pp. 19–29

Alfred the Great. Asser's Life of King Alfred and Other Contemporary Sources, trans. by Simon Keynes and Michael Lapidge, Penguin Classics (Harmondsworth: Penguin, 1983; repr. 1985)

Alfredian Prologues and Epilogues, ed. and trans. by Susan Irvine (Oxford: Oxford University Press, 2024)

Ancient Laws of Ireland, ed. by William Neilson Hancock, Thaddeus O'Mahony, Alexander George Richey, and William Maunsell Hennessey, 4 vols (Dublin: HMSO, 1865–1901); repr. in 4 vols (Buffalo, NY: Hein, 2000)

'An Edition of the Pseudo-historical Prologue to the *Senchas Már*', ed. by John Carey, *Ériu*, 45 (1994), 1–31

An Introduction to Early English Law, trans. by Bill Griffiths (Norfolk: Anglo-Saxon Books, 1995)

'*Apgitir Chrábaid*: The Alphabet of Piety', ed. by Vernam Hull, *Celtica*, 8 (1968), 44–89

A Raven's Battle-Cry: The Limits of Judgment in the Medieval Irish Legal Tract Anfuigell, ed. and trans. by Charlene M. Eska, Medieval Law and Its Practice, 27 (Leiden: Brill, 2019)

Asser, *Life of King Alfred*, ed. by William Henry Stevenson (Oxford: Clarendon, 1904; repr. 1998)

Audacht Morainn, ed. and trans. by Fergus Kelly (Dublin: Institute for Advanced Studies, 1976)

Augustine of Hippo, *Sancti Avreli Avgvstini Opera, 8.II: De perfectione iustitiae hominis, De gestis Pelagii, De gratia Christi et de peccato originali libri dvo, De nvptiis et concvpiscentia ad Valerivm comitem libri dvo*, ed. by Charles Urba and Joseph Zycha, Corpus Scriptorum Ecclesiasticorum Latinorum, 42 (Vienna: Tempsky, 1902)

Augustine of Hippo, *Sancti Avrelii Avgvstini Opera, 7.II: De Sermone Domini in Monte Libros Duos*, ed. by Almut Mutzenbecher, Corpus Christianorum Series Latina, 35 (Turnhout: Brepols, 1967)

———, *Answer to the Pelagians I*, trans. by Roland J. Teske, The Works of St Augustine: A Translation for the 21st Century, I.23 (New York, NY: City, 1997)

Bechbretha: An Old Irish Law-Tract on Bee-Keeping ed. and trans. by Thomas M. Charles-Edwards and Fergus Kelly, Early Irish Law Series, 1 (Dublin: Institute for Advanced Studies, 1983)

Bede, *Ecclesiastical History of the English People*, ed. and trans. by Bertram Colgrave and R. A. B. Mynors, Oxford Medieval Texts (Oxford: Clarendon, 1969; repr. 2007)

Biblia Sacra Iuxta Vulgatam Versionem, ed. by Robert Weber and Roger Gryson, 5th edn (Stuttgart: Deutsche Bibelgesellschaft 2007)

The Bishop's Synod ('*The First Synod of St Patrick*'), ed. and trans. by M. J. Faris (Liverpool: Cairns, 1976)

Biskupa Sögur I: Kristni saga; Kristni þættir, ed. by Sigurgeir Steingrímsson, Ólafur Halldórsson, and Peter Foote, Íslenzk fornrit, 15, 2 vols (Reykjavík: Hið íslenzka fornritafélag, 1998–2003)

Bretha Comaithcheso: An Old-Irish Law Tract on Neighbouring Farms, ed. and trans. by Thomas Charles-Edwards, Early Irish Law Series, 9 (Dublin: Institute for Advanced Study, 2022)

Briefe, Abhandlungen und Predigten aus den Zwei Letzten Jahrhundereten des Kirchlichen Alterthums und dem Anfang des Mittelalters, ed. by Carl Paul Caspari (Christiania [Oslo]: Mallingsche, 1890; repr., Brussels: Culture et Civilisation, 1964)

Cáin Adomnáin and the Canones Adomnani, ed. and trans. by Pádraig P. Ó Néill and David N. Dumville, Basic Texts for Gaelic History, 2, 2 vols (Cambridge: Department of Anglo-Saxon, Norse, and Celtic, 2003)

'Cáin Domnaig', ed. and trans. by J. G. O'Keefe, *Ériu*, 2 (1905), 189–211

'Cáin Domnaig', ed. and trans. by Vernam Hull, *Ériu*, 20 (1966), 151–77

Cáin Lánamna: An Old Irish Tract on Marriage and Divorce Law, ed. and trans. by Charlene M. Eska (Leiden: Brill, 2010)

Cath Maige Mucrama: The Battle of Mag Mucrama, ed. and trans. by Máirín O Daly, Irish Texts Society, 50 (Dublin: Irish Texts Society, 1975)

Charlemagne: Translated Sources, trans. by P. D. King (Moresdale Hall: King, 1987)

Chronicum Scotorum, ed. and trans. by William M. Hennessey, Rerum britannicarum medii ævi scriptores (Rolls Series), 46 (London: Longmans, 1866; repr. 1964)

Chronicon Scotorum, ed. by William M. Hennessy, trans. by William M. Hennessy and Gearóid Mac Niocail, electronic edn by Beatrix Färber and Ruth Murphy, *CELT: Corpus of Electronic Texts* (Cork: University of Cork, 2012–), <https://celt.ucc.ie/published/G100016/> [accessed 19 September 2023]

Collection of the Laws and Canons of the Church of England from its First Foundations to the Conquest, trans. by John Johnson (Oxford: Parker, 1720)

The Colloquy of the Two Sages, ed. by Whitley Stokes (Paris: Bouillon, 1905)

Columbanus, *Sancti Columbani Opera*, ed. and trans. by G. S. M. Walker, Scriptores Latini Hiberniae, 11 (Dublin: Institute for Advanced Studies, 1957)

———, 'Columbanus, Letter 1: Translation and Commentary', trans. by Robert Stanton, *Journal of Medieval Latin*, 3 (1993), 149–68

Concilia, Decreta, Leges, Constitutiones in Re Ecclesiarum Orbis Britannici, ed. by Henry Spelman, 2 vols (London: Warren, 1639–1664)

Concilia Magna Britanniae et Hiberniae, ed. by David Wilkins, 4 vols (London: Gosling, 1737)

Corpus Iuris Hibernici: ad Fidem Codicum Manuscriptorum, ed. by Daniel A. Binchy, 6 vols (Dublin: Institute for Advanced Studies, 1978)

Córus Bésgnai. An Old Irish Law Tract on Church and Society, ed. by Liam Breatnach, Early Irish Law Series, 7 (Dublin: Institute for Advanced Studies, 2017)

Councils and Ecclesiastical Documents Relating to Great Britain and Ireland, ed. by Arthur West Haddan and William Stubbs, 3 vols (Oxford: Clarendon, 1869–1878)

Councils and Synods with Other Documents relating to the English Church, trans. by Dorothy Whitelock, 2 vols in 4 (Oxford: Clarendon, 1964–1981)

Críth Gablach, ed. by Daniel A. Binchy (Dublin: Institute for Advanced Studies, 1941; repr. 1979)

Cummian, *Cummian's Letter 'De Controversia Paschali' and the 'De Ratione Conputandi'*, ed. and trans. by Maura Walsh and Dáibhí Ó Cróinín (Toronto: Pontifical Institute of Medieval Studies, 1988)

Decrees of the Ecumenical Councils, I:, *Nicaea I to Lateran V*, ed. and trans. by Norman P. Tanner (Washington, DC: Sheed & Ward, 1990)

Die Admonitio Generalis Karls des Großen, ed. by Hubert Mordek, Klaus Zechiel-Eckes, and Michael Glatthaar, Monumenta Germaniae Historica, Leges, Fontes iuris, 16 (Hanover: Hahn, 2012)

Die Alten Lateinischen Thomasakten, ed. by Klaus Zelzer, Texte und Untersuchungen zur Geschichte der Altchristlichen Literatur, 122 (Berlin: Akademie, 1977)

Die Gesetze der Angelsachsen, ed. and trans. by Felix Liebermann, 3 vols (Halle: Niemeyer, 1903; repr. Clark, NJ: Lawbook Exchange, 2007)

Die Irische Kanonensammlung, ed. by Herrmann Wasserschleben (Leipzig: Tauchnitz, 1885; repr. Aalen: Scientia, 1966)

The Early Irish Linguist. An Edition of the Canonical Part of the 'Auraicept na nÉces', ed. and trans. by Anders Ahlqvist (Helsinki: Societas Scientiarum Fennica, 1983)

Ecclesiastica Historia, integram Ecclesiae Christi ideam, quantum ad Locum, Propagationem, Persecutionem, Tranquillitatem, Doctrinam, Hæreses, Ceremonias, Gubernationem, Schismata, Synodos, Personas, Miracula, Martyria, Religiones extra Ecclesiam, & statum Imperii politicum attinet, secundum singulas Centurias, perspicuo ordine complectens: singulari diligentia & fide ex vetustissimis & optimis historicis, patribus, & aliis scriptoribus congesta: Per aliquot studiosos & pios viros in urbe Magdeburgica, ed. by the Magdeburg Centuriators, 13 vols (Basel: Wolfenbüttel Herzog August Bibliothek Basileae Oporinus, 1561–1574)

English Historical Documents, I: *c. 500–1042*, trans. by Dorothy Whitelock, 2nd edn (Oxford: Oxford University Press, 1979)

The Hibernensis: Book I, A Study and Edition and Book II, Translation, Commentary and Indexes, ed. and trans. by Roy Flechner, Studies in Medieval and Early Modern Canon Law, 17, 2 vols (Washington, DC: Catholic University of America Press, 2019)

The Holy Bible. Douay-Rheims Version, rev. by Bishop Richard Challoner and ed. by Archbishop James Cardinal Gibbons (Rockford, IL: Tan, 1899; 1989)

Iona. The Earliest Poetry of a Celtic Monastery, ed. and trans. by Thomas Owen Clancy and Gilbert Márkus (Edinburgh: Edinburgh University Press, 1995; repr. 2003)

Irenaeus of Lyons, *Against Heresies*, trans. by Peter Kirby, Early Christian Writings (2001–) <http://www.earlychristianwritings.com/irenaeus.html> [accessed 8 January 2024)

Irish Litanies: Text and Translation, ed. and trans. by Charles Plummer, Henry Bradshaw Society Publications, 62 (London: Harrison, 1925)

The Irish Penitentials, ed. and trans. by Ludwig Bieler (Dublin: Institute for Advanced Studies, 1963)

The Irish Sex Aetates Mundi, ed. and trans. by Dáibhí Ó Cróinín (Dublin: Institute for Advanced Studies, 1993)

Isidore of Seville, *Etymologiarum siue originum libri xx*, ed. by Wallace Martin Lindsay, Scriptorum classicorum bibliotheca Oxoniensis, 2 vols (Oxford: Clarendon, 1911)

———, *The Etymologies of Isidore of Seville*, trans. by Stephen A. Barney, W. J. Lewis, J. A. Beach, and Oliver Berghof (Cambridge: Cambridge University Press, 2006)

Íslendingabók; Landnámabók, ed. by Jakob Benediktsson, Íslenzk fornrit, 1 (Reykjavík: Hið íslenzka fornritafélag, 1986)

Íslendingabók – Kristni Saga, The Book of the Icelanders – The Story of the Conversion, trans. by Siân Grønlie, Viking Society for Northern Research Text Series, 18 (London: Viking Society for Northern Research, 2006)

King Alfred's Old English Prose Translation of the First Fifty Psalms, ed. by Patrick P. Ó Néill (Cambridge, MA: Medieval Academy of America, 2001)

King Alfred's West-Saxon Version of Gregory's Pastoral Care, ed. and trans. by Henry Sweet (London: Early English Texts Society, 1871)

King of Mysteries: Early Irish Religious Writings, trans. by John Carey (Dublin: Four Courts, 2000)

The Laws of the Earliest English Kings, ed. and trans. by F. L. Attenborough (Cambridge: Cambridge University Press, 1922; repr. New York, NY: AMS, 1974)

Lebor Gabála Érenn, The Book of the Taking of Ireland, ed. and trans. by R. A. S. Macalister, Irish Texts Society, 34; 35; 39; 41; and 44, 5 vols (Dublin: Irish Texts Society, 1938–1956)

Lebor na hUidre, ed. by R. I. Best and Osborn Bergin (Dublin: School of Celtic Studies, 1929)

Lex Baiwariorum, ed. by Ernst Schwind, Monumenta Germaniae Historica: Leges nationum Germanicarum, 5.ii (Hanover: Hahn, 1926)

The Liber de ordine creaturarum, ed. and trans. by Marina Smyth, Brepols Library of Christian Sources, 5 (Brepols: Turnhout, 2023)

Libri Epistolarum Sancti Patricii Episcopi, ed. by Ludwig Bieler (Copenhagen, 1951; repr. Dublin: Royal Irish Academy, 1993)

Lost and Found in Early Irish Law Aidbred, Heptad 64, and Muirbretha, ed. and trans. by Charlene M. Eska, Medieval Law and Its Practice, 36 (Leiden: Brill, 2022)

Marriage Disputes: A Fragmentary Old Irish Law-Text, ed. and trans. by Fergus Kelly, Early Irish Law Series, 6 (Dublin: Institute for Advanced Study, 2015)

Medieval Handbooks of Penance, trans. by John T. McNeill and Helena M. Gamer (New York, NY: Columbia University Press, 1938)

Nennius, *British History and the Welsh Annals*, ed. and trans. by John Morris (Totoaw, NJ: Rowman & Littlefield, 1980)

The Oecumenical Councils from Nicea I to Nicaea II (325–787), ed. by Giuseppe Alberigo, Corpus Christianorum Concilium Oecumenicorum Generaliumque Decreta, 1 (Turnhout: Brepols, 2006)

The Old English Orosius, ed. by Janet Bately, Early English Texts Society, s.s. 6 (Oxford: Oxford University Press, 1980)

Old Irish Wisdom Attributed to Aldfrith of Northumbria: An Edition of Bríathra Flainn Fhína maic Ossu, ed. and trans. by Colin Ireland (Tempe, AZ: Arizona Center for Medieval and Renaissance Studies, 1999)

The Patrician Texts in the Book of Armagh, ed. by Ludwig Bieler (Dublin: Institute for Advanced Studies 1979)

Pauca problesmata de enigmatibus ex tomis canonicis. Praefatio De Pentateucho Moysi, ed. by Gerard McGinty, Corpus Christianorum Series Latina Scriptores Celtigenae, 173 (Turnhout: Brepols, 2000)

Pelagius, *Expositions of the Thirteen Epistles of St Paul*, I: *Introduction*, ed. by Alexander Souter, Texts and Studies, 9, no. 1 (Cambridge: Cambridge University Press, 1922)

———, *Life and Letters*, trans. by Brinley Roderick Rees (Woodbridge: Boydell, 1991)

———, *Commentary on St Paul's Epistle to the Romans*, trans. by Theodore de Bruyn (Oxford: Clarendon, 1993)

Prosper Tiro, 'Epitoma Chronicon', in *Chronica minora saec. IV, V, VI, VII*, ed. by Theodor Mommsen, Monumenta Germaniae Historica: Auctores Antiquissimi, 9 (Berlin: Weidman, 1892), pp. 341–499

Pseudo-Cyprian, *De xii abusivis saeculi*, ed. by Siegmund Hellmann, Texte und Untersuchungen zur Geschichte der altchristlichen Literatur, 34 (Leipzig: Hinrichs, 1909), pp. 1–61

'*Sanas Cormaic*: An Old-Irish Glossary', ed. by Kuno Meyer, in *Anecdota from Irish Manuscripts*, ed. by Kuno Meyer, Osborn Bergin, R. I. Best, and J. G. O'Keeffe, 5 vols (Dublin: Hodges, Figgis & Co., 1907–1913), IV, pp. i–xix; 1–128

Sedulius Scottus, *The Harmonius Organ of Sedulius Scottus. Introduction to his Collectaneum in Apostolum and Translation of Its Prologue and Commentaries on Galatians and Ephesians*, ed. and trans. by Michael Sloan (Berlin: De Gruyter, 2012)

'The Settling of the Manor of Tara', ed. and trans. by R. I. Best, *Ériu*, 4 (1910), 121–72

'The Seventh-Century Hiberno-Latin Treatise Liber de ordine creaturarum. A Translation', trans. by Marina Smyth, *Journal of Medieval Latin*, 21 (2011), 137–222

Sulpicius Severus, 'Chronicorum, quae vulgo inscribuntur historia sacra, libri duo', in *Quinti saeculi scriptorum ecclesiasticorum qui ad S. Hieronymum usque floruerunt, nonnullis tantum exceptis, melius alibi collocandis, ut in eorum loco adnotabitur, opera omnia*, ed. by Jean-Paul Migne, Patrologia cursus completus: series latina, 20 (Paris: Garnier, 1845), cols 95A–160A

———, *The Works of Sulpicius Severus*, trans. by Alexander Roberts, in *A Select Library of the Nicene and Post-Nicene Fathers of the Christian Church*, ed. by Philip Schaff and Henry Wace, 14 vols (New York, NY: Christian Literature Company, 1894), XI, pp. 1–122

Táin bó Cúailnge: Recension 1, ed. and trans. by Cecile O'Rahilly (Dublin: Institute for Advanced Studies, 1976)

Thesaurus Palaeohibernicus, ed. by Whitley Stokes and John Strachan, 2 vols (Cambridge: Cambridge University Press, 1901–1903; repr. Dublin: Institute for Advanced Studies, 1987)

Uraicecht na Ríar: The Poetic Grades in Early Irish Law, ed. and trans. by Liam Breatnach, Early Irish Law Series, 2 (Dublin: Institute for Advanced Studies, 1987)

Secondary Sources

Anlezark, Daniel, 'Sceaf, Japheth and the Origins of the Anglo-Saxons', *Anglo-Saxon England*, 31 (2002), 13–46

d'Arbois de Jubainville, Henri, 'Le manuscrit cottonien Otho E.xiii. La Saisie Irlandaise et Galloise, la Saisine Bretonne', *Revue Celtique*, 7 (1886), 238–40

Bately, Janet, 'The Alfredian Canon Revisited: One Hundred Years On', in *Alfred the Great. Papers from the Eleventh-Centenary Conferences*, ed. by Timothy Reuter (Florence: Taylor and Francis, 2003), pp. 109–20

———, 'Old English Prose before and during the Reign of King Alfred', *Anglo-Saxon England*, 17 (1988), 93–138

———, *The Literary Prose of King Alfred's Reign, Translation or Transformation? An Inaugural Lecture in the Chair of English Language and Medieval Literature Delivered at University of London King's College on 4th March 1980* (Binghamton, NY: Center for Medieval and Early Renaissance Studies, 1984)

———, 'Lexical Evidence for the Authorship of the Prose Psalms in the Paris Psalter', *Anglo-Saxon England*, 10 (1981), 69–95

———, 'Compilation of the Anglo-Saxon Chronicle, 60 BC to AD 890: Vocabulary as Evidence', *Proceedings of the British Academy*, 64 (1978), 93–127

———, 'King Alfred and the Old English Translation of Orosius', *Anglia*, 88 (1970), 289–322

———, 'The Old English Orosius: The Question of Dictation', *Anglia*, 84 (1966), 255–304

Baumgarten, Rolf, 'Etymological Aetiology in Irish Tradition', *Ériu*, 41 (1990), 115–23

———, 'Placenames, Etymology, and the Structure of *Fianaigecht*', in *Fiannaíocht: Essays on the Fenian Tradition of Ireland and Scotland — The Heroic Process: Form, Function and Fantasy in Folk Epic*, ed. by Bo Almqvist, Séamas Ó Catháin, and Pádraig Ó hÉalaí, Béaloideas, 54/55 (Dublin: An Cumann le Béaloideas Éireann, 1987), pp. 1–24

———, 'A Hiberno-Isidorian Etymology', *Peritia*, 2 (1983), 225–28

Bieler, Ludwig, 'Editing Saint Columbanus. A Reply', *Classica et Mediaevalia*, 22 (1961), 139–50

Binchy, Daniel A., 'The Pseudo-historical Prologue to the *Senchas Már*', *Studia Celtica*, 10/11 (1975–1976), 15–28

———, 'Irish History and Irish Law: 1', *Studia Hibernica*, 15 (1975), 7–36

———, 'Distraint in Irish Law', *Celtica*, 10 (1973), 22–71

———, 'Ancient Irish Law', *The Irish Jurist*, 1 (1966), 84–92

———, 'The Linguistic and Historical Value of the Old Irish Law Tracts', *Proceedings of the British Academy*, 29 (1943), 195–227; repr. *Celtic Law Papers Introductory to Welsh Medieval Law and Government*, ed. by Dafydd Jenkins, Studies Presented to the International Commission for the History of Representative and Parliamentary Institutions, 42 (Brussels: Les Éditions de la Librairie encyclopédique, 1973), pp. 71–107

Bischoff, Bernhard, 'Wendepunkte in der Geschichte der Lateinischen Exegese im Frühmittelalter', *Sacris Erudiri*, 6 (1964), 189–279; repr. Bernhard Bischoff, *Mittelalterliche Studien: Ausgewählte Aufsätze zur Schriftkunde und zur Literaturgeschichte*, 3 vols (Stuttgart: Hiersemann 1966–1981), I, pp. 206–73; trans. by Colm O'Grady, 'Turning-points in the History of Latin Exegesis in the Early Middle Ages', in *Biblical Studies: The Medieval Irish Contribution*, ed. by Martin McNamara, Proceedings of the Irish Biblical Association, 1 (Dublin: Dominican, 1976), pp. 74–160

Bleich, J. David, 'Judaism and Natural Law', *The Jewish Law Annual*, 7 (1988), 5–42

Boadt, Lawrence, and Alice Thomas Ellis, *The Book of Job: Why do the Innocent Suffer?* (New York, NY: Palgrave Macmillan, 1999)

Bonner, Ali, *The Myth of Pelagianism* (Oxford: Oxford University Press, 2018)

Boyle, Elizabeth, *History and Salvation in Medieval Ireland*, Studies in Early Medieval Britain and Ireland (London: Routledge, 2020)

Bracken, Damian, 'Juniors Teaching Elders. Columbanus, Rome and Spiritual Authority', in *Roma Felix - Formation and Reflections of Medieval Rome*, ed. by Éamonn Ó Carragáin and Carol Neuman De Vegvar (Aldershot: Ashgate, 2007), pp. 252–73

———, 'Authority and Duty: Columbanus and the Primacy of Rome', *Peritia*, 16 (2002), 168–213

———, 'The Fall and the Law in Early Ireland', *Irland und Europa im Früheren Mittelalter: Texte und Überlieferung / Ireland and Europe in the Early Middle Ages: Texts and Transmission*, ed. by Próinséas Ní Chatháin and Michael Richter (Dublin: Four Courts, 2001), pp. 147–69

———, 'Immortality and Capital Punishment: Patristic Concepts in Irish Law', *Peritia*, 9 (1995), 167–86

Bradshaw, Henry, *The Early Collection of Canons Known as the Hibernensis: Two Unfinished Papers* (Cambridge: Cambridge University Press, 1893)

Brady, Lindy, *The Origin Legends of Early Medieval Britain and Ireland* (Cambridge: Cambridge University Press, 2022)

———, and Patrick Wadden, eds, *Origin Legends in Early Medieval Western Europe* (Leiden: Brill, 2022)

Brasington, Bruce, '*Congrega seniores provinciae*: A Note on a Hiberno-Latin Canon Concerning the Sources of Authority in Ecclesiastical Law', in *Plenitude of Power: The Doctrines and Exercise of Authority in the Middle Ages: Essays in Memory of Robert Louis Benson*, ed. by Robert Charles Figueira (Aldershot: Ashgate, 2006), pp. 1–10

Breatnach, Liam, *The Early Irish Law Text Senchas Már and the Question of its Date*, Quiggin Pamphlets on the Sources of Mediaeval Gaelic History, 13 (Cambridge: Department of Anglo-Saxon, Norse, and Celtic, 2011)

———, 'Satire, Praise and the Early Irish Poet', *Ériu*, 56 (2006), 63–84

———, *A Companion to the Corpus Iuris Hibernici* (Dublin: Institute for Advanced Studies, 2005)

———, 'Law', in *Progress in Medieval Irish Studies*, ed. by Kim McCone and Katherine Simms (Maynooth: Department of Old Irish, Saint Patrick's College, 1996), pp. 107–21

———, 'On the Glossing of the Early Irish Law-Texts, Fragmentary Texts, and Some Aspects of the Laws Relating to Dogs', in *Celtica Helsingiensia; Proceedings from a Symposium on Celtic Studies*, ed. by Anders Alqvist (Helsinki: Societas Scientiarum Fennica 1996), pp. 11–20

———, 'The Ecclesiastical Element in the Old Irish Legal Tract *Cáin Fhuithurbe*', *Peritia*, 5 (1986), 36–52

———, 'Canon Law and Secular Law in Early Ireland: The Significance of *Bretha Nemed*', *Peritia*, 3 (1984), 439–59

Breen, Aidan, 'Pseudo-Cyprian *De duodecim abusivis saeculi* and the Bible', in *Irland und die Christenheit. Bibelstudien und Mission / Ireland and Christendom. The Bible and the Missions*, ed. by Próinséas Ní Chatháin and Michael Richter (Stuttgart: Klett-Cotta, 1987), pp. 230–45

Brüning, Gertrud, 'Adamnans Vita Columbae und ihre Ableitungen', *Zeitschrift für Celtische Philologie*, 11 (1917), 213–304

Bullough, Donald A., 'The Career of Columbanus', in *Columbanus: Studies on the Latin Writings*, ed. by Michael Lapidge (Woodbridge: Boydell, 1997), pp. 1–28

———, 'Albinus deliciosus Caroli Regis', in *Institutionen, Kultur und Gesellschaft im Mittelalter: Festschrift für Josef Fleckenstein zu seinem 65. Geburtstag*, ed. By Josef Fleckenstein, Lutz Fenske, Werner Rösener, and Thomas Zotz (Sigmaringen: Thorbecke, 1984), pp. 73–92

Carella, Bryan (who now publishes under the name 'Kristen Carella'), 'The Earliest Expression for Outlawry in Anglo-Saxon Law', *Traditio*, 70 (2015), 111–44

———, 'Asser's Bible and the Prologue to the Laws of Alfred', *Anglia*, 130 (2012), 195–206

———, 'Alcuin and the Legatine Capitulary of 786: The Evidence of Scriptural Citations', *Journal of Medieval Latin*, 22 (2012), 221–56

———, 'Divine Law in the Pauline Commentary of the Eighth-Century, Hiberno-Latin *Reference Bible*', *Proceedings of the Harvard Celtic Colloquium*, 31 (2012), 74–90

———, 'Evidence for Hiberno-Latin Thought in the Prologue to the Laws of Alfred', *Studies in Philology*, 108 (2011), 1–26

———, 'The Source for the Prologue to the Laws of Alfred', *Peritia*, 19 (2005), 91–118

Carella, Kristen, *Northumbrian Law before the Vikings*, Quiggin Pamphlets on the Sources of Mediaeval Gaelic History, 25 (Cambridge: Department of Anglo-Saxon, Norse, and Celtic, 2024)

———, 'Northumbrian Law before the Vikings: A Preliminary Assessment of the Evidence', in *Languages of the Law in Early Medieval England. Essays in Memory of Lisi Oliver*, ed. by Stefan Jurasinksi and Andrew Rabin, Mediaevalia Groningana, n.s. 22 (Leuven: Peeters, 2019), pp. 45–54

———, 'The Historical and Literary Context of the Legatine Capitulary of 786 in England and Abroad', in *Law, Literature, and Social Regulation in Early Medieval England*, ed. by Andrew Rabin and Anya Adair (Woodbridge: Boydell and Brewer, 2023), pp. 137–50

Carey, John, 'Native Elements in Irish Pseudohistory', *Cultural Identity and Cultural Integration: Ireland and Europe in the early Middle Ages*, ed. by Doris Edel (Dublin: Four Courts, 1995), pp. 45–60

———, *The Irish National Origin-Legend: Synthetic Pseudohistory*, Quiggin Pamphlets on the Sources of Mediaeval Gaelic History, 1 (Cambridge: Department of Anglo-Saxon, Norse, and Celtic, 1994)

———, 'The Ancestry of Fénius Farsaid', *Celtica*, 21 (1990), 104–12

———, 'The Two Laws in Dubthach's Judgment', *Cambridge Medieval Celtic Studies*, 19 (1990), 1–18

———, 'The Origin and Development of the Cesair Legend', *Éigse*, 22 (1987), 37–48

Carney, James, 'The Dating of Archaic Irish Verse', in *Mündlichkeit und Schriftlichkeit in der Frühen Irischen Literatur / Early Irish Literature – Media and Communication*, ed. by Stephen N. Tranter and Hildegard L. C. Tristram, Script Oralia, 10 (Tübingen: Narr, 1989), pp. 39–55

Charles-Edwards, Thomas M., *Early Christian Ireland* (Cambridge: Cambridge University Press, 2000)

———, *The Early Mediaeval Gaelic Lawyer*, Quiggin Pamphlets on the Sources of Mediaeval Gaelic History, 4 (Cambridge: Department of Anglo-Saxon, Norse, and Celtic, 1999)

———, 'The Context and Uses of Literacy in Early Christian Ireland', in *Literacy in Medieval Celtic Societies*, ed. by Huw Pryce (Cambridge: Cambridge University Press, 1998), pp. 62–82

———, 'Early Irish Law', in *A New History of Ireland, I: Prehistoric and Early Ireland*, ed. by Dáibhí Ó Cróinín (Oxford, 1972; repr. 1993), pp. 342–43

———, 'Celtic Kings: "Priestly Vegetables?"', in *Early Medieval Studies in Memory of Patrick Wormald*, ed. by Stephen David Baxter (Farnham: Ashgate, 2009), pp. 65–80

Clement, Richard W., 'The Production of the *Pastoral Care*: King Alfred and his Helpers', in *Studies in Earlier Old English Prose*, ed. by Paul Szarmach (Albany, NY: State University of New York Press, 1986), pp. 129–52

Cook, Albert S., 'Alfred's "Word for Word" Translation', *Academy*, 30 (1886), 108

Corning, Caitlin, *The Celtic and Roman Traditions. Conflict and Consensus in the Early Medieval Church* (New York, NY: Palgrave MacMillan, 2006)

Corthals, Johan, 'Zur Frage des mündlichen oder schriftlichen Ursprungs der Sagen *roscada*', in *Early Irish Literature – Media and Communication*, ed. by Stephen Norman Tranter and Hildegard L. C. Tristram, Script Oralia, 10 (Tübingen: Narr, 1989), pp. 201–20

———, 'Early Irish *retoirics* and their Late Antique Background', *Cambridge Medieval Celtic Studies*, 31 (1996), 17–36

Cubitt, Catherine, *Anglo-Saxon Church Councils, c. 650–850* (London: Leicester University Press, 1995)

Dailey, Erin T., 'To Choose One Easter from Three: Oswiu's Decision and the Northumbrian Synod of 664', *Peritia*, 26 (2015), 47–64

Davies, Luned Mair, 'The Biblical Text of the Collectio Canonum Hibernensis', in *Irland und Europa in Früheren Mittelalter / Ireland and Europe in the Early Middle Ages*, ed. by Próinséas Ní Chatháin and Michael Richter (Stuttgart: Klett-Cotta, 1996), 17–41

Davies, Wendy, 'Alfred's Contemporaries: Irish, Welsh, Scots and Breton', in *Alfred the Great. Papers from the Eleventh-Centenary Conferences*, ed. by Timothy Reuter (Florence: Taylor and Francis, 2003), pp. 323–37

Davis, Craig R., 'Cultural Assimilation in the Anglo-Saxon Royal Genealogies', *Anglo-Saxon England*, 21 (1992), 23–36

Davis, Kathleen, 'National Writing in the Ninth Century: A Reminder for Postcolonial Thinking about the Nation', *Journal of Medieval and Early Modern Studies*, 28 (1998), 611–37

Dictionary of Medieval Latin from British Sources, ed. by R. E. Latham, D. R. Howlett, and Richard Ashdown (Turnhout: Brepols, 2015) <https://clt-brepolis-net.ezp-prod1.hul.harvard.edu/dmlbs/Default.aspx> [accessed 11 January 2024]

The Dictionary of Old English: A to I, ed. by Angus Cameron, Ashley Crandell Amos, and Antonette DiPaolo Healey (Toronto: University of Toronto Pres, 2007–) <https://tapor-library-utoronto-ca.lib.assumption.edu/doe/> [accessed 28 December 2023]

Discenza, Nicole Guenther, '"Wise Wealhstodas": The Prologue to Sirach as a Model for Alfred's Preface to the *Pastoral Care*', *Journal of English and Germanic Philology*, 97 (1998), 488–95

Donahue, Charles, 'Beowulf and Christian Tradition: A Reconsideration from a Celtic Stance', *Traditio*, 21 (1965), 55–116

———, 'Beowulf, Ireland, and the Natural Good', *Traditio*, 7 (1949–51), 263–77

Doorly, William J., *The Laws of Yahweh. A Handbook of Biblical Law* (New York, NY: Paulist, 2002)

Dumville, David N., *A Palaeographer's Review: The Insular System of Scripts in the Early Middle Ages*, Kansai University Institute of Oriental and Occidental Studies Sources and Materials, 20.1, 2 vols (Suita: Institute of Oriental and Occidental Studies, 2007)

———, 'The West Saxon Genealogical Regnal List and the Chronology of Early Wessex', *Peritia*, 4 (1985), 21–66

———, 'Late Seventh- or Eighth-Century Evidence for British Transmission of Pelagius', *Cambridge Medieval Celtic Studies*, 10 (1985), 39–52

———, 'Kingship, Genealogies, and Regnal Lists', in *Early Medieval Kingship*, ed. by P. H. Sawyer and Ian Wood (Leeds: University of Leeds, 1979), pp. 72–104

———, 'The Anglian Collection of Royal Genealogies', *Anglo-Saxon England*, 5 (1976), 23–50

eDIL 2019: An Electronic Dictionary of the Irish Language, based on the Contributions to a Dictionary of the Irish Language (Dublin: Royal Irish Academy, 1913–1976) <www.dil.ie> [accessed 29 December 2023]

Edmonds, Fiona, *Gaelic Influence in the Northumbrian Kingdom. The Golden Age and the Viking Age* (Woodbridge: Boydell, 2019)

Esposito, Mario, 'On the New Edition of the *Opera Sancti Columbani*', *Classica et Mediaevalia*, 21 (1960), 184–203

Etchingham, Colmán, 'Conversion in Ireland', in *The Introduction of Christianity into the Early Medieval Insular World*, ed. by Roy Flechner and Máire Ní Mhaonaigh (Turnhout: Brepols, 2016), pp. 181–207

———, 'Bishops, Church and People: How Christian Was "Early Christian Ireland?"', in *L'irlanda e gli irlandesi nell'alto medioevo*, Settimane di studio della Fondazione Centro italiano di studi sull'alto Medioevo, 57 (Spoleto: Presso la sede della Fondazione, 2010), pp. 325–48

Evans, Nicholas, *The Present and the Past in Medieval Irish Chronicles* (Woodbridge: Boydell and Brewer, 2010)

Flechner, Roy, and Sven Meeder, *The Irish in Early Medieval Europe: Identity, Culture and Religion* (New York, NY: Bloomsbury, 2016)

Foot, Sarah, 'The Making of *Angelcynn*: English National Identity before the Norman Conquest', *Transactions of the Royal Historical Society, Sixth Series*, 6 (1996), 25–49

Fournier, Paul, '*Liber ex lege Moysi* et les tendances bibliques du droit canonique irlandais', *Revue Celtique*, 30 (1909), 221–34

Frantzen, Allen, 'The Form and Function of the Preface in the Poetry and Prose of Alfred's Reign', in *Alfred the Great. Papers from the Eleventh-Centenary Conferences*, ed. by Timothy Reuter (Florence: Taylor and Francis, 2003), pp. 121–36

———, *King Alfred* (Boston: Twayne, 1986)

Gerriets, Marilyn, 'Theft, Penitentials and the Compilation of the Early Irish Laws', *Celtica*, 22 (1991), 18–32

Gill, Paramjit S., Tim B. Swartz, and Michael Treschow, 'King Alfred's Scholarly Writings and the Authorship of the First Fifty Prose Psalms', *The Heroic Age* (= *The Journal of Early Medieval Northwestern Europe*), 12 (2009) <https://jemne.org/issues/12/treschowgillswartz.php> [accessed 19 September 2023]

———, 'A Stylometric Analysis of King Alfred's Literary Works', *Journal of Applied Statistics*, 34 (2007), 1251–58

Oxford Latin Dictionary, ed. by P. G. W. Glare (Oxford: Clarendon, 1968–1982)

Godden, Malcolm, 'Did King Alfred Write Anything?', *Medium Ævum*, 76 (2007), 1–23

———, 'Wærferth and King Alfred: The Fate of the Old English *Dialogues*', in *Alfred the Wise. Studies in Honour of Janet Bately on the Occasion of her Sixty-fifth Birthday*, ed. by Jane Roberts and Janet L. Nelson, with Malcolm Godden (Cambridge: Brewer, 1997), pp. 35–51

Goodrich, Peter, and Yifat Hachamovitch, 'Time out of Mind: An Introduction to the Semiotics of Common Law', *Dangerous Supplements: Resistance and Renewal in Jurisprudence*, ed. by Peter Fitzpatrick (Durham, NC: Duke University Press, 1991), pp. 159–81

Gougaud, Louis, *Christianity in the Celtic Lands* (London: Sheed and Ward, 1932; repr. Dublin: Four Courts, 1992)

Grabowski, Kathryn, and David Dumville, *Chronicles and Annals of Medieval Ireland and Wales: The Clonmacnoise-Group Texts* (Woodbridge: Boydell, 1984)

Gwynn, Aubrey, and Richard Neville Hadcock, *Medieval Religious Houses, Ireland* (London: Longmans, 1970)

Hardinge, Leslie, *The Celtic Church in Britain* (London: S.P.C.K., 1972)

Harris, Stephen J., *Race and Ethnicity in Anglo-Saxon Literature* (New York, NY: Routledge, 2003)

———, 'The Alfredian *World History* and Anglo-Saxon Identity', *Journal of English and Germanic Philology*, 100 (2001), 482–510

Hartmann, Hans, 'Was Ist "Wahrheit"', *Zeitschrift für Celtische Philologie*, 49/50 (1997), 287–309

Hay, M. V., 'Columbanus and Rome', *Revue Celtique*, 38 (1920/1921), 315–19
Herren, Michael W., and Shirley Ann Brown, *Christ in Celtic Christianity: Britain and Ireland from the Fifth to the Tenth Centuries*, Studies in Celtic History, 20 (Woodbridge: Boydell, 2002)
Howe, Nicholas, *Migration and Mythmaking in Anglo-Saxon England* (New Haven, CT: Yale University Press, 1989)
Hughes, Kathleen, 'Evidence for Contacts between the Churches of the Irish and the English from the Synod of Whitby to the Viking Age', in *England Before the Conquest*, ed. by Peter Clemoes and Kathleen Hughes (Cambridge: Cambridge University Press, 1971), pp. 49–67
———, *The Church in Early Irish Society* (Ithaca, NY: Cornell University Press, 1966)
Jenkins, Dafydd, 'The Medieval Welsh Idea of Law', *Tijdschrift voor Rechtsgeschiedenis*, 49 (1981), 323–48
Johnston, Elva, *Literacy and Identity in Early Medieval Ireland*, Studies in Celtic History, 33 (Woodbridge: Boydell, 2013)
Jón Hnefill Aðalsteinsson, *Under the Cloak: A Pagan Ritual Turning Point in the Conversion of Iceland*, 2nd extended edn (Reykjavík: Háskólaútgáfan, 1999)
Jurasinski, Stefan, 'Slavery, Learning, and the Law of Marriage in Alfred's Mosaic Prologue', *Secular Learning in Anglo-Saxon England: Exploring the Vernacular*, ed. by Lászlo Sándor Chardonnens and Bryan Carella (who now publishes under the name 'Kristen Carella'), Amsterdamer Beiträge zur älteren Germanistik, 69 (Amsterdam: Rodopi, 2012), pp. 45–64
Kelly, Fergus, *A Guide to Early Irish Law* (Dublin: Institute for Advanced Studies, 2005)
Kelly, Joseph F. T., 'Das Bibelwerk: Organization and Quellenanalyse of the New Testament', in *Irland und die Christenheit: Bibelstudien und Mission / Ireland and Christendom: The Bible and the Missions*, ed. by Próinséas Ní Chatháin and Michael Richter (Stuttgart: Klett-Cotta, 1987), pp. 113–23
———, 'Pelagius, Pelagianism, and Early Christian Ireland', *Mediaevalia*, 4 (1978), 99–124
———, 'Augustine in Hiberno-Latin Literature', *Augustinian Studies*, 8 (1977), 139–49
Kenney, James F., *Sources for the Early History of Ireland*, I: *Ecclesiastical* (New York, NY: Columbia University Press, 1929; repr. Dublin: Four Courts, 1993)
Kéry, Lotte, *Canonical Collections of the Early Middle Ages (ca. 400–1140)*, History of Medieval Canon Law Series (Washington, DC: Catholic University of America Press, 1999)
Kottje, Raymund, 'Der *Liber ex lege Moysis*', in *Irland und die Christenheit: Bibel und Mission / Ireland and Christendom: The Bible and the Missions*, ed. by Próinséas Ní Chatháin and Michael Richter (Stuttgart: Klett-Cotta, 1987), pp. 59–69
———, *Studien zum Einfluss des Alten Testamentes auf Recht und Liturgie des Frühen Mittelalters*, Bonner Historische Forschungen, 23 (Bonn: Röhrscheid, 1963)

Ladner, Gerhart B., 'On Roman Attitudes toward Barbarians in Late Antiquity', *Viator*, 7 (1967), 1–25
Lapidge, Michael, and Richard Sharpe, *Bibliography of Celtic-Latin Literature, 400–1200* (Dublin: Royal Irish Academy, 1985)
Levison, Wilhelm, *England and the Continent in the Eighth Century* (Oxford: Oxford University Press, 1946)
MacCana, Proinsias, 'The Three Languages and the Three Laws', *Studia Celtica*, 5 (1970), 77–78
Mackey, James P., 'The Theology of Columbanus', in *Irland und Europa im früheren Mittelalter: Bildung und Literatur / Ireland and Europe in the Early Middle Ages: Learning and Literature*, ed. by Próinséas Ní Chatháin and Michael Richter (Stuttgart: Klett-Cotta 1996), pp. 228–39
MacNeill, Eoin, 'Ancient Irish Law. The Law of Status and Franchise', *Proceedings of the Royal Irish Academy*, 36 (1921/1924), 265–316
Mac Niocaill, Gearóid, *The Medieval Irish Annals* (Dublin: Dublin Historical Association, 1975)
Markus, Robert Austin, 'Pelagianism: Britain and the Continent', *Journal of Ecclesiastical History*, 37 (1986), 191–204
Markús, Gilbert, *Conceiving a Nation: Scotland to 900 A.D.* (Edinburgh: Edinburgh University Press, 2017)
Martin, Lawrence T., and Thomas N. Hall, 'The Enumeration of Laws Motif in the Middle English Homily *An Bispel*', in *Models of Holiness in Medieval Sermons*, ed. by Beverly Mayne Kienzle, Textes et Études du Moyen Âge, 5 (Louvaine-La-Neuve: Fédération internationale des Instituts d'études médiévales, 1995), pp. 47–65
Mathisen, Ralph W., 'Barbarian Bishops and the Churches "in barbaricis gentibus" during Late Antiquity', *Speculum*, 72 (1997), 664–97
———, *Roman Aristocrats in Barbarian Gaul: Strategies for Survival in an Age of Transition* (Austin, TX: University of Texas Press, 1993)
Mayr-Harting, Henry, *The Coming of Christianity to Anglo-Saxon England*, 3rd edn (University Park, PA: Pennsylvania State University Press, 1991)
McCann, Sarah, 'Bede's "Plures De Scottorum Regione": The Irish in the "Historia Ecclesiastica Gentis Anglorum"' (unpublished doctoral thesis, National University of Ireland, Galway, 2013)
McCone, Kim, *Pagan Past Christian Present in Early Irish Literature*, Maynooth Monographs, 3 (Maynooth: An Sagairt, 1990)
———, 'Dubthach maccu Lugair and a Matter of Life and Death in the Pseudo-Historical Prologue to the *Senchas Már*', *Peritia*, 5 (1986), 1–35
Magoun, Francis P., 'Some Notes on King Alfred's Circular Letter on Educational Policy Addressed to His Bishops', *Medieval Studies*, 10 (1948), 93–108
McCarthy, Daniel P., 'The Chronology of the Irish Annals', *Proceedings of the Royal Irish Academy: Archaeology, Culture, History, Literature*, 98C.6 (1998), 203–55
McKitterick, Rosamond, *The Frankish Church and the Carolingian Reforms 789–895* (London: Royal Historical Society, 1977)

McLeod, Neil, 'A True Companion to the *Corpus Iuris Hibernici*', *Peritia*, 19 (2005), 136–63

———, 'The Concept of Law in Ancient Irish Jurisprudence', *The Irish Jurist*, 17 (1982), 356–67

McNally, Robert E., '"Dies Dominica": Two Hiberno-Latin Texts', *Medieval Studies*, 22 (1960), 357

McNamara, Martin, 'Midrash, Apocrypha, Culture Medium and Development of Doctrine. Some Facts in Quest of a Terminology', *Apocrypha*, 6 (1995), 127–64

———, 'Sources and Affiliations of the *Catechesis Celtica* (MS. Vat. Reg. lat. 49)', *Sacris Erudiri*, 34 (1994), 185–237

———, 'Midrash, Culture Medium and Development of Doctrine. Some Facts in Quest of a Terminology', *Proceedings of the Irish Biblical Association*, 11 (1988), 67–87

———, 'Plan and Source Analysis of *Das Bibelwerk*, Old Testament', in *Irland und die Christenheit: Bibelstudien und Mission / Ireland and Christendom: The Bible and the Missions*, ed. by Próinséas Ní Chatháin und Michael Richter (Stuttgart: Klett-Cotta, 1987), pp. 84–111

———, *The Apocrypha in the Irish Church* (Dublin: Institute for Advanced Studies, 1975)

Meeder, Sven, 'The *Liber ex lege Moysi*: Notes and Text', *Journal of Medieval Latin*, 19 (2009), 173–218

Meens, Rob, 'Politics, Mirrors of Princes and the Bible: Sins, Kings and the Well-being of the Realm', *Early Medieval Europe*, 7 (1998), 345–57

Meroney, Howard, 'Studies in Early Irish Satire I–II', *Journal of Celtic Studies*, 1 (1949/1950), 199–226

———, 'Studies in Early Irish Satire III', *Journal of Celtic Studies*, 2 (1953–1958), 59–130

Moisl, Hermann, 'The Church and the Native Tradition of Learning in Early Medieval Ireland', in *Irland und die Christenheit / Ireland and Christendom*, ed. by Próinséas Ní Chatháin and Michael Richter (Stuttgart: Klett-Cotta, 1987), pp. 258–71

———, 'Anglo-Saxon Royal Genealogies and Germanic Oral Tradition', *Journal of Medieval History*, 7 (1981), 215–48

Molyneaux, George, 'Did the English Really Think They Were God's Elect during the Anglo-Saxon Period?', *Journal of Ecclesiastical History*, 64 (2014), 721–37

———, 'The *Old English Bede*: English Ideology or Christian Instruction?', *English Historical Review*, 125 (2009), 1289–323

Nagy, Josef Falaky, *Conversing with the Angels and Ancients. Literary Myths of Medieval Ireland* (Ithaca, NY: Cornell University Press, 1997)

Nelson, Janet L., 'Presidential Address: England and the Continent in the Ninth Century: II the Vikings and Others', *Transactions of the Royal Historical Society*, Sixth Series, 13 (2003), 1–28

———, '"...*sicut olim gens Francorum...nunc gens Anglorum*": Fulk's Letter to Alfred Revisited', in *Alfred the Wise: Studies in Honour of Janet Bately on the occasion of her 65th Birthday*, ed. by Malcolm Godden, Jane Roberts, and Janet L. Nelson (Woodbridge: Brewer, 1997; repr. *Rulers and Ruling Families in Early Medieval Europe. Alfred, Charles the Bald, and Others*, ed. by Janet L. Nelson (Brookfiled, VT: Ashgate, 1999)

———, 'The Political Ideas of Alfred of Wessex', in *Kings and Kingship in Medieval Europe*, ed. by Anne Duggan (London: King's College London Centre for Late Antique and Medieval Studies, 1993), pp. 125–58

Nerney, D. S. 'A Study of St Patrick's Sources: II – The Doctrine of Divine Vocation', *Irish Ecclesiastical Record*, 72 (1949), 14–26

———, 'A Study of St Patrick's Sources: IV – Proof of Divine Vocation', *Irish Ecclesiastical Record*, 72 (1949), 263–80

Ní Chatháin, Próinséas, and Michael Richter, eds, *Irland und Europa im früheren Mittelalter: Texte und Überlieferung / Ireland and Europe in the Early Middle Ages: Texts and Transmission* (Dublin: Four Courts, 2002)

O'Brien, Conor, 'The New Israel Motif in Early Medieval Origin Legends', in *Origin Legends in Early Medieval Western Europe*, ed. by Lindy Brady and Patrick Wadden (Leiden: Brill, 2022), pp. 239–58

Ó Cathasaigh, Tómas, *Táin Bó Cúailnge and Early Irish Law*, Osborn Bergin Memorial Lecture, 5 (Dublin: Faculty of Celtic Studies, University College Dublin, 2005)

Ó Corráin, Donnchadh, 'Irish Vernacular Law and the Old Testament', in *Irland und die Christenheit: Bibel und Mission / Ireland and Christendom: The Bible and the Missions*, ed. by Próinséas Ní Chatháin and Michael Richter (Stuttgart: Klett-Cotta, 1987), pp. 284–307

———, 'Irish Law and Canon Law', in *Irland und Europa: die Kirche im Frühmittelalter / Ireland and Europe: The Church in the Early Middle Ages*, ed. by Próinséas Ní Chatháin and Michael Richter (Stuttgart: Klett-Cotta, 1984), pp. 157–66

———, Liam Breatnach, and Aidan Breen, 'The Laws of the Irish', *Peritia*, 3 (1984), 382–438

———, 'Early Irish Churches: Some Aspects of Organisation', in *Irish Antiquity*, ed. by Donnchadh Ó Corráin (Cork: Cork University Press, 1981), pp. 320–41

———, 'Nationality and Kingship in Pre-Norman Ireland', in *Nationality and the Pursuit of National Independence*, ed. by T. W. Moody (Belfast: Appletree, 1978), pp. 1–35

Ó Cróinín, Dáibhí, 'New Heresy for Old: Pelagianism in Ireland and the Papal Letter of 640', *Speculum*, 60 (1985), 505–16

O'Loughlin, Thomas, *Celtic Theology* (London: Continuum, 2000)

———, 'Tradition and Exegesis in the Eighth Century: The Use of Patristic Sources in Early Medieval Scriptural Commentaries', in *The Scriptures in Early Medieval Ireland*, ed. by Thomas O'Loughlin, Instrumenta Patristica, 31 (Turnhout: Brepols, 1999), pp. 217–39

———, 'The Library of Iona in the Late Seventh Century; The Evidence from Adomnán's *De Lociis Sanctis*', *Ériu*, 45 (1994), 33–52

Ó Néill, Pádraig P., *Biblical Study and Mediaeval Gaelic History*, Quiggin Pamphlets on the Sources of Mediaeval Gaelic History, 6 (Cambridge: Department of Anglo-Saxon, Norse, and Celtic, 2003)

———, '*Romani* Influences on Seventh-Century Hiberno-Latin Literature', in *Irland und Europa: Die Kirche im Frühmittelalter / Ireland and Europe: The Early Church*, ed. by Próinséas Ní Chatháin and Michael Richter (Stuttgart: Klett-Cotta, 1984), pp. 280–90

O'Reilly, Jennifer, 'Islands and Idols at the End of the Earth: Exegesis and Conversion in Bede's *Historia Ecclesiastica*', in *Bède le Vénérable: Entre tradition et postérité / The Venerable Bede: Tradition and Posterity*, ed. by Stéphane Lebecq, Michel Perrin, and Olivier Szerwiniack (Lille: Ceges, 2005), pp. 119–45

O'Sullivan, Tomás, '"Let deaths be died": Dubthach's Judgement and the Justification of Capital Punishment in a Christian Society' (unpublished MA thesis, University College Cork, 2000)

Oxford English Dictionary (Oxford: Oxford University Press, 2000–) <https://www.oed.com> [accessed 9 January 2024]

Poppe, Erich, *Of Cycles and Other Critical Matters. Some Issues in Medieval Irish Literary History and Criticism*, Quiggin Pamphlets on the Sources of Mediaeval Gaelic History, 9 (Cambridge: Department of Anglo-Saxon, Norse, and Celtic, 2008)

Pratt, David, *The Political Thought of King Alfred the Great* (Cambridge: Cambridge University Press, 2007)

Qiu, Fangzhe, 'The Ulster Cycle in the Law Tracts', *Ulidia*, 4 (2017), 9–22

———, 'Law, Law-books and Tradition in Early Medieval Ireland', in *Law | Book | Culture in the Middle Ages*, ed. by Thom Gobbitt, Explorations in Medieval Culture, 14 (Leiden: Brill, 2021), pp. 126–46

Rabin, Andrew, 'Law and Justice', in *The Blackwell Handbook of Anglo-Saxon Studies*, ed. by Jacqueline Stodnick and Renee Trilling (Oxford: Blackwell, 2012), pp. 85–98

A Revised Medieval Latin Word-List, ed. by Ronald Edward Latham (London: Oxford University Press, 1965)

Reynolds, Susan, 'What Do We Mean by "Anglo-Saxon" and "Anglo-Saxons"?', *The Journal of British Studies*, 24 (1985), 395–414

Russell, Paul, review of *The Hibernensis: Book I, A Study and Edition and Book II, Translation, Commentary and Indexes*, ed. and trans. by Roy Flechner (2019), *North American Journal of Celtic Studies*, 5 (2021), 116–27

Ryan, Martin J., 'Archbishop Ecgberht and His *Dialogus*', in *Leaders of the Anglo-Saxon Church: From Bede to Stigand*, ed. by Alexander R. Rumble (Woodbridge: Boydell & Brewer, 2012), pp. 41–60

Scheil, Andrew, *The Footsteps of Israel. Understanding Jews in Anglo-Saxon England* (Ann Arbor, MI: University of Michigan Press, 2004)

Scowcroft, R. Mark, '*Recht Fáide* and Its Gloss in the Pseudo-historical Prologue to the *Senchus Már*', *Ériu*, 53 (2003), 143–50

———, '*Leabhar Gabhála*, Part I: The Growth of the Text', *Ériu*, 38 (1987), 79–140

———, '*Leabhar Gabhála*, Part II: The Growth of the Tradition', *Ériu*, 39 (1988), 1–66

Sdralek, M., *Wolfenbüttler Fragmente: Analekten zur Kirchengeschichte des Mittelalters aus Wolfenbüttler Handschriften* (Münster: Schöningh, 1891)

Sharpe, Richard, *A Handlist of the Latin Writers of Great Britain and Ireland before 1540*, Publications of the Journal of Medieval Latin, 1 (Turnhout: Brepols, 1997; reissued with additions and corrections, 2001)

Sims-Williams, Patrick, and Erich Poppe, 'Medieval Irish Literary Theory and Criticism', in *The Cambridge History of Literary Criticism*, II: *The Middle Ages*, ed. by Alistair Minnis and Ian Johnson (Cambridge: Cambridge University Press, 2005), pp. 289–309

Sisam, Kenneth, 'The Authorship of the Verse Translation of Boethius' *Metra*', in *Studies in the History of Old English Literature*, ed. by Kenneth Sisam (Oxford: Clarendon, 1953), pp. 293–97

———, 'Anglo-Saxon Royal Genealogies', *Proceedings of the British Academy*, 39 (1953), 287–348

Smit, Johannes Wilhelmus, *Studies on the Language and Style of Columba the Younger (Columbanus)* (Amsterdam: Hakkert, 1971)

Stacey, Robin Chapman, *Dark Speech: The Performance of Law in Early Ireland* (Philadelphia, PA: University of Pennsylvania Press, 2007)

———, 'Law and Literature in Medieval Ireland and Wales', in *Medieval Celtic Literature and Society*, ed. by Helen Fulton (Dublin: Four Courts, 2005), pp. 65–82

———, 'Law and Order in the Very Old West: England and Ireland in the Early Middle Ages', in *Crossed Paths. Methodological Approaches to the Celtic Aspect of the European Middle Ages*, ed. by Benjamin T. Hudson and Vickie Ziegler (Lanham, MD: University Press of America, 1991), pp. 39–60

Stancliffe, Claire, 'Red, White and Blue Martyrdom', in *Ireland in Early Medieval Europe: Studies in Memory of Kathleen Hughes*, ed. by Dorothy Whitelock, Rosamond McKitterick, and David N. Dumville (Cambridge: Cambridge University Press, 1982), pp. 21–46

Stokes, Whitley, 'Old Breton Glosses', *Revue Celtique*, 4 (1879/1880), 324–48

Story, Joanna, *Carolingian Connections: Anglo-Saxon England and Carolingian Francia, c. 750–870* (Farnham: Ashgate, 2009)

Strachan, John, review of *Fled Bricrend*, ed. and trans. by George Henderson (1899), *Zeitschrift für Celtische Philologie*, 3 (1901), 410–24

Summerfield, Thea, 'Filling the Gap: Brutus in the Historia Brittonum, Anglo-Saxon Chronicle MS F, and Geoffrey of Monmouth', in *The Medieval Chronicle VII*, ed. by Juliana Dresvina and Nicholas Sparks (Amsterdam: Rodopi, 2011), pp. 85–102

Thurneysen, Rudolf, 'Morands Fürstenspiegel', *Zeitschrift für Celtische Philologie*, 11 (1917), 65–106

Treschow, Michael, 'The Prologue to Alfred's Law Code: Instruction in the Spirit of Mercy', *Florilegium*, 13 (1994), 79–110

Wadden, Patrick, 'The Pseudo-Historical Origins of the *Senchas Már* and Royal Legislation in Early Ireland', *Peritia*, 27 (2016), 141–58

Wallace-Hadrill, J. M., *Early Medieval History* (Oxford: Blackwell, 1975)

Warntjes, Immo, 'Introduction: State of Research on Late Antique and Early Medieval Computus', in *Late Antique Calendrical Thought and Its Reception in the Early Middle Ages. Proceedings of the Third International Conference on the Science of Computus in Ireland and Europe. Galway, 16–18 July, 2010*, ed. by Dáibhí Ó Cróinín and Immo Warntjes (Turnhout: Brepols, 2017), pp. 1–42

———, 'Victorius vs Dionysius: The Irish Easter Controversy of AD 689', in *Early Medieval Ireland and Europe: Chronology, Contacts, Scholarship. A Festschrift for Dáibhí Ó Cróinín*, ed. by Pádraic Moran and Immo Warntjes (Turnhout: Brepols, 2015), pp. 33–98

———, 'Computus and Scientific Thought in the Early Medieval West', in *The Irish in Early Medieval Europe: Identity, Culture and Religion*, ed. by Roy Flechner and Sven Meeder (New York, NY: Bloomsbury, 2016), pp. 285–321

———, 'The Mechanics of Lunar Calendars and the Modes of Calculating Easter, AD 400–1100: Contexts and Perspectives', in *La Conoscenza Scientifica nell'Alto Medioevo: Spoleto, 25 aprile – 1 maggio 2019* (Spoleto: Fondazione Centro Italiano di studi sull'Alto Medioevo, 2020), pp. 273–310

Watson, Daniel, review of Ali Bonner, *The Myth of Pelagianism* (2018), *Irish Theological Quarterly*, 85 (2020), 421–45

Whitelock, Dorothy, and David N. Dumville, eds, *Ireland in Early Mediaeval Europe: Studies in Memory of Kathleen Hughes* (Cambridge: Cambridge University Press, 1982)

———, 'The Old English Bede', *Proceedings of the British Academy*, 48 (1963), 57–90

———, 'The Prose of Alfred's Reign', in *Continuations and Beginnings. Studies in Old English Literature*, ed. by Eric Gerald Stanley (London: Nelson, 1966), pp. 67–103

Wormald, Patrick, *The Making of English Law: King Alfred to the Twelfth Century* (Oxford: Blackwell, 1999; repr. 2000)
———, '*Engla Lond*: The Making of an Allegiance', in *Legal Culture in the Early Medieval West*, ed. by Patrick Wormald (Rio Grande: Hambledon, 1999), pp. 359–82
———, 'The Venerable Bede and the "Church of the English"', in *The English Religious Tradition and the Genius of Anglicanism*, ed. by Geoffrey Rowell (Oxford: Oxford University Press, 1992), pp. 13–32
———, 'Bede, the *Bretwaldas* and the Origins of the *Gens Anglorum*', in *Ideal and Reality in Frankish and Anglo-Saxon Society*, ed. by Patrick Wormald, D. A. Bullough, and Roger Collins (Oxford: Blackwell, 1983), pp. 99–129
———, '*Lex Scripta et Verbum Regis*: Legislation and Germanic Kingship from Euric to Cnut', in *Early Medieval Kingship*, ed. by Peter H. Sawyer and Ian N. Wood (Leeds: University of Leeds, 1977), pp. 105–38
Wright, Neil, 'Columbanus's *Epistulae*', in *Columbanus: Studies on the Latin Writings*, ed. by Michael Lapidge, Studies in Celtic History, 17 (Woodbridge: Boydell, 1997), pp. 29–92
Yorke, Barbara, *Kings and Kingdoms of Anglo-Saxon England* (New York, NY: Routledge, 1990)
Zimmer, Heinrich, *Pelagius in Irland*, Texte und Untersuchungen zur Patristischen Literatur (Berlin: Weidmann, 1901), trans. by A. Meyer, *The Celtic Church in Britain and Ireland* (London: Nutt, 1902)

General Index

Medieval Texts and Cultures of Northern Europe

All volumes in this series are evaluated by an Editorial Board, strictly on academic grounds, based on reports prepared by referees who have been commissioned by virtue of their specialism in the appropriate field. The Board ensures that the screening is done independently and without conflicts of interest. The definitive texts supplied by authors are also subject to review by the Board before being approved for publication. Further, the volumes are copyedited to conform to the publisher's stylebook and to the best international academic standards in the field

Titles in Series

Drama and Community: People and Plays in Medieval Europe, ed. by Alan Hindley (1999)

Showing Status: Representations of Social Positions in the Late Middle Ages, ed. by Wim Blockmans and Antheun Janse (1999)

Sandra Billington, *Midsummer: A Cultural Sub-Text from Chrétien de Troyes to Jean Michel* (2000)

History and Images: Towards a New Iconology, ed. by Axel Bolvig and Phillip Lindley (2003)

Scandinavia and Europe 800–1350: Contact, Conflict, and Coexistence, ed. by Jonathan Adams and Katherine Holman (2004)

Anu Mänd, *Urban Carnival: Festive Culture in the Hanseatic Cities of the Eastern Baltic, 1350–1550* (2005)

Bjørn Bandlien, *Strategies of Passion: Love and Marriage in Old Norse Society* (2005)

Imagining the Book, ed. by Stephen Kelly and John J. Thompson (2005)

Forms of Servitude in Northern and Central Europe: Decline, Resistance, and Expansion, ed. by Paul Freedman and Monique Bourin (2005)

Grant risee?: The Medieval Comic Presence / La Présence comique médiévale. Essays in Honour of Brian J. Levy, ed. by Adrian P. Tudor and Alan Hindley (2006)

Urban Theatre in the Low Countries, 1400–1625, ed. by Elsa Strietman and Peter Happé (2006)

Gautier de Coinci: Miracles, Music, and Manuscripts, ed. by Kathy M. Krause and Alison Stones (2006)

The Narrator, the Expositor, and the Prompter in European Medieval Theatre, ed. by Philip Butterworth (2007)

Learning and Understanding in the Old Norse World: Essays in Honour of Margaret Clunies Ross, ed. by Judy Quinn, Kate Heslop, and Tarrin Wills (2007)

Essays in Manuscript Geography: Vernacular Manuscripts of the English West Midlands from the Conquest to the Sixteenth Century, ed. by Wendy Scase (2007)

Parisian Confraternity Drama of the Fourteenth Century, ed. by Donald Maddox and Sara Sturm-Maddox (2008)

Broken Lines: Genealogical Literature in Medieval Britain and France, ed. by Raluca L. Radulescu and Edward Donald Kennedy (2008)

Laments for the Lost in Medieval Literature, ed. by Jane Tolmie and M. J. Toswell (2010)

Medieval Multilingualism: The Francophone World and its Neighbours, ed. by Christopher Kleinhenz and Keith Busby (2010)

The Playful Middle Ages: Meanings of Play and Plays of Meaning. Essays in Memory of Elaine C. Block, ed. by Paul Hardwick (2011)

Emilia Jamroziak, *Survival and Success on Medieval Borders: Cistercian Houses in Medieval Scotland and Pomerania from the Twelfth to the Late Fourteenth Century* (2011)

Normandy and its Neighbours, 900–1250: Essays for David Bates, ed. by David Crouch and Kathleen Thompson (2011)

Historical Narratives and Christian Identity on a European Periphery: Early History Writing in Northern, East-Central, and Eastern Europe (c. 1070–1200), ed. by Ildar H. Garipzanov (2011)

Multilingualism in Medieval Britain (c. 1066–1520): Sources and Analysis, ed. by Judith Jefferson and Ad Putter with the assistance of Amanda Hopkins (2013)

The Social Life of Illumination: Manuscripts, Images, and Communities in the Late Middle Ages, ed. by Joyce Coleman, Markus Cruse, and Kathryn A. Smith (2013)

Stefka Georgieva Eriksen, *Writing and Reading in Medieval Manuscript Culture: The Translation and Transmission of the story of Elye in Old French and Old Norse Literary Contexts* (2014)

Keith Busby, *French in Medieval Ireland, Ireland in Medieval French: The Paradox of Two Worlds* (2017)

Medieval Francophone Literary Culture Outside France: Studies in the Moving Word, ed. by Nicola Morato and Dirk Schoenaers (2019)

Colmán Etchingham, Jón Viðar Sigurðsson, Máire Ní Mhaonaigh, and Elizabeth Ashman Rowe, *Norse-Gaelic Contacts in a Viking World* (2019)

Crossing Borders in the Insular Middle Ages, ed. by Aisling Byrne and Victoria Flood (2019)

The Chronicles of Medieval Wales and the March: New Contexts, Studies, and Texts, ed. by Ben Guy, Owain Wyn Jones, Georgia Henley, and Rebecca Thomas (2020)

Making the Profane Sacred in the Viking Age: Essays in Honour of Stefan Brink, ed. by Irene García Losquiño, Olof Sundqvist, and Declan Taggart (2020)

The Cult of Saints in Nidaros Archbishopric: Manuscripts, Miracles, Objects, ed. by Ragnhild M. Bø and Jón Viðar Sigurðsson (2022)

Crusading and Ideas of the Holy Land in Medieval Britain, ed. by Kathryn Hurlock and Laura J. Whatley (2022)

Celts, Gaels, and Britons: Studies in Language and Literature from Antiquity to the Middle Ages in Honour of Patrick Sims-Williams, ed. by Simon Rodway, Jenny Rowland, and Erich Poppe (2022)

Multi-Disciplinary Approaches to Medieval Brittany, 450–1200: Connections and Disconnections, ed. by Caroline Brett, Paul Russell, and Fiona Edmonds (2023)